Men singing in the forest during the wai'a

AKWẼ-SHAVANTE SOCIETY

BY

DAVID MAYBURY-LEWIS

CLARENDON PRESS
OXFORD
1967

© *Oxford University Press 1967*

**Printed in Great Britain
by W. & J. Mackay & Co. Ltd., Chatham**

To Pia

PREFACE

Nimuendajú's monographs on certain Gê-speaking tribes (1939, 1942, 1946) are important landmarks in Brazilian anthropology. They not only provided detailed ethnographic accounts, such as are sadly lacking for the majority of Brazilian tribes, based on a prolonged and intimate acquaintance with the peoples concerned; but they were the first series of related studies to be carried out anywhere in Brazil. Nimuendajú worked among the Apinayé (Western Timbira) and the congeries of Eastern Timbira tribes (see Map 1), both belonging to the northern branch of the Gê linguistic group. He also published a study of the Sherente, who may be classed as Central Gê, together with the Shavante. Towards the end of his life he was engaged on a study of the Kayapó, who are closely related to the Apinayé, but he died before his results were published.

Americanists were fascinated and at the same time perplexed by the societies he described. They were characterized on the one hand by a savannah culture and technological backwardness, and on the other by institutional complexity linked with various forms of dualism. Lévi-Strauss took the view that these people had been expelled from the forests they originally inhabited, and that each of the cultures described by Nimuendajú '. . . represented an attenuated replica, on account of a new unfavourable geographic surrounding, of the higher life of the forest area' (1944: 46). Haekel contested this (1952), but felt nevertheless that the Gê tribes could not have developed these social complexities of their own accord. He therefore restated a thesis he had advanced over a decade earlier (1939), according to which the 'Zweiklassensystem' of Central Brazil was traceable to centres of diffusion in the High Andes and even in Middle America. Lowie, in a brief interpretative summary of Nimuendajú's personal communications to him from the field (1941), argued, in the absence of any evidence to the contrary, in favour of the Gê tribes' having developed their institutions independently.

Amidst this welter of speculation about the origins of Gê

institutions there were few who devoted much scholarly attention to how they actually worked. Jules Henry, who had himself
experienced the difficulties of carrying out field research among
bands of macro-Gê 'Kaingang' (Aweikoma) in the south of
Brazil (1941a), pointed out in a perspicacious review of *The
Apinayé* (1941b) that Nimuendajú's outline of the marriage
system failed to provide information on certain crucial points.

Typically, however, it was Lévi-Strauss who first attempted
to analyse Nimuendajú's material. He mentioned the parallel
descent system which had been described for the Apinayé
(1949: 61–62, 287) and promised an elucidation of it in a
future work. Later, in a brief but closely argued communication
to the XXIXth International Congress of Americanists (1952),
he presented a schematic analysis of Nimuendajú's data, together
with a discussion of the Bororo, who are culturally and linguistically closely related to the Gê.[1] He concluded that further
field work was required among these people, and that it should
be undertaken with a view to making a comparative study of
their institutions.

The Northern and Central Gê are so closely related linguistically that Greenberg (1960) classed them all simply as Gê,
without further discrimination. They have shared a common
habitat for a very long time. While some of them practised more
agriculture than others, all of the tribes approximated to the
stereotype of hunters and gatherers. Moreover, Nimuendajú's
sociological information suggested a range of institutional variation which inevitably reminded anthropologists of the Austra-
lians. These societies thus offered an opportunity for controlled
comparison which was not to be missed.

Such a comparison could not, however, be made without a
deeper understanding of the functioning of Gê societies than
could be gleaned from Nimuendajú's reports. I therefore undertook to do further work among the Central Gê. I re-studied the
Sherente in order to supplement Nimuendajú's information and
to prepare for research among the Shavante. Subsequently I
visited the Shavante, and had the opportunity to observe a Gê

---

[1] Greenberg (1960) distinguished a Macro-Gê subfamily of the Gê-Pano-
Carib linguistic family. This subfamily was in turn divided into three groups:
Macro-Gê, Bororo, and Karajá. The Gê are the main branch of the Macro-
Gê group.

people whose social organization had not been appreciably modified by outside contacts. In 1962, thanks to a grant from the National Institutes of Health, I was able to organize further research among the Northern Gê tribes. The following work has already been carried out in connexion with this project:

Terence and Joan Turner (Harvard University) studied the Northern Kayapó in 1962–3.

Jean Carter and Dolores Newton (Harvard University) studied the Krĩkatí (Eastern Timbira) in 1963–4.

Julio Cézar Melatti (Museu Nacional) visited the Krahó (Eastern Timbira) in 1962, 1963, and 1964.

Roberto da Matta (Museu Nacional) visited the Apinayé in 1962 and is at present doing further work among them.

J. Christopher Crocker (Harvard University) is at present working among the Bororo.

I attach particular importance to this simultaneous prosecution of field research and armchair analysis. There has been a tendency in anthropology lately for structural analyses to become increasingly elegant at the expense, or preferably in the absence, of data. On the other hand I feel that an over-insistence on ethnography can in the long run only prove stultifying. We have therefore tried, in our work on the Gê, to formulate structural hypotheses which were capable of some sort of verification.

This has required some restraint, for the Gê material is likely to prove at least as fascinating as the Australian data, and it lends itself easily to formal analysis. Indeed one might be forgiven for supposing that the Gê themselves were experimenting with the various sociological possibilities open to them, such is the range of combinations we have encountered.

This book then is offered as the first of a series of related publications on the Gê. I shall here concentrate on a description and analysis of Shavante institutions, with references to the unpublished material of my collaborators kept down to a minimum. In the final chapters I shall attempt to place my Shavante analysis provisionally in its comparative context.

ACKNOWLEDGEMENTS

This book is based on research financed initially by the Horniman Foundation through an Emslie Horniman Studentship, awarded in 1957. Since 1962 my work in Brazil has formed part of a project (No. MH 06185) financed by the Public Health Service of the United States. I am exceedingly grateful to them both for their generous assistance. I would also like to acknowledge the support of the Brazilian Government, which made a contribution towards my research expenses in 1958.

My warmest thanks are due to the Brazilian Air Force. It was the willingness of its pilots in the interior to ferry me and my family to remote places under difficult conditions which enabled us to bring our work to a successful conclusion. The Salesian Missions in Mato Grosso were also extremely hospitable and generous with information about the Shavante. I particularly wish to thank Padre Mario Panziera for his assistance and Mestre Adalbert Heide who gave me much help with my Shavante texts. In the absence of material on the Shavante language I had to make do as best I could linguistically but I wish to express my especial gratitude to Ruth McLeod, Joan Hall and Eunice Burgess of the Summer Institute of Linguistics who generously put their preliminary language data at my disposal in the final stages of my research. The Anthropological Division of the National Museum in Rio de Janeiro, and particularly its present director, Dr. Roberto Cardoso de Oliveira, gave us and continues to give us friendly and unstinting help. And when our problems defeated all other agencies we found that we could turn to the Danish Consul General in São Paulo, Mr. Adam von Bülow, and rely on him to solve them. We are deeply grateful to him and Mrs. Virginia von Bülow for their extraordinary hospitality.

In fact we were obliged to depend so heavily on our friends in Brazil that this bare acknowledgement of their assistance seems ludicrously inadequate. Professor Herbert Baldus of the Museu Paulista, with whom I studied Brazilian Ethnology, has been a staunch friend and adviser. Mr. Donald Darling, while he was in São Paulo, handled our bizarre problems with skill, wit, and perseverance. Mr. and Mrs. Anders Glens were unforgettably hospitable. Mr. Manuel Klabin came to our assistance when we most needed it. Mrs. Vera Königsberger did likewise. Mr. Robert Parry was the kindest of mentors and it was through his efforts that I was able to continue my work in São Paulo. Mr. Harold Schultz and his wife Wilma Chiara Schultz tutored us in the ways of the interior, and were generous not only with advice but with assistance and hospitality. Mr. and Mrs. Frantisek Schur were always ready with help and hospitality, as was Miss Astrid Sternberg, who became virtually a one-woman committee for handling our affairs. To all these people we owe a profound debt of gratitude. The final draft of the manuscript was completed at the Center for Advanced Study in the Behavioral Sciences at Stanford during my tenure of a fellowship there in 1964–5. I am nostalgically grateful for their assistance and for the scholarly haven they provided.

My intellectual debts are harder to specify. So many people have influenced the course of my work in the past years that it would be impossible to identify them all. The ideas in this book have been discussed in seminars at Harvard and Rio de Janeiro with the other members of the Harvard-Central Brazil Project, and I am grateful to my collaborators for their part in shaping them. Dr. Rodney Needham of Oxford University was my tutor at the time when I wrote the first draft. I am deeply grateful for his constant interest and unsparing advice. He has not only influenced my thinking but has set an analytical standard which I have tried to emulate. Finally it should be clear to my readers that I owe a great deal to Professor Lévi-Strauss. It gives me particular pleasure to acknowledge my debt to him, since I have disagreed with him before and do so again in this book. Nevertheless my argument is one which derives from his pioneering work in Brazilian anthropology. The work of the Harvard-Central Brazil Project is in some respects a dialogue with Professor Lévi-Strauss, and we are keenly aware of our good fortune that this is the case.

CONTENTS

LIST OF PLATES

LIST OF MAPS

LIST OF FIGURES

LIST OF TABLES

SPELLING OF SHAVANTE WORDS

In my spelling of Shavante words I have made use of the following conventions:

Consonants have approximately the same value as in English.
Vowels have approximately the same value as in Spanish.
(~) over a vowel or a consonant nasalizes its pronunciation.
(,) under a vowel shortens it (e.g. ę is pronounced like unaccented e in English *the*).
(') represents a glottal stop.

The word *Shavante* itself is, in Portuguese, usually rendered as *Chavante* or *Xavante*.

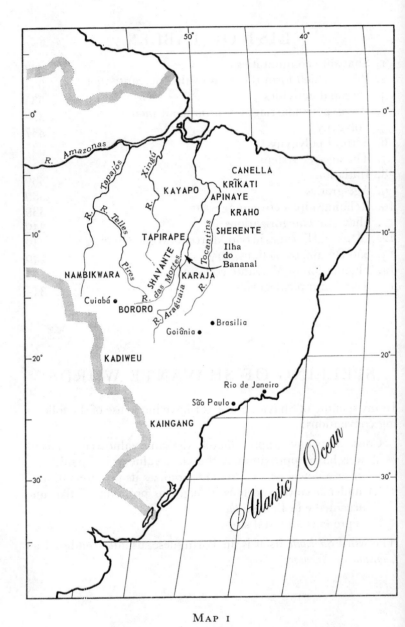

MAP I

Location of principal tribes mentioned in the text.

INTRODUCTION

ANTHROPOLOGISTS are frequently reticent about the circumstances of their field-work. I find this regrettable. It is surely as important to know the conditions under which a field study was carried out as it is to know the conditions of an experiment. Admittedly the 'conditions' of field-work are difficult to set down. For many anthropologists it is a crucial experience entailing a total involvement of mind and personality with the people studied, something quite foreign to the physical sciences. I would certainly not wish to underestimate the value of this empathic aspect of the undertaking. But empathy alone is not enough. A field-worker may feel he knows something about the people he studied, but he has to show his colleagues how he knows (or at least thinks) he knows it. This can only be done if he attempts to describe the manner in which he arrived at what he now asks his readers to accept as 'knowledge'.

I am aware that such descriptions are unlikely to satisfy everybody. But that is insufficient grounds for omitting them or, worse still, for providing an inadequate summary of the circumstances of a particular piece of research. Most anthropological reports nowadays specify how long the author spent in the field, but they do not always indicate how much of that time was actually spent in daily contact with the people studied and how much elsewhere—for example in a near-by city. Nor do they always mention other pertinent details of such contacts. We are not always told how the field-worker was received by the people he studied and how he went about collecting his information. It is often difficult to discover whether he shared living quarters with the people, or occupied a separate dwelling in the same community, or one at some distance from the community, or whether he commuted from another community altogether.

Of course it is the quality of the interaction that counts, not the quantity. A good field-worker may obtain better data in six months than an indifferent one in two years. Nor will a daily breakfast with his subjects make up for an anthropologist's lack of perception. But this is all the more reason for insisting that the quality of this experience should be described as minutely as possible, so that readers of the ensuing report may be in a proper position to evaluate its content. Such descriptions may prove embarrassing. Anthropologists are often reluctant to admit the extent to which they were bewildered or unable to understand their informants. Some of us may not even like to admit to ourselves what sort of a figure we cut in the eyes of the people we studied, and would certainly not like to have the matter discussed dispassionately by our colleagues. We therefore acquiesce publicly in the convention that a field-worker's statements can only be challenged on theoretical grounds or if they are inconsistent, never because we have good reason to believe that he was not in a position to make them in the first place. Such suggestions are taboo and therefore relegated to anthropologists' gossip, where, I have noticed, they occupy a prominent place.

I suggest that it is time we abandoned the mystique which surrounds field-work and made it conventional to describe in some detail the circumstances of data-collecting so that they may be as subject to scrutiny as the data themselves. This could improve anthropological scholarship in that we might be less inclined to take the writings of our colleagues on trust;[1] it might also eliminate some of the cant from field-reports. Once field-work was viewed dispassionately it would come to be realized that there are difficult field situations and less difficult ones, just as there are difficult languages and less difficult ones. There need therefore be no stigma attached to an anthropologist whose data in difficult circumstances are less 'rich' than those of his colleagues, provided that he makes no exaggerated claims on the basis of them. It would seem better to have a few, well attested, facts than a mass of poorly established ones, yet all too often anthropologists judge a field-report in terms of quantity rather than this sort of quality.

It may seem that this preamble is offered here in order to disarm criticism of the field-report which I am about to present. Indeed, I do consider that the circumstances of my work among

---

[1] Evans-Pritchard has consistently maintained that anthropologists tend to be uncritical in their use of documentary sources, which of course include field reports (see 1962: 50).

the Shavante were, by normal anthropological standards, difficult. Nevertheless, I specify those circumstances to the best of
my ability, as a matter of principle. I am quite aware of some
of the inadequacies in my data and I do not believe that any
scholarly purpose is served by seeking to gloss over them. On the
contrary, I shall call attention to them where possible. Finally,
if my specification of the conditions under which this work was
carried out is found to be unsatisfactory, I can at least plead that
I have had few models to go on.

I have made five field trips to Central Brazil. In 1955–6 I
worked among the Sherente and the Krahó, returning to spend
the summer among the Sherente in 1963. Meanwhile I had
worked among the Shavante in 1958, returning for the summer
in 1962 and again for a short visit in 1964. This book deals
primarily with the Shavante and it is the circumstances of my
research among them which I now describe.

This research was planned in 1954. At that time the first
Shavante had barely established peaceful relations with the outside world and it was not thought advisable for anthropologists
to work among them. Moreover, they could not be expected to
speak Portuguese, so that the problem of communication for a
field-worker would have been serious. I therefore planned to
work first among the Sherente. They were reputed to speak 'the
same language' as the Shavante and had had a long period of
contact with the Brazilians, so that many of them spoke some
Portuguese. I hoped to be able to learn Sherente through
Portuguese and at the same time to acquire some experience of
Central Brazil before embarking on the more difficult Shavante
research. I assumed too that a knowledge of Sherente would
enable me to learn Shavante in the field.

The whole project depended on a progression from one
language to another. I should therefore state that my under-
graduate training had been in languages.[1] When I came to
Brazil in 1953, I spoke fluent Spanish but no Portuguese. I was
able to make the change to Portuguese by 1954, and for eighteen
months I studied ethnology at the Escola de Sociologia e Política

---

[1] But not in linguistics. I have a good ear and a certain facility for
languages. When I arrived in Brazil I spoke fluent French, German, and
Spanish, good Danish and quite good Russian. My first degree from Cam-
bridge University is in Spanish and Russian.

(University of São Paulo) under Professor Baldus. During that time I read all the available material on both the Sherente and the Shavante. I spoke Portuguese when I first went into the field. My wife and I worked for seven months among the Sherente. We were then obliged to leave them, owing to lack of funds and consequent ill health.[1] There was at that time little linguistic material available for the Sherente and nothing approaching either a grammar or a dictionary of the language. I was therefore obliged to learn it as I went along. By the end of our stay I was able to understand Sherente conversation and could express myself with reasonable fluency on a limited range of topics. With some help I could understand anything that was said in Sherente, but I could only get the gist of rapid conversation or of the formal speeches which Sherente frequently deliver.

In December 1957 we returned to Brazil with the intention of spending approximately a year among the Shavante. Unfortunately bureaucratic difficulties, of which the most intractable was the refusal of the Brazilian customs to release our equipment for three months, made it impossible for us to reach the field as quickly as we had hoped or to stay there as long as we had wished.

In February 1958 I was flown by the Brazilian Air Force to the Indian Protection Service post at São Domingos on the Rio das Mortes,[2] in order to make a preliminary reconnaissance among the Shavante. I discovered that this Shavante group had established itself about fifteen minutes' walk from the post. It was not until the beginning of April that I was able to go definitively into the field. I was then flown to the same post, accompanied by my wife and son, who had just had his first birthday.[3]

On our arrival in São Domingos we were lodged in a hut at the Indian post. A number of Shavante from the village had come to the airstrip when our plane landed and helped to carry our baggage to the post. They set it down at the feet of an elderly

---

[1] Our total budget for the year, to include all field expenses, was the equivalent of £650. We did not therefore take food supplies into the field. Unfortunately the Sherente were not themselves well supplied with food. Consequently our health suffered; my wife, particularly, became ill from malnutrition.

[2] See Map 2.

[3] A popular account of the circumstances of our field-work among the Sherente and the Shavante can be found in Maybury-Lewis 1965a.

man, who we discovered was the chief of the village. He clearly expected us to open the trunks then and there and distribute their contents. It was difficult for us to refuse him, since these Shavante had grown accustomed to being wooed with gifts. It was not five years since high-ranking army and air force officers had felt it worthwhile to fly into Central Brazil and visit these newly pacified Indians, to make them elaborate presents on behalf of the government and to have their photographs taken in affectionate embraces with dignitaries such as this chief.

I finally persuaded him that we would make a major distribution of presents as soon as we moved into the house which I hoped his people would build for us in their village. The hut was completed approximately two weeks after our arrival and we were then able to move into the village. Meanwhile I had discovered that there was enough difference between Shavante and Sherente, especially as regards pronunciation, to make it extremely hard for me to understand what was being said, but also enough similarity for me to be able to make myself understood in an elementary fashion.

Four days after we had moved into the village (at the end of the third week in April) the community left to go on trek[1] in the region of the Serra do Roncador. I did not accompany them since I was waiting for the arrival of some manioc flour which I had commissioned. The supply plane which was supposed to visit São Domingos had not arrived,[2] and some of the workers from the post had been sent up river by canoe to purchase food. I needed the manioc flour so that I should have something to offer the Shavante in return for my presence in their camps, and also so that I might have an independent food supply. Meanwhile I worked with the few Shavante, including the chief, who had remained behind in the village and tried to improve my knowledge of their language.

The flour arrived five days later and I set out with a single Shavante guide to join the others. I trekked with them during the entire months of May and June, while my wife and child remained behind. When I returned to São Domingos I found

---

[1] Shavante treks are discussed fully in Chapter II.

[2] This supply plane was taken off its run as a consequence of the need for air support during the building of Brasilia. It never came during the time we were at São Domingos.

that my son was ill and needed medical care. It was our good fortune that a missionary up-stream from our post had decided to close his mission and sell his boat. He therefore had to make the journey right down the Rio das Mortes to its mouth and then up the Araguaia to Aragarças, where he could hand over the craft to its purchaser. He agreed to take my wife and child to Aragarças, where they could arrange to be flown to the coast, but only on condition that I accompanied them. We therefore made a twelve-day journey up the Araguaia.

From Aragarças I was immediately flown back to São Domingos by the air force. It was now mid-July. From 16 to 28 July I accompanied a group of hunters who were killing game for the culmination of the initiation festivals. We returned to the village, where the ceremonies were completed by 4 August.

On 7 August the community moved off on trek again. I travelled overland to another Shavante group at the Salesian mission of Santa Terezinha. I discovered, however, that this community was also out on trek. There were a few Shavante there who had stayed behind, however, and I was able to work with them. In particular they listened with fascination to my tapes recorded in São Domingos and not only explained them to me, but also commented freely and unfavourably on the affairs of that community.

At the beginning of September a private plane brought a passenger to the mission and I was able to fly back with it to Campo Grande and make my way to São Paulo.

Two weeks later I arranged with the air force to have my family and myself flown back to São Domingos. The members of that community were just beginning to straggle in from their trek. I stayed with them until the end of November, when I left the Shavante definitively. I had been in the field for a total of just over seven months, not counting the time spent away from the Shavante.

During those periods when the Shavante were in their base village, near São Domingos, my family and I lived in a small hut next door to that of the chief. Our household differed from other Shavante households only in so far as it was the 'home' of no more than a single family. But our home was in this case far from being our castle. Shavante came and went in it all day more freely than they would in each other's houses. They normally come and go in the houses of their kin and avoid those of their affines. Since the chief treated me as, and addressed me by the term for, 'son', we were automatically treated as kin by the members of his clan. But the members of other clans did not really regard me as an affine. We were therefore in the position of having to keep open house for the entire community. This had its advantages, in that we did get to know everybody, but it had its disadvantages as well.

Those people who were most prone to hang around our hut were often the ones who had least to say and their presence inhibited other Shavante on the rare occasions when they seemed disposed to talk. Furthermore, the chief's numerous sons were our closest 'relatives' both spatially and conceptually. As a result they virtually lived under our roof. They were the most difficult Shavante to deal with and the most demanding of presents and favours. They were in some ways the least helpful informants, yet I tended to be identified with them, which created feelings of jealousy and hostility towards me in the minds of other Shavante whose company I would often have preferred.

The complete and perpetual lack of privacy imposed a strain on us which became almost intolerable as the months passed. There were always Shavante lolling or sleeping in our hut. Some of them invariably spent the night with us; others came to while away the hot hours in the middle of the day under our roof, dozing and begging from us alternately. This created a number of problems. Some of them were personal. We did not mind most Shavante habits but we did object to their spitting on our small patch of floor or voiding their phlegm in the thatch of our hut. They were most amused by this idiosyncrasy of ours and used to hawk loudly and make as if to spit whenever they wanted to catch my attention, as for example when I was trying to write my notes. More serious was the fact that it was impossible to arrange to have a private conversation with any Shavante. It would occasionally happen that I could talk to one of them alone by finding him alone in his hut, but such encounters could not always be anticipated and were not necessarily with the right people. At the same time it was very difficult for me to get enough privacy to write up my notes, let alone analyse my data. I could of course do this with Shavante present, but it imposed a considerable strain. It became virtually impossible during the period when the chief's hut was being re-thatched. All its occupants moved into our house while theirs was being repaired. Since it poured with rain on the following days, the thatching could not proceed and we were cooped up with seventeen people and their pets in a hut the size of a small room.

During the early days of my work in São Domingos I made a plan of the village, which at that time contained sixteen houses plus a bachelors' hut. I then tried to establish who lived in which house. This was not as easy as it sounds. The Shavante were unused to being visited in their huts and on occasion gave me clearly to understand that I was not welcome. They resented my questions and their answers were reluctant and incomplete. Before I had even got to know everybody in the village, let alone establish his residence, the community split up into three groups and moved off on trek.

I travelled with one of these groups for approximately five weeks. During that period I lived in a shelter occupied by the chief's sons (my brothers), his daughter and son-in-law. These shelters provide just enough covered space for their inmates to lie in, like so many sardines in a tin. If there are many people to a shelter, as there were to ours, then not all of the occupants of it can lie on their backs at once, or the people sleeping at the ends are pushed into the thatch. If a tall man stretches his legs, then his toes stick out of the entrance. It took me some time to learn to sleep in these shelters, for I had perforce to lie intertwined with the other sleepers and was kept awake by the jarring of their knees and elbows or by having them roll over on top of me. Shavante seemed able to push and shove for themselves without waking up. Moreover the sleepers were always thickest in my vicinity, for I had blankets, and the nights get bitterly cold on the high Central Brazilian plateau. Shavante usually sleep until the chill wakes them irrevocably, and then go outside to squat over their fires until sunrise. In my shelter there were invariably at least three people who preferred a portion of my blanket to this other alternative.

During the day I accompanied the men on their various activities until I felt that I knew approximately what everybody was doing and how. After that I would spend the day going from place to place and talking with different people. I found them more communicative than they had been in the village.

They were intrigued by the fact that I was accompanying their trek, a thing no outsider had done previously, and this piqued their curiosity about me, especially that of the women. I had made myself *persona grata* in my shelter by giving them half my supply of manioc flour on arrival. Subsequently, whenever I made any food for myself, I always shared it with two or three members of the shelter. This consisted of various mixtures of my four ingredients, powdered milk, powdered soup, sugar, and manioc flour. In return I was given a share of the food which came into the shelter. It came in less regularly than I was accustomed to, and I had not developed the Shavante habit of eating prodigiously when it was there and then going without. Consequently I asked for and received a smaller share than the others, which did not displease my hosts.

While we were on trek I found that I was progressively cast in the role of camp jester, or perhaps mascot. The guide who had accompanied me from São Domingos reported to the men's council, as was customary, on the evening of his arrival. There he gave a detailed report on our two-and-a-half-days' journey, expertly mimicking my clumsy Shavante and recounting everything I had said and done *en route*. This included all the things I had failed to see and the fact that I could not find the pack-horse one morning after it had wandered, hobbled, for miles over hard ground the previous night. The Shavante found this uproariously funny, and were obviously amused by my general ignorance and incompetence in their habitat.

This feeling crystallized on the day when I lost my way back to camp after accompanying a group of hunters. I had set out with them in the early morning when excited shouts of 'Pig, pig, quick after the pigs!' had brought most of the men running from their shelters. I had run too, gun in hand, under the impression that a flock of peccary were near by. Instead I found myself included in a hunting party which had not killed by midday but had seen enough tracks to whet their appetites. They planned therefore to stay out for two days or more. The prospect was both strenuous and uncomfortable. Worse still it was unproductive. I had already accompanied innumerable hunts and my companions were much too busy to be communicative. I was looking for a way of bowing out without losing face. This was provided when they killed a deer and wanted someone to carry it back to camp. I volunteered for the task. On the way back, however, I lost myself in a thick patch of jungle.

I must have been lost for little more than an hour, but it was an unpleasant experience. I had taken my clothes off to avoid getting them caked with deer's blood and entrails, with the result that I was severely cut and scratched as I tried various ways out. I tried wading down a stream until it crossed a trail, but it became deeper all of a sudden and I submerged, deer and all. In the process my hunting knife was jerked out of its sheath and lost. When I got back to camp I was therefore physically marked by my experience and the Shavante noted (before I did) that the knife was gone. These details were woven into a story about me which was guaranteed to produce guffaws in the men's circle and which was retold on every occasion.

Nevertheless, these eccentricities of mine produced a kind of amused tolerance for me among the men, which I found far more productive than their previous surly hostility. If we joked at my expense, at least we joked, and could then go on to talk of other things. My command of Shavante was still so rudimentary, however, that the talk could not progress very far. I was unable to do much more than observe, note the composition of the band and the relations within it, and embark on preliminary discussions of Shavante institutions, of which I had only the haziest notion.

Later I journeyed to another of the São Domingos bands, where I lived in the bachelors' hut. This was, if possible, more uncomfortable than the previous shelter I had occupied. The boys in it did their own thatching, a job done by the women for all the other shelters. This was so poorly done that the hut was sunbaked and infested with insects by day, windy and moon-swept by night. Moreover the boys assisted me in finishing my flour supply in no time and I was therefore obliged to live on a Shavante diet.

Once I had obtained data on these two bands I could calculate the composition of the third by elimination. By the time we returned to São Domingos at the end of June, therefore, I had the essential data for the community and was in a position to be able to ask intelligent questions, if not to phrase them properly.

This language barrier was the most difficult one of all, and I never overcame it satisfactorily. There was no means of improving my knowledge except by the direct method. There are still no grammars or dictionaries of Shavante,[1] and the few published word-lists were antiquated and useless. Furthermore, there were no Shavante in this community who spoke any Portuguese at all. Towards the end of my stay in the field I went out of my way to find a reputedly bilingual Shavante in a nearby township. His Portuguese consisted of a few words and was much worse than my Shavante. Similarly, the only whites I met who were indicated as 'speaking Shavante' commanded a smattering of the language which amounted to less than my own knowledge of it. I therefore had no option but to pick up the language in the course of my work. The Shavante of São Domingos were poor teachers, however. They still lived active lives and were little inclined for the tedium of instructing a foreigner in their tongue. I could not even get them to tell me stories. The sight of my microphone, whether carelessly arranged close by or openly given to them to talk to, invariably dried them up completely. They even reacted negatively to any suspicion of an 'interview', so that all of my work had to be conducted on the basis of informal chats with this person and that.

The most frustrating thing was to listen nightly to the impressive oratory of the speakers in the men's circle without being able to understand more than the gist of what they were saying. If I turned to my neighbours for explanations, they were not usually of much assistance, for they had no experience at that time either of translation or of paraphrase. They either repeated what had been said, perhaps louder, or 'explained' it by saying 'He is very angry' or 'He said very much.' There were certain recurrent phrases which I had to learn by hearing them repeatedly in context and then puzzling out their meaning, an extremely time-consuming process.

In any case the Shavante had an acute distrust of white people, which made the initial stages of my research even less productive than they might have been. Even when we had, to some extent, succeeded in overcoming this reserve, we found them naturally so taciturn that I sometimes despaired of getting information from them. Much of their time and ours was in any

---

[1] The Summer Institute of Linguistics is at present working on the preparation of these.

case occupied with activities such as hunting, food-getting, and travelling, which discourage conversation.

By the end of June 1958 we had established what might be considered a satisfactory relationship with the São Domingos Shavante, for research purposes. They had come to accept our presence and to include us in their activities. They had even come to accept that we might wander into their houses to talk in the same way as they wandered into ours. The presence of my son was a great help in this respect. He played with the village children and thus gained us an *entrée* into households where we had not previously been made welcome. When my wife had to take him to the coast, the Shavante seemed genuinely concerned and pestered me with questions about when they were coming back again. It was largely for this reason that we took the decision to bring him back to the field when he had recovered from his illness. It was in the days after my wife and son had returned to the community in September, and brought fresh gifts, that I began to feel that our presence was not entirely irksome to our hosts. For the first time Shavante came to visit us without begging or demanding anything, and for the first time they would talk freely with me instead of my perpetually having to cross-question them.

At this time I also had a better perspective of my data from São Domingos, due to my work in Santa Terezinha. Accordingly, the bulk of my understanding of the Shavante, such as it was in 1958, was acquired during those months of October and November, before I was obliged to return to England. My doctoral dissertation was based on these data.

In 1962 I was able to return to Brazil and revisit the Shavante. My objectives were to assist a team of geneticists in their research on the Shavante; to note the changes which had taken place since 1958; but above all to obtain data from other Shavante communities in order to check my conclusions from the study of São Domingos.

I was flown to São Domingos with the geneticists on 17 July. There I was warmly received by the Shavante and immediately took up residence in the village, while the team of geneticists stayed at the Indian Protection Service post.[1] On this occasion

[1] The Indian agent at São Domingos made it clear on this occasion that he did not wish to receive me at his post. This did not interfere with my

there was no problem of *rapport*. Many things had changed since 1958. The Shavante were no longer haughty in their dealings with outsiders. Their lands had been infiltrated. The population of the community was half its former size, owing to epidemics and internecine warfare. A number of its inhabitants had broken away and gone to live on the other side of the Rio das Mortes, at a place called Ẹ Tõ (Still Water). Moreover the São Domingos Shavante had developed a taste for the products of the outside world. They were therefore more forthcoming with outsiders who came bearing gifts. I believe, however, that they remembered us, particularly my wife and child, favourably. In fact they expressed great disappointment that I had returned to them alone. In any case the chief built me a private shelter with his own hands, and I do not think there was ever a night when less than a dozen people slept in it with me.

I spent eleven days in São Domingos and during that time I made one journey to Ẹ Tõ. Its inhabitants were all away on trek but I was able to make a plan of the village. My guide was an inhabitant of Ẹ Tõ who happened to be visiting São Domingos. He told me the names of as many of the occupants of each house as he could remember, so that I could get some idea of the composition of the community and make a guess at its total population.

From São Domingos I returned with an air force plane to Aragarças. From there I took an air taxi to the Salesian mission at São Marcos, where I spent ten days. During that time I stayed at the mission and spent each day working in the village, which was situated about a hundred yards away. I

---

plan of research, but I note it here in order to give as complete a picture as possible of the prevailing conditions. He was the same agent who had been at São Domingos during my previous research. When we left the Shavante in 1958 relations between us had been cool, but I for my part did not feel as strongly about him as he obviously did about me. It would be invidious to try and describe the difference between us; but it is relevant to point out that Indian agents in Brazil generally resent social anthropologists who work with their charges. Social anthropologists remain a long time in the field and therefore introduce an unwelcome external element into the relation between agent and Indians. If the agent has claims to being an amateur expert on the Indians at his post, then the anthropologist also threatens this position. Since anthropologists carry authorizations from the directorate of the Indian Protection Service, the agent is theoretically obliged to assist them. Such an obligation cannot of course be enforced. Most anthropologists are content if the agent does not actively obstruct their work, as has sometimes happened.

made a rough census and established the residential and factional alignments of the people in the village. I was able to obtain a great deal of information on the Shavante of the communities I had studied previously, since they were heartily disliked in São Marcos and people were ready and willing to wash their dirty linen for them.

At the same time I received valuable assistance from Adalbert Heide, a lay brother who had been with the Shavante since 1958. He was the first outsider I had met with a good command of the language. He generously provided me with linguistic glosses, texts, and other notes, which enabled me to clear up many points. In the more sedentary atmosphere of the mission elderly Shavante could be more easily persuded to recount stories, so I was able to record a number of tapes.

After leaving São Marcos I was flown to Xavantina, where I tried to obtain a boat to take me to a Shavante village at Areões. This took some time, since Xavantina, incredible though it may seem, had not a single serviceable boat at the time of my arrival. Finally I managed to hire a canoe and visit Areões, only to find that its inhabitants were out on trek. I stayed at the Indian Protection Service post, however, and enlisted the assistance of a Shavante informant who happened to come back to the village. I was thus able to do as I had done in Ẽ Tõ: make a plan of the village and put in the names of the occupants of the houses. I also obtained information as to their factional alignments, which was important, since the community was a recently constituted amalgam of a number of bands who had been involved in warfare on the lower reaches of the river.

I then returned to Xavantina and waited there for a week until a lorry could be found to undertake the difficult journey to Aragarças. In Aragarças I was held up a further week, since the air force plane which would have taken me to Cuiabá was grounded with engine trouble. On arrival in Cuiabá I hired an air taxi and flew to the Indian Protection Service post at Simões Lópes.

The post was flanked on one side by a village of highly acculturated Bakairí and on the other by a village of Shavante, who had been there since 1956. They appeared to be more acculturated than any Shavante group I had previously met.

I was lodged in a spacious guest house belonging to the post and about a hundred yards away from the huts of the Shavante community. I came and went as I pleased in the village although I took my meals at the post. The house I occupied had been for some time used by some girls from the Summer Institute of Linguistics who were engaged on a study of the Shavante language. They were not at Simões Lópes during my stay there but were kind enough to lend me some of their analytical material on another occasion. As a result of their efforts, these Shavante were accustomed to sitting down and talking to field-workers for long periods. In fact the men were eager to do so, since the previous workers had predominantly made use of women informants. At this time I was particularly investigating Shavante factionalism and its relation to the kinship system, so I preferred male informants.[1] I was also interested in obtaining taped material in the form of stories or Shavante discussions of topics which puzzled me. I was able to record some hours of tape. Finally I was also able to observe the closing stages of the initiation ceremonies. After ten days at Simões Lópes I was obliged to leave in order to be in time for the beginning of term at Harvard.

My final visit to the Shavante took place in March–April 1964. I was in Brazil at that time, engaged on a different study, and took the opportunity to spend ten days at São Marcos. My objective was to elucidate certain points in my analysis of Shavante institutions with the assistance of Shavante informants. I therefore selected São Marcos, since I hoped to be able to count on the linguistic ability of Adalbert Heide and to find there Shavante who were sophisticated enough to explain certain concepts to me.

Adalbert Heide had left the mission, but I was able to accomplish my purpose by virtually holding Shavante seminars in the mission. I enlisted the participation of three elder Shavante and questioned them about the matters which per-plexed me. They explained them as best they could and I recorded the discussions. I then went over the tapes with younger Shavante who were skilled in paraphrase and could assist me to understand them fully.

At the same time I was able to make some observations con-cerning changes that had taken place at São Marcos between

[1] Women are not involved in Shavante politics.

1962 and 1964. I was also fortunate in meeting a group of Shavante who had left São Domingos for Ẽ Tõ and finally fled to São Marcos. Some of them were people I had known well, and seen in 1958 and 1962. I could therefore observe (with all the relevant data in hand) how they were assimilated into the São Marcos community.

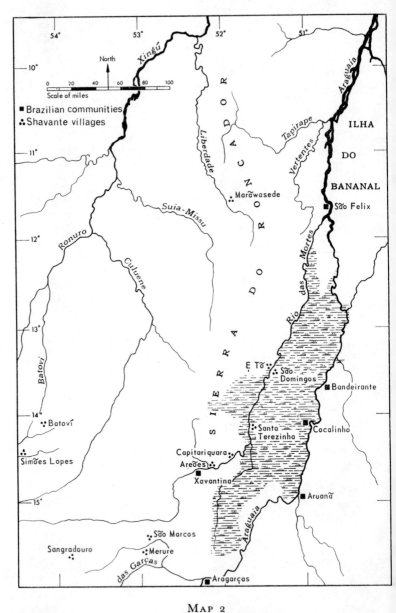

MAP 2

Location of Shavante communities.

I

ABOUT THE SHAVANTE

1. HISTORICAL

THE Shavante enjoy a certain notoriety in Brazil. They burst upon the national consciousness thirty years ago when they proved unremittingly hostile to missionaries, adventurers, and agents of the Brazilian Government who were trying to open up the interior of the country. Local backwoodsmen told tales of vast numbers of intractably ferocious Indians in the region of the Rio das Mortes. The Brazilian Air Force flew sorties to look for them, and brought back photographs of horseshoe villages built on the open savannah and of big, naked men firing arrows at the low-flying planes. A press photographer hired a small plane to take some photographs of his own, and reported that a muscular Shavante had actually hit it with a well aimed club at a height of over fifteen feet (five metres). These widely publicized stories soon established the Shavante as prototypical of the naked savages of the interior and of the backwardness (*atraso*) which Brazil had to overcome. Civilization had caught up with the Shavante, but not for the first time.

Although little is known about their history, it has been established that until the early part of the nineteenth century they lived in the northern part of the state of Goiás, between the Tocantins and the Araguaia rivers (Maybury-Lewis, 1966a). This region, like most of the central plateau of Brazil, was occupied by tribes of the Gê linguistic family, who were probably already there before the great migrations of the Tupí.[1] Of these the Shavante and the Sherente were clearly very closely related, if not actually the same people. I have elsewhere (1966a, 1966b) discussed the relationship between them, which is a difficult one to establish with any precision, since the early chroniclers used both names rather loosely.

It is not even possible to give the derivations of the names.

[1] See Mason 1950: 288 and Métraux 1927.

Their etymology is Portuguese but nobody knows who first used them or why (Nimuendajú, 1942: 3–4). *Shavante* was applied indiscriminately to a number of tribes on the savannahs of the interior (Almeida, 1869; Siqueira, 1872: 41–42) but finally came to be restricted to three groups:

(1) The *Oti-Shavante*, who are now to be found in the western part of the State of São Paulo.

(2) The *Ofaié (Opaié)-Shavante*, who are located in the far south of the State of Mato Grosso.

(3) The *Akwẽ-Shavante*, who are to be found west of the Rio das Mortes (Mato Grosso).

These three groups are linguistically and culturally quite distinct (Nimuendajú, 1942: 2–3; Ribeiro, 1951; Baldus, 1954). We shall here be concerned exclusively with the *Akwẽ-Shavante*, and wherever I use the word *Shavante* by itself, it refers to them. The qualifier *Akwẽ* is a term in current use among Brazilianists and refers to both Sherente and Shavante. It is in fact the word the Sherente use to refer to themselves and their own language. The modern Shavante cognate is *A'wẽ* or *Auwẽ*.

It seems that the definitive separation between the two branches of the *Akwẽ* took place in the 1840s. At that time they were fighting the settlers who were coming into Goiás in increasing numbers and occupying the land along the Tocantins. In all probability the present-day Sherente were pushed back to the east, away from the river, while the Shavante were similarly driven westwards. Indeed the distinction between Shavante and Sherente may date from this time (Maybury-Lewis, 1966a).

In any case, the Shavante moved south-westwards to avoid the colonists and found their way into a sort of no-man's-land in eastern Mato Grosso. They were definitely located west of Aruanã according to a report dated 1862 (Couto de Magalhães, 1938: 99). During the three final decades of the nineteenth century they remained comparatively unmolested in the region of the Rio das Mortes. They attacked any intruders, as when for example they forced Colonel Tupí Caldas' expedition to turn back in 1887 (Ehrenreich, 1891: 118). They were also reputed to be at war with neighbouring Indians (Ehrenreich, 1895: 149).

After the turn of the century their activities began for the first time to be reported by writers to the west of them. Salesian

missionaries were already working among the Bororo, with
whom the Shavante clashed when they moved into their new
habitat. They reported persistent Shavante attacks on the
Bororo in the early years of the twentieth century. There is even
a mention of an attack on the Mission at Merure where
numbers of Bororo had taken refuge (Colbacchini and Albisetti,
1942: 150; Carlette, 1928: 28–30). As homesteaders began to
arrive in the region between the Araguaia and the Rio das
Mortes, Shavante took to ambushing and killing the intruders.
By the 1930s they had thus established a local reputation for
ferocity. People feared to camp overnight anywhere on the
west bank of the Araguaia, from the Ilha do Bananal up to and
including the Rio das Garças. Even today the Karajá Indians,
who are some of the best watermen in the whole area, prefer to
moor their canoes in mid stream if they have to spend a night
on the river south of São Felix.

The first serious attempts to re-establish peaceful contact with
the Shavante were made in the 1930s. Two Salesian fathers,
Sacilotti and Fuchs, went up the Rio das Mortes in 1934 and
tried to make friends with them. They were killed on the bank
of the river in full view of their companions. Another Salesian,
father Chovelon, built a hut on the east bank of the river, at a
site which he named São Domingos, and tried to induce the
Shavante to enter into friendly relations with him. He was
unsuccessful. The Shavante made their desire to be left alone
only too plain. They even returned from time to time and
destroyed the crude cross and memorial which the missionaries
erected and re-erected at the spot where Sacilotti and Fuchs
were killed.

Meanwhile there was fighting between Shavante and Brazilians far to the west in the neighbourhood of Merure. A group
of Indians killed a settler's child in 1936 and stole its hammock.
The father of the child obtained permission from the governor
of Mato Grosso to mount a reprisal expedition. When the
Salesians got to hear of it, they intervened with the governor and
explained that the consequences of such an expedition could
be disastrous in terms of Indian-white relations, and might
threaten the peace of the region and the safety of its inhabitants.
The governor withdrew his permission, but by that time the
expedition had already left.

The expeditionaries, well mounted and heavily armed, were accompanied by Bororo auxiliaries. They travelled for four days without meeting any Shavante, and were about to turn back, when they sighted a village. They dismounted and entered it on foot, finding it occupied by women and children. The expeditionaries reported that they shot a child as it came running out of one of the huts, and then beat a retreat, fighting off the Shavante men as they returned from the hunt. Their Bororo companions told a different story. According to them the leader of the expedition went into one of the huts and saw what he took to be his child's hammock hanging there. Then he went berserk, shooting and killing every Indian in sight, to a total of about thirty.

By this time the Shavante were beginning to have quite a reputation in the Brazilian popular press. In 1937 and again in 1938 parties of adventurers from São Paulo tried to establish contact with them. On the first expedition they did not meet any Shavante at all, but came upon one of their deserted encampments and went through it collecting artefacts and leaving presents in exchange. The second group tried to force its way into a Shavante village with the aid of fireworks and fusillades, but beat a retreat when they saw that the Indians were prepared to defend themselves. They were subsequently ordered back by the government at the request of the Indian Protection Service.[1]

In 1941 the Indian Protection Service sent its own expedition to make friendly contact with the Shavante. They established their base in Father Chovelon's disused hut at São Domingos, and from there crossed the Rio das Mortes and made their way into the Serra do Roncador. There they met and conversed with a group of Shavante, who received them exceedingly cautiously. That night the leader of the expedition, Dr. Pimentel Barbosa, seeing that his men were nervous, decided that it would be wiser to disarm them all, rather than risk a battle with

[1] Indian Protection Service is the translation used throughout this study to refer to the *Serviço de Proteção aos Indios*. This is a department of the Brazilian Ministry of Agriculture, and is responsible for the protection of Amerindian rights throughout the country, as also for the administration of certain Amerindian communities which are in peaceful contact with the outside world. It maintains a section devoted to anthropological research, and on occasion organizes attempts to make contact with tribes that have hitherto been living outside the effective national territory.

the Shavante due to a chance shot. The following day the Indians attacked and killed them all. Only the Sherente interpreters, who had been out reconnoitering the Shavante village, escaped.

Nevertheless the Indian Protection Service established a post at São Domingos, where the expeditionaries were buried. Persistent attempts were made to persuade the Shavante to exchange presents and to visit the post. Parties of Indian Protection Service men would cross the Rio das Mortes and search for trails which looked as if they were frequented by the Indians. Then they would leave gifts there and go away. For some years this tactic was unsuccessful. The gifts were either destroyed or scattered in the jungle. In 1946 they finally succeeded in persuading a group of Shavante to exchange presents. Five years later, in 1951, Shavante came to visit the post (now called Pimentel Barbosa) at São Domingos. In 1953 one community consented to move its base to within walking distance of the São Domingos. This was the first continuous and amicable contact with the Shavante since the late eighteenth century.[1]

[1] The circumstances under which other Shavante groups established peaceful relations with the whites are discussed in Section 3.

2. GEOGRAPHICAL

It is estimated that there are, at present, about 2,000 Shavante, although, in the absence of a census or even of a reliable count, this figure must be taken as a very rough guide. It seems unlikely that the population is more than 2,500 at the outside, and it definitely exceeds 1,500.

The Shavante share a common language and a common culture. It seems that until recently they also occupied a continuous tract of territory. As they are a semi-nomadic people, this 'occupation' of their lands rather took the form of enforcement of their own right of usufruct within a given region, and the denial of such rights, including the right of settlement, to outsiders. In 1958, when I first visited the Shavante, their groups were to be found at intervals for the entire length of the Rio das Mortes. Only those north of (down-river from) Xavantina exercised any sort of control over limited tracts of land both east and west of the river, and this only in the absence of Brazilian interest in the regions concerned. By the time of my return in 1962 the situation had already changed dramatically. The banks of the river between Xavantina and Areões were dotted with small homesteads. Downstream from Areões there were few settlers, but the land had in large part been bought by companies based in São Paulo, and occasionally gangs of workmen with even a tractor or two would be sent to clear these holdings. The powerful Shavante bands that had previously managed to keep settlers off these reaches had been reduced to enclaves, which were, for the first time, aware of their impotence in the face of encroachment.

The situation of the western Shavante, located down-stream from Xavantina or over on the headwaters of the Xingú, is similar. In the vast wasteland of eastern Mato Grosso they were harried and hemmed in by the settlers until they were driven to seek the patronage of either the Salesian missions or the Indian Protection Service posts.

Under Brazilian law the Shavante do not own any land. 'Unassimilated' Indians may not own lands themselves, but there are legal provisions for their land to be guaranteed and held in trust for them, preferably by the Indian Protection Service. Other agencies, such as the Central Brazil Foundation[1]

[1] This translation will be used to refer to the *Fundação Brasil Central*, a

or an authorized mission, may also be legally empowered to hold lands on behalf of Indian wards. These provisions are, however, difficult to put into effect. State governments are notoriously unwilling to grant land titles to Indians or their representatives; and where they do so, they usually frame the legislation with loopholes that render it nugatory.[1] As far as I am aware, however, there are no lands even held in trust for the down-stream Shavante. There are two Indian Protection Service posts authorized to protect their interests, but the Service does not own either the land on which the posts stand or any adjacent territory. The situation of the western Shavante is little better. Their patrons, respectively, are two Indian Protection Service posts and two Salesian missions. These agencies only control the lands on which they are situated and are in no position to guarantee Shavante territory, even if the extent of it could be determined.

This problem of land is at the heart of the Indian question in Mato Grosso, ironic though this may seem in a state which is the size of France, Germany and Great Britain combined, and has a population of about a million. Land speculation is, however, the major economic activity of the state, and the rights of the Indians are difficult to protect against powerful economic interests. Darcy Ribeiro's account (1962: 109–12) shows the lengths to which speculators are prepared to go. The State Assembly voted a law in 1957 under the terms of which the land previously guaranteed by the Federal Government to the Kadiwéu Indians reverted to the State of Mato Grosso for sale on the open market. The Kadiwéu were to be left with lands close to the Paraguayan frontier, which were not only flooded and uninhabitable for half of each year, but were also unsaleable, owing to a federal law which prohibits the private ownership of land in border zones except under special circumstances. The Governor of Mato Grosso vetoed the bill but the Assembly voted it a second time over his veto, and it became law in April 1958. The state deputy who had proposed the bill then went to the official printing press and had two copies of

---

federal agency created by President Getulio Vargas in order to promote the 'opening up' of the interior.

[1] For a discussion of this problem, see Darcy Ribeiro 1962 *passim*.

the *Diário Oficial* printed with the new law in it. One copy was deposited in the state archives. He took the other one with him to Campo Grande, where the State of Mato Grosso maintains the department which deals with lands in the region where the Kadiwéu are located. There, on the grounds of the official promulgation of the law contained in the *Diário Oficial*, he was able to buy tracts for himself and his friends and relatives, as also were other deputies who had voted for the law and were party to the machinations. The Indian Protection Service took the case to the Supreme Court of Mato Grosso, where judgment was in effect given against them. Finally, the Federal Supreme Court ruled for the Indian Protection Service in 1961, on the grounds that the State of Mato Grosso could not dispose freely of lands which it did not receive from the United States of Brazil at the time of union in 1891, when jurisdiction over unoccupied lands passed from the federal to the state governments. At that time the Kadiwéu already had their lands guaranteed by federal legislation.

Under these circumstances the position of Indians such as the Shavante, who have only recently come into contact with the outside world and therefore have no legal title to their lands, is an unenviable one. Nevertheless, in 1952 the President of Brazil sent a bill to Congress which would have created an enormous reserve of land in north-eastern Mato Grosso as the exclusive preserve of various Indian tribes which were retreating before the settlers. This project, to set up what became known as the Indian Reserve on the Xingú (*Parque Indígena do Xingú*), was not approved as it stood. It was not until 1961 that a law was passed setting up the *Parque Nacional do Xingú* and reserving a much smaller area to the Indians.

This modification directly affected the Shavante. Originally they were to have been guaranteed under separate legislation a tract of territory extending from the west bank of the Rio das Mortes to the south-eastern corner of the *Parque Indígena do Xingú*. When the *Parque Indígena* was whittled down to the *Parque Nacional*, the Shavante were left well to the east of the proposed reserve. In any case the State of Mato Grosso was complicating the issue between the state and the federal governments by selling off tracts of territory which had been earmarked for the Indians (Oliveira, 1955).

In 1956 Mato Grosso enacted legislation which provided for the cession of a tract of land on the west bank of the Rio das Mortes to the Indian Protection Service on behalf of the Shavante, with the proviso that if this land was not surveyed by the Service and a valid claim to it staked within two years it would revert to the state. The state authorities appear to have assumed that this would in fact happen, since lands within the reserve were being sold to private buyers long before the period of grace expired.[1] In fact the Indian Protection Service had neither the funds nor the personnel to carry out such a survey and they made no move to do so. The lands therefore reverted to the State of Mato Grosso on 15 December 1958.

Although the Shavante do not own any lands *de jure*, they have until very recently been in *de facto* control of a large region. It is impossible to give precise geographical limits for it, since it was not in fact occupied by the Shavante but rather denied to outsiders through fear of Shavante attack. Darcy Ribeiro points out (1962: 107) that the possibility of such attacks even served to reduce the pressure on lands occupied by other tribes, such as the Tapirapé and the Karajá. There has thus been a region of Central Brazil where land was virtually not negotiable as a result of Shavante bellicosity. Yet it was only part of this region that the Shavante considered their own and over which they regularly trekked. Recently even this part has been shrinking extremely rapidly.

Its heart consisted of those lands bounded on the west by the tributaries of the Xingú and on the east and south by the Araguaia and the Rio das Mortes. The northern limit was rather vague. Shavante have sometimes been reported on the Tapirapé river but in general they seem to have kept to the south of the Rio Xavante (or Vertentes). This region is well known throughout Brazil as the Serra do Roncador or Snoring Mountains, although the name is misleading, for there is no real *serra* (highlands) in these parts but merely an escarpment, whose moderate elevation is only remarkable because of the general flatness of the surrounding countryside. Ten years ago

---

[1] This information is taken from reports from Indian agents to the chief of the Indian Protection Service and to the chief of the 8th Regional Inspectorate of the Indian Protection Service which I was permitted to consult.

this territory was not unexplored, but it was by common consent Shavante country. If Brazilians ventured into it, they did so in parties and comparatively well armed. The fringes of it were in any case only sparsely settled.

At one time the Shavante clearly considered that the Araguaia was the eastern boundary of their domain, for they regularly attacked people who tried to establish themselves on the west side of it. Later they retreated behind the Rio das Mortes, but they still trekked over the lands between the Rio das Mortes and the Araguaia, so that it was only the hardiest Brazilian who would settle there. Even after the Indians had been 'pacified', their wanderings east of the Rio das Mortes were a cause of concern to the local population; and the inhabitants of distant settlements such as Cocalinho or Aruanã were as late as 1958 both frightened and embarrassed when bands of Shavante came to town.

To the present day there are only two settlements right at the edge of Shavante country. One of them, Xavantina, was founded by the Central Brazil Foundation and still retains the character of a forward base in the penetration of the interior. The other, São Felix, has grown up as small villages do along the Araguaia, which is the main artery of communication in this part of Brazil. There have been conflicts with the Shavante at both points. The founders of Xavantina, however, were federal employees with orders to establish friendly relations with the Shavante and provided with the necessary gifts for distribution to help them accomplish this purpose. As a result there was no fighting with the Shavante in the neighbourhood of their base after the mid 1950s. At São Felix things were different. The inhabitants of the settlement were Brazilian settlers and backwoodsmen with an ingrained horror of Indians and neither the desire nor the resources to woo them. Consequently, clashes with the Shavante continued in this area until 1962 at least. It is clearly no coincidence that these Shavante remained hostile long after other communities had made their peace with the whites.[1]

[1] When I last visited the tribe in April 1964 I heard unconfirmed reports that the Shavante near São Felix had made peace with the whites. This was alleged to have been as a result of the activities of a large concern which had moved bulldozers and workmen into their territory and started to clear an air strip.

Meanwhile the Shavante have no longer much contact with other Indian tribes. They may once have fought the Tapirapé to the north, but there is no record of their having done so for a long time. In fact Baldus reported that, as long ago as 1935, the Tapirapé knew nothing of the Shavante and had not even seen their smoke[1] (1948: 157). In 1958 I was told by Brazilians who had worked on the upper Xingú that the tribes of that region reported clashes with wild Shavante to the east of them who did not even have knives, or in other words had no contact with the Brazilians. These Shavante are presumably identical with, or close to, the ones that are reported to have just made peace with the whites.

Similarly the Shavante I met had little recollection of past contacts with the Sherente (Maybury-Lewis, 1966a). When they spoke of the Sherente, it was invariably to refer to Sherente individuals who had either been brought over to act as interpreters by the Indian Protection Service or who had drifted into Shavante territory of their own accord. Significantly they did not have a word of their own to refer to the Sherente.[2] Nor are Shavante and Sherente mutually intelligible languages nowadays.

There are only two Indian tribes whom the Shavante clearly recognize as neighbours and also as enemies: the Karajá and the Bororo. The Bororo joined the Portuguese to fight against the Shavante in the eighteenth century (Maybury-Lewis, 1966a). Later they moved westward into Mato Grosso where the Shavante followed them. The Salesians record that the tribes waged war for the possession of *urucú*[3] in the late nineteenth century (Colbacchini and Albisetti, 1942: 150). In this century the western Shavante continued fighting the Bororo until about

[1] All over the interior of Brazil Indians and non-Indians alike practise a slash-and-burn type of cultivation. Even those tribes which are not enthusiastic cultivators fire the savannahs, so that neighbouring peoples are always traceable through their smoke.

[2] I thought for some time that the Shavante word for Sherente was *S'rõzasé-tdé'wa* = people who use a certain type of basket (S'rõzasé). I discovered, however, that a Sherente by the name of S'rõzasé had lived for some time among the Shavante and I now believe that *S'rõzasé-tdé'wa* simply means S'rõzasé's people. I am likewise of the opinion that when Shavante nowadays 'remember' the old contacts with the Sherente, they are in fact referring to what they have been told about these contacts by outsiders.

[3] A fruit whose crushed seeds provide the red paint which is of such ceremonial importance.

ten years ago, when the Salesians persuaded some to settle at mission stations where Bororo were already living.

The eastern Shavante have no contacts with the Bororo now. Their enemies were always the Karajá, whom they called *woradzú-toro* (from *woradzú* = stranger). They have been fighting each other since the eighteenth century at least (Pinto de Fonseca, 1867: 382–90). As the Shavante came less and less to the Araguaia but kept to the west of the Rio das Mortes, they had progressively less to do with their old enemies. Yet in this century it was always the Karajá who suffered when Shavante raiding parties appeared on the Araguaia. As the Shavante made peace with the Brazilians they learned to accept the Karajá as well, so that at the time I was working amongst them it was only the hostile Shavante near São Felix who were still reputed to fight the Karajá.

Although they may have given up fighting, the two tribes are still reserved in their relations toward each other. They meet infrequently, usually when the Shavante visit one of the Brazilian settlements along the Araguaia or when Karajá boatmen are hired by somebody to go up the Rio das Mortes. A very small amount of trading has been done during these encounters. The few trade beads which the eastern Shavante possess were obtained by barter from the Karajá.

The Shavante despise the Karajá and fear them, for they say that they infect them with sickness, either by contagion or sorcery, depending on the mood of the informant. Karajá, as we have seen, also fear the Shavante. Their word for them is a synonym for devil.

3. SHAVANTE COMMUNITIES

The Shavante are not a political unit. Their communities are autonomous and rarely less than a full day's journey apart. Since Shavante calculate travelling time on the basis of distances which can be covered on foot, this means that Shavante communities are generally separated by at least thirty miles. In fact most of them are even further apart, as can be seen from Map 2.

Until recently the Shavante were semi-nomadic. The 'location' of a community was therefore the site where they built large, beehive-shaped huts intended to last for a number of years. All treks started and finished at this site, but the villagers might spend the better part of each year away from it. When they were on the move they built much smaller shelters, which were occupied for perhaps a single night, perhaps a week or two but never more.

This semi-nomadic pattern of exploiting the surrounding country has been considerably modified in the last few years. In 1958 I heard of no Shavante group which had abandoned it, although there were indications that one or two were beginning to go on trek less frequently than they might have done. In 1962 there was evidence that certain groups were in the process of giving up this way of life, though the Shavante would have denied it strenuously. In 1964 I met Shavante who were prepared to admit they no longer planned to go out on trek.

I discuss these treks in Chapter II. At this stage I shall do no more than give a brief survey of the known Shavante communities, indicating their locations and giving some information as to their present circumstances. These communities are listed in Table 1. They are distributed between three distinct regions: on the tributaries of the Xingú river (shown in the table as *Xingú*), along the Rio das Mortes west of Xavantina (*Upstream*), and along the Rio das Mortes north-east of Xavantina (*Downstream*). There is little contact between Shavante of different regions. Yet there appears to be more contact between the Xingú and the Upstream Shavante than between either of these and the Downstream Shavante. The tribe is thus effectively divided into two parts which have comparatively little to do with each other and even differ as regards certain details of their social institutions. These are referred to in the table as Western Shavante and Eastern Shavante respectively. On the other hand there is a great deal of coming and going between the villages of a single region.

Table I gives an illusory impression of the stability of Shavante communities. This is because the locations listed for both Xingú and Upstream Shavante are in fact Indian Protection Service posts (Xingú) or missions (Upstream) to which Shavante groups have become attached. I shall later develop the argument that Shavante communities were usually highly unstable aggregates, whose composition fluctuated and whose very existence over a period of years could not be taken for granted. Something of these fluctuations can be seen from the data for the Downstream Shavante. At least two communities which existed in 1958 had ceased to exist in 1962. At least one new one had appeared. Meanwhile there had been considerable rearrangement of population in new and old communities alike.

The present circumstances of these communities are as follows:

Western Shavante

The Western Shavante were reported by the Salesians to have fought the Bororo along the upper reaches of the Rio das Mortes in the early part of this century. They attacked the missions at Sangradouro and Merure where Bororo were living, and at one time the Bororo of Sangradouro were so nervous of them that they would not willingly cross a small river only two kilometres from the settlement that was regarded as the frontier between the two tribes.[1] It seems that by the 1930s these Shavante were already divided between those who roamed the lands near the affluents of the Xingú and those who remained in the Upstream region.

Xingú Region

1. *Batoví*. I have not visited this village. My information is taken from the Indian agent at Simões Lópes, from inhabitants of Batoví whom I met at Simões Lópes, and from the Shavante of Simões Lópes themselves.

Shavante have been reported on the upper reaches of the Batoví and the Rio Sete de Setembro since the early 1950s (Simões, 1955: 24). At that time they were not settled near any of the Indian Protection Service posts in the region but merely

---

[1] This information was given to me by the Salesians at São Marcos.

visited them occasionally for short periods. It was not until 1955 that a Shavante community established its base at what I here call Batoví. When I worked among the Eastern Shavante in 1958, I was not aware that there were Western Shavante already in regular contact with the Indian Protection Service.

2. *Simões Lópes*. These Shavante remembered the names of a few men in the São Domingos group and claimed kinship with that community. One informant, aged about 40, specified that he was very small when his group left the region of the Eastern Shavante. It seems then that these people may have wandered westwards about 1930. I could obtain no coherent details about their relationship with the Upstream Shavante.

They were regular visitors to their present location in the early 1950s, as were the group now at Batoví. The village at Simões Lópes was established in 1955, some months after the one at Batoví. I visited it in August 1962.

The Indian Protection Service Post at Simões Lópes is one of the largest and best supplied of all in Brazil. It has its own air strip. The agent's house is well built and so are the numerous other houses and dependencies of the post, which form a lane nearly a quarter of a mile long down to the river. It was originally established for the Bakairí Indians and it still has a Bakairí village on one side. These Indians are highly acculturated. They live in Brazilian-style houses, wear Brazilian-style clothes and behave by and large like Brazilian back-woodsmen. They still speak Bakairí among themselves, though the majority of them also speak fluent Portuguese. It is they who are employed as workers at the post, especially in any jobs that require riding or the care of cattle.

The Shavante village is on the other side of the post and is a squalid affair by comparison. In 1962 it consisted of sixteen houses (see Fig. 1), nine of which were oblong Brazilian-style constructions and only seven of which were the typical round thatched huts of the Shavante. The oblong houses were poorly built and poorly furnished. Many of them contained only the traditional Shavante sleeping-mats and baskets, with the addition of any manufactured goods the residents had managed to scrounge.

All of these Shavante went clothed, save for a few of the children, and many of them had even taken to wearing boots.

During their ceremonies, when they would previously have appeared naked (save for penis-sheaths on the men) and painted, they no longer wish to do so. The men usually obtain clean white shorts from the Indian agent and they are worn for the ceremonial period. The women have taken to wearing clothes, and make-up if they can get it. Both sexes cut their hair short, the men to the same length as Brazilian men and the women to a shoulder-length bob. The men no longer wear their penis-sheaths or their ear-plugs, although the boys of the community still have their ears pierced at initiation. Even this custom may have died out. The Indian agent was invited to watch the previous initiation, and told that it was the last time the ear-piercing would be performed.

Every house has its own plantations, which are at some distance from the village.[1] At those periods of the year when much work in the plantations is necessary, the members of a household normally build shelters by their gardens and live there for extended periods. The community has entirely abandoned trekking. On occasion, though, a group of men will go out for days at a time to hunt, especially before a festival. There is still plenty of game and the Shavante, especially now that they have .22 rifles, usually bring back large quantities of meat. Soon after my arrival in the village a group of hunters came back with five tapir and two or three deer for the initiation ceremonies.

They must request permission from the Indian agent before going out on excursions such as this. Since they are now dependent on his goodwill for their supplies of food and manufactured goods from the post, they take care at least to make a show of obeying his instructions, of working when he tells them to and leaving off only when he says they may.

Work in this case consists either of agricultural labour on their own plantations or of tasks connected with the post and its lands, which the villagers carry out in return for a supply of such items as matches, tobacco, soap, and food. The arrangement is fluid and irregular. The agent gives general directives for the work that the Indians should do and does not enquire too closely into how they set about doing it. Certainly 'working hours' are not rigidly enforced. The Shavante for their part come in a constant

---

[1] I was unable to visit these plantations.

stream to the post, asking for this and that. The women come more frequently than the men and I noticed during my stay that certain women went virtually every day.

A few Shavante have regular jobs; for example two women and one man work around the house for the Indian agent. In general, though, the village as a whole sees itself as working for the post. This leaves room for individual variation. People may spend time on their own domestic tasks, or go out hunting or collecting very much as they feel inclined. In 1962, however, the Shavante of Simões Lópes were not self-sufficient as regards food. Since they had acquired a taste for a number of products which they could only obtain through the post, they were both dependent on, and being subsidized by, the post.

They also enjoyed the facilities the post offered. A Saturday-night dance, organized by the Bakairí, was well attended by Shavante. The women in particular oiled their hair, put on their cleanest clothes, and make-up if they had any, and showed obvious enthusiasm for the occasion. This struck me especially, since in traditional Shavante communities it is the men who do all the preening and most of the dancing, not the women. Certainly the Shavante did not dance as much on this occasion as the Bakairí, yet most of the dancing they did do was between couples of women.

On the other hand the community had not abandoned its traditional ceremonies. I observed the closing stages of the initiation, and the ritual was the same as I had witnessed in São Domingos in 1958. There were some modifications in the circumstances of the ceremonies which I shall discuss below. However, they refused to accede to the request of the Indian agent to hold the climax of the ceremony on Indian Day, a Brazilian holiday which he felt would have been appropriately celebrated in this fashion. They insisted instead that there was a proper time for this festival, which was at the height of the dry season.

Upstream Region

1. *Sangradouro*. This mission was established by the Salesians who came from Cuiabá to proselytize the Bororo. The Shavante of the region were consistently hostile until the early 1950s. At about that time their own situation became precarious. It seems

that they moved towards Xavantina with the idea of establishing contact with the Brazilians, possibly as a result of reports that other Shavante groups had done so and received many presents in return. But in 1954 they clashed with some Eastern Shavante in the vicinity of Xavantina and consequently turned westwards again.

By 1956 these Shavante had acquired considerable knowledge of the white man's ways, since a group of them were reported to be travelling in the direction of Cuiabá 'to see the governor'.[1] It was this group which eventually sought out the Salesians and were accommodated in the settlement at Sangradouro.

I have not visited this village, so my information is taken from the reports of the Salesian missionaries at São Marcos. According to them the Sangradouro Shavante no longer build their houses in the traditional style, but live in oblong Brazilian-style houses. These are not arranged in the traditional crescent but in rows at one side of the mission. It is also reported that these Shavante are more literate than the São Marcos Shavante and that they have 'fully adapted themselves' to their new way of life as a community of peasants attached to the mission.

2. *São Marcos*. The original nucleus of this community was the group of Shavante who did not set out for Cuiabá in 1956. Afflicted with epidemics and harried by the local settlers, they camped on land belonging to a certain Manuel Garcias. He planned to exterminate them by giving them poisoned provisions. The Salesians got to hear of the plan, however, and forestalled it by inviting the whole group to live on their mission station at Merure. There the Shavante and the Bororo could not get along together, so in 1958 the Salesians set up a mission at São Marcos especially for the Shavante from Merure and any others who cared to live there.

This is now the largest of all the Shavante communities. In 1962 it numbered fifteen houses. In 1964 there were thirty-two houses (Fig. 2). It can be seen from Table 1 that the population has not doubled in that interval. It has increased, but the striking increase in the number of houses reflects a shrinking of the average size of the household, a phenomenon which I shall discuss elsewhere.[2] Nevertheless, in 1962 all the houses were

---

[1] This information was given to me by the Salesians at São Marcos.
[2] In a paper, now in preparation, on social change among the Shavante.

Shavante-style huts, and in 1964 all but three of them were. Moreover the village still retains its traditional layout.

There is one important modification in the spatial arrangements. The *hę*, which I shall throughout translate as 'bachelors' hut', is not located at one extremity of the village. The missionaries, with a view to indoctrinating the young people of the community, insisted that the bachelors' hut should be located at the mission. There they built an octagonal house where all the boys of the village sleep.[1] One of the lay brothers also sleeps there with them.

In 1962 the older men of the village still spoke as if their stay at São Marcos were simply a rather longer interval between treks than usual. They went hunting in the vicinity, and occasionally went out in a band for a few days at a time to get meat for ceremonies. The boys in the bachelors' hut were however completely caught up in the routine of the mission. They attended Mass at 7.00 a.m. to start the day, intoning the responses (many of them in Latin) with gusto. During the morning they worked at jobs around the mission and after their midday meal they all attended school. Here they were taught how to read and write, were given religious instruction, and practised hymns and patriotic songs. After school they were free and most of them visited their families in the village. Their day ended with more prayers before they were all shepherded over to their dormitory to go to sleep. If their elders wished them to come and 'sing round the village', then they would do so, but they always came back to sleep at the mission.

As a result of this regime, the boys were not free to go out hunting with their elders and certainly not to go on trek. They appeared to enjoy the mission life, with the result that it became increasingly difficult for their parents to get them away. The missionaries took the position that the Shavante were welcome to go on trek if they wished to, but that they should not coerce their children if they did not want to go too. On the other hand the mission fathers also made it clear that they considered trekking a wasteful form of activity. Thus Shavante who remained at São Marcos and worked could expect more favours

---

[1] These included the boys not only of the age-set which would normally be in the bachelors' hut but of two other age-sets as well, to a total of seventy-four.

from the mission, to say nothing of wages, than those who did not.
By 1964 the missionaries had managed to wean the community
from its semi-nomadic life. People still left the village occasionally, but they were of two kinds: those who for one reason or
another were angry with the mission and were therefore walking
out, and those who were irked by the mission restrictions and
wished to go off, 'live it up' for a while, and then return. The
community as a whole no longer moved out on trek.

Instead they worked for the mission. The fathers gave
instructions to certain men who then had the responsibility of
mustering the various age-grades to their respective tasks. One
man similarly organized the women. Most of the work was
agricultural. The mission provided tools and by 1964 had a
truck to take its workers to the farthest fields. It also had a
certain amount of machinery for processing rice, manioc and
other products. The Shavante worked the mission lands and in
return they were fed, provided with manufactured goods by the
mission, and on occasion given payment in other ways. For
example the mission promised the men a total of eleven .22
rifles in 1962 if they would clear certain stretches of land, an
exceedingly hard and lengthy job. When it became apparent
that the job would take even longer than anticipated, the payment was raised to thirteen. Usually, however, payment is made
in items such as clothes and knives that the Shavante may obtain
from the mission store in return for the vouchers they earn by
working for the mission.

As a result these are perhaps the most affluent Shavante. All
of them possess more than a single change of clothes and many
of them have acquired suitcases to house their possessions.
Nevertheless, they have not abandoned the long hairstyle for
both men and women, and they continue to pierce the ears of
boys at initiation, even though the same boys do not subsequently wear ear-plugs. Meanwhile the boys are learning to
read and write.

There were two young men in 1964 who had completed the
equivalent of two years of Brazilian schooling. They had been
singled out to lead the boys in their various activities and they
took their duties very seriously. They also led the prayers and
could do this without any need for mission staff to be present.
One of them explained the details of the Passion, Crucifixion,

and Resurrection in the vernacular during the Mass on Palm Sunday. The other boys have not reached the same level but were certainly beginning to read and write.

The missionaries concentrate on instructing these boys, but there are regular prayers and Masses held for the village as a whole. These were much more frequent in 1964 than they were in 1962. The Shavante participated with apparent enthusiasm in these activities. Sunday Mass was well attended. On weekdays only workers could come to be fed at the mission, whereas on Sundays only those who attended Mass could claim food. But they appeared to enter into the spirit of the occasion. Thus some young Shavante motioned a Brazilian couple to remove their baby, which was crying too much during the Mass. Another indignantly kicked away a dog which was excreting outside when the Palm Sunday procession came past. Shavante are not so particular about their own ceremonies.

Finally these Shavante have developed a passion for, one might even say an addiction to, soccer. Everybody played it, young and old, and at all times. The missionaries did not permit the mission ball to be used during working hours, but the village had obtained a ball at some time or other and there was always a straggling game in progress there. People joined or left it as the fancy took them, and when all the men got tired of playing, then the women took over.

Eastern Shavante

Downstream Region

1. *Areões*. Between 1945 and 1950 there was apparently a difference of opinion between Eastern Shavante groups as to the desirability of entering into friendly relations with the whites. A certain chief Ẽribiwẽ led a community out of the Roncador region and made contact with the Brazilians a little way downstream from Xavantina in about 1950. Ẽribiwẽ himself was made much of by the Brazilians he met and he soon became known up and down the river as the Shavante who went about in a silk shirt with two revolvers. In the years that followed, his people did not move far from the Central Brazil Foundation's base at Xavantina, which they visited with a regularity that the Brazilians found embarrassing. It was Ẽribiwẽ's group which fought off the Western Shavante who came down towards

Xavantina in 1954. Finally they established themselves on the other bank of the Rio das Mortes, right opposite Xavantina itself.

It was clear that they intended to live in Xavantina, and, as far as possible, off its inhabitants. This threatened to paralyse the settlement, for the Shavante were ubiquitous and were accused of helping themselves to whatever they fancied as they went about its houses and storerooms. It also constituted a serious problem for a town which was so precariously supplied. Xavantina had been established as a base of penetration. An air strip was built there and a detachment of the Brazilian Air Force now runs its airport, which is of some importance in Brazil's transcontinental communication system. But the place has never been self-supporting. A high proportion of its inhabitants are functionaries and technicians who do not grow food. On the other hand, since Xavantina was until the mid 1950s exposed to Shavante attack, no sizeable peasant population settled by the base. Consequently it has to be supplied from the air, even to the present day.

Ẹribiwẽ's village therefore threatened to overtax the settlement's supplies. Up to this time the Central Brazil Foundation had been content to accept the *kudos* of 'pacifying' such intractable Indians. Now it appealed to the Indian Protection Service, in spite of the rivalry and antagonism which existed between the two agencies, and demanded that they should do something. The Service sent up an agent with instructions to establish a post well downstream from Xavantina, get the Shavante to settle there, and thus take the pressure off the town. In the meantime an American Fundamentalist missionary had also arrived in Xavantina and persuaded a dissident group of Ẹribiwẽ's people to settle at the mission which he proposed to establish for them.

This took place in 1955. In 1956 the group was located at Areões by the mission. I did not visit Areões at the time when it was a mission station, so that my information for this period is supplied by the Shavante themselves and by the missionary who once took me up the Araguaia river in his boat. The mission at Areões had a great deal against it at the time of its foundation. Since the missionary had attracted to it a group of Indians who had split off from the community which the Indian Protection

Service was trying to relocate, he incurred the bitter enmity of the Indian agent responsible for relocation. His mission was therefore not favoured by the Indian Protection Service. It could not count on local support because he was Protestant, and anyway the people of Xavantina felt that Areões was still too close. Similarly a Protestant mission, worse still an American Protestant mission, would have difficulty exercising political pressure in Rio de Janeiro to safeguard its position.

During the years of its precarious existence the mission tried hard to reshape the lives of these Shavante. They were instructed to build sanitary houses in straight lines instead of a semi-circle of palm leaf huts. They were exhorted to give up trekking and to devote themselves enthusiastically to agriculture. Above all they were admonished not to go into Xavantina and be corrupted by the local Brazilians. Although the Shavante complied as regards housing, they still went on trek and they still continued to visit Xavantina and prosecute their own private feuds. Thus the Areões Shavante killed Ẽribiwẽ when he was visiting their community in 1958. Fighting then broke out between Areões and Capitariquara and the mission was obliged to close down.[1] The last missionary left in September 1958. The Shavante then moved to Santa Terezinha. In 1959 they were attacked there by the Shavante from Capitariquara. The following year they counterattacked Capitariquara.

Now Capitariquara and São Domingos joined forces against them, so that the Shavante representing the villages of Areões and Santa Terezinha took refuge in Xavantina itself. They camped at one end of the airfield in a high state of alarm, hourly expecting to be attacked by their enemies from further

[1] The Indian agent at Capitariquara reported to the Indian Protection Service that the missionary had incited his Shavante to attack Capitariquara, or at least connived at their doing so. The missionary meanwhile had made his position in Mato Grosso difficult by broadcasting to his friends in the U.S.A., over an unlicensed transmitter, to reassure them of his personal safety during the 'Shavante war'. The Indian Protection Service protested to the National Security Council that a foreigner had no business to operate an unlicensed transmitter and communicate with other countries from Central Brazil.

Unfortunately the various agencies working with the Shavante are so busy with their own feuds that they tend to interpret the fluctuations in Shavante groups in the light of the relations between their patrons. The relations between the Shavante themselves have never claimed their attention.

downstream. Late in 1961 the Indian Protection Service sent an agent to relocate this group once again. He made use of the deserted settlement at Areões to establish a new village there, this time under the patronage of an Indian post.

It was this post which I visited briefly in 1962. The agent received me warmly[1] and told me that the Areões Shavante were still maintaining their old pattern of trekking for most of the year, although they had cleared extensive plantations, which I was able to inspect. He also told me that they were still very nervous about the prospect of attack from further downstream and that he feared they might get involved in fighting with other Shavante bands while they were travelling in the Roncador.[2]

2. *Capitariquara.* This post was established by the Indian Protection Service in 1956 with the same purpose as the mission at Areões, to draw the Shavante away from Xavantina. Like the Areões mission it was perpetually in difficulties, but the reasons were different.[3]

The first agent was a young man who had had a course of training in the methods of settling immigrants in the Brazilian interior. He hoped to apply similar techniques to persuade the Shavante to renounce their nomadism and settle down to tilling the soil. His post was supplied with a certain amount of equipment and provisions to start it off, but the Shavante accepted these gifts without apparently realizing that they were supposed to be the basis of a new way of life for them. Later the agent instructed them that they were not to waste time hunting. They were to work in their plantations, and if necessary he would send out men to hunt and provide meat, or alternatively he would slaughter a steer for the workers. The Shavante took this as an opportunity to eat off the post while doing the minimum of work. Consequently the post very soon ran through its supplies of equipment and provisions.

At the same time the funds for the purchase of new items and for the payment of employees were either held up interminably by bureaucratic delays or were expropriated before they reach the post. Finally the shopkeepers in Xavantina

---

[1] I mention this because the agent had been second in command of the post at São Domingos during our stay there in 1958.

[2] For a plan of this village and a skeleton genealogy, see Figs. 3 and 3a.

[3] I was never able to visit this post. My information is taken from the Shavante and from conversations with employees of the post.

stopped its credit, many of the unpaid employees deserted, and the agent himself procured a transfer. A new agent was appointed in 1958, but he was so appalled by conditions at the post that he spent very little time there. Instead he lived in Xavantina and ignored his agency.

This built up great resentment among the Shavante. They had been used to receiving largesse from the Brazilians for nearly a decade. Now they felt that they had been supplied with an official patron in the form of a post, and instead of the bounty being augmented, it had inexplicably dried up. Chief Ẽribiwẽ was particularly incensed, and he was actually trying to rally support for an attack on his own post when he was murdered at Areões. For a year or so after that the Downstream communities were busy with their own attacks and counterattacks, but in 1960 the Capitariquara Shavante finally drove out the remaining Brazilians from their post at gun point, set fire to the buildings and destroyed the whole venture. After which the community moved off into the Roncador, where it split into various factions which went their several ways.

3. *Santa Terezinha.* This mission was founded in 1954 by the Salesians with the specific purpose of attracting Downstream Shavante and proselytizing them. Two Shavante groups settled there, one being a band which did not get on either with Ẽribiwẽ's group or with those still out in the Roncador, and the other a band which had wandered in from the Xingú region. Although they settled at the mission they still continued to go on trek and were actively involved with the neighbouring Shavante communities. Thus nearly half of the community moved to Capitariquara in early 1958.

When I visited Santa Terezinha in August 1958 I found that the Shavante had just finished building a new village. It consisted of seven traditional huts arranged in a semi-circle with a bachelors' hut, still incomplete, at one end of it. This village had been moved closer to the mission. It was then about 200 yards away.

The regime at the mission was essentially similar to the one I have described for São Marcos, but its influence over the Shavante was not so great. I did meet some teen-age boys who spent much of their time hanging around the mission and were eager to do odd jobs for the missionaries in order to acquire the manufactured goods which set them apart from their fellows. But these boys were in any case untypical, or they would have been on trek with the rest of the community. It must be remembered, too, that at this time the Shavante did not possess manufactured goods in the same quantity as they did in 1962 and there was still considerable eagerness to obtain them. These teen-agers at Santa Terezinha were inordinately proud of their clothes and their snakeskin belts because their fellow Shavante still went naked in the village.

Such villagers as had not gone on trek simply worked for the mission, in order to get fed and to obtain payment in kind. They did not otherwise spend a great deal of time there. Indeed they would sometimes 'strike' by staying away from work *en masse*. During such 'strikes' the missionaries would feed any children who presented themselves at the mission, but would not permit them to take any food back to their families.

Afternoon classes were held for the children and teen-age boys, but few of them had made much progress at the time of my visit. Indeed I found little evidence of serious modification of the Shavante's way of life. The Shavante themselves were only conscious of one important change—that they were having difficulty in performing the *wai'a* ceremony, which involves the ceremonial rape of selected women by the officiating age-set. One woman had managed to avoid this by fleeing to the mission, where she had been afforded sanctuary. At subsequent *wai'a* other women had done the same thing until, by the time of my visit, it seemed doubtful whether the Santa Terezinha Shavante could perform the ceremony without breaking off their contact with the mission. They could of course perform it while they were out on trek and that is what they did, but the missionaries would always get to hear of it and would try to apply such sanctions as lay in their power to indicate their displeasure. This was something of a bone of contention between the mission and the Shavante at that time.

In 1958 this village was joined by the Shavante from Areões. At about the same time the Capitariquara Shavante split up and some of them went to São Domingos. The fighting between Areões and Capitariquara was therefore continued between Santa Terezinha and São Domingos. São Domingos attacked Santa Terezinha in 1960. Later in the year the Santa Terezinha people cut to pieces a band from São Domingos whom they found out hunting. Then, as the reports of planned reprisals came in, the whole community, which was now on bad terms with the mission, retreated to Xavantina in the hope that the proximity of the Brazilians would protect them. They were subsequently resettled, as we have seen, at Areões. Meanwhile the Salesians closed down the mission in 1961.

4. *São Domingos.* I have already described the circumstances leading up to the arrival of a Shavante community which built its base village near the Indian Protection Service Post at São Domingos in 1953. Ironically, in view of the hostility these Shavante had shown towards the whites, this was the first such community to enter into permanent peaceful relations with the outside world. This was due to the strenuous efforts of the Indian Protection Service in this area. Other Shavante groups which were more anxious to make friends with the whites found that after the first shower of presents the whites did not really know what to do with them and wished they would go away again. These Shavante, by contrast, found an Indian post already set up to deal with them.

The community which settled at São Domingos was, and still is, under the chieftaincy of Apҫwẽ, an old Shavante renowned among his compatriots and also among the local Brazilians as a 'strong chief'. When I worked among his people in 1958, they were the most powerful, most numerous and least acculturated of all the Downstream Shavante. They built their village about 15–20 minutes' walk from the post. A small creek separated the two, so that during the wet season one had either to swim or to use a canoe in order to communicate between them. Some Shavante were nevertheless at the post nearly every day, but there were those who hardly ever went there. I discovered that a great deal went on in the village of which the people at the post were ignorant; and it even happened, though this was much less frequent, that the Shavante in the village were uninformed about events at the post.

At that time the presence of the post had exercised little influence on the Shavante. The Indian agent had no authority over the village. He could advise, but the Shavante accepted his advice only when it suited them. He was unable either to prevent or punish acts of what would be considered murder under

Brazilian law. He had been unsuccessful in persuading the Shavante to abandon nomadism or to take up agriculture systematically.

Meanwhile the Shavante rarely spent more than a week or two in their base village, usually on the occasion of an important festival. They regarded the post as a source of provender and of manufactured goods. The influence of the Indian agent seemed to be directly proportional to his supply of gifts. He was careful to give the lion's share of these to the chief and the members of his lineage, so that even if the community as a whole did not feel warmly towards him at a particular time, he could be certain that its most influential people would not side against him.

There was no regular work which the post commissioned and asked the Shavante to carry out. Occasionally the agent would ask to have a specific task carried out and the payment for it, preferably a slaughtered steer, would be negotiated with Apçwẽ in advance. Apçwẽ would then see that the job was done. But the post interfered minimally in the lives of the Shavante. The agent could make himself understood in Shavante but his knowledge of the language had not improved with the years, and he did not attempt to instruct his Indians beyond exhorting them to take up agriculture.

When I returned to São Domingos in 1962 I found this situation substantially altered. In 1958 the village had comprised seventeen huts, plus a bachelors' hut (Fig. 4). In 1962 there were only ten, and a bachelors' hut. There had been a considerable decrease in its population due to epidemics and internecine warfare. A number of its inhabitants had seceded and gone to live at Ę Tõ. Moreover, the village site had been moved closer to the post, which was now only a few minutes' walk away.

Its inhabitants still went out on trek, but they were equally inclined to go on begging trips to the nearest Brazilian cities. During my stay there a plane landed for a moment or two on the air strip and took off again. We discovered that it had brought back eight young men who had been to Goiânia in search of clothes. They had been taken into the local barracks and looked after by the military, who had given them gifts of clothing and arranged for them to get a lift back to their village.

They were very well dressed on their return and all sported small airline bags or suitcases. They had not learned any Portuguese or even worked at anything much, but simply acquired things.

By now most of the inhabitants of the village went about clothed, though not a single one had in 1958. In order to acquire clothes and soap to wash them, and the other goods which they now desired, they were much more dependent on the post than they had been before. The position of the Indian agent was correspondingly strengthened.

Besides this, the Shavante had learned by now of their comparative impotence, and they were acutely conscious of their own dwindling numbers, a topic to which they returned again and again in conversation with me, who had known their village in the days when it was numerous and strong. They were therefore more inclined to imitate the ways of the outside world. They had for instance planted a much larger area than they ever did in 1958, and had adopted the cultivation of manioc, a thing they had resolutely refused to do before.

Even in 1962, however, I was able to verify that they were much involved in their old feuds, in spite of the fact that they were as much interested now in the doings of Brazilians both near and far as they were in the activities of their fellow Shavante. Similarly they had not abandoned their ceremonies, not even the *wai'a*.

5. *Ẽ Tõ*. A diagram of this village will be found in Fig. 5. I have already described the circumstances of my visit to it. This is the only Shavante village of known location which is not attached to either a mission or an Indian Service post. Its present circumstances are somewhat obscure, since it was perpetually threatened by São Domingos, and a number of its inhabitants even seceded in 1963 and made their way to São Marcos.

6. *Marãwasede*. This community had not been contacted as late as 1962. My information concerning it is taken from a number of São Domingos Shavante who were originally members of it. They told me that it was located at least three days' journey (close to 100 miles) away to the north and that it was fighting with the Brazilians and on occasion with other Indians (non-Shavante). It was also on bad terms with São Domingos.

These were the Shavante who were reported to be making peace in 1964.

I tried in 1958 to visit the uncontacted Shavante of Marã-wasede, but was finally defeated by lack of guides, lack of transport and lack of time. The men who could have guided me to it were all refugees from the community and were understandably reluctant to go back there. I should in any case have had to take a large quantity of gifts with me, and there were no pack-horses available which were capable of making such a journey. Moreover, I knew from experience that travelling with a pack-horse in the Roncador region is cumbersome and exceedingly slow. I should have had to spend weeks on the journey there and back.

At one time I succeeded in interesting an influential São Paulo newspaper in supplying me with air transport for such a journey in return for an exclusive report on my visit. But it transpired that there was nowhere for conventional planes to land, and that helicopters could not be flown into Central Brazil without setting up a special chain of fuel dumps for them. In any case the only helicopters available were those of the Brazilian air-rescue service, which could not be spared for such a purpose. I was therefore reluctantly obliged to abandon the proposed journey.

It is quite possible that this list does not exhaust all the Shavante communities. The Shavante themselves say that there are 'more villages' in the country between the Rio das Mortes and the Xingú, but they cannot give precise details of them and the villages are in any case highly mobile.

II

ECOLOGY

1. HABITAT

SHAVANTE country forms part of the plateau which is the western section of the Brazilian highlands. It is high savannah, saved from extremes of heat and humidity by the fact that it is about 2,000 feet above sea level. There is a clearly marked dry season from May to September, when even a shower of rain is most unusual and travellers whose routes lie away from the larger rivers may suffer seriously from thirst. During this period the lakes of the wet season are marked by a few sparse blades of green grass in the middle of an expanse of dried mud, which crackles underfoot like gelatine. It is possible to dig water-holes in the middle of these 'lakes' to the full extent of a man's reach and still to get no more than a cupful of dirty water out of them. The rains come in October and are customarily heavy. By January or February the land is usually water-logged, so that hunters and Indians get used to walking perpetually in a foot or more of water. The traveller's difficulty then is to find a dry spot to make his camp at night, or even one on which he can lie down and sleep.

The soil is of sandstone, conglomerate, and shale (Sauer, 1950: 323), and is generally known to be of poor quality. The broad western plateau of the Brazilian highlands is sometimes regarded as country rich in mineral deposits, but otherwise good for nothing but cattle-raising and not always very well suited for that. The mines of the state of Minas Gerais at one time provided the whole basis of Brazil's wealth. Gold was mined in Goiás. Gold and diamonds are still mined near Cuiabá in Mato Grosso, and the extraction of quartz is becoming increasingly important throughout the region. There are in fact rumours of fabulous wealth to be acquired in the lesser-known intervening regions, such as that of the Serra do Roncador, yet nobody has discovered mineral deposits of any great value in Shavante-land. The Rio das Mortes is supposed originally to have acquired its name from a group of pioneers who mined gold near its banks at the beginning of the eighteenth century, and subsequently massacred each other while quarrelling over the division of the spoils; but no subsequent prospectors have succeeded in locating these veins. The existence of these deposits has now become part of the folk-lore of the region, and is believed in by optimistic backwoodsmen in Mato Grosso and Goiás, but probably the last outsider to take the legend really seriously was Colonel Fawcett, who lost his life in the attempt to prove that it had some foundation.

In the circumstances it is understandable that the Shavante have been permitted to rove about 'their' lands comparatively unmolested for so long. But when Shavante-land is referred to as 'savannah' it must be understood that it is not open grassland or prairie. Brazilians call such open grassland *campo limpo* (clean country) and it is highly valued for cattle grazing. Shavante-land consists, however, of another type of savannah—the *campo cerrado* (closed country). One geographer has described the *campo cerrado* as 'a savanna with scattered thickets of deciduous scrub forest' (James, 1941: 505). It may occasionally be productive land, but in general (and this applies to Shavante-land) it is poor country and some of the most sparsely populated in the whole of Brazil.

The Shavante like it because it is open country compared with the tropical jungles of which there are patches all over their territory, and which they have seen to the west of the head-waters of the Xingú River. These local jungles are known by the Brazilians as *galerias* (galleries) because they are usually found in broad bands along the water courses, so that even the smaller creeks wind their way through tunnels of thick foliage. The Shavante appreciate the gallery forests because in them they invariably find water and the most abundant supplies of the wild roots and fruits which are the basis of their diet. Often, though not always, the stands of *buriti* palms (*Mauritia* sp.) whose leaves provide the bast for their ceremonial regalia are to be found in the galleries, as also are the trees whose woods they use for the manufacture of various artifacts. Here too is the best soil for the cultivation of their meagre crops; and finally the gallery forests are usually good places to start game, for the game animals are drawn to the well-watered shade of these jungles.

The Shavante consider these forests, however, to be a convenience and no more. Hunting is the activity which interests them above all else, on which they spend most energy, and about which they talk unceasingly. They discuss at length where particular game was sighted and all the details of its tracking and killing, down to the exact spot at which the fatal arrow entered it, at what angle and with what effect. In their monotonous scrub, where I was unable to tell one bush or thicket from another, and was frequently under the impression that I had travelled through a particular patch of trees only a little while previously, the Shavante can remember the exact place where a kill was made months or even seasons previously and narrate its circumstances in detail. Yet hunting can be carried on as successfully in open country as in the jungle. There is enough game for the Shavante's requirements out on the savannah, so that they do not have to seek out the gallery forests when they want meat. On the other hand the thrill of stalking, and more especially of pursuing, their game is heightened for the Shavante when they are in the open. Even the toughest Indian cannot crash through thickets of thorns in the same way as a tapir does, and the detours he is obliged to make and the perpetual concern to prevent his bow and arrows getting tangled in the lianas put him at a disadvantage when he is hunting in the jungle. The inhospitable tangle of the undergrowth and the ubiquitous thorns sometimes even daunt Shavante who are out on a collecting trip, looking for fruit rather than for game. I have often heard men come back empty-handed from such trips, with the explanation '*ro pipá-di*' (literally 'I was afraid of the country'). There is no reason, then, for Shavante to associate open country with scarcity and jungle with abundance. They do require jungles for clearing when they plant their crops, but these crops are not vital to the Shavante diet, as we shall see.

On the other hand the Shavante make no secret of their detestation of close country. They call it *ro was'té-di* (*ro* = country, *was'té* = bad, an expression of disgust which is invariably uttered with a perjorative accentuation of the final syllable). They refer to the savannah as *ro pse-di* or *ro wẽ-di* (*pse* = good, *wẽ* = pretty, beautiful) and on it they live their lives. Their villages are invariably built out in the open, on ground from which even the sparse savannah vegetation has been meticulously cleared. When they are on the move they travel through the savannah, avoiding as far as possible the belts of the jungle, even if this means going short of water in the dry season. While they are travelling they set fire to patches of particularly close jungle, simply, as they say, 'to clear the country' (*ro wē da*). In short they think of the jungle as alien and ugly and are contemptuous of peoples who make it their home. This attitude is fully shared by the Sherente, who even use the same words (*ro pse-di* and *ro wasté-di*) for open and close country. Nimuendajú reports similarly for the Timbira (1946: 1): 'The predominant part of the Timbira steppes consists of *campos cerrados*, that is, grass tracts with more or less dense stands of trees and bushes. Absolutely pure steppes I have seen only in the upper Pindaré country, and even these were only of minor extent. The two Timbira tribes of that region—Krīkatí and Pukóbye—are accordingly called by other members of their branch Popéykateye[1] (inhabitants of the true (or beautiful), pey, steppes, põ).'

[1] Jean Carter, who has worked among the Krīkatí, informs me that this designation would be more correctly rendered as Pŏpéykateye, the spelling which Nimuendajú uses on page 18.

2. SUBSISTENCE ACTIVITIES

In this section I shall describe the manner in which Shavante exploited their environment prior to their contacts with the Brazilians in recent decades. The information is taken from my study of the community at São Domingos in 1958, at a period before substantial modifications had set in. These modifications and their influence on Shavante culture will be treated separately elsewhere.

Hunting

It has often been thought that the tribes which inhabit the upland savannah of Central Brazil subsisted primarily, if not exclusively, on hunting and gathering. The Gê tribes were therefore considered hunters *par excellence*, and their agriculture was thought to be rudimentary in the extreme, or even non-existent. The researches of Nimuendajú (1946: 57) and Lowie (1946: 480) did much to correct this impression, for they showed that all the then-known Gê tribes had probably always practised a significant modicum of agriculture, while, among the Timbira at least, farming was of considerable importance. The Shavante also farmed, but they devoted so little time, energy or thought to their agriculture that they conformed more closely to the stereotype of 'hunters and collectors' than did the other Gê tribes already studied.

On the other hand meat was not the basis of the Shavante diet, as has often been supposed even by people who knew them quite well. This misconception was due to the Shavante interest in hunting and their passion for meat, which they regard as the prime delicacy. Those who have had to resist the importuning of a band of Shavante begging to have a steer killed for them, or have seen these Indians returning from a hunting trip, each with perhaps 100 lb. of meat in his carrying basket, and witnessed the subsequent carnivorous orgy, may be excused for assuming that, broadly speaking, 'the Shavante lived on meat'. In fact they subsisted primarily on wild roots, nuts, and fruits which they gathered in their wanderings. If I have elected, then, to discuss hunting before the economically far more important activity of gathering, it is because I range these pursuits in the order which the Shavante would assign to them.

For them there is no question as to which is relatively more

'important'. Meat far and away transcends other forms of food
in the Shavante esteem, and food in general plays a very large
part in their interests and in their conversation. While any small
item of news or gossip is faithfully related in the men's circles
and commented on at length, often on a number of evenings
over a period of weeks or longer, the two subjects which most
occupy the men are what food there is in the community (and
where, i.e. at whose hut it may be found), and hunting details,
including past feats and future prospects. The plans for a
communal hunt are usually discussed for days beforehand,
whereas the decision that people should go out collecting is often
taken as the men are already getting up to leave the meeting,
while they are dusting the sand off the skins they have been
sitting on. Nor is this interest in meat and its acquisition confined only to the men. Shavante women will discuss the prospects
of getting meat at great length and will send their children out
to spy for them (if they have not already gone of their own
accord), to see what meat is coming in to which household.
While they have not the interest in, or the knowledge of, the
technicalities of hunting, which are such a perennial topic
among their menfolk, they are quite as interested in the end
product. They receive an unsuccessful hunter with a marked
coldness, even when there is plenty of other food in the household. A successful hunter, on the other hand, flings down his kill
for the women to prepare and goes to lie down on his sleeping
mat with an appearance of studied indifference which masks his
feelings of self-importance.

  Hunting is the most common expression of virility. Shavante
men enjoy it for its own sake and delight in it, if they are good
at it, because it enables them to make a public exhibition of
their manliness. Shavante, as we shall see, prize endurance and
fleetness. Wakefulness and watchfulness are also qualities on
which the men pride themselves. The successful conclusion of a
hunting trip shows that they are endowed, in some measure,
with all of these.

  A man (or a group of men) usually decided without any
formality to go out after game and simply stayed out either until
he had sufficient meat or he was too tired to continue. On such
occasions hunters left the camp before daybreak and went off
armed with the best long-range weapons they possessed. These

were most commonly bows and arrows. By 1958 most Shavante communities had some guns. São Domingos, for example, possessed three .22 rifles, and a hunter would always take one of these in preference to his bow, if he could get it and ammunition to go with it. By 1962 Shavante could rarely be bothered to go hunting without a gun. Clubs were never carried on such informal hunting excursions, nor were dogs taken to help the hunters.[1] Shavante did their own tracking and hounding of the game they pursued.

In this they are both astute and fleet. They will sometimes run down the young of peccary or deer and capture them while hunting the full-grown animals. They then bring the young animals home and rear them as pets. Eventually, however, they are eaten, particularly in the case of peccary, an animal whose meat the Shavante especially enjoy.[2]

Hunters give different calls to indicate the various species of game they are following; and the call for peccary, if heard in the encampment, invariably sends men leaping for their bows and running to join the hunting party. The Shavante class tapir with peccary, as can be seen from the following table of equivalences:

SHAVANTE	ENGLISH
uhędę	tapir
uhę	wild pig (*Tayassu tajacu*)
uhę-ri	peccary (*Tayassu pecari*)
uhębį	pig (domestic)

[1] The Shavante seem to own very few dogs. Certainly there were not more than five or six in São Domingos in 1958. These dogs are used as pets and watchdogs and never used for tracking game—not even jaguar, which backwoodsmen in Mato Grosso will not hunt without trained dogs. It is interesting to compare this attitude towards dogs with that of the Sherente, who rely on their hunting-dogs to track, start, and often to corner their game for them. Sherente frequently gave as an excuse for an unsuccessful hunt that the dogs were no good. Consequently, perhaps, the Sherente dogs were kept half starved and were usually received with kicks and missiles in the huts, where they were invariably thieving food. Shavante dogs tend to be pampered and well-fed by their owners.

[2] The Shavante told me that they would be eaten, though I never actually saw an animal reared as a pet and subsequently eaten by its owners. It seems likely that peccary at least were reared for food, not only because the Shavante find them delicious eating but because they are bad-tempered and dangerous animals to have about the house.

Tapir are highly prized since they are the largest game animals in Shavante-land. The other major class of fauna which the Shavante hunt down systematically is deer.

The generic term for what we should call 'deer' is *po*, and Shavante often use the phrase *po da* (after deer) as a synonym for hunting in general. They make the following discriminations between species of deer:

SHAVANTE	ENGLISH
po-ne	deer (*Mazama americana*)
po-nĕri	deer (*Mazama simplicicornis*)
po-dze	deer (*Ozotocerus bezoarcticus?*)
(po-dze-wasede)	cattle
(po-dze-was'té)	

It is interesting to note that they assimilate cattle to the class of deer, and malformed deer at that, for *wasede* = bad, whereas the Sherente word for cattle designates them as belonging to the other major class of game animals. Sherente call a steer *ktĕku*, where *ktĕ* = tapir, and thus assign it to what is essentially a porcine class. On the other hand the largest species of deer in Shavante-land (*Dorcelaphus bezoarcticus*) is, for reasons I did not discover, not classed as a variety of *po* at all but referred to as *aihĕ*.

When the men are planning the general direction in which the community should move while on trek, their deliberations are specially influenced by the possibility of finding deer or peccary in particular regions according to the latest reports available. But any game is hunted and eaten. Besides peccary and deer, the greater and lesser ant-eater are fairly plentiful. I have also seen the Shavante eat steppe rats and various species of monkey and armadillo. They eat most birds except carrion birds but would hunt only certain species: the pampa ostrich and the sariema, both of whom provide a great deal of meat; parrots for their feathers and the arara (macaw) for its long tail feathers, which they use in their ceremonial regalia. The appearance of a macaw causes a flurry of excitement as everybody within reach of a bow or a club takes a shot at it.

On the other hand I have never seen Shavante eat reptiles. They are not, in any case, very plentiful on the savannah, and the Shavante certainly do not seek them out at the water's edge.

PLATE I

Men returning from the hunt with a captured peccary

They do, however, kill and eat turtles at the end of the dry season, but this is done *en passant*. Their real interest is in collecting the turtles' eggs, for a single nest will provide large numbers of these extremely nourishing and fatty eggs and an experienced collector can find a number of nests on a single riverain beach in the right season.

When out hunting in this way the Shavante men carry nothing but their weapons. Very occasionally they will also take a small carrying-basket with them, containing a few nuts to eat by the way, and—invariably nowadays—matches. They move at a quick, shuffling pace (which is extremely difficult for an outsider to get used to), faster than a walk but not quite a trot. They can keep this up all day if necessary, interspersed with the darting or running after any game that may present itself. When they wish to rest they nearly always climb a tree. This affords an excellent vantage point from which to spy out the land amidst the thickets and stunted trees of the savannah, and further, offers a dry resting place in the rainy season.

While they are in search of game they eat anything that they come upon in the way of fruits, nuts, or roots, but they keep a particular watch for wild honey. Several varieties of bee are to be found on the savannah. Shavante distinguish a large number of varieties whose peculiarities are all well known, especially as regards whether they give much honey and how good it tastes. I list some of these varieties here:

putédi	no honey
puteté wawẽ	no honey
utętororiné	bad honey
datomnęre-bumorõĩ'wa	good honey
nęnçre	good honey
wamnęnęrirẽ-pré	good honey
pató	?
tsiprí	good honey
amdzę	good honey
u'mra	good honey
u'mra zę-pré	good honey
mrõmęrtõri	bad honey
pi'ú	hornet (see Chapter VII)
m'honé-ri	termite

I have included their word for 'termite' in the list, since they also refer to the sticky secretion around these grubs as *ĩ-pnĩ*, the generic word for what we should refer to as 'honey', and they eat it when they can get it. Since most of these bees are stingless, a Shavante who catches sight of a bee's nest immediately climbs the tree in question, breaks open the nest, and eats its contents, bees and all. Shavante will do the same with certain termites' nests and will endure considerable pain in the process, for the bite of a termite is sometimes sharp enough to draw blood. My companion on a hunting trip was once covered with angry termites, even down to his genitals, as he struggled and hacked at a particularly resistant nest, but he did not run off to rid himself of them until he had prized the nest clear. The disadvantage of eating large quantities of wild honey when out hunting is that very often there is no water near at hand to slake the acute thirst it induces. Shavante are well aware of this and will sometimes, though rarely, miss the opportunity of raiding a bee's nest because of the absence of water in the neighbourhood. Usually, however, they will eat the honey and contain their thirst until they come to water; or, alternatively, will try to tap some ground water, if the dry season is not so far advanced as to make this impossible.

This is done by digging a water hole to the depth of a man's reach, or, in more favoured circumstances, by finding some grasses growing in a shady spot and uprooting them. A small hole about eighteen inches deep is then dug and in this 'clean mud' water slowly collects. It is then drunk off quickly before it dirties. I thought it tasted horrible, but it was apparently quite harmless.

When an animal has been killed it is either roasted on the spot (if the hunters intend to stay out till the following day or longer) or it is carried back to be cooked by the women. Shavante men know how to make small baskets out of two intertwined palm-leaves, which can be plaited in a few moments and are used for carrying pieces of meat. Usually, though, they do not bother to make any receptacle for their kill, but merely tie its feet together with a strip of bark, place the bark around their foreheads and carry it home in this way. The animal may or may not be cleaned first, depending on how far the hunter has to walk to get back to camp, and on how tired he is. He may decide, for example, that it is less trouble to empty out the contents of a tapir's stomach than to carry the extra weight all the way back.

If meat has to be kept for any length of time, then it is roasted on the embers of the fire. This roasting is done long and thoroughly, for the meat is well protected by a covering of ash and earth. When the cooking is completed the roast meat can be kept for a week, or even more, without becoming inedible. Admittedly, by the end of a few days after roasting there are maggotts in the centre of the meat, but the Shavante do not mind this or the accompanying stench, and simply cut the good meat off the rotten part and eat it. I found that, once I had overcome my initial repugnance, I could also eat this meat without any ill effects.

This type of hunting, in which the Shavante indulge throughout the year, is undertaken on the initiative of any individual, and is referred to as *aba* or *ai'wa*. If more than one hunter should go out, then the party is composed of friends who have joined forces for the purpose. The distribution of kills on their return is described in Chapter V.

There is, however, another type of hunt, which is a communal enterprise, ordered and directed by the mature men[1] on behalf of the community as a whole. Such hunts, known as *hɛmono*, are invariably held in conjunction with ceremonies in which the entire community participates and are terminated by a formal distribution of the meat by official distributors. Communal hunts in connexion with important ceremonies are characteristic of the Gê tribes; and it will be remembered that the Sherente had two permanent meat distributors, one from each moiety, who officiated on such occasions (Nimuendajú, 1942: 18). There is no office of meat-distributor among the Shavante, but certain men of the dominant lineage in the community, who are in certain respects recognized as leaders and arbiters, invariably distribute meat (and other things) on formal occasions.

A communal hunt differs from an ordinary one in that it is

---

[1] Shavante men pass through four age-grades: children, boys (in the *Hɛ* or bachelors' hut), young men (initiated but not regarded as mature), and mature men (all the senior age-sets). The mature men are those who take all decisions affecting the community, and wherever I use the term 'men's council' I refer to their forum, unless I specifically state otherwise.

planned in the men's circle and usually lasts a number of days. Sometimes it is decided in the men's circle that a particular group—usually the young men—should go out hunting on behalf of the community and directions are given to that effect. But this is not the same thing as a formal hunt. The members of the age-set which has been instructed to hunt may or may not comply with the instructions, and generally they are accompanied by other hunters who happen to feel like joining them. Furthermore, there is no formal distribution of the spoils on their return, but the meat is swiftly distributed among kin in a manner that will be described later. In a communal hunt, on the other hand, the majority of the able-bodied men of the community take part. They set out more or less together and their hunting is directed by the elders. They return together and they surrender their game for distribution in the village.

Such hunts invariably produced huge quantities of meat—enough to feed the hunters while they were out, and to feed the entire community for three or four days after their return.[1] The economic reason for holding them in conjunction with festivals, when people were too busy to procure food, is therefore obvious. But the reasons are not entirely economic, for the Shavante, in common with other Gê tribes, value meat and maize as the basis of all ceremonial prestations. They cannot in theory be substituted in ceremonial by any other food of which they may happen to have a surplus. In the same way, other Gê tribes, faced with the disappearance of game due to the encroachments of cattle breeders on their hunting lands, scoured the countryside for weeks to obtain the necessary meat for their ceremonies (see, for example, Nimuendajú, 1946: 64).

One method, which the Shavante still use to ensure the success of these communal hunts, is that of firing a circular area of the savannah in the dry season and then stationing large numbers of hunters at the mouth of the circle, where they club or shoot the animals who come out terrified by the flames and often stupefied by the smoke.

The ceremonial game drives are not preceded or accompanied by any rites designed to ensure a successful hunt or to promote the abundance of game. I have only once come across an instance of hunting-magic of this kind. A man was squeezing

[1] This is no longer true for the Upstream Shavante.

the juice of a potato-like root over his arms, and he told me that he did it in order to ensure that he would kill many deer. This may well not have been a 'magical' practice and I never obtained a satisfactory explanation of it. Apart from this doubtful instance I have only hearsay evidence that the Shavante perform special rites and wear special ear-plugs[1] for hunting jaguar. On the one occasion when I hunted jaguar in their company, however, ours was an informal expedition and the Shavante did not behave any differently, apart from being more excited, than they would have done had they been hunting other game. It is perhaps surprising that hunts of a pronounced ceremonial character should be unaccompanied by any sort of rites, especially among a people to whom hunting means so much.[2] I can only suggest as an explanation that it is because the rites are performed instead on the occasion of the manufacture of the hunting arrows. There is a special form of the *wai'a* (see Chapter VII) which is celebrated in the locality where Shavante collect their arrow-canes and said to be 'for the arrows'. I have not, unfortunately, been able to attend this particular *wai'a*, though I have attended others.

Gathering

Without hunting, Shavante culture would have been very different; but without gathering, the Shavante could not have existed at all. In 1958 the São Domingos Shavante did not eat meat every day and even went without meat for a number of days at a stretch when they were too busy to hunt. A day never went by, however, when the wild products of the region were not available in the community.

These products were basically of three kinds: roots, nuts, and fruits. Sketches of the roots will be found in Table 2. I am unable to identify them by other than their Shavante names, as the Brazilians in Central Brazil neither eat them nor, as far as I know, have words for them. I was similarly unable to obtain a

[1] This is consistent with the symbolic significance that the Shavante attach to ear-plugs, discussed in Chapter VII. The information was given to me, however, by the Salesian missionaries, who had little experience of Shavante custom, and I was unable to confirm it through informants.

[2] We know in any case that societies which consider hunting important do not invariably have specific 'hunting rites' (see Lévi-Strauss, 1962, for more on this topic).

satisfactory identification of the specimens I took back with me for laboratory analysis in São Paulo.

They are gathered in large quantities in certain parts of the savannah and provide a nourishing, if starchy, diet. Usually the loads of roots are brought in during the late afternoon or at dusk, the fires are lit (or revived), and half the tubers are put over them to boil in a pot while the other half are roasted in the embers. The roasted ones are ready first and may be eaten with their skins on (rather like potatoes in their jackets), or peeled, according to the whim of the individual. Whether a Shavante bothers to take it off or not seems to depend on how much earth and carbonized matter is adhering to the skin. In general they like a certain amount of it and they tend to eat a great deal of incidental earth and ash with their food. The boiled roots are similarly eaten when they are ready.

The Shavante eat huge quantities of these roots throughout most of the year. This starchy base to their diet probably accounts for the fact that Shavante children are markedly pot-bellied, though it is unusual for any of them to suffer from undernourishment. Similarly, Shavante find it necessary to break wind incessantly after these starchy meals. The discussions in the men's council are punctuated by these noises, which are not considered indecorous. On the other hand it is regarded as bad form to call attention to them in any way.

The roots are available all the year round, but are particularly important in the Shavante diet from April to June, during the first half of the dry season. In April, 1958, the Shavante were saving what was left of the maize harvest for the initiation cere-monies due to take place in the middle of the dry weather. Accordingly, they were no longer eating maize by the end of the rains and were relying almost entirely on roots and *palmito* shoots. At about this time the beans started showing green in their plantations, and I was told that this was the signal for the group to leave on trek. In this way the impatient and the immature are prevented from eating the young beans and spoil-ing the harvest. It was not until they returned at the end of June that they ate the rest of their maize, together with the harvest of beans and pumpkins (see Table 3).

In the meantime the basis of their diet, apart from roots, was palmito and nuts. These are also year-round staples. *Palmito* i

PLATE II

Women around an earth oven

the Brazilian word for the edible shoots of the palm tree of that name (*Chamacrops* sp.), which is found all over the interior of the country. These shoots are often used as a vegetable by Brazilians and are even exported to the larger cities. Shavante collect the shoots in lengths and eat the younger ones (as well as the heart of the thicker ones) raw. They also collect palm shoots as much as six inches thick, which are usually cooked in an earth oven. This process takes a long time, so that on occasion the shoots may be put into the earth oven at night and taken out again the following morning. Alternatively, the Shavante get up after their first sleep and settle down to eating the cooked plants.

Among the Shavante the earth oven is made by scraping out the embers of the fire to provide a flat surface of hot ash. Stones are placed on this and covered with leaves.[1] The food to be cooked is spread out on the bed of leaves and earth is heaped on top of it. The fire is then shovelled back on top of the earth oven and left to smoulder there while the food is cooking. Leaves are seldom placed on top of the food, as is generally the custom among the Timbira tribes. Instead, the Shavante simply remove the embers and dig their food out of the earth when it has been cooked. The food most commonly cooked in this way is palm shoots; but earth ovens are also used to roast haunches of meat that would not cook right through if they were simply placed in the embers, and to prepare the maize pies that are sometimes baked.

Finally, nuts are a perennial source of food. Many varieties are found in Shavante-land, but by far the most important is the nut of the *babassú* palm (*Orbignya* sp.). These palms grow in stands all over the tropical savannah of Brazil and are an important source of oil. The Shavante regularly collect *babassú* as part of their day-to-day activities and sometimes they will even go out in bodies to bring in large quantities of it. On one occasion during my stay with them the women went out as an organized group to collect *babassú* for a festival while the men were away engaged in a game drive for the same purpose.

Nuts, and particularly *babassú* nuts, are the commonest snack. When they wake in the morning Shavante eat whatever they have left over from their meal the night before. If there is

---

[1] The stones and leaves may be omitted where the food (e.g. a maize cake) can easily be dug out and dusted off after cooking.

nothing very much then they rummage in their personal baskets and take some of their store of nuts. During the day, whenever they feel hungry, the most usual thing is for them to help themselves to more nuts. Everyone therefore takes care to keep a good supply of nuts at hand with which to eke out the time between the big 'meals' when a consignment of food is brought in to the household. Furthermore, nuts are the only form of food that is regarded as a 'private' commodity. A Shavante may help himself to nuts from his carrying basket without offering them to present kin in a way that he would find unthinkable with any other food. Men are especially careful to keep a supply of nuts, because their milky juice, when chewed and mixed with saliva, is the Shavante's favourite cosmetic, and the men are more careful of their appearance than the women. They oil their hair and their bodies at least once a day in this fashion, while those of the age-grade that I have called the 'young men' spend much of the day preening themselves when they are in the encampment. Coconuts, because of their soft flesh and their abundant milk, are thus more highly valued than *babassú* nuts, but they occur far more rarely in Shavante-land and it is only occasionally that the Shavante have them.

Finally, both before and during the rainy season the Shavante collect quantities of wild fruits. The carob or ceretona tree (*Ceretona* sp.), whose pods are commonly known as St. John's bread, bears fruit in July. From then until the end of the year carob fruit is a staple food. In August other fruits, particularly that of the *buriti* palm (*Mauritia* sp.), which is reputed to have the highest vitamin-C content in the world, begin to be plentiful. In October, at the beginning of the rains, there is a large harvest of *piqui* (*Caryocar* sp.). Carob, *buriti*, and *piqui* are the most important fruits in the Shavante diet and provide them with their basic food supply throughout the rainy reason. Other fruits, such as mangoes, *genipapo* (*Genipa americana*), and a number of species that I was not able to identify, are also gathered and eaten to supplement this diet. By February and March, when the Shavante have exhausted the fruits of the regions through which they wander, the maize harvest is ready for collection.

Shavante-land, then, is naturally well endowed to support a small migratory population of hunters and gatherers. An efficient collector can feed a number of mouths without undue difficulty. As collecting is primarily a women's activity, it follows that women are an economic asset to their household. Men sometimes go out collecting too, since they do not consider that gathering is beneath them. It just so happens that much of their time is taken up with hunting and with the social and ceremonial life of the community, in which women play little part. In fact, collecting trips with other women represent one of the few opportunities for social intercourse outside the household that is offered to a woman. The result is that women enjoy going out gathering and they usually contrive to return in the early afternoon, if the encampment has a good water supply, and take a long and frolicsome bathe together. Men only go out collecting if they can think of nothing better to do. Consequently the women's contribution to the household food supply, while not so highly esteemed as the men's, is both sufficient and essential for the survival of the group. In these circumstances it is clear why the Shavante find it convenient to practise polygyny, which leads, as we shall see, to a state of affairs where the elder men have a number of wives while the younger ones are impatiently waiting for immature girls to reach a nubile age.

Agriculture

The Shavante are inefficient cultivators because they are bored by the drudgery of agricultural work, and because they have no pressing need for crops to supplement their abundant diet. Aboriginally they planted maize (*Zea mays*), beans (*Phaesolus* sp.) and pumpkins (*Cucurbita* sp.), which are hardy crops that require virtually no tending.

Of these the most important was maize. Shavante distinguish a number of different varieties of maize:

nõdzę	nõñęmę'ubutí
nõdzę-pré	nõñęmęhębį
nõdzę-p-a	
nõdzę-wawẽ	
nõdzę-p-mrãri	

These are considered to be their very own crops and maize cakes figure prominently in Shavante ceremonial exchanges. There is an origin myth explaining how they acquired maize, which is, to my knowledge, unique among crops in this respect. The Shavante refer scornfully to the fact that the Brazilians only had a single variety of maize, which they distinguish as *waru wawĕ*.

Their nomadic way of life would have made more intensive agriculture difficult. They used to spend only three weeks, or at the most a month, of the year at their plantations, devoting roughly a week to clearing and planting, a week to harvesting the maize, and a week to harvesting the beans and pumpkins. In between these visits they would either remain at their village (which was usually at least a day's journey away from the plantations) or would go on trek. Someone occasionally went to have a look at the plantations and see that they did not get too overgrown, otherwise the crops received no care.

The harvests were thought of less as providing the essentials for the life of the community than as bonuses to be used for celebrations. Many Shavante festivals require the ceremonial preparation of maize pies, and a glance at Table 3 will show that the two important stages of the initiation ceremony in 1958 were held respectively at the time of the maize harvest and at the time of the harvest of beans and pumpkins. The crops that the Shavante sowed and harvested in their haphazard way were adequate for these purposes. Similarly, the cotton they required for the preparation of ceremonial regalia grows wild in the region. They therefore had little incentive to adopt the cultivation of new crops.

The Indian Protection Service tried very hard to persuade the Shavante to cultivate various other crops, particularly manioc (cassava), rice, and bananas. The reasons for this are easy to see. While the Shavante continued their nomadic existence they made uneconomic use of their lands. They occupied tracts of territory that could support a larger farming population. In the course of time it was certain that this area of Mato Grosso would be 'opened up' to settlement and that the Shavante would have to face the problem of how to provide for themselves on a fraction of their former territory. If they could be induced to take up farming, it would have the advantage of enabling them to adapt themselves slowly to the inevitable and would also make the task of administering them very much easier. With this end in view, the personnel of the Indian Protection Service at São Domingos cleared and planted gardens, which were to supply the post during the period when the Shavante were being 'attracted', and were subsequently to be handed over to the Indians in order that they should take up agriculture. When the Shavante had been contacted and it was discovered that they had a passion for manioc flour, it was thought that they could easily be persuaded to cultivate manioc and that this would initiate the changes that the administrators hoped to bring about in Shavante culture.

The Shavante, however, perceived that if they followed the advice of the Indian agent they would have to modify or even give up their roving way of life. They therefore accepted the plantations but failed to keep them up. They planted only the aboriginal crops, which they had been accustomed to plant. They took endless pains to discover which Brazilians for many miles around had supplies of manioc flour, and made special expeditions to beg, extort, or steal it from them; yet they obdurately refused to plant manioc themselves. Even the banana trees that were left to them were destroyed. They were too careless in burning off the undergrowth in the plantations and burned down the trees as well. No seed bananas were saved, so the community had no bananas in 1958.

Originally, so the Shavante say, they used to clear their planatations by burning off a patch of gallery forest. This method of cultivation is still used by Brazilian backwoodsmen all over the tropical savannah today. They set fire to the vegetation of their chosen site and then clear away the growth which the fire left behind. The clearing can then be sown after the first rains have softened the earth. Such plantations are full of the trunks and stumps of trees, with here and there tangled branches that have escaped the burning, so that one has to pick one's way through a 'clearing' at the planting season. Shavante plantations are (as one would expect) even more untidy and overgrown than those of the Brazilians, even though the Indians are nowadays supplied with the same tools—hoes and bush knives—with which to clear away the subsidiary growth after the forest has been burned. Originally, when they had no means of clearing other than repeated burnings, and no agricultural implements but the digging-stick, their crops must have been cultivated in a tangle of extraneous vegetation.

They would burn their clearings as soon as they had collected the harvest of beans and pumpkins, which in 1958 was in early July. They would return with the first rains, usually late in October, clear away some of the undergrowth, and then plant their three crops. Towards the end of the rains, usually about February, they collected the maize harvest and this was the sum of their agricultural activity.

The household is the economic unit among the Shavante and it was therefore the members of a household who cleared, planted, and harvested a plantation in common. A household was responsible for keeping its own stock of maize sewn up in a plaited bag, its own stock of pumpkin seeds in a sealed gourd, and its own stock of beans in a similar container. These stocks were carefully preserved by each household group for planting at the following rains. When the time came for agricultural work, a decision was taken in the men's circle that the community should, for example, do their planting within the next few days. Accordingly each household decided when it would set off for the plantations, and generally all the members of it went together. When they arrived, however, they did not by any means apply themselves solely to the task at hand. The burning and clearing of the plantations devolved on the men, while the planting was done jointly. The men dug the holes and the women went out collecting or lazed in their shelters. The men, too, took time off from their work in the clearings to go collecting or, more often, hunting.

Although each step in the process of cultivation was undertaken in concert by the whole community, there was no formality about the procedure. Household groups and even individuals left on different days for the plantations and came back on different days, so that for about a week there was a trickle of coming and going between the village and the clearings. In the plantations themselves, and in the men's circle at the plantations, men who had the status of *ǫmãdǫ'ǫ'wa* or *ĩdzú* delivered long harangues. But these were neither directives nor of any ritual significance. They were purely exhortatory. The Shavante certainly require exhortation to encourage them in what they find a thoroughly uncongenial task. When they return from the plantations, having done the minimum of agricultural labour, the same men who can perform feats of endurance on the hunt complain of stiffness and pains all over. They besiege the Indian posts with requests for palliative injections,[1] and often bleed themselves as well to effect a cure in the traditional Shavante manner.

Fishing

Fishing was probably unimportant among the Shavante until after they were re-contacted by the Brazilians. Their preference for land travel and for open country meant that they did not spend much time by the rivers. They are not, in any case, very good at shooting fish in the water with a bow and arrow and do not have specially tipped arrows which pierce rather than glance off fish scales. They use no fish traps and I suspect that they have only recently learned, from the Brazilians, how to drug and capture fish with the sap of a creeper known as *tingui* (*Jacquinia* sp.). They are still unable to make canoes and have only learned how to handle them, which they do on the whole very badly, from the Brazilians or from the Indian Protection Service. Originally they used rafts to cross broad rivers (Szaffka, 1942) or would cross them swimming and holding on to a floating tree trunk. Nowadays they usually contrive to borrow a canoe to ferry their party across, in the absence of which they will make long detours to find a fording place. In general they are poor watermen and are uninterested in the potentialities of rivers, regarding them rather as hindrances that bar their way. It is therefore reasonable to suppose that they shared the lack of interest in fish and fishing that has been reported for neighbouring Gê tribes (Nimuendajú, 1939: 93; 1942: 33; 1946: 71).

Now, however, the introduction of metal hooks and nylon line has transformed them into passionate fishermen. The

[1] The medical profession and the pharmaceutical companies in Brazil have convinced the lay public that the most efficient way of taking medicines is via injection. A corollary of this view is the attitude, which is now characteristic even of backwoodsmen living in the remotest regions, that injections are the only 'real' medicine. Consequently store-keepers far removed from medical centres stock ampoules and syringes for their customers' complaints and most people are content to inject themselves. The Indian Protection Service has made much use of injections in its every-day treatment of Indians with minor ailments, apart from the periodic vaccinations and innoculations which they arrange for those groups of Indians who can be persuaded to accept them. As a result, those Indians who do not object violently to this form of treatment, as did the Shavante until recently, have come to look on it as particularly effective.

promise of hooks and line is the most effective incentive that can
be offered them to do anything; and in the same way the most
effective sanction that an Indian agent can employ in order to
get them to respect his wishes is the threat of cutting off their
supply of these commodities.

There is no doubt that the Shavante interest in fishing was
awakened by the introduction of the hook-and-line method. It
is used at present to the virtual exclusion of all others, and when
Shavante have run out of hooks or line they do not fish. Another
circumstance, however, has been instrumental in persuading
Shavante groups to take up fishing. As soon as they came to
value the commodites that they could get from the Brazilians
there was a tendency for Shavante communities to build their
base villages near their patrons. This meant that their villages
were located near sites that Brazilians had chosen because they
were easily accessible by river and were reasonably close to
good ground for plantations. These sites were not such as the
Shavante would have chosen for themselves, and the immediately surrounding countryside usually could not provide
food for the community for more than short periods at a time.
Normally, faced with a similar situation, the Shavante would
simply have moved on. Now, however, they were anxious to
remain a little longer in their village so that they could extract
the maximum from their patrons. They are expert in the technique of importunity and have discovered that, given time, they
can often get what they want if it is available at all. In order
to give themselves time they turned to fishing and discovered
that, with the expenditure of little time and labour, a man with
a hook and line could catch enough fish to feed a whole household.

Fishing is therefore an activity which is important only when
the Shavante are temporarily sedentary. Otherwise it may be
indulged in by men who go on an occasional fishing excursion
because they do not feel like hunting or because there are good
fishing waters in the vicinity. It is only regularly practised by
boys. Women never fish, except with a pan or sieve, which they
use to catch loads of tiny *piabinha* fish. These are enjoyed as a
delicacy, but are of little importance in the Shavante diet.

3. TREKS

There was little seasonal variation in Shavante life. They were able to go hunting and collecting as well in the rains as in the dry season and by these means they were assured of a constant and abundant food supply. There was only one proviso: that they should keep on the move.

They were nomads, but not in the sense that their home was wherever they happened to be at a given moment. They had their villages, which they thought of as semi-permanent settlements. Such settlements might be abandoned without too much difficulty and similar half-circles of huts erected on a new site; but they did not generally abandon them without good reason and would do so as infrequently as possible, in order to spare themselves the labour of erecting new huts. Yet they spent little time in these base villages. For much of the year they were out on trek.

A trek starts from the base village and may last as little as six weeks or as much as three or four months. It is deliberately planned by the elders in the men's circle so that the community may move over certain country with a view to exploiting specific resources. It is not unusual for a community to split into bands that travel in different directions but come together again after a comparatively short interval. It seems that each trek moved in a different direction from others that had been undertaken in the same year, so that the rhythm of Shavante life was not seasonal but approximately annual. Roughly speaking they exploited the territory dominated by their own community in the course of the year. Alternatively, it might be said that the territory of any particular community was that area which it was able to exploit in the course of a year's wanderings.

Each Shavante village held proprietary rights in common over an area of land and its products, but it did not recognize specific boundaries between its own territory and that of other groups. Nor was the composition of the village group or local community in any way a constant factor, determined by descent or any other principle. Shavante felt free to wander out of 'their own' territory if they were prepared to risk a clash with other Shavante groups, who might resent the intrusion. Similarly the individual Shavante felt free to transfer his allegiance from one community to another.

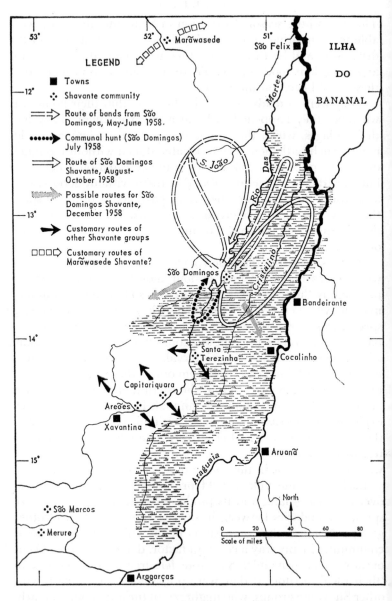

MAP 3

Shavante treks.

Map 3 shows how the Shavante of São Domingos exploited the surrounding country in 1958. In May and June the community split into three bands. Two of these travelled west and then north-west from São Domingos and joined forces again near the upper reaches of the Rio São João. From there they trekked back again to São Domingos, thereby completing a full circle. These bands went primarily in search of *buriti* bast, with which to manufacture the regalia for the forthcoming initiation ceremonies, of scleria seeds for the same purpose, and of arrow canes. As they moved they lived mainly on gathered roots and nuts, though the men occasionally hunted and brought in peccary meat. The third band, which travelled north-east along the right bank of the Rio das Mortes, was also collecting *buriti* bast, but in that region there were no arrow canes or scleria seeds. On the other hand game, particularly deer, was more abundant and it was this that had attracted them.

Shavante bands keep track of each other by watching for the columns of smoke which go up when they fire the steppe. Travellers also 'make smoke' as they go, so that their own group may be able to keep track of their movements and other groups may know that their intentions are peaceful. Shavante would regard with suspicion anybody who approached without giving a smoke signal, for they interpret this as a sign of hostility.

In the second half of July a communal hunt was organized. This time the men went south-westwards along the Rio das Mortes and returned in the opposite direction, having crossed the river. The women made a short excursion to the west to collect *babassú* nuts.

From mid August to late October the whole community now trekked to the north-east and back, covering substantially the same region as had previously been visited by the third band in May–June.

There would be another trek during the rains, possibly to the south-east towards the Araguaia river, or possibly to the south-west in the direction of the Rio Curuá and the affluents of the Xingú. It was impossible for me to get precise information about the direction of this trek, as the Shavante themselves were unable to tell me where they would go until it had been discussed and decided in the men's circle. My attempts to interest my infor-

mants in a discussion of the hypothetical possibilities were unsuccessful. I was told, however, that the previous rainy-season
trek, which had finished just before my arrival in February 1958,
had been 'over towards the Araguaia'.

It is noteworthy that the Shavante of Santa Terezinha
usually trekked southwards on either side of the Rio das Mortes
rather than in the opposite direction. They were on bad terms
with the Shavante of São Domingos and were afraid of them.
They were consequently forced to celebrate their initiation
festivals without the necklaces of scleria seeds, which are an
essential part of the regalia. When I visited them I was wearing
a scleria necklet made for me by a Shavante in São Domingos,
and put on so tightly around my throat that I was unable to
remove it without cutting it off. The Shavante of Santa
Terezinha begged me persistently and frantically for this small
bead chain, explaining that they had no such beads where they
were and felt the lack of them very keenly. They had only to
trek north-westwards towards the source of the Rio São João to
reach an area that was rich in these seeds, but that would have
brought them into close proximity with the Shavante of São
Domingos.

In 1962 the community at Areões, which, it will be remembered, included the group from Santa Terezinha, was nervous
at the prospect of an attack from São Domingos. They therefore
went on trek to the north-west, keeping well away from their
enemies to the north-east.

Similarly the Shavante of São Domingos make their bows of
a wood which is only found in large quantities some way to the
north of the Rio São João. They had procured a certain number
of bow staves on their last visit to this area, but by the time of
my visit many of them had snapped and others had been
bartered with the personnel of the Indian agency.[1] When I
attempted to procure bows for the ethnographic collection I was
making I found it almost impossible. The explanation I was
given was that it was a long way to the country where the good
wood for bows was to be found and that they were frightened of
going there because of the Shavante from Marãwasede. When
I was accompanying these same Shavante on trek in the neighbourhood of the upper São João I noticed that if a hunter found

[1] Who sell them to anybody who wants a souvenir of the Shavante.

PLATE III

Loaded women setting off on trek

PLATE IV

Man making a sleeping mat. This picture shows a group of shelters such as Shavante built for themselves when out on trek

human tracks, however old, to the north and north-east these were the subject of lengthy discussion and interpretation in the men's circle.

Shavante do not move on every day even when they are on trek. At a good camping place, i.e. where there is a creek that provides water and a place to bathe, and where the surrounding country offers plenty of game or other natural resources, they may remain for up to two weeks. If they find their camp unsatisfactory, and especially if there are too many insects there, they may spend only one night in it.

The decision to move on is taken in the men's circle, which meets in the evening. Before dawn the following day the young men set out for the next site, taking nothing but their weapons with them. At sunrise the whole camp is astir and the married men are helping their women to pack all the household belongings into the large carrying-baskets used to transport them. Each household moves off together. The women have the big carrying-baskets slung from their foreheads and supported on their backs, and all the extras that would not fit in are either piled on top of, or hung from them. Babies and toddlers too small to walk the short distance to the next camp must also be carried in the women's carrying-baskets. Babies are cradled in them but toddlers perch on top, together with any small pets, usually birds, that may be travelling with the household. Girls help their elders in carrying the household goods, and even tiny girls three or four years old bear miniature carrying-baskets containing a few odds and ends. Men and boys are free to carry their weapons, though a married man may sometimes carry something for his wife. The small boys, meanwhile, skip in and out of the heavily laden procession, revelling ostentatiously in their freedom of movement.

The pace is that of the slowest and the distances between camps are never great. The Shavante try to have the shelters at their next camp already built before midday, so as to give protection from the heat of the sun. This means that the distance between one camp and the next is a matter of about two hours' walk. Once, when I was following in the track of a group of Shavante on trek, my guide and I used to pass about four of their camps in each day's journey.

The new site is usually on a patch of ground that has been

artificially cleared by being burned over. This is done in advance, generally on the previous day, by the young men who are sent out to choose a camping place. The group then builds its semi-circle of shelters in this ash-covered clearing. The relative positions of these shelters are constant and correspond exactly to the order of the huts in the base village. There is, however, no prescribed relation of the village semi-circle to the cardinal points. It may even be turned 'inside out', provided that each household group keeps the same neighbours.

On arrival at the new site the women immediately set about building the shelters. Men help, if necessary, with the work of clearing the actual floor-space of the shelter and procuring the trees out of which its frame is constructed. If there are young trees close to the site, then they leave this work to the women and lounge by their possessions or go off to the men's circle. The young men invariably form their own circle and sit there gossiping until the shelters have been built for them. It is also the men who, at this stage, dig a water-hole if there is no natural water supply near by.

The shelters are miniature versions of the huts in the base village. A circle of pliant saplings is bedded firmly in the ground and their tops are bent over and lashed together with strips of bark. This frame is then covered with palm fronds and branches. Such a shelter is usually no more than three feet high and about six feet in diameter. It cannot, of course, accommodate all the members of a household, whose hut in the village may be fifteen feet high at the apex and about twenty-five feet in diameter. On trek, therefore, the Shavante shelters are grouped about common fires, so that a household group occupies a number of shelters but still feeds together.

Living in these shelters is like living in a chimney, for they are built on a layer of ash. Their inhabitants are soon hopelessly grimy, for where water is drawn from a water-hole there is none to spare for washing.

All that Shavante will do when they are unable to bathe is to take a mouthful of water and squirt it over their hands, and this only if their hands are covered with some especially glutinous substance. The entrances to the shelters soon fill up with offal. The girls who sit round the cooking fire throw rejected morsels of food, pieces of intestine, animal and vegetable skin, and so on, to one side, which means that they remain at the entrances to the shelters. Meanwhile the men in the shelters also toss their waste into the entrances and the accumulation is very soon quite nauseating. I found it especially distasteful that food from the cooking fires was always thrown casually over to the men in the shelters and invariably landed in the patch of refuse just beyond our feet, to be picked up, dusted off, and eaten. It was always a great relief to me when we moved camp.

4. EXPLOITATION OF THE ENVIRONMENT

The Shavante had an extremely simple technology, which was, until recently, adequate for all their requirements. They made much use of fire: to burn off the savannah; to clear their plantations; to fell trees; to drive game; and even to shape and harden their clubs. They made it with a fire-drill, twirling between their palms a thin stick inserted into the surface of a thicker one until the friction produced sparks and the sparks ignited the sawdust that had been thrown up by the boring process. Their rudimentary agriculture required no more implements than the digging-stick, carefully pointed at one end and with a butt at the other, so that it could be handled more comfortably and do double duty as a club.

Digging-sticks, war clubs, and bow staves were planed with tools consisting of a smooth, sharp-edged stone lashed with strips of bark or native cord to a wooden handle such as would fit comfortably into the palm of the hand. The string in its turn was made out of plaited *tucum* fibre, from which the Shavante make a strong and durable twine. Their only other tools were the teeth, bones, and claws of the animals they killed. They sharpen small bones into efficient needles, which they use for tasks such as piercing scleria seeds to make bead chains, piercing the young men's ears at initiation, and hem-stitching the deer-skins on which the men sit. They use the teeth of the dangerous *piranha* fish as a cutting instrument, and some Shavante prefer these to scissors for hair-cutting even to this day. They use the claw of the great armadillo when they require a sharp instrument, and also as a ruler to get their fringes straight when they are having their hair cut.

The delicate task of making an arrow can be quickly and neatly performed with these tools. The bamboo canes are cut and notched with the stone scraper. The feathers are gummed on with beeswax and bound with string made from wild cotton. Finally the feathering is trimmed by heating a spare bamboo cane in the fire and then burning the feathers off in a straight line.

The making of household utensils and furniture required no tools whatever. Everything inside the hut is kept in baskets hung from the thatch or from a forked pole planted in the ground and these baskets are made by the women out of three super-imposed sets of two palm fronds plaited together. Around the walls are sleeping mats which the men plait out of *buriti* bast. Cooking did not necessarily require pots, as we have seen. It seems that the Shavante probably did make clay pots originally, but these have been entirely superseded by metal ones among all the groups in contact with the Brazilians. Water and other precious things, such as seeds or magical powders, are kept in gourd bottles, which may be sealed with lumps of beeswax if they are not in constant use. Finally, the women plait an all-purpose palm-leaf mat, which may be used to sit on, or to fan the fire with, or to hand hot food from the cooking fires to the waiting men. A man will never sit on one of these, however. He either lies on his sleeping mat, when he is in his hut, or he sits on a deerskin outside.

The way in which Shavante make use of a seemingly un-promising environment to supply their needs is a feature of their life which strikes an outside observer most forcibly. Blades of the sharp rank grass (Portuguese *capim*) which grows on the savannah are used for cleaning purposes—to wipe the sweat off the body, to clean oneself after defecating, to clean the tongue on awaking and so on. There is another type of grass which has a barbed stem, and with this they pluck out the hairs of their face and body when they beautify themselves. A Shavante out on the savannah will tear the bark from a tree with his teeth in order to use it as a carrying sling or as a bandage for a hurt foot. He can make himself a carrying-basket out of green palm fronds in a matter of minutes. He never goes short of food and can usually find water or wait till he finds it. He can build himself a shelter in less than an hour out of materials that are everywhere available. In short, Shavante life was so well adapted to their environment that as late as 1958 a visitor got an impression of abundance and efficiency in their villages, which was in striking contrast to the feeling of poverty and inadequacy conveyed by Brazilian settlements in Central Brazil.

III

THE DOMESTIC GROUP

1. INTRODUCTION

I HAVE now given sufficient background information about the Shavante to enable me to embark on a description of their social institutions. It is always difficult to know where to start such an account. A thorough discussion of any aspect of a people's life presupposes knowledge of other aspects which have yet to be described. I have chosen to begin with the discussion of the domestic group as a matter of convenience. I do not regard this as the 'initial situation' in some Malinowskian sense, nor do I start here because I feel that Shavante institutions are determined by their child-rearing practices. I wish merely to develop an argument which will depend on a structural analysis of Shavante society. It will derive its ethnographic support particularly from my interpretation of the data relating to factionalism, relationship terminology, and ritual. I shall argue that a certain code, common to these domains, provides a model which leads to a certain type of understanding of the Shavante, and may be useful for comparative purposes. I shall do my best to show ethnographically in what sense this model can be said to 'explain' Shavante institutions and in what sense it is inadequate for such a purpose, but in order to be able to do this I must first present a certain amount of arbitrarily categorized information.

2. BIRTH

Shavante appear to desire children. They have neither contraceptives nor abortifacients. The immediate reason for this is not far to seek. Patrilineages form the core of Shavante factions, so that children are the basis of a man's political support. It is still not clear why Shavante women do not seek to limit their pregnancies, in view of the fact that they start child-bearing in their early teens, and that it considerably affects their general state of health.[1]

Shavante, however, speak only of measures to ensure conception. The most usual of these are repeated copulation, the wearing of reddened ear-plugs during sexual intercourse, and the manipulation of a powder known as *wede-dzu* (*wede* = wood and *dzu* = dust). I discuss the use of this powder more fully in Chapter VIII. Since it is associated with sorcery, Shavante are reluctant to go into detail about its use, and I did not learn *how* it was employed to promote fertility, simply that it was. The symbolic significance of ear-plugs is also discussed later. Here it need only be said that Shavante think of the cylindrical ear-plug as piercing the lobe of a man's ear in the same way as his penis may pierce a woman, now that he has attained maturity. Reddened ear-plugs thus have special procreative properties when associated with the sexual act.

Clearly then they understand the relationship between coitus and conception. However, they appear to view the fashioning of the child as a process induced by repeated copulation. Men have on two occasions expressed it for me this way: '*tsihúri, tsihúri, tsihúri, tsihúri, tsihúri ahẽ-di. wasã. tsihúri, tsihúri, tsihúri, waptãr.*' (copulate, copulate, copulate, copulate, copulate a lot. pregnant. copulate, copulate, copulate, born.) They ticked the process off on their fingers so that 'pregnant' fell on the fifth finger and 'born' fell on the ninth. Other Shavante spoke of the father 'making his child' by repeated intercourse with its mother. It seems then that they believe a man fashions his child during the first months of gestation, and that it is only fully 'made' (and the woman, therefore, properly speaking 'pregnant') by the fifth month, which is also about the time when her condition becomes unmistakably apparent.[2]

[1] See Maybury-Lewis, 1964: 110.
[2] It might seem that pregnancy would be obvious before then, since the

Contrary to the impression given by the informant's description above, men do not usually have intercourse with their wives during the last months of pregnancy. This seems, however, to be a matter of preference not of prohibition. As the time of birth approaches, the prospective father should observe a series of restrictions. He should not kill an armadillo (*węrã-ri*), since that would prevent the baby's coming out. Nor should he kill a great armadillo (*węrã-wawê*), since that would cause his wife a long and painful childbirth. He should also avoid killing python, pampa ostrich, macaws, and certain species of fish, particularly the *barbado* (*Pirinampus pirinampus*) and the *cachorro* (*Auchenipterus striolatus*). One elderly informant also insisted, over the skeptical denials of younger men, that a prospective father should neither hunt nor eat the meat of the red curassow, for if he did it would cause his wife to die in childbirth. There was general agreement, however, that a man should abstain altogether from eating meat just before his wife gives birth, for this is 'strong' food and would harm the child in the imminent crisis of childbirth. Nor should he have intercourse with any woman during this time, as this would also be harmful to the baby, who is still weak.

The expectant mother, on the other hand, is not bound by any restrictions and usually manages to carry on with her every-day life until two or three days before her baby is born. I have seen women in the last stages of pregnancy go out collecting roots with the others, and come staggering back to the encampment with heavy loads on their shoulders. A woman will retire to her hut when she feels that labour is imminent. She is attended by her close kinswomen, usually assisted by one or other of the older women of the community who are regarded as experienced midwives. Men, and particularly the father of the child, stay away

As soon as the child is born, the umbilical cord is cut about a foot from its navel. The baby is then taken outside where the midwife nurses it on her lap for the crowd which always collects on these occasions to see. Later, when the afterbirth has been

---

women wore no clothes at the time this information was obtained. However Shavante women tend to be pot-bellied at an early age, and I was often surprised to discover that women whom I had seen daily without realizing that they were pregnant were on the verge of giving birth. Of course they were so active that I probably tended to assume that they could not be expecting children.

expelled and the soiled mats used for the lying-in taken away and destroyed, the husband goes in to his wife and customarily remains with her and his child.

For some days immediately after the birth (in two actual instances the number was five) the husband should live quietly in and around his hut. He may work on the making of weapons or of anything else he is currently manufacturing, but he should not go out hunting or fishing and he should not eat meat. The Shavante emphasize that he should moderate his activities during this period. He must eat and drink little. He must not attend the men's councils or be involved in discussion or argument. He must not have sexual intercourse with any woman. He must, in short, live a quiet life.

I hesitate to call this a form of *couvade* because the word has come to be used as a blanket term for various practices all over the world, which have been classed together simply because they are all connected in some way or other with the activities of a father at the time of the birth of his child. It seems that we have to thank Tylor for the application of the term *couvade* to what he called 'the whole set' of these customs (1870: 293), and for some of the resultant confusion. Writers have tried to interpret them in the light of a single principle, either as a fiction which enabled the father to be thought of and to act as a second mother (a view first put forward by Bachofen, 1861 : 256), or as a male imitation of a woman's labour, or as a method of establishing agnatic descent. It was Frazer who pointed out (1910: 244–55) that at least two different kinds of customs have been designated as *couvade*: the rites performed by a father for the benefit of his child, and the simulation of childbirth by the mother's husband. He further pointed out that neither of these customs appeared to have anything to do with establishing the rule of descent in societies that practised them. Finally he was perspicacious enough to doubt the accounts of 'simulated childbirth' as being external interpretations of observers who were generally ignorant of the native beliefs connected with the custom.

I do not propose here to attempt a redefinition or a re-examination of the concept of *couvade*.[1] I would suggest, however,

---

[1] Fock (1960; 1963: 145–51) has made a valuable contribution in this respect. He points out, among other things, that many theorists have overlooked or underrated the restrictions on the mother in cases of 'couvade'.

that no useful generalizations can be made about the institutions which have hitherto been referred to by that name until they are understood and described in terms of the beliefs about the father-child relationship held in the societies where they are found.

The Shavante view of this relationship is aptly expressed in Frazer's description as 'one of intimate physical sympathy' (1910: 247). They believe that a child is 'soft' (*ua-di*) from the time just before its birth to a time some days after it. Since it is especially vulnerable during the period of its birth, its father must take special precautions not to harm it. The activities of its mother are not vital to its health in the same way. The mother of a new-born infant may therefore, and often does, go out foraging for food while her husband lies in his hut and minds the baby. I know of only one instance where a father ignored these restrictions and went out hunting the day after the birth of his child, and even he would not eat the meat that was brought in. Moreover, his case was atypical, since he suspected his wife of having committed adultery and had already accused a member of another lineage of being her lover. Since he was executed shortly afterwards by the community[1] I was unable to elucidate the circumstances from his point of view.

The Sherente, who were thoroughly acculturated when I studied them first, held similarly that a bond united father and son throughout their lives. Thus when a child fell ill they looked for the cause of its illness in the excesses (often alcoholic) of the father. A man who got drunk while his child was ill was subsequently regarded as its murderer if it died. I was unable to discover whether the Shavante believed that the activities of the father influenced his child as long as the father lived or only in the crisis of birth. The relationship is however definitely asymmetrical—a child cannot prejudice its father's health.

This leads him, however, to overemphasize the role of the mother in a general theory of couvade. Shavante birth customs, for example, affect only the father of the child, and there are other similar instances.

[1] See Chapter V.

3. CHILDHOOD

From the very beginning, a Shavante baby is bound by this intimate link to its father. Whenever the father is present it is he rather than the child's mother who will handle the baby and play with it. It is he who will pet it and attempt to distract its attention when it cries, even if it is obviously crying for the breast. I have often seen fathers trying in this way to amuse their howling children for perhaps a quarter of an hour, until the mother came over, took up the infant with very bad grace and thrust it onto her breast, scolding her unfortunate husband the while for his inability to keep it quiet. A father will never smack, and very rarely use any sort of physical coercion on his child, seldom even pushing it out of the way. A mother will only smack her child when she is exasperated beyond endurance, for the Shavante are extremely permissive in bringing up their children. Nevertheless, it is noticeable that whatever disciplining the child gets in this way comes from its mother and not from its father.

Yet it would be misleading to make too much of this contrast. A tiny baby spends the greater part of its time with its mother or with her sisters, who may be its mother's co-wives and are in any case co-resident with her. It lies curled up in one of the big carrying-baskets, shaded from the sun, if necessary, by an inverted basketry bowl which acts as a lid for its cradle. Its mother, or whoever else is looking after it, wears this basket perpetually suspended from her head for it is very light compared with the loads that Shavante women are used to carrying. When the baby cries the woman swivels her shoulders backwards and forwards while carrying on with whatever she may be doing. This rocks the cradle and usually puts the baby to sleep, unless it is very hungry. If it keeps up its squalling it is given the breast. If the mother is not present, then it may be suckled at the breast of any of its kinswomen, whether they have milk or not. Sometimes this soothes it. When it does not, then it may even be fed slops from the mouth of one of the women present. Grandmothers are particularly fond of feeding their tiny grandchildren in this way, and I have seen a five-day-old baby take this sort of nourishment without any apparent ill effects. In general, though, babies are given the breast whenever they want it during the first few months, and a mother will often lie down while suckling her child and take an obvious pleasure in the relaxation this affords her. A baby thus spends the first years of its life in intimate contact with its mother. She rarely leaves it altogether, though she may hand it over to someone else in the household to look after. As soon as it can crawl it learns to make its way to its mother when it wants the breast, and it usually gets it, irrespective of what she is doing.

By the time a baby learns to toddle it is used to being petted and made much of by all around it. If it cries, then people try and distract it or they feed it. If it urinates or defecates, it is simply held at arm's length and the mess is cleared up by someone else. It is allowed to help itself to anything it can get hold of, even such things as knives and fish hooks, precious though the latter are. Shavante become expert at intelligent anticipation of a baby's movements and usually manage to avoid having to take things from it by removing them out of its reach in advance. Nor do they ever coerce the child or remonstrate with it at this stage. There is nothing it may not touch except the fire and babies learn to avoid that before they can even toddle. There is little it may not do and nothing that it has to learn, or rather, nothing that adults are anxious to teach it. The adults keep all their possessions in baskets suspended out of reach, so that the entire floor space of their huts or shelters is virtually a small child's undisputed domain. Even the dogs, which are savage and suspicious, permit themselves to be used as playthings by these small tyrants, for this is what children soon become.

By the time children can talk and run about, i.e. around the age of three, they are already exceedingly spoilt by our standards. They react violently if they are thwarted and fly into tantrums that they are sometimes able to prolong for as much as half an hour. Their elders deal with these by ignoring them

One small child received a smaller piece of maize cake than it had expected one day. It bawled lustily and promptly kicked first its mother and then its sister, without receiving any remonstrance from either of them or from its father, who was lying beside them. Another little boy, aged about four, wanted some of the food his sister (a couple of years older than he) was eating. She did not give it to him so he rushed about screaming with rage and finally flung himself down on the ground. He lay pummelling the ground for some time and then rolled over on his back and lay there kicking and still screaming. The whole performance took about ten minutes before he quieted down. Nobody paid any attention to him and when he was silent at last and got up from the ground his sister offered him a fruit, which he accepted. Perhaps the most comical instance of all the ones I saw, however, was when a small boy who felt offended about something or other leaned on his toy bow, just as he had seen the mature men do when they were making an important speech in the men's council, and wailed for half an hour.

Children cry easily until they are 5 or 6 years old, but usually from indignation rather than from other causes. Their elders are only indifferent or positively amused when they cry in anger, but they may be ashamed if they cry in pain, especially if it is a boy that is crying. My 'sister's son' (the son of the daughter of the chief of São Domingos) was a little boy of about 4 and more indulged even than most. He was high-spirited and thoroughly disrespectful of his elders by our standards. On one occasion his father took a splinter out of his finger with a bone needle. The child screamed, tried to escape, and made a huge fuss. This provoked his mother to scold and even to slap him, the only time I ever saw her do such a thing.

The only occasions on which I have heard children scolded were for crying overmuch when hurt, for refusing to run errands for their elders, and for refusing to run away when told to. Yet such scoldings were never followed up by coercion or physical punishment. A child asked to do something or to fetch something would often just stand there and refuse to move. In such a case the person who asked would either go and do it himself, telling the child at the same time what a lazy good-for-nothing it was, or he would scold the child and leave the errand undone.

It was always much more difficult to get children to go away when they were not wanted, since they were usually allowed to go where they pleased and were not trained to be obedient. They were tolerated in the mature men's council, which even the young men could not attend except by express invitation. Fathers and grandfathers would often take a small son or grandson to the council with them and let him fall asleep in their laps. Similarly children were always allowed to run in and out and around the participants in all ceremonies, except the *wai'a*, which was restricted to initiated men. They would, in fact, often burlesque the proceedings at no great distance without ever provoking any remonstrance. On the rare occasions, then, when the children were wanted out of the way, a mere injunction to go had not the slightest effect. Men would sometimes get exasperated by a throng of children around them, especially when they were arranging an exchange of presents with me, and would leap up, seize a weapon and make as if to attack them. This always effected a temporary clearance. The older children accepted it as part of the game and skipped nimbly out of the way, but the tiniest ones were usually left rooted to the spot with fright and crying bitterly. The men would consider this a great joke and would take no further action against the sobbing child, who was allowed to stay after all.

The only other times at which men would use physical force on children were on those occasions when they wished to imbue them with strength by making incisions in their flesh with the claws of animals or birds. Shavante have a strong belief in the therapeutic efficacy of bleeding. They bleed each other as the commonest way of treating ailments; when they are tired; in order that they may not feel tiredness; and in certain other situations (e.g. a pregnant woman may bleed her husband, when she is approaching childbirth). I have occasionally seen a Shavante pick up a claw and decide that he will bleed his sons and any other small boys that happen to be about. He does not, however, chase them and catch them but invites them to come over to him. If they do so, then he seizes them and does not release them until he has made incisions on their arms or legs or both. The older boys are too wily to approach him in such a situation and it is, once again, usually some small toddler who gets caught and lacerated.

A woman, on the other hand, may get provoked beyond endurance by the importunities of her children and give one of them a beating. One elderly and energetic woman with grown-up sons also had a baby daughter who was always crawling all over her. The mother would tolerate the child's disturbances and was usually ready to give it the breast whatever she was doing. One day she had come in from a gathering trip and was trying to cook some of the food. The child made such a nuisance of herself that she belaboured it with a straw mat. This induced an explosion of grief and rage from the girl, who was quite unused to being treated in this way. On similar occasions children who have provoked their mothers into striking them make as if to hit back. Some of them actually do, which the mother accepts quite calmly after her own outburst. Others take hold of a stick or other weapon to threaten their mothers with, or make as if to burn down the hut by thrusting a burning brand into the thatch. They are encouraged in these displays by their fathers, who are intensely amused by such episodes. Men sometimes go as far as to provide the indignant child with a twig and direct it to go and get its own back on its mother.

Shavante were shocked by the way in which we smacked our child in order to discipline him. They would often come to tell me that my wife had smacked the baby, and if they were present when it happened they would give him a stick to retaliate with, just as they did with their own children. They were not interested in the fact that frequently our baby was smacked because he took advantage of their children. Shavante never intervene in children's affairs. They leave them to play and to fight together, knowing that any child who wishes to can leave the play group and return to its own household, thereby opting out of any situation which displeases it. The parents do not therefore bother about the rights and wrongs of childish quarrels. If a child returns howling to his household they comfort it and leave it at that. There is never friction between adults because of what their children do to each other.

As soon as children can run about—that is, from late in their second year—they begin to venture outside the household or the household cluster of shelters and play together. They wander in droves about the encampment and play out on the steppe and at the nearest watering place. If this means going some distance from the huts, then the older ones see that the tiniest come to no harm; but this is only necessary for a very short time. Shavante children are usually self-sufficient by the age of about three and quite capable of looking after themselves, provided they stay in the immediate neighbourhood of their homes. They spend their time playing games and seeing what is happening around the village. It is this ubiquitous presence of casual groups of children which ensures that everybody's activities in Shavante communities are public knowledge. The Shavante themselves are insatiably curious about the doings of their fellows and the children provide them with their intelligence of these doings. Long before a hunter has got back to his household with his kill, the children have usually alerted the community, and he finds a swarm of people gathering to share in it. Similarly, when a man and a woman wish to go out onto the steppe for sexual purposes, they must go a fair distance from the village and procure some well-concealed place if they do not want their activities to be spied on. Nor is this always sufficient, for all comings and goings in the village are remarked upon. Anybody leaving is always asked by any person who happens to see him '*N'mumu teptaimõri?*' or simply '*N'mumu?*' ('Where are you going?' or just 'Where?'). A failure to give an answer is regarded as boorish, if not downright suspicious, and might induce a curious child to follow, merely to see where his interlocutor was in fact going and for what reason.

When children are not hanging about watching the adults or waiting to be given snacks by them, they play games imitating their elders. They run log-races with sticks instead of logs or they run flat races as the boys do during the initiation ceremonies. They fight mock battles with straws or they play at hunting. Most of all they enjoy dancing as their elders do or playing games in which they represent various animals.

This is an important stage in a child's development, because it is now that it becomes conscious of the distinctions which are so important in Shavante life: the distinction between boys and girls; the distinction between people of the same age and their seniors (also grouped into age-sets and age-grades); the distinction between kin and affine.

Even among the four-year-olds there is a tendency for boys and girls to play separately. When they play together the boys order the girls about. If they are shooting with bows and arrows the girls are given the task of retrieving the arrows and bringing them back to the boys to be fired again. Girls tend to be excluded from the races because children only see males participating in them among adults. Dancing is, in the same way primarily a masculine activity and so the girls go off to have a frolic in the water and play with their gourds (which they use both as dippers and as dolls), leaving the boys to the stamping and grunting that go with Shavante dances. Boys' games meanwhile grow progressively rougher. The six-year-olds enjoy wrestling and throwing each other about and, if they should really get angry with each other, indulge in a form of duelling which is highly stylized. One hits the other on the arm or body, usually the arm, but never in a more vulnerable spot. The other then hits back in the same way. They go on exchanging alternate blows until one of them gives up or bursts into tears. These exchanges are sometimes friendly jousts. Sometimes they start off as such but end up as anything but friendly. Sometimes they are angry from the start and the punches are then delivered with force and science in order to hurt, but never more than one at a time and always with a pause to wait for the retaliatory blow. I have never seen Shavante children fighting in any way but this.

In the years between weaning, which takes place between the ages of 2 and 3 (though a child may be given the breast even later on occasions), and his entry into the bachelors' hut a boy leads a carefree life. Boys of this age are usually singing and dancing and in boisterous high spirits. The girls, by contrast, are obliged much earlier to develop a sense of responsibility. They are expected to help in the house as soon as they are physically capable of it, and I have seen girls who could not have been older than 3 go out with minute carrying-baskets to accompany their mothers on short collecting trips. By the time a girl is five she usually has a younger sibling to look after, and she may well be married. When she is seven she is already being watched carefully both by her kin and by her husband, for she will soon be considered physically able to cohabit with a man. Accordingly a girl of about six tends to behave like a small, weak, and underdeveloped woman. A boy of the same age gives the impression of being still a child.

In about his sixth year a boy is given a well-made *sö'rebzu* necklet by his mother's brother. It is made out of plaited cotton and the ends of it are fluffed out, so that when it is bound around his neck they look like the ends of a bow-tie. At the nape he has a feather gummed onto the necklet with latex. This piece of finery, which is worn in addition to the ordinary *sö'rebzu* cords, is standard wear for all Shavante males and is always worn at festivals, unless it is superseded by any more elaborate neck ornament. The giving of it by the mother's brother to his sister's son accompanies the bestowal of a name by the former on the latter. The lack of a name in his early years is of no particular inconvenience to a Shavante since he is, during this period, addressed either by a kinship term or as 'boy' or 'girl', as the case may be. Even in later life his name will only be used to address him on very rare occasions. Nor are those names normally transferred by a maternal uncle to his sister's son such as have any social significance outside the system of nomenclature.[1] Girls, on the other hand, are named in a public ceremony by the representatives of the community as a whole.[2]

At this age Shavante boys are usually eager to be in the bachelors' hut, to take part in the singing and dancing, the joint hunting and collecting trips, and the other group activities that go with it. So much so that little boys often hang around the bachelors' hut and accompany its occupants on their various excursions. They are usually tolerated, although from time to time the *hę'wa* chase them away with a great show of irritation, merely to emphasize the difference in their respective statuses.

Then the boys band together and remain outside the bachelors' hut imitating the behaviour of their elders. They roam the savannah together and hold impromptu dances in the village, though never in the middle of it. In 1958 the boys who were waiting to enter the bachelors' hut in São Domingos were going about and behaving like a junior age-set long before the incumbents of the hut had been initiated. They were laughed at by their elders, who referred to them jocularly as 'little children', even when they had built their own bachelors' hut and moved into it subsequent to the initiation ceremonies. Socially they remained children until they had been formally inducted into the bachelors' hut as the junior age-set.

The girls of their own age were already married. They were not cohabiting with their husbands and indeed their husbands would have strenuously denied, if asked, that any marriage existed at all. But the marriage ceremony had been performed and the young men were in fact only waiting for their wives to mature sufficiently to have sexual intercourse.

[1] Certain Shavante names, e.g. Páhiri'wa and Tebe, are connected with particular offices, and their incumbents automatically have to perform the functions of these offices after receiving the names. Among the Eastern Timbira (Nimuendajú, 1946: 77–79) names belong to particular social groups. A person is affiliated to one or other of these groups, depending on which names have been transferred to him.

[2] Names and naming are discussed in Chapter VI.

4. MARRIAGE

The Eastern Shavante are divided into three exogamous patriclans which are called respectively Tpereya'óno, Ę Wawẽ, and
Topdató. They regard it as incestuous to marry within the clan.
Spouses may be selected from either of the other clans indiscriminately.

The marriage rules of the Western Shavante are slightly
different. The same three patriclans are found there, although
there are minor variations in the names of two of them, which
are rendered as Poriya'óno or Poriza'óno and Toprdató.[1]
Ę Wawẽ remains unchanged. They are said to be 'the same
clans' as those in the east. However the Western Shavante insist
that the Ę Wawẽ and Toprdató do not intermarry. Both of
them exchange wives with the Poriya'óno. They thus have a
system of exogamous moieties with two clans in one moiety and
one clan in the other. They too regard it as incestuous to marry
within the moiety. In fact they strenuously denied my statement
that members of the Toprdató and Ę Wawẽ had been known
to intermarry in the east. When I cited instances of such
marriages, they reluctantly admitted that such things could
happen but only among shameless people.

In São Marcos there were two marriages (Genealogy 2: 148,
149) not only within the moiety but within the clan. There were
two more (Genealogy 2: 165, 192) between the Ę Wawẽ and
Toprdató. My informants assured me that this could not be so,
yet my best efforts to check the genealogies could not show these
marriages to be otherwise. I do not claim absolute accuracy for
my genealogies and I could be mistaken, but it seems to me
unlikely that so many instances are all uniformly erroneous.
Instead I would suggest that objectively 'incestuous' marriages
do sometimes take place, although they are not seen as such. It
is significant that the marriages within the Ę Wawẽ clan were
between two men of the Uhę lineage and two fatherless girls
of the newly arrived Wamãrĩdzu. I doubt if they could have
been contracted with girls of the same faction or whose people
were not newcomers in the community.

The Shavante term for incest (*tsiwamnãr*) is interestingly

---

[1] I noted other dialectical differences between Western and Eastern
Shavante pronunciation and the Shavante themselves are conscious of the
difference.

enough the same word as is used in Shavante legends to refer to metamorphosis, usually when people change into animals or vice-versa. Their notion of incest is thus clearly that of passage from one state to another or confusion of statuses. We shall see later how important the distinction between Kin and Affine is, and thus be in a position to appreciate how serious the confusion of them would be for Shavante society. Similarly there is a terrifying monster which appears in Sherente stories and is referred to by them as a *romsiwamnãrí* from *ro* = countryside, creation, things in general + *siwamnãr* = metamorphosis, confusion, incest. This monster is the spirit of confusion; he has everything mixed up.

Shavante practise polygyny. We have already noted that wives are an economic asset. Lévi-Strauss stressed this function of polygyny among the Nambikwara, a nomadic people who roam in bands across the savannah some 450 miles to the west of the Shavante. Among them men with sufficient influence took more than one wife, even if it meant depriving others of women altogether. Polygyny was accordingly an essential privilege of a chief. It also provided him with the means to act in the way a chief was expected to. A man with a number of wives could acquire a food surplus which enabled him to be generous to others, or alternatively to devote his time to matters of public concern rather than to the domestic business of providing for his family (Lévi-Strauss, 1948: 60–62, 86–90). A Shavante does not need the economic contribution of more than one wife to enable him to exercise authority.

Nevertheless, Apęwẽ, the chief of São Domingos, has been married to at least five women and has had at least three wives simultaneously. His offspring constituted a remarkably high proportion of the total population of his village in 1962 (Maybury-Lewis, 1964: 94). On the basis of these data it might be supposed that it was the prerogative of the chief to marry a large number of wives. The situation is not quite so simple however. Apęwẽ is an unusual chief.[1] In Table 4 I show the number of wives possessed by certain prominent Shavante, and it can be seen at once that Apęwẽ has more than most of the

[1] My original account of the institution of chieftaincy among the Shavante (1960) was somewhat distorted because I knew Apęwẽ best of all and assumed that he was a typical chief. In fact he is an unusually 'strong' one.

others. Shavante are quite aware of this. In São Marcos, a community bitterly hostile to São Domingos, and to Apęwẽ personally, I was frequently told that Apęwẽ was evil. The specific charges against him were that he had many people killed and he took many women for himself. It seems that his many marriages were not his prerogative as chief but rather his spoils as a successful man. This is consistent with the fact that Shavante chiefs do not necessarily have the most wives in their community. The number of wives a man may acquire depends on a combination of factors such as the initial marriage his parents arranged for him, the availability of 'sisters' of his wife whom he can take as further wives, his own age and so on. It is thus quite possible for a prestigious senior man who was lucky enough to marry into a prolific family to have more wives than the theoretically more powerful chief of his community, especially since many Shavante communities have more than one chief, with correspondingly diminished authority for each.

There is no doubt that Shavante men like having more than one wife. Furthermore their wives appreciate the help that co-wives can give in doing the domestic chores and particularly in the business of moving from place to place, constructing shelters and generally taking care of the household while on trek. It is therefore customary for a man to take another wife if he can. If he has sufficient good fortune and prestige he may continue throughout his life to take a series of wives. If the wives bear him sons early then they will increase his potential prestige by making him the head of a strong lineage, and this in turn may enable him to take extra wives.

There is of course a demographic limit to this process. Given that the number of women in a community rarely exceeds the number of men by a large margin, polygyny cannot be the norm nor can senior men acquire unlimited numbers of wives. That they do not in fact can be seen from Table 5, where I present the data on polygynous marriages for three communities. Well over half the adult males of each community had only one wife.[1] Some of these had a wife only in the sense

[1] In São Domingos just over half of the marriages were polygynous. This is due to the severe feuding and consequent killing of men which has taken place there. There is thus some statistical justification for the feeling in other Shavante villages that the São Domingos people 'kill many and take their women for themselves'.

that they had been married once but were, at the time the data was collected, living without her, either because she was dead or because they had separated. A very small proportion were living with as many as three wives simultaneously.

Even so the additional wives have to come from somewhere, and they are made available by the fact that Shavante men marry much later than Shavante women. The age-set of small boys who are inducted into the bachelors' hut remains there for five years. At the completion of this period it is initiated and all of its members are married at a joint ceremony.[1] At that time the youngest of them is generally at least 12 years old and the oldest may be as much as 17. The available girls of their age are however already married to older men. They must therefore marry girls considerably junior to them. When I witnessed such a ceremony in São Domingos (1958) all the brides were immature, and some of them were carried out to be married on their mothers' hips. At Simões Lópes in 1962 the ceremony was not performed in full because the girls were even younger. I was even told of a woman from Simões Lópes who took her daughter to Batoví and had her married there at the age of two months.

Such a first marriage is a process, not an act. The Shavante speaking of getting married as 'moto ti-mrõ' (lit. 'went to the husband', or 'to the wife' as the case may be). In this case the approximation takes a number of years.

The arrangements are made initially by the parents of the parties concerned; they are not difficult, since marriages rarely have political consequences, and there are no significant payments or presents involved. Since the prospective bride and bridegroom are so young, their wishes are not usually taken into consideration. The girls are frequently too small to understand the negotiations anyway. The boys, on the other hand, may manage to have their preferences considered by their elders. They are usually interested in securing a bride who is as old as possible so that they will not have to wait over-long before they are able to consummate the marriage. On the other hand no boy would deign to take any vigorous part in the negotiations

---

[1] This practice has been discontinued in São Marcos, where the members of the young men's age-grade are not automatically married on initiation but may have to wait for some time before obtaining wives.

concerning his own marriage, a subject which causes him acute
embarrassment and shame. When he has completed his initiation and become a member of the age-grade of young men, he
will have participated in a ceremony of marriage to a small girl
chosen for him by his parents. Yet he will neither live in her
house nor visit it if he can possibly avoid it, and he will go out
of his way to avoid his parents-in-law as well, so as not to have
to address them as *īmāpari'wa*. If anybody questions him during
this period about his wife (and nobody except an anthropologist
would do such a thing, unless to tease him) he will strenuously
deny that he has one at all.

Boys, therefore, have very little to do with their prospective
brides before marriage and, as far as possible, nothing at all to
do with them afterwards. There is no 'courtship' among the
Shavante and, though men often treat their wives and children
tenderly by European standards, one never sees Shavante
couples make mutual demonstrations of affection.

The entire boys' age-set is married on the day that they
emerge from the bachelors' hut for the last time and perform the
final rites of the initiation ceremonies. On the occasion when I
watched such a marriage the bachelors' hut was dismantled in
the early morning as soon as the initiation ceremonies had been
completed, and the boys' age-set had been given a brand by the
mature men to start their own fire. During the morning the boys
were 'run in' as mature men in a ceremonial race. After this
the newly-constituted young men's age-set built itself a shelter
of leaves and branches in the middle of the village, over the
spot where they were to have their meeting-place.

In the early evening the Atẽpá age-set[1] (at that time 'young
men') gathered in their meeting place and sang. They then
proceeded round the village singing before each house. Meanwhile the Ai'riri, who were sponsoring the Tírowa initiates,
gathered by the mouth of the Tírowa shelter. The newly
initiated young men were all present in their shelter, lying on
their sleeping mats face downwards or at least with averted eyes.
The brides of the Tírowa were now led to the shelter by their
mothers. Each mother gave a small maize cake to the Ai'riri,
and then took her daugher into the shelter. There the girl's
prospective husband was lying on his side, his head turned

[1] See Chapter IV for the names of the age-sets.

away from her and covering his face with his hands. She lay down for a moment on the mat beside him, although he kept his back to her the whole time, and was then taken away again by her mother. Some of the girls married in this way were toddlers who had to be carried to the shelter where their husbands were waiting for them. They were frightened by the row of solemn young men, lying inert in their ceremonial paint, and they cried and shrieked bitterly as their mothers pulled them into the shelter and made them lie down for an instant behind their husbands.

When all the brides had been formally brought to their husbands in this way the Ai'riri ate the maize cakes which they had received for sponsoring the Tírowa. At the same time a huge maize cake, which had been prepared in an earth-oven with contributions of maize from all the households supplying brides or grooms that day (virtually all the households in the community), was carried to the meeting place of the mature men and there shared out among them. This closed the marriage ceremony.

A marriage among the Shavante is not therefore an occasion on which social cleavages are emphasized. The kin of the bride are not opposed either ritually or politically to the kin of the groom. Indeed the arrangement of a marriage is not a matter which is held to be the concern of the kin-groups (in this case patrilineages) of the man and the girl involved. It is left to their parents or paternal uncles to arrange the match and they do it with little fuss. No transfer of property is involved, nor can judicious marriages enable the spouses or their kin to acquire prestige. Shavante do not even use the marriage tie for political purposes as one might expect them to, for instance by arranging that their daughters should marry suitable young men, who could then be persuaded to throw in their lot with their in-laws' patrilineage, by choosing to stress their affinal rather than their descent link to a particular political group. On the contrary the marriage of a newly-initiated age-set is a community affair. The entire community is involved in it through being directly related to one or other of the newly-weds, and the entire community sponsors and conducts the marriage ceremony. The social recognition of the individual marriage ties that bind the members of the initiated age-set to their several brides is n more than a function of the recognition given by the community as a whole to a state of wedlock which the recently matured age-set must enter without delay. It is a public matter that these young men should be married. To whom they are married is only of domestic concern.

They are now fully-fledged *ritai'wa* (members of the young men's age-grade). Although they have no prestige as such, for the affairs of the community are directed entirely by the council of mature men, they are nevertheless regarded as the most virile and handsome group in the village, and this is a source of great pride to them.

If the community were involved in any warfare all its able-bodied men would fight, yet the *ritai'wa* are regarded as the warriors *par excellence*. This was brought home very clearly on one occasion when the news reached our group of a fracas to the south in which the chief of another Shavante community had been killed. This report aroused a heated debate in the mature men's council, which was punctuated at intervals by remarks to the effect that the Atẽpá (currently the young men's age-grade) were very angry. They would be sure to take action. The Atẽpá would not let it pass . . . and so on. In fact I discovered that the Atẽpá were entirely bewildered and apathetic about the whole matter. It was their elders who were bellicose. Yet because bellicosity is supposed to be a characteristic of the young men's age-grade, it had to be implied that it was really the Atẽpá who felt this way on behalf of the community.

Ideally a young man is not supposed to have sexual relations with a girl until he has become a *ritai'wa*. In fact it is very rare for him to have had any previous experience of this kind. As a boy he will have been inducted into the *hę* (bachelors' hut) as a member of an age-set whose ages vary between 7 and 12. Although the boys in the bachelors' hut are by no means secluded, they live separately and chastity is enjoined on them. In fact they have little opportunity for sexual experience since the girls of their own age are already married to men in the senior age-sets. The husbands are anxiously awaiting the maturity of their child brides in order to have sexual intercourse with them, and certainly would not permit them to have adulterous liaisons with uninitiated boys. There are, of course, rumours that this nevertheless takes place, and I have heard boys teased by their age-mates on account of their supposed interest in the wives of senior men; but I have never obtained any evidence that a boy in the bachelors' hut actually had a liaison with a girl. Nor have I ever heard of a boy having sexual relations with an older woman, even one who was temporarily without a husband through death or separation. It appears that they conform to the ideal of chastity expected of them, simply because they have little alternative.

The missionaries suspected that a good deal of homosexuality was practised in the bachelors' huts. Among the São Domingos Shavante at any rate this did not seem to be the case. I have lived for periods in the bachelors' hut and did not notice any homosexual attachments, although I was looking for them. There was one boy who was markedly effeminate both in his appearance and in his behaviour. The only occasions on which I noticed homosexual horseplay all involved him. At other times I saw members of the young men's age-grade perform a panto-mime of copulation with him during their bawdy discussions about women. I would say that he was a passive homosexual in the sense that he enjoyed provoking men into making pseudo-erotic assaults on him. He was extended a good-natured tolera-tion by his fellow Shavante and took part in all masculine pursuits on equal terms with the others. He suffered no disability or censure, other than having to put up with laughter and teas-ing if his performances fell far below that of his companions. On the other hand he could turn this laughter to his own account by clowning, and thus coming to be relied upon to provide the light relief on most occasions.

It seems then that these boys do not, as a rule, indulge in homosexual activities during their period in the bachelors' hut, and they have little opportunity for heterosexual experiences prior to their initiation. Even when they have been admitted to the status of young men, which will be when they are between the ages of 12 and 17, and are formally married, they will not necessarily have any opportunity for sexual intercourse, since their wives are generally too young for it even by Shavante standards.[1] It would be reasonable to expect that, once the

---

[1] I am uncertain as to the criteria according to which the Shavante deem a girl to be old enough for sexual intercourse. Girls are normally deflowered long before their first menses and before there has been any significant

physiological maturity of the boys' age-set had been socially recognized and they had been admitted to the status of young men, with the concomitant sexual privileges implied by that status, any further frustration of their sexual impulses would create social tensions. In fact, though there are tensions between the *ritai'wa* (young men) and the *predu* (mature men), these have not the intensity of the rivalries between age-sets characteristic of some societies,[1] where juniors may revolt and come into physical conflict with their seniors in order to oblige them to hand over their privileges. Shavante young men are prepared to wait their turn because it comes more quickly. In five years they will be promoted to the age-grade of *predu* (mature men), and by that time their wives will be nubile (or very nearly so) by Shavante standards. The older a boy is at his initiation the older the girl his parents try and obtain for him as a wife. Since a man starts cohabiting with his wife when she is somewhere between the ages of 8 and 10 years old, it follows that the oldest boys to be initiated will not have long to wait before they are able to have sexual intercourse with their wives.

Nevertheless, there is a waiting period of some sort for each young man just at the time when he has been received into the age-grade that is socially acknowledged to be the most virile and handsome in the community.

Ritai'wa are thus much preoccupied with sex. Shavante on the whole are prudish and not much given to bawdy conversation. Sexual matters are rarely mentioned in the mature men's circle and then only when some unusual phenomenon, such as a woman's haemorrhage, makes them a matter for public concern. The young men, on the other hand, talk about sex most of the time when they are gathered by themselves, and often when others are present too. Some of them could seldom see a

---

development of their breasts. It seems to depend largely on the size of the individual girl. Her husband will sleep with her as soon as he considers her to be big enough, which is usually between the ages of 8 and 10 as far as I could judge.

[1] e.g. the Masai (Fosbrooke, 1948: 29) and, to a certain extent, the Kipsigis (Peristiany, 1939: 32). In the latter case there is physical conflict between the age-set which must shortly retire and the age-set which will assume its privileges; the actual transfer of these privileges, however, does not come as a direct result of these clashes but through the mediation of the elders.

woman pass by without turning to a companion and telling him with appropriate gestures that they were longing to copulate with her. They used to joke about the boys in the bachelors' hut and say how much they copulated, which was quite untrue, and a perennial topic among them was who copulated a lot and who did not. Sometimes they would insist that they were above that sort of thing. Others, they said, copulated a great deal. The mature men copulated a lot, even the boys were always at it, but they, the *ritai'wa*, could do without it. One young man who had just become a father, and who was very fond of his baby, stoutly maintained that he never copulated at all, while at the same time insisting that I must have copulated a great deal in order to have such a large child. His attitude was one of the two extremes between which the *ritai'wa* oscillate. Forced as most of them are to remain continent at a time when they are expected to indulge themselves sexually, they react either by hungering openly for sexual gratification, or by ostensibly rejecting it as effeminate and inappropriate for people as actively masculine as themselves.

In the circumstances it is perhaps surprising that more of them do not have affairs with the wives of older men. I heard of only one case of this nature, which resulted in the plaintiff's being killed. Generally speaking, the young men wait until their wives are old enough and then go to visit them regularly at night, though they would be ashamed to be seen anywhere near their houses by day.

A consequence of this disparity in ages between husband and first wife is that Shavante girls are usually deflowered by an impatient man when they are barely old enough for it. It is commonly a painful experience, and many girls complain that they do not like it and that it hurts a lot when their husbands force their attentions on them. Yet the pain that many women associated with the first occasions on which they had sexual relations with their husbands does not seem to have traumatic consequences. Frigidity is unintelligible to Shavante of both sexes, whose attitude towards sex is usually summed up in the phrase 'to copulate is good'.

As soon as a young man starts visiting his wife in her house at night her kin construct a thatch partition within the hut ostensibly so that the couple are afforded privacy that they may not be ashamed (*ĩ-sem-di*). When the community goes on trek and the household group is occupying a number of small shelters, the girl builds herself a separate shelter within the household cluster. She will only do so, however, if her husband is accompanying the particular band she is in. On one occasion I was present when two bands of Shavante from São Domingos, which had been travelling separately, joined forces again. Certain young girls, accustomed to receiving the nocturnal visits of their husbands, had nevertheless been sleeping in their parents' shelters because the husbands' households were travelling in the other band. The day the bands reunited, these girls built themselves private shelters beside those of their parents.

This is the second stage in the marriage process. At first the wife was an immature girl whom her husband rarely saw. Now he visits her by night for sexual purposes only. The third stage comes when she is mature enough for her husband to take up residence with her.

The transition from the first to the second stage is less important than the transition from the second to the third, which completes the process of getting married. When a man begins to sleep with his first wife, the event is marked by no more than the erection of the partition already mentioned and a certain amount of amused gossip, especially on the part of the wife's kin. They take a delight in opposing the young man's pretensions to chastity by telling in circumstantial detail how they see him come to their household by night, how long he stays, when he leaves, and how he is so sluggish and sleepy that he slinks away when the rest of the household is already astir. The man himself strenuously denies it all, usually maintaining that he has no wish whatever to sleep with any woman, let alone the girl he is said to be visiting; and that if he had, he would know how to come and go like a shadow in the night without her household being so much as aware that anyone had had intercourse with her.

Young men resent this type of gossip about them because it is at once an aspersion on their individual independence (their ability to do without sexual gratification), and an insinuation of their social dependence on their affines, particularly on their parents-in-law. The daughters' husbands in a Shavante household are the inferiors of their wives' fathers and of their wives' brothers. A young man therefore postpones as long as possible the time when he must accept the status of daughter's husband in his wife's house. He tries to sleep with his wife without admitting that her brothers are his *ĩ'ãri* and that her parents are his *ĩmãpari'wa*. Not only does he avoid his wife's parents, but he tries to avoid mentioning them in conversation until the time comes when he is obliged to take up residence in their house and to accept his father-in-law as head of his own household.[1]

This he must do either when his wife bears a child or when his age-set is promoted to the age grade of mature men. One of the characteristics of maturity among the Shavante is that a man should be married and the process of getting married is not complete until the husband has actually taken up uxorilocal residence in his wife's household.

Under the circumstances it is remarkable how well husbands and wives get on together. Quarrels are very rare and I do not recollect having seen them use violence on each other. This is by no means because Shavante women are submissive. On the contrary, many of them are sharp-tongued and sarcastic and, though they may defer to their husbands' wishes in the end, they seek to influence them by a type of vigorous back-chat, which few men seem able to counter. If the relations between Shavante spouses are in general harmonious, it is probably because they expect no more from marriage than what it automatically gives: economic co-operation, sexual partnership, and children. If a woman is barren, her husband can always take an additional wife, and I have never heard of a married man being impotent. Since inter-group tensions concern only the men in each group they do not affect the relations between a man and his wife. Perhaps even more important as a factor in reducing possible friction between spouses is the circumstance that a man need not spend too much time in the company of his wife. At dawn and at dusk he can and usually does go out to the men's circle, where he sits gossiping with the other mature men. During the day he is either engaged in some sort of activity outside his house or he can go off to his parents'

---

[1] One Shavante in the young men's age-grade had a deep cut in his hand, but he declined to come to the shelter where I slept to have it dressed because it was the shelter of his wife's father, a circumstance of which I was unaware at the time.

hut and lounge there. Near every Shavante encampment the men select a shady spot or perhaps a number of such spots (known as *marã* = jungle) where they can spend the day together talking and manufacturing artefacts. It is only those men without sisters in the community in which they live (and such men are usually refugees from another Shavante group) who have no 'home' to go to and must therefore stay in their wives' households in their idle moments. Such men tend to be the minority in any community. Finally, if a man gets tired of his wife he can often find another girl to marry as well, so that he is not forced to spend so much time in the sole company of the first one.

Polygyny is ideally and frequently, though not always, sororal. As marriage is uxorilocal it is clearly much easier for a man to marry a number of uterine sisters, so that there is no problem as to where he should live and he acquires only one set of in-laws. Furthermore, Shavante say that sisters get on better together than more distantly related co-wives. If a man takes a second wife who has not been brought up in the same household as the first one, then she leaves her house and comes to live with him in the house of his first wife. Such an additional wife is therefore usually a widow or a girl whose parents are dead, for no parents would permit their daughter to go out as a wife, rather than to bring a son-in-law into the household, if they could possibly help it. It does happen occasionally that an older man who is head of his own household (his wife's parents being by this time dead or incapacitated) will take a younger girl as an extra wife while at least one of her parents is still alive, and yet will arrange for her to move in with him and his older wife. In those cases where I have a record of such a situation arising, the new wife had only her mother still living. Whether her husband would have been able to make the same arrangement if her father had been alive remains doubtful. In fact the system of uxorilocal polygynous marriage is given flexibility by the short expectation of life among Shavante men. A woman with no father can only get her husband to move into her house if he is also unmarried and therefore has no 'affinal' house to go to. On the other hand, if he is already living as son-in-law in another household, or has graduated to head of his own household, then he will have his new wife to live with him there.

Ideally, then, full sisters try and remain in the same household and they will often marry a single man. Conversely full brothers and lineage mates also try to stick together. The best marriages, from a Shavante point of view, are those which unite a group of brothers with a group of sisters. In this way patrilineages are not broken up through the rule of post-marital residence. It can be seen from Genealogy 1 that fully half the houses in Simões Lópes (A, C, I, L, M, N, O, P) are constituted wholly or in part by such marriages. Their incidence is somewhat less in São Marcos, where only a quarter of the households are made up in this way (Genealogy 2: D, E, P/Q, T, α/β). In São Domingos about a third of them are built around marriages of brothers with sisters (Appendix 4: B/C, F, K, M, N, P, X). I shall discuss the political effects of this custom in Chapter V.

In polygynous households junior wives[1] are therefore treated by senior ones as if they were younger sisters, which they usually are. They are bossed around a certain amount and frequently instructed to do odd jobs which their seniors feel too lazy to do, such as fetching water when the gourds are empty in the heat of the day, or going out to cover up a hole in the thatch when the sun moves. Sometimes they do them, but they may also refuse, which has no consequence other than that the person who gave the original injunction scolds and grumbles without anybody else paying particular attention. If a man's wives happen to be lying beside him on his sleeping mat instead of squatting in the middle of the hut as women generally do, then when a male visitor comes, he will motion the junior one off to make room for his guest. Apart from such small indications of her inferior status, a junior wife is treated both by her husband and by her co-wives as being the equal of her senior co-wives. Wives seem to be happy to co-operate with each other in collecting and preparing food, in moving and building house and in minding each other's babies. Rivalry appears to be quite uncharacteristic of their relationship nor do they compete

---

[1] Junior here means 'younger'. Younger wives are often those that a man has subsequently married and therefore junior on both counts. This is not always the case, though, and when a man takes as an extra wife a woman who is older than or the same age as the wife (or wives) to whom he already married, then the new wife will be treated by the previous one as an equal.

sexually for their husband's favours. A man will not in any case have intercourse with his wife for some time after the birth of each child nor while she is menstruating. It thus happens that a man often has only one wife with whom he may have sexual relations at any given time. Even when this is not the case, his wives do not seem to resent his having intercourse with their co-wives.

Nor do the wives in these polygynous marriages commonly seek sexual satisfaction in adulterous relationships. Adultery, and virtually all extra-marital intercourse comes under this heading since girls are married at such an early age, is extremely rare. It is possible that it is accomplished so discreetly that I was unaware of the majority of occurrences, but I find it difficult to believe that those gossips and know-alls, the old women, to whom I spent so much time talking, would not have mentioned it more often had it occurred more often. Furthermore, if adultery were practised more frequently than I thought, the aggrieved parties themselves would not have been ignorant of it, for secrecy is almost impossible in Shavante communities. We should therefore have to assume that the cuckolds took little notice of it, since these presumed cases never became issues. This seems highly unlikely, in view of the fact that Shavante men are touchy and truculent in their relations with other men, and that the few cases of adultery I know of had very serious consequences.

Thus the schism which took place at Santa Terezinha just before my arrival in 1958 was caused by the fact that the chief's wives both died within a short time of each other. Their kinsmen accused the chief of killing them through sorcery and refused to allow him to marry other women of their clan.[1] He seduced one of them anyway, while most of the village was away on trek, and this led to a break-up of his community.

On another occasion a man at São Domingos accused one of Apẽwẽ's sons of seducing his wife. Subsequently members of Apẽwẽ's lineage fell ill and sorcery was suspected. The accusing husband was therefore killed as a sorcerer.[2]

[1] They could do this because Pepetinho, the 'chief' in question, was not a proper chief by Shavante standards. He was the son of a powerful man who had acquired the knack of dealing with Brazilians and had therefore been appointed 'chief' by the mission.

[2] These cases are further discussed in Chapter V.

It may be that adultery only becomes a serious issue when it involves men of different factions and is therefore complicated by sorcery. Certainly no Shavante would ever take issue with a fellow member of his lineage over such a matter, and I believe (although I could not confirm this) that a man traditionally had sexual access to his brother's wife. A man sometimes cedes a wife to his brother, who then marries her; and a man is expected to marry and care for his brother's widow. Similarly men who are actual brothers like to marry actual sisters and frequently do (see Table 6). In the same way the members of a lineage who address each other as 'brother' regularly marry into adjoining houses, so that sections of the village semi-circle are taken over in each generation by lineage brothers. I do not believe that a member of such a group would charge another member of it with adultery. Such accusations appear to be inter-factional matters, which would lead one to suppose that the Shavante conceive of adultery not simply as the infringement of the sexual prerogatives of a husband by another man but rather as the infringement of his sexual prerogatives by a man of another faction.

I have heard reports of husbands' beating their wives for suspected adultery but have never confirmed that this actually happened, nor managed to elicit subsequent evidence of action taken by the husband towards his wife's lover such as would confirm the reported beating. It would be consistent if a husband punished his wife in this way, without taking further action against the man who had had relations with her, in cases where that man was too close a kinsman for this to be advisable. Yet if this were so, one would expect cases of adultery involving men of different factions to lead to both punishment of the wife and an inter-factional dispute. But wives are not always beaten when adultery becomes a factional matter, and in the one instance where I was present, the wife was certainly not in any way punished by her husband. I therefore incline to the view that these reported beatings are exaggerations; that Shavante may on occasion say that a husband beats his adulterous wife because they have learned that the neighbouring Brazilians regard this as the proper thing to do.

5. DIVORCE

It is as difficult to make precise statements about Shavante divorce as it is to make them about the Shavante notion of adultery. The difficulty stems from the fact that it is virtually impossible to describe the particular concatenation of Shavante rules and relationships with which we are concerned in this chapter in terms of general categories such as *marriage, adultery,* and *divorce*. Such terms are useful, in that they indicate general areas of interest, but their specific connotation requires to be stated afresh in each study.[1] Thus before we can discuss the circumstances under which Shavante might consider a marriage to be jurally terminated, we must be clear as to what rights are involved in 'marriage' among the Shavante in the first place.

I would argue that in most societies marriage is seen to be a process. The jural consequences of a rupture of the marriage tie vary according to the stage which the process has reached. We have already seen that a 'first marriage' among the Shavante passes through three clearly distinct stages. The ceremony at which brides are presented to recently initiated young men starts the first stage. The husband is thereby guaranteed exclusive rights in his wife's sexuality. Yet this is a promissory guarantee, since the wife is not usually old enough for him to exercise them. Consequently he may refuse to admit that he is actually her husband, or rather that he is the daughter's husband in relation to her father. His wife's father may claim him as a son-in-law, thereby stressing that an affinal link has been established between them through the daughter, but the young man can deny this until he starts having intercourse with the daughter. Nor does the father-in-law attempt at this stage to demand that his daughter's husband perform the duties of a son-in-law. In a sense, then, this period corresponds to what we

[1] I agree therefore with Leach (1955) that the attempt to establish precise definitions of categories such as *marriage* is fruitless. I would go further and add that it is probably misleading. Gough (1959), for example, replied to Leach, arguing that such definitions were required so that cross-cultural work could proceed. Yet it is my contention that much cross-cultural work is hampered by a failure to appreciate that the anthropologist's category may do violence to the data. Cross-cultural statements about 'marriage as we have defined it' tend to become statements about 'marriage', and from these are deduced theorems about marriage in different societies; in this way legitimate deductions from clear premises become illegitimate inferences.

would call the 'engagement', especially since a marriage can be more easily broken up at this stage than after it has been consummated. In Shavante thought, however, a man is 'married' as soon as the first ceremony has been performed. There is no ceremonial recognition of the beginning of the second stage, when the marriage is consummated.

During the second stage the husband still tries to deny that he has entered into any affinal relationship with his wife's kin. They nevertheless erect a partition inside their household for him and his bride. This is only ostensibly to afford them privacy. Shavante are accustomed to seeking privacy outside the hut if they should want it (which they seldom do). In any case, they usually consider that darkness, or the cover afforded by a sleeping mat, provides sufficient concealment for sexual activities. The partitition for the newly-weds is therefore erected as a public statement by the wife's kin that the marriage has been consummated and that the young husband is now contractually bound to them. He is expected to send portions of the game he kills over to their household. If his wife should become pregnant, then he will be regarded as father of her children, even if he has been away from the community for some time. When she gives birth he must move into her household if he has not already done so.

The Shavante refer to a separation of spouses as *tsi-remĕ*, a word with connotations of being parted or disjoined. But they also use the same term to refer to spouses who no longer live in the same household. It is thus difficult to determine whether certain couples would in our terms be considered 'separated' or whether they should more properly be classed as 'divorced'. Indeed it is questionable whether the Shavante would consider the jural tie of marriage as either severed or dissolved unless it was accompanied by the physical separation of the spouses to the extent that they no longer lived in the same community. *Mutatis mutandis*, there is evidence that desertion in this sense is sometimes equated with divorce, so that if a spouse leaves the community for a long time both partners consider themselves free to remarry.

It sometimes happens that an elderly woman no longer lives with her husband but establishes a separate household in the same village. She is still considered the wife of the man to whom she was married, even though they do not cohabit. She cannot take another husband, nor may she have sexual relations with other men, unless she is prepared to put up with her husband's displeasure. Her children usually live with her, but they come and go in their father's house on equal terms with the children of the wife with whom he lives. Some of her children may even live in the father's household. It does not make much difference.

There is some ambiguity, on the other hand, if a spouse goes away. It depends on the circumstances of his or her going whether it will be considered as breaking the marriage or not. If the husband flees from the community as the result of some factional dispute, then his wife has a choice of going after him in her own time, and thus preserving the marriage, or remaining behind, which is equivalent to divorcing him. If she remains behind she may take another husband. Her husband's actions do not similarly affect the jural status of their marriage, for he may take a second wife without divorcing the first one. It may, however, affect her decision as to whether or not she will bother to follow him, if she hears that he has moved into another woman's household as her husband. I knew three men in 1958 who had fled to São Domingos from Marãwasede, leaving their wives and children behind. At least one of them, Rìntimpsé, assured me that his wife would follow him, and that if she did not he would go back to Marãwasede and fetch her. In 1964 I met him again in São Marcos, where he had remarried.

It is not only the husband who might leave the community for political reasons. Sometimes a dissident faction moves away *en bloc*, and a wife may accompany her parents while her husband remains behind. An instance of this is the case of Hitã, daughter of old Aihí're at São Marcos (Genealogy 2: 95). When her brother Sebastião led a dissident group away from Capitari-quara, she left her husband there and went with her kin. She was remarried in São Marcos.

On the other hand, if a spouse leaves the community under less dramatic circumstances, and is away for a long period, the other partner may remarry. This can lead to misunderstandings. A young man left São Marcos immediately after initiation and was away for nearly two years. When he returned he found that his wife, who he had thought would be barely old enough to consummate the marriage, had already been married and deflowered by another man. He demanded that she be given up to him, but the girl's kin refused. He appealed to the missionaries, who consulted the girl and learned that she preferred to remain with her present husband. They therefore took no action. Next the plaintiff went to the mission at Sangradouro and persuaded its director that he had been wronged. A letter was sent to the director of the São Marcos mission asking him to intervene on behalf of the wifeless young man. The director at São Marcos tried again without success. Eventually the young man went off and married a widow at Sangradouro.

This case shows clearly that the Shavante regard desertion as equivalent to divorce. The young man could obtain no redress from his own people, even though he had been through the marriage ceremony with the girl in question. On the other hand it would be misleading to suggest that desertion is the only grounds for divorce, though it is the sole way of effecting it. A spouse sometimes 'goes away' specifically in order to terminate the marriage. The only case in my notes of a divorce consequent upon a quarrel between the spouses concerns a man in Santa Terezinha who was so incensed with his wife that he hit her over the head with a club while she was asleep. I was unable to learn much about the girl, but she was obviously not living in the house of her kin or her husband would not have been foolhardy enough to adopt this tactic. After she had been injured she was taken to 'her people' in another house and she subsequently left both her husband and the village.

In general, however, marriage is remarkably stable, jurally speaking, among the Shavante. The rarity of divorce is probably a function of the fact that it entails the removal of one of the spouses to another village.[1] Men do not need to divorce one wife in order to take another; and for a woman the requirement that she should leave the community if she wishes to divorce her husband is a severe deterrent, unless her kin are also leaving.

The children of the divorced couple remain with the spouse who is deserted, except in the very unusual circumstance that it is the mother who is going away and she has tiny children. In that case, Shavante say, the children would accompany her;

[1] In 1958 I had so little data from other Shavante villages that I believed divorce was virtually non-existent.

have no record of such an instance, and can therefore only suggest that in all probability the mother would simply go off on trek with the toddlers and not return if she really planned to desert her husband. I do not otherwise see why he would permit her to take the children with her.

6. THE HOUSEHOLD

Shavante build the houses in their base villages in the same way as they do on trek. Saplings are collected by the men of the household, embedded on the periphery of a circular patch of cleared ground, and then bent over at the top and lashed together. The women of the household assist the men in the task of binding them together and it is they who undertake the final thatching of the structure. All houses face inwards towards the middle of the village. A hole large enough for a stooping person to pass through is left in the thatch to serve as an entrance. This may be blocked up by a load of palm fronds held in position by a heavy log which is leant at an angle against them during high wind and driving rain, a combination which is frequently encountered in Shavante-land. On either side of this entrance a screen of stakes is erected, which serves to separate those who lie to the left of the entrance from those who lie to the right of it.

Conventionally, the head of the household and his wife live on one side of this 'tunnel' while their daughter and her husband live on the other side. They are thus mutually invisible when they remain on the sleeping mats, which are laid to each side of the entrance around the periphery of the hut. This convention does not, however, have the force of a rule which allocates one side of the hut to a particular group and the other side of it to the other. In the first place, if there are a number of married daughters, then they and their 'families' will be ranged all round the circumference of the hut. In this way, if the parents-in-law live to the right of the entrance and their eldest daughter to the left of it, other daughters and their husbands may occupy other positions all round the hut until there is also a son-in-law to the right of the parents-in-law. Secondly, there is no rule as to which side of the entrance the parents-in-law must live and which side must be kept for their daughters' families, even at the stage of the initial dichotomy between wife's parents and eldest daughter's husband. A man enters a household with the status of a son-in-law and graduates later to the status of father-in-law. When, in turn Ego's son-in-law comes to live in the house he will occupy the living space that was once occupied by Ego's father-in-law, now dead. In this way, if parent-in-law is to the right of the entrance in one generation and son-in-law

PLATE V

A house under construction

to the left, then in the succeeding generation the juxtaposition will be reversed. Finally, if the parents-in-law of a particular household are dead, then one daughter and her husband usually live to one side of the entrance while her sister and sister's husband live to the other. As far as possible, however, the men in a household group who come into the category of *ĩ-za'mũ* in relation to the others (i.e. have married the women of the household) keep spatially separate from those whom they address as *ĩ'ãri* (wife's brother) or *ĩmãpari'wa* (wife's father).

When Apęwę's hut in São Domingos had to be rebuilt, all its inhabitants moved in with us next door. For two days afterwards it rained incessantly, so that they were unable to proceed with the work of construction and remained cooped up with us. At the end of the third day, as soon as enough thatch had been put on to provide a modicum of shelter, the old man's son-in-law, together with his wife and two children, moved back into the partly finished hut. He considered that living right on top of his in-laws was inappropriate, and he took the very earliest opportunity to re-establish the conventional spatial division between himself and them.

The work of rebuilding that large hut took a long time because the only men engaged on it were the chief and his son-in-law. Meanwhile his sons and adopted sons (members of his patrilineage who spent most of their time in his hut and usually slept there as well) lounged on their sleeping mats watching the progress of the work. Although the house that was being contructed was their home, they did not belong economically to that household group. They were already members or potential members of other households (their wives' households) and it was to those household groups that they owed their labours. They had an obligation to help their parents-in-law build or rebuild the houses that they would not refer to as their homes but as their wives' houses. Similarly they had an obligation to co-operate with the members of their wives' household groups in the clearing, planting, and harvesting of their gardens. They could (and sometimes did) deny this obligation while they were still young enough to do so, especially since their wives were either too young to be their sexual partners or at least young enough for them to deny having had sexual relations with them.

A young man who avoids his *īmãpari'wa* and even denies this relationship in public can still get away with shirking the services he is supposed to perform for his father-in-law. His justification is that, as he does not have sexual relations with his wife, he has not, in a sense, fully entered into marriage with her and is not therefore bound by any concomitant obligations to her kin. Sooner or later, however, he is forced to give up this pretence—either when the screens are erected in his wife's home to enable him to visit her in private or, at the very latest, when the time comes for him to move into the father-in-law's house. A Shavante man thus sees marriage as a state in which he is obliged to work for, and is in a sense subordinate to, his wife's father. It is this contrast between being the pampered son in his natal household and being the outsider in his wife's that leads a young man who is anxious for the sexual privileges of marriage to cling to his 'freedom' by maintaining that he does not have intercourse with his wife, or even that he is not married at all.

A Shavante boy is thus born into a household where his father is an outsider. He himself is petted by everybody, by the women of the household, by his father, by his maternal uncles, and by his maternal grandfather. His mother's brothers may still be resident there and, even if they are married and living with their wives, they still use his mother's hut as their home. The head of the household is his maternal grandfather, who is likely to be a particularly fond relative. Many grandfathers are inseparable from their daughters' children once these can run around and no longer require their mothers' constant care. They take them out with them when they leave the village; they take them onto their sleeping mats at night; in fact they enjoy having them close to them at all times.

The structure of the household in a boy's infancy is schematically represented in Fig. 6.1. It will be seen that there are basically four male positions in the structure of the household at whichever stage of the developmental cycle we choose to examine it.[1] At any given moment at least two of these positions

[1] It should be emphasized that these are structural positions, not representations of individuals. For example, in Fig. 6.3a Ego is shown as having a sister's husband and an immature sister's son co-resident with him in the same household. Clearly there might be a number of men who are his

are connected by a tie of descent, and their incumbents, if they are adult or on the verge of adulthood, will form the dominant group in the household. The proviso is important. In Fig. 6.1, for instance, Ego and his brothers are linked to their father by a tie of descent, but as they are immature the dominant group in the household (represented by the block) is that of Ego's maternal grandfather and maternal uncles. As Ego grows up he comes to realize that he lives in a divided household. His father treats his mother's father and his mother's brothers with respect, which serves to emphasize the cleavage between them. His father is expected to assist his maternal grandfather and if necessary to provide for him, yet it is his maternal uncles who have the run of the house. Whenever important matters are discussed in the household, it is his maternal kin who discuss them, and they may even be embarrassed by the presence of his father across on the other side of the entrance partition. Furthermore, as a boy gets bigger he finds that his father will increasingly look to him as an ally while others will similarly tend to think of him as a member of his father's patrilineage. This does not mean that he will have to side either with his father or with his mother's brothers. The necessity for taking sides within the household itself is obviated by the fact that Ego (in the stage represented by Fig. 6.1) is bound by close affective ties to all the individuals resident there, irrespective of their mutual relationships in the household structure. It is not until he is nearing adulthood—usually at the stage when he is in the bachelors' hut—that he becomes a full member of his father's block within the household (see Fig. 6.2).

At this stage (Fig. 6.2) Ego's maternal grandfather is either dead or aged. His maternal uncles are established in their own 'affinal' households and have less to do with the household of their sisters. The group that dominated Ego's household in his infancy fades out of the picture. It is replaced by the group

---

sisters' husbands, all of whom would normally come to live with their wives in Ego's natal home, but they all stand in the same structural relationship to Ego and are represented by a single symbol in the diagram. This is a commonplace of kinship diagrams, but it needs to be stressed here because the fact that some structural positions have a number of possible incumbents is highly significant at the level of relations between persons in the household, although the structure of the domestic group remains unaltered.

consisting of Ego's father and his sons. A boy does not therefore come to be allied with his father against his maternal kin. It is when his mother's patrilineage relinquish control of his natal household that he and his father come to represent the dominant group as against his sister's husband.

It should now be clear why the Shavante arrange for fellow clansmen to marry the women of a particular household. If the young men coming into a household belong to different clans, then, when their father-in-law abdicates and their brothers-in-law transfer their control to their 'affinal' households, there will be members of two rival groups in the structural positions of Ego and Ego's father (Fig. 6.2). Since Shavante conceive of their domestic life in terms of a dichotomy between the in-group and the out-group in a particular household, such a splitting of either of these groups to introduce a third element would render the everyday life of the members of the household extremely complicated. In fact I was able to discover few cases where men of the same generation who married wives resident in a single household did not also belong to the same clan.

In Simões Lópes, household B, a man from the Ẹ Wawẽ and another from the Topdató (Genealogy 1: 86, 78) appear to have married two Tpereya'óno sisters. It will be remembered that these Shavante insisted that the Ẹ Wawẽ and Topdató were one, so it is perhaps surprising that this is the only instance of its kind which appears. The explanation is that the Shavante household is ordered according to a factional dichotomy. This normally coincides with a division between two clans, but if a Topdató man and an Ẹ Wawẽ man should belong to the same faction, they could well marry into the same household.

In Simões Lópes, household D, a Tpereya'óno man (Genealogy 1: 27) and a Topdató man (Genealogy 1: 63) of the same generation are both in-married spouses in a Ẹ Wawẽ house.

Simões Lópes, Household D

This was regarded by the Shavante as a special case. It was explained to me that the wife of 63 would normally have taken her husband to live with her mother in household L, but it was too small to accomodate them. She therefore moved in with her brother in D and brought her husband with her. Her husband meanwhile was anxious to fall in with the arrangement, or may even have insisted on it, since in this way he was able to move close to his brothers in households A, B, and C. Thus the chief's lineage of the Topdató consolidated its locus at one end of the village and also occupied the household at the other extremity of the community, thereby taking over both the ceremonial end houses.

I have recorded one other case of this kind, in São Domingos, household D. There the young men who married into the household are respectively Tpereya'óno (Genealogy 3: 50) and Ẹ Wawẽ (Genealogy 3: 119). But in this case 119 was a man who had 'gone over' to the Tpereya'óno, so that socially speaking no conflict arose.

Fig. 6.2 shows the structure of the Shavante household when Ego is approximately at the state of being a boy in the bachelors' hut. Figs. 6.3a and 6.3b show the households of which Ego is a member during the period when he belongs to the young men's age-grade. He calls his natal household (Fig. 6.3a) *iñõrowa*. When he is there other people will say that he is *aisõrowa'u* (gone to his home). He calls the household of his wife *ĩ-mrõ'u* (gone to the wife) and so long as his sisters are still alive he will continue to use these designations. At this period he occupies complementary positions in the two households. In his natal home he is a member of the in-group, *ĩ-ãri* to his sisters' husbands. In his wife's house he is an outsider, an *ĩ-za'mũ*.

The relationship between *ĩ'ãri* and *ĩ-za'mũ* is a critical one, not only for the household but for the Shavante in general. The hostility between kin groups, which is characteristic of Shavante society as a whole, is felt in the domestic group particularly between these affines. The Shavante realize this and attempt to neutralize it by prescribing a system of etiquette to regulate the behaviour of the *ĩ-za'mũ* and the *ĩ'ãri* towards each other. They should address each other politely and be mutually generous. They should help each other and stand by each other. A man should not object to his *ĩ'ãri* using his property. The *ĩ'ãri* should

reciprocate by giving presents to his *ĩ-za'mũ*. I was frequently
questioned by Shavante men about my wife's brothers. How
did they treat me? Were they good to me (*zawi-di*)? Were they
mean (*zõiti-di*)? What did I give them? and so on. To a
certain extent, Shavante conform to these precepts. *ĩ'ãri* and
ĩ-za'mũ are formal and polite with each other. They ostentatiously share food when they are together. Frequently a man
to whom I offered a present or some food would say 'give it to
my wife's brother'. When this gesture had been made and the
present given, he would then turn his attention to getting a
duplicate for himself. *ĩ'ãri* make use of their *ĩ-za'mũ*'s property
without hesitation, though there is little reciprocity in such
matters, and *ĩ-za'mũ* often grumble about their predatory
brothers-in-law.

The relationship is overtly one of formal courtesy and covertly
one of suspicion and resentment. This is symbolically expressed
in the Shavante myth concerning the acquisition of fire, which
describes how two brothers-in-law go out hunting together.
ĩ-za'mũ holds a tree-trunk in place for his *ĩ'ãri* to climb up to a
rock and get some macaw eggs. *ĩ'ãri* tries to deceive *ĩ-za'mũ* by
pretending there are no eggs up there and only throwing down
stones when he is asked for proof. *ĩ-za'mũ* gets angry, takes away
the tree and deserts his *ĩ'ãri*, who is subsequently rescued by a
jaguar.[1] Similarly a Shavante will ask for presents on behalf of
his brother-in-law, but at the same time will be jealous of what
he gets and will strongly resent it if his brother-in-law is given
anything in his absence. In the same way, he and his brother-
in-law may assist each other on the hunt, but they will also
watch each other, for they know from the discussions in the
men's council that they belong to potentially hostile groups.
Such hostility is implicit in the relationship itself and is therefore anticipated by brothers-in-law and engendered between
them, where none may have existed before.

Since the Shavante anticipate hostility from their affines and
since this hostility must be restrained by the rules of etiquette
to make any sort of domestic life possible, they come to regard

[1] The Sherente have an identical myth concerning the acquisition of
fire. The theme of co-operation in theory and betrayal in practice of the
ai'ãri and the *i'za'mũ* (Sherente: *aikãri* and *ĩ-zakmũ*) also occurs in a number
of other Sherente stories (see Nimuendajú, 1944).

their affines with a great deal of suspicion. They suspect them perennially of harbouring designs against them, and consequently they tend to explain death and misfortune as being due to affinal malevolence. A man's affines are therefore the first people to be suspected of sorcery. I discuss these suspicions and their consequences, also how they are manipulated for political ends, in Chapter V.

The relationship between a man and his wife's father is also one of respect veiling hostility, but in this case the respect is more easily accorded since his wife's father is an older and senior man, while the hostility is less marked as there is less competition between the two. A man usually treats his father-in-law with deference, asks his advice, and makes a show of asking his permission about what to do and where to go. He is expected to give him presents, and most Shavante who came persistently to me to get things were doing it on behalf of their wives' fathers. On the other hand, every Shavante knows that the parent-in-law relationship is a trying one for the son-in-law, and jokes about it are as common as they are in our own culture. When a man says 'ĩmãpari'wa udzee ubtábi-di' (my parent-in-law is very ill) drawing out the 'eeee' for comic effect, this is a sally which never fails to evoke roars of laughter. Nevertheless, the reality is earnest enough and the son-in-law of an important man must watch his step.

It will be seen, then, that when a man leaves the security of his natal household (Fig. 6.3a) and begins the process of transfer to that of his wife (Fig. 6.3b) he is, in a sense, going as a hostage into the enemy camp. Throughout the period shown in Fig. 6.4, when his own children are too young to give him any support, he must resign himself to being an outsider, perpetually on his guard. He is fortunate if his sister's home is in the same community, because then he can return to it as often as he wishes and there he is able to relax among his own kin. It is not until his children are growing up that he can really consider his wife's house as his own. Then the same process that has already taken place in his natal household is repeated, only this time he occupies the structural position occupied by his father in the previous cycle. Fig. 6.5 shows how his wife's father retires and his wife's brothers lose their connexion with the household. In Fig. 6.6 he is left as the head of the household, that is as head of the dominant group in the household, which consists of the members of his own patrilineage.

A girl, on the other hand, does not feel the stresses resulting from the changes in composition of the domestic group. In the normal course of events she is born and brought up and subsequently spends her life in the same household. In her infancy this household will be dominated by her mother's patrilineage, and for most of the rest of her life by that of her father. Only at the death or retirement of her father will her house become the 'home' of her affines, i.e. of her husband's people. But by this time she and her husband are usually elderly and they have grown-up sons. She comes to be regarded as, in a sense, belonging to her husband's patrilineage. In any case she is largely by-passed by the inter-group rivalries that divide the men into factions. I have never heard of a woman being accused or suspected of sorcery, which is a sure indication that women are not involved in the system of alliances and enmities that engenders such accusations. Sorcery, like adultery and so much else in Shavante life, is a function of politics, and Shavante politics is based on competition between groups of males.

In such a system uxorilocal marriage seems anomalous indeed. It is an anomaly to which we shall have to return in a general discussion of the structural principles of Shavante society.

IV

THE AGE-SET SYSTEM

1. THE BACHELORS' HUT

SHAVANTE see their own society as being divided at any given moment into a number of age-sets arranged in a hierarchical order of seniority (see Table 7). These age-sets unite those who have passed through the bachelors' hut together, who have been initiated together, and who have been married at a joint ceremony. Such men are set apart from others who have shared these common experiences either previously or subsequently.

The bachelors' hut is therefore the cornerstone of the age-set system. It is the place where a Shavante boy first feels what it is to belong to an age-set and participates in the comradeship, cross-cutting distinctions of clan and lineage, which such membership implies. A boy does not belong to an age-set until he has been formally inducted into the bachelors' hut, so that before that time he is, in a sense, not a full member of society. He has no place in a system where social and ceremonial activities are largely carried out by the age-sets. He belongs to an undifferentiated class of 'children' who are no more than social potential. He ceases to be treated and addressed as a child only when he and his age-mates have been formally inducted into the bachelors' hut.

Recognition of the new age-set is given ceremonially on an appointed day by the *predu* i.e. by all the 'mature men' in the community. The prospective members of the bachelors' hut paint themselves scarlet from head to foot. They then put leaves on their shoulders so that the *urucú* will not soil their regalia and don broad collars of white cotton. Over the collars they wear bead necklaces terminating in two macaw's tail fathers. They are then fetched one by one from their houses and led out into the middle of the village by one of the *predu* who bears the name of Páhiri'wa. From there they are led over to the bachelors' hut where all the mature men of the village are assembled. Each boy sits down and has his collar removed by one of the *predu* and placed on the ground. He then enters the bachelors' hut and sits on the far side, facing the back wall. His penis sheath is given to him by the mature men and he puts it on. This is the outward sign that he has now left childhood behind. From that time on he is a *hę'wa* and must live in the bachelors' hut.

A boy may be anything between the ages of 7 and 12 when he is inducted in this way, depending on whether he was only just too young to be incorporated into the previous age-set or whether he was a toddler at the time that they entered the bachelors' hut. I doubt whether any boy would actually have to wait till he was 12 before entering the *hę* (and therefore till he was 17 before initiation) unless he were rather undersized. The Shavante do not keep count of the actual ages of their children before they are old enough to belong to an age-set; after that their relative ages, i.e. the age-set to which they belong, are all that matters. In practice any boy who looks and behaves as if he is old enough to be with the members of the new age-set is permitted to be incorporated into it.[1]

Once he has put on the penis sheath he is no longer a child. He will never be seen without it again for the rest of his life. He even wears it while bathing. The sheath itself is a tiny conical spiral of palmito bark. A man pulls his prepuce over the glans penis, moistens the sheath in his mouth and places it over the folds of his foreskin. The sheath therefore covers only the tip of his genital organ, and apart from this covering he goes entirely naked. Nevertheless, Shavante consider it exceedingly immodest for any male not a child to be seen without this covering. They are much embarrassed should the sheath fall off, as it sometimes does during athletic activities such as dancing or racing, and the man concerned is obliged to cover his genitals with his hand until he can get a new one or until someone brings him the one he has lost. During the races which are an integral part of the initiation ceremonies small boys are detailed to stand by the 'track' to retrieve such lost sheaths and return them to their owners. The only occasions on which a man removes his penis

---

[1] In Simões Lópes (1962) I saw small boys who could barely walk being 'inducted' into the bachelors' hut. I believe this was a recent development prompted by feeling in the community that this might be the last age-set ever to be inducted.

sheath are those on which he is obliged to do so by physiological necessity: when urinating or copulating. It is for this reason (in order to hide the uncovered penis) that Shavante men squat down to urinate. Women invariably stand up to do so.

The wearing of a penis sheath is a symbolic affirmation of physiological maturity. The sheath 'conceals' the erect penis and therefore indicates sexual potency, and at the same time the social control to which inherently dangerous sexual powers are submitted.

Soon after the new age-set has been introduced to the bachelors' hut they take part in a ceremony known as *oi'o*.[1] I have never seen this ceremony, but according to my informants the procedure is as follows:

The *hę'wa* come out at dawn, when the mature men are all gathered about their fire in the middle of the village, and assemble in two groups at each extremity of the village semi-circle.

One of the mature men now goes to join each of these groups. He makes the boys form a circle and then gets them to deposit the reddened clubs they are carrying in the middle of it. These clubs are known as *um'ra* and are little more than lightwood sticks about 2 feet long and reddened with *urucú*. They are the insignia of the *hę'wa* and are carried by them on all ceremonial occasions. The man who has gone to direct the group of boys now leans on his bow stave and delivers a harangue, after which he deposits his bow on the boys' clubs. The two groups are then led to the centre of the village and drawn up in lines facing each other.

The mature men have in the meantime selected two of the boys' light clubs and weighed them in their hands to see that they are much the same size and weight. They then call forward one boy from each of the two lines, taking care to select a pair who are of approximately the same size, and give them the clubs. The boys hold them in one hand, leaving the other hand free or clasping the wrist of the clubbing arm. They then duel, clubbing each other over the back and shoulders. They make

[1] Some informants gave me to understand that the *oi'o* was coterminous with the induction ceremony, when the junior age-set entered the bachelors' hut. It seems more likely however that it is performed on a number of occasions during the years that the boys spend in the bachelors' hut, one of which might be the induction ceremony.

great efforts not to cry or show pain when they are hit, and their elders stand by to shout encouragement and stop the bout if necessary. If one boy cries, or simply when the contest has gone on long enough, the elders stop the bout and call out a fresh pair. The men re-arrange the contestants so that each boy fights a number of bouts, and they try to ensure that the stronger take on the stronger, leaving the weaker to fight the weaker. The duelling continues as long as the men see fit.

The *oi'o* is only one of a number of ceremonial activities in which the boys in the bachelors' hut are obliged by their elders to take part. The purpose of their seclusion is not only that they may have the time and opportunity to develop a corporate spirit, but also that they should be available for instruction. This instruction proceeds not so much by oral teaching as by example and emulation.

While they are in the bachelors' hut they are treated as a group apart and therefore obliged to act in concert. This corporate solidarity is further encouraged by the institution of ceremonial partnership. Each boy acquires at this stage one or two *ĩ-amõ* (literally 'my other' or 'my partner'). He enters into a formal relationship with them, characterized by ceremonial partnership, friendship, and mutual assistance. He is supposed to sleep between them in the bachelors' hut and dance between them during ceremonial. Shavante age-sets perform their dances in a circle holding hands, so that it is theoretically possible for everyone to stand between his two *ĩ-amõ*. In the bachelors' hut, where the boys generally sleep in a row, this is more difficult. In practice this is of no significance. It does not matter particularly whether Shavante do in fact dance or sleep beside their *ĩ-amõ*. It is the ideal notion that counts, and according to that, each boy enters into a special relationship with all the members of his own age-set whom he would class as affines. They are collectively his *ĩ-amõ*. In an ideal age-set there would be equal numbers of all clans, so that every boy would have affines on either side of him whenever the age-set stood in a circle. The two affines who stood beside him would be his especial *ĩ-amõ*. Few age-sets are ideal age-sets, however. A boy may have only one *ĩ-amõ*, or he may have two, of which one or both are away. But that is immaterial. The important aspect of the institution is that a man is bound throughout his life by formal friendship

ies to at least one member of his age-set who belongs to a
different clan. In practice, however, the bond is only operative
during the years when his age-set is ceremonially active.

It is important here to realize that when we speak of the
'seclusion' of boys in the bachelors' hut the term is used in a
relative sense. The *hę'wa* are not debarred from contact with
the rest of the community. They may visit their homes and
spend much of the day there if they wish. They may even sleep
there on occasion, though it would not be considered proper if
a boy regularly slept in his home rather than in the bachelors'
hut. They are secluded only in the sense that their age-set has
been formally lodged in a hut apart from the village. This
spatial separation symbolizes their social separation from the
community. They are not children and they are not initiated
adults. They are recognized as the incumbents of a particular
age-set but their age-set is regarded as still immature and, in a
way, marginal to the system.

The focus of their activities is therefore apart from the village
—in the bachelors' hut. But just as they are permitted to leave
this hut and come into the village whenever they wish, so the
hut itself is used as a male club by any men who wish. Even
children may spend a lot of their time there, though they may
also be chased away. The older men, for obvious reasons, are
not chased away. Nor are women positively forbidden to enter
it. Younger girls frequently do, and are often sent over from
their households with food for their brothers. Even older women,
though they rarely go near the *hę*, can and do enter it if they
wish to speak to any of its inmates. It is accordingly not true to
say of the modern Shavante that they ensure the chastity of their
uninitiated boys by secluding them and thus preventing their
having access to the girls.[1] Chastity, as we have already seen, is
indeed enjoined on uninitiated males, and they may even be
exhorted to remember this when their elders visit the bachelors'
hut and harangue them, but their 'seclusion' is conceptual
rather than physical and neither can nor does have the purpose
of preventing their having pre-marital sexual relations.

During their years in the bachelors' hut the *hę'wa* live a
comparatively free life. They have few obligations and no

[1] Martius (1867, I: 112) mentions this as a practice characteristic of the
Shavante.

responsibilities. Their families provide them with a certain amount of food, and whenever they are hungry they are able to send a messenger to one of the households to bring back more. If ever a kill or any other large quantity of food comes into a household which has a boy in the bachelors' hut, the *hę'wa* immediately send a representative to bring their share. Food that comes in this way is always distributed among all the boys present. Sometimes shares are even kept for those who are absent, which is contrary to the usual practice among the Shavante. The *hę'wa* are, however, particularly careful about sharing. For example, when I was living in the bachelors' hut, boys would occasionally give me gifts of food, usually fish that they had caught. When I reciprocated with gifts of food (manioc flour) or other items (e.g. fish hooks) my presents were always shared out. In this way the two or three who were especially generous towards me came off badly, for they gave to me personally and yet received from me only as members of the group.

But the boys have no difficulty in getting enough to eat. They have no dependents to feed and little to do save forage for themselves, apart from the fact that they are still provided for by their families. As a result they are probably those Shavante who have the most leisure. They do not even make very many artefacts, for their elder kin can usually be persuaded to give them the implements they need. They must plait their own sleeping mats, but in fact they seldom do, so that their mats are usually the most tattered and filthy of any in the village. In the same way their sisters do not help them with the thatching of the *hę*, so that the bachelors' hut is an uncomfortable place to live. It is badly covered, so that the sun scorches its inmates by day and the moon keeps them awake by night, and it is frequently infested with insects. But in general the *hę'wa* live a life of carefree ease. They go out hunting and collecting only when they feel like it, and usually prefer to go fishing if they have hooks and line, because it is less strenuous. They spend much time bathing and playing games in the water, in the same spirit as they play games and run races on land. Whenever there are Brazilians in the neighbourhood it is the *hę'wa* who have the most time to hang around their houses, partly out of curiosity and partly in the hope of getting something out of them. At

São Domingos, for instance, the boys from the bachelors' hut spent most of their time at the Indian Post, whose inhabitants sometimes felt persecuted by their perpetual presence from first light till well after dark.

Nevertheless, the five-year period in the bachelors' hut is not one of complete idleness for the boys. During this time they are taught the skills, both practical and ceremonial, which they will need in adulthood. Older men accompany them on the hunt and teach them how to track and kill the various game animals on which the Shavante rely. Such hunting instruction is mostly confined to the *hęmono*, those short hunting trips prior to festivals in which the entire community takes part. Then the entire age-set of the *hę'wa* are usually present and their elders can show them what to do during a concentrated spell of hunting. Boys usually know a great deal about fishing and gathering before they enter the bachelors' hut. While they are there, they are taught how to make their own weapons and to plait their sleeping mats. But by far the greater part of their instruction is devoted to ceremonial and to the making of regalia for the various ceremonies in which they have to take part.

They have, in the first place, to learn the songs of the tribe. These are of two different kinds: public and private. By public songs I mean songs which are the property of the community and are sung on specific occasions, during initiation, before a log-race, during the *wai'a* and so on. Private songs, on the other hand, belong to individuals who literally 'dream them up'. These songs come to their owners in dreams, and if the owners are of sufficient standing they are subsequently able to teach the songs to the community. The method of doing this is to go over to the bachelors' hut during the night and wake up all those who are sleeping there. The song can then be sung over a few times with the boys, after which the owner of the song leads the *hę'wa* in a singing tour of the village. Outside each house (or outside as many as he can be bothered to) he gathers the boys in a circle and leads them in the singing of his song. Any mature man has the right to take the boys out at night in this way, but in fact the right is exercised more by people of strong character than by others. A man who is shy about pushing himself forward will not be one to go and order out the boys,

especially if it is a cold night and they are liable to come ou
reluctantly, muttering and grumbling.

Those who most commonly take the boys out singing are the
members of the junior age-set in the mature men's age-grade
When I was in São Domingos the Tírowa were in the bachelors
hut and it was usually members of the Ai'riri who made them
sing (See Table 7). A special relationship exists between these
two age-sets, for it is always the junior age-set of the mature
men's grade which sponsors the education, initiation, and
marriage of the *hę'wa*. Alternate age-sets are linked by an
especially close tie, which is to some extent expressed by
opposition to their intermediaries. In São Domingos the Tęrã
were linked to the Atẽpá in opposition to the Ai'riri and the
Tírowa. These were the only active age-sets. In 1958 the four
senior age-sets in the community had a total membership of
only seven. This meant that, in practice, they had ceased to
function as separate age-sets. Their members would get together
to work and talk outside the village, but simply as *predu* (mature
men), not as members of specific age-sets. Even the Tęrã very
rarely sang or danced together. On the other hand the Ai'riri
the Atẽpá, and the Tírowa frequently undertook particular
tasks as age-sets and often danced together and sang round the
village during the night.

For much of 1958 the boys in the bachelors' hut at São
Domingos were engaged in the manufacture of regalia for the
initiation ceremonies. It seems that the Shavante no sooner
complete one ceremony or ceremonial series but they start
planning for the next. They must, for example, ensure that the
group treks through country which provides the raw materials
for the manufacture of their regalia. Furthermore, these treks
must be planned to coincide with a season of comparative
abundance of some crop in the required region so as to leave
people free to work on their artefacts. Finally, the actual processes used in the making of much of their ceremonial outfit
are frequently laborious and long drawn out. The dance-masks
required for the initiation ceremonies took months to make. In
the meantime the boys in the bachelors' hut were engaged in
the manufacture of the traditional bead necklaces.

This involved the collection of tiny seeds (*Scleria* sp.) which
had to be carefully singed so that they hardened on the outside

This is difficult to do without setting fire to the entire cutting and requires a great deal of care and skill to be accomplished successfully. The blackened 'beads' were picked off their stems, with the result that each one had a tiny hole in one side. A boy would then sit for hours on end taking up each separate bead, inserting a bone needle into the hole and pressing the spitted seed into the flesh of a scooped-out gourd. The bead was thus driven a little way into the meat of the gourd before the needle broke through to the other side. The flesh of the gourd held the tiny bead together and prevented it from shattering, so that after each operation one cleanly perforated bead was left embedded in the rind. The boys then had to manufacture string out of plaited grass, and thread these beads into necklets and into decorative chains such as are required by most Shavante ornaments.

These *a'é* beads were their principal contribution to the initiation regalia, but it was a contribution which took a long time and much effort to prepare. During the months before the final ceremonies which completed their initiation the two Ai'riri who were acting as masters of ceremony (Páhiri'wa and S'rizamdí) visited the bachelors' hut every evening and harangued the boys, telling them what was expected of them and urging them to get on with their preparations. They were also visited by the chief himself, or by his eldest son, who delivered similar injunctions.

When that phase of the initiation ceremonies which involved ceremonial races at dawn and before dusk every day was reached, the boys had also to manufacture the huge grass capes which were worn on successive days by the man who led their processions.

The boys therefore spend a great deal of their time preparing their own regalia, but they are also preparing themselves physically and mentally for the series of ceremonies in which they take part during their time in the bachelors' hut. Not only do they learn the words of the tribal songs, but they sing them at night to demonstrate that they are 'wakeful' as Shavante men should be. Not only do they learn the steps of the dances, but they learn to stamp in the masculine fashion which Shavante admire. The purpose of ceremonies such as the *oi'o*, which is repeated a number of times during their period as *hę'wa*, is to make them tough. They are taught to wrestle and are called out from time to time for ceremonial bouts with their elders. On these occasions they paint themselves scarlet and emerge one by one from the bachelors' hut to wrestle with two or three mature men, who have challenged them. Each boy wrestles with his opponent individually, the larger boys first while the man is fresh and later the smaller ones when he is getting tired. It is, of course, usually the boy who is thrown, after which he takes up a ceremonial stance[1] in front of the bachelors' hut. When the entire age-set has wrestled it is harangued by the mature men and that completes the ceremony. Later on, the initiation ceremonies themselves consist largely of ceremonial exercises designed to develop physical resistance and fleetness. They are in fact the culmination of a series of athletic rites which are interspersed over the entire period of seclusion in the bachelors' hut.

[1] A posture characterized by a bent head, set expression with eyes fixed on the ground, relaxed body, arms hanging loose at the sides and one foot forward with that leg flexed at the knee.

2. INITIATION (See table 8)

First Phase

In São Domingos the initiation ceremonies for the Tírowa began at the end of February 1958. The first phase consisted of a form of trial by immersion. The Tírowa were taken down to the creek by representatives of the Ai'riri and each boy was directed to stand in the water with his arms together and held out in front of him. He bent his arms at the elbows and made a cup with his hands. Then he was told to leap up, bringing his body clear of the surface of the stream and at the same time scooping water over his own head with his outstretched arms. As he fell back into the water again he should bring his forearms down on it with a resounding thwack. The initiates are supposed to leap in unison so that the splash as they jump and the boom as they smack the surface of the water can be heard a long way away.

For about three weeks the Tírowa were led out daily to perform this exercise.[1] Their first spell would be well before dawn when the water was cold and the boys soon got very chilled. When they could stand it no longer they would send some of their number out on to the bank to build a fire and take it in turns to crouch over it to get warm. The older men, who left them to get on with their jumping while they themselves went back to sleep or else sat over the morning fire in the centre of the village, sometimes noticed that the splashing had diminished in volume or died away altogether. They would then send someone down to the river to catch the boys unawares. If he was successful, he rushed in among them buffeting them and pushing them back into the water. They would in any case be tumbling over themselves to get back in there and go on with their test of fortitude. The indignation of the mature men when they found the Tírowa shirking was assumed, however, for it was accepted that the initiates would let up whenever they could. It was virtually a game to see whether the initiates could avoid their exercise without being caught or whether their elders could steal up on them and catch them in the act of shirking.

Finally they would be permitted to return to the bachelors' hut. At intervals throughout the day, that is for at least two

[1] I am unable to give exact details as this phase of the initiation ceremonies took place in my absence.

further spells, they would be taken out for more diving, and there was usually a final exercise after dark before they were permitted to go to sleep. During the night they might be woken again by one of the Ai'riri and taken singing round the village. It was therefore a strenuous time for the Tírowa. They complained of stiffness and aches and pains all over their bodies. Some of them developed colds. In between their periods in the river they spent most of their time sleeping.

It was finally decided by the mature men that this phase had continued long enough, so the chief gave instructions for the boys to have their ears pierced as a sign that they were entering the final stages of their initiation. The Tírowa were led out of the bachelors' hut as usual at dawn on the appointed day, but they were not taken down to the river. Instead each boy was seated on a mat in front of his parents' house and had the lobes of his ears pierced with a bone needle. Tiny cylinders of wood were then inserted in the holes. These would be progressively replaced by larger cylinders until the boys were capable of wearing full-sized ear-plugs. This closed the first phase of the initiation.

Second Phase

The community set out on trek on the first day of May, and throughout May and most of June all the adult males were collecting raw materials for the regalia to be used in the second phase. The actual manufacture of these items, particularly of the *wamñõrõ* 'dance-masks',[1] took the better part of three months.

These masks are made out of a fine bast procured from the fronds of the *buriti* palm. During May the men went out collecting the fronds. The finest strands (known by the Brazilians as '*buriti* silk') then had to be separated from the coarser ones and only the former were used. They were dried in the sun and hung up on strings between the shelters, where the men would stand plaiting them for hours on end. When the community returned to São Domingos towards the end of June each man had a

---

[1] The *wamñõrõ* are, strictly speaking, not really masks. They are bast cones, open at the bottom and with a slit down the side. They may be worn ceremonially suspended from the wearer's head while his face and arms protrude through the slit, but they are more usually carried as tassels in the right hand and swung by the dancers during the initiation ceremonies. I call them 'dance-masks' merely for want of a better word.

number of bunches of these *buriti* strands, which were then ready to be woven together into masks. Work on the *wamñõrõ* was interrupted, however, during the harvesting of the beans and pumpkins which took place immediately after the return from the trek (see Table 3). Later the entire community went out on a communal hunt to procure meat for the final ceremonies in the initiation cycle. During this time little work could be done on the preparation of the masks. As soon as the hunt was over, all energies were concentrated on this task and for a few days the men did nothing else but work on them to get them ready.

Meanwhile the boys were passing through the second phase of initiation. As soon as the community returned from its trek the men cleared a race track starting outside the village and finishing in its centre. The cleared space began some fifty yards outside the village, included houses H and I (Fig. 4), and the meeting place of the mature men. Two saplings were transplanted and set up to act as finishing posts in the middle of the village.

While the men were preparing the village the boys were busy making huge grass capes known as *no'oni*. These are made by plaiting together the ends of outsize palm fronds, and then cutting off the stem so that the blades hang free like a long comb from the top line where they have been plaited together. The string down the centre of each individual blade is then pulled out so that the cape consists of a collection of thin strands.

The second phase of the initiation ceremonies was opened on the afternoon of 27 June. All the male members of the community except the very oldest and the very youngest were painted with *urucú* on the back and stomach and were wearing clean cords at the neck, wrists, and ankles. Those with the seniority of *hę'wa* or over also had their calves painted black, with either two or three white lines drawn vertically down them, depending on which ceremonial moiety they belonged to.[1] The master of ceremonies was a man named Manõwaúmurtuwẽ. He was a member of the Ai'riri age-set, who sponsored the initiation, and of the Dzutsí lineage, who have the prerogative of performing this particular ceremonial function. For example, when

[1] These ceremonial moieties operate only during the *wai'a* (Chapter VII), although men wear their distinctive paint styles on their legs on virtually all ceremonial occasions.

Manõwaúmurtuwẽ fell ill later on and was unable to carry out his duties, they were taken over by his brother Siẽ'mõwẽ. On the final day Siẽ'mõwẽ was late for the ceremonies and the elders got impatient and detailed another brother, a new arrival from Capitariquara who was not painted or prepared for the rite in any way, to deputize for him. The master of ceremonies on the opening day was painted scarlet all over and had his hair bound up at the back, in the way which Shavante affect when they are engaged either in ceremonial or in warfare.

To begin with, however, it was not he who carried the *no'oní* cape but a bystander arbitrarily conscripted from among the crowd. Since the man chosen was commonly regarded as the village clown he was almost certainly selected in order to provide a little light relief before the proceedings proper began. He had to sling the cape on its loop from his forehead so that it hung down over his back and then lead the members of whichever age-set chose to follow him round the village in an anti-clockwise direction. He took them from the finishing posts to the bachelors' hut and from there round the village until he reached household H. The procession would then follow him along the left-hand edge of the cleared track moving away from the centre of the village until they reached the starting line. The leader turned right, walked to the middle of the line, and took up his position there while the members of the accompanying age-set ranged themselves on either side of him. The start of the race was signalled by the master of ceremonies flinging the cape to one side off his shoulders. The members of the performing age-set then ran down the track and into the village, towards the spectators gathered behind the finishing posts. Each man touched one or other of the posts and then joined the crowd again. After each run the cape-bearer was supposed to bring the cape back to the finishing posts at a ceremonial trot and to lead off with a new age-set.

In fact the first few runs were made by members of the Anõrowá and Tẹrã age-sets respectively and for them the full ceremony was not observed. After they had run four times, Prapá, the senior man of the Dzutsí lineage, gave a demonstration of how the cape should be carried in procession and how it should be run back to the finishing posts. While in procession the cape-bearer virtually has to dance with it, taking a long

PLATE VI

a. Initiates being led in procession around the village

b. Men dancing in the jungle with the dance masks

stride forward, moving his weight onto the front foot, and then swinging his body back before repeating the performance on the other foot. Similarly, when running it back to the finishing posts he has to bend double, take long hopping strides, and at each pace slap the cape with one arm so that his passage is marked by the rhythmic beating of his hands against the grass.

Manõwaúmurtuwẽ then led out the Ai'riri age-set, for whom the full ceremonial was observed. They walked to the bachelors' hut, processed round the village arc, walked to the starting point and then ran to the finishing post. After their run the cape was brought ceremonially back to the finish. The Tírowa were then led out to repeat the process. The Ai'riri ran once or twice but the Tírowa were obliged to run no less than seven times. The Atẽpá did not take part in the running.

These runs are not races in that there is no element of competition involved. They are ceremonial displays in which each performance is judged on its individual merits. Men who are ill or tired make a point of running just the same, but lope along well behind the others without exciting any adverse comment. If a strong runner gets off to a bad start, however, or is idling through his race and being accompanied or outdistanced by people weaker or younger than he is, there are shouts and jeers from the spectators. He may ignore them if he does not feel like exerting himself. Often he puts on a terrific spurt which causes intense excitement among the onlookers. The spectators act as a stimulus, especially for the boys, who run with great dash when there is a crowd, but laze through the performance when there is not.

Finally the elders decided that the Tírowa had done enough running and the ceremony was declared finished.

Immediately the Ai'riri, together with any women members of their age-set whom they could persuade to join them, danced a round dance in the centre of the village. We shall have occasion to refer to this dance later in our discussion of the initiation ceremonies as a whole. For the moment it is only necessary to mention that it was danced by the Ai'riri every evening before the men's council assembled and every morning before dawn, throughout this phase of the initiation. Correspondingly, every morning after the Ai'riri had danced, the *no'oni* cape was borne in procession and the Tírowa ran a number of races (never less than three) until the sun came up. Every afternoon 'when the sun was hanging' the cape would be taken in procession again and the Tírowa would run a further series. The afternoon runs usually attracted a few spectators and the boys were obliged to go on longer than they did in the mornings, when the men kept an eye on them from their fire at the edge of the track. The chief usually presided at both the afternoon and morning runs. It was he who gave permission for the running to cease and who made a notch in the trees by the finishing post every day so as to keep track of the progress of the initiation.

After a few days of running the Tírowa began to complain of stiffness and soreness all over. They besieged the Indian Post to obtain pills and injections to make them feel better, but they never shirked the actual runs. On the other hand they were not obliged by any overt sanctions to attend them. A boy could absent himself from them without the circumstance arousing much comment. I had the impression, though, that they themselves would have regarded it as dishonourable to be absent from the runs without any good reason. Certainly boys who were not well did not therefore avoid the ceremonies, though they complained bitterly about them, and trotted along far behind the others without making any show of running all out.

On some days members of other age-sets would join them in their runs, either accompanying them as individuals or running as separate groups. The Atĕpá (young men) were particularly fond of displaying their prowess in this way and on one or two occasions they appeared in full paint and regalia and ran half a dozen races.

Every evening, after the men's council had broken up, two members of the Ai'riri, usually Páhiri'wa and S'rizamdí, though others sometimes deputized for them, went over to the bachelors' hut. There they took down the double-barrelled flutes which are the insignia of the boys in the bachelors' hut and played them. Each player sounded one note which was answered by his opposite number. They gradually decreased the intervals between notes until the blasts followed almost immediately after each other, working up to a climax and then ceasing altogether. The men in the huts all round the village used to listen for this signal from the bachelors' hut and the chief,

when he had heard it, invariably broke out into the con-
gratulatory exclamation '*Hé wa-t-p'rĩ!*'

When the men went out to collect the harvest of beans and
pumpkins the Tírowa were left in the village to carry on with
their running. Their first break came on 16 July, when the
running had been going on for exactly twenty days.

The entire community then went out to collect a stock of
food for the forthcoming rites. The men went out together on a
hęmono (communal hunt). The women, accompanied by only a
few men, went in a different direction to gather *babassú* nuts.
The men were away twelve days, during which time the Tírowa
interrupted their running to join in the hunting. They were
instructed as a group in hunting techniques by the older men.

By this time the corporate nature of the age-set was being
particularly stressed as far as the Tírowa were concerned. Two
of their number were to receive the name Páhiri'wa at the
coming initiation and they bore long ceremonial lances, painted
scarlet, which were the emblems of the age-set. They also
carried, tied round their necks, the double-barrelled flutes for
the Ai'riri to blow on their behalf. At each camp the lances
were stuck in the ground by the bachelors' hut and the flutes
were hung from them, one on each. The boys were expected
to do most things together, and though their running had been
temporarily suspended, their sponsors made up for it by insisting
that they sang each night.

The hunters arrived back in São Domingos at mid afternoon.
They approached from the west so that a canoe had to be sent
over to ferry them and their game across the river. Contrary
to usual Shavante practice, the first ones over, instead of making
straight for home, sat down and waited for the other boatloads,
just as the women had done on their return a few days earlier.
They went as a group in single file back to the village, where
the Tírowa were immediately led out to run again.

All the game was deposited in a big heap at the entrance to
the village and was formally distributed. The distributors were
Apęwẽ, the chief, Waarodí, his eldest son, Páhiri'wa, his next
most influential son, and Sibupá. The three younger men leaned
on their bows (or guns), as influential Shavante do when they
wish to emphasize their standing, and directed the division of
the huge quantity of meat, while the chief himself presided over

the distribution. Three outsize baskets were filled with about 200 lb. of meat each and were carried away to the households from which a boy was to be named Tebe and two others Páhiri'wa. The rest of the pile was divided between the men present. As many of them had brought back over 100 lb. in their carrying baskets and no one had returned with less than about 30 lb., there was plenty all round. The formal distribution did not, however, put an end to the meat exchanges. For the rest of the evening people were hurrying to and fro with meat which they had either begged from or were taking to their kinsmen in other huts.

The following day the men all adjourned to a working place (*marã*) which had been especially well cleared in the bush. Here a semi-circle of poles was erected on which to hang the dance-masks while the finishing touches were put to them. Each man had his own pole and when he was not actually working on his mask it was hung there to await his return.

The work in the clearing was occasionally interrupted for periods of singing and dancing. These were invariably led by the Páhiri'wa of the Ai'riri age-set, if he happened to be present. Sometimes he would gather those present around him and they would sing a certain song (without meaningful words) while he beat time by striking the palm of his hand with a deer's hoof rattle. After the singing one or more of the elder men usually performed a stamping dance.[1] At other times, if there were sufficient men present, they would take their dance masks and leave the clearing. They then rushed back and sprinted round and round Páhiri'wa in an anti-clockwise direction, waving the masks as they ran. After a minute or so they would stop running and congregate in a circle around Páhiri'wa. He would then lead them in the singing of the same song, while they danced, waving their masks to and fro in the right hand. This continued all day until the Ai'riri had to leave and dance their customary dance in the village at evening. The Atĕpá meanwhile had to sleep in the clearing in order to guard the dance-masks. For two days the initiated men continued their preparations in the bush while the initiates carried on with their running in the village.

[1] This dance, which can best be described as a dance of aggression, is discussed in Chapter VII in connexion with the *wai'á*.

On 30 July the running phase of the initiation was cere-monially closed. All the men took part just as in the opening ceremony, only this time they were painted black all over instead of red. The only man painted scarlet on his breast and back was Páhiri'wa of the Ai'riri age-set, the sponsor of the ceremony.

The men gathered in the afternoon and soon the majority of the community was present. The Tírowa, Atẽpá, and Ai'riri age-sets were all fully painted. Some of the other men had painted but some had not. Siẽ'mõwẽ, the bearer of the cape, took such a long time over his toilet that the elders became impatient. There were mutters from the crowd about how low the sun was and it was finally decided to start the proceedings without him. His brother was therefore directed to carry the cape, which he did most reluctantly and with obvious embarrass-ment. After the first age-set had run he brought the cape back to the finishing posts and set off again on his procession round the village without waiting to see if the next lot were ready to follow him. In fact the runners were taking such pains to deck themselves out that they were not ready. They were still taking over some of the ceremonial head-dresses and hair-sheaths that had been worn by the previous age-set, and trying to bind them into their own hair, when the cape-bearer was half way round the village. As a result some of the runners had to cut across the village to join in the run without taking part in the procession, and this happened each time a new age-set was taken to the start. Finally Siẽ'mõwẽ came out to take over the cape. His stand-in did not trot round to the forked pole on which all the capes were hung and put it up there as he should have done; he simply brought it back to the finish and threw it on the ground.

From then on the proceedings went smoothly. They were deliberately protracted so that a large number of races could be run. Towards the end there was no pretence that age-sets were running as groups. Small batches went off from particular age-sets (the chief indicating how many were to go) and they were accompanied by anybody else who felt like running.

Finally the elders decided that there had been enough run-ning and the chief therefore approached Probuwairõ, the senior man present who held the name of Páhiri'wa, and asked him if he would care to dance with one of the outsize *no'oní* capes which had been specially made for the closing ceremony. He agreed and put on the cape, together with a rattle of pendant deer's hooves, which he bound round his right leg. He took up a stance with his back to the left-hand finishing post and the crowd assembled behind him. Then he danced across to the right-hand post, the dance consisting of a movement in which he raised his right knee as high as he could and stamped ferociously while taking a pace to the right. He repeated the movement until he reached the right-hand post and then continued back again until he stood right between the posts. At that point he stopped stamping and flung the cape off backwards so that it lay between the posts.

He was followed by a Páhiri'wa belonging to the Tẹrã age-set, one belonging to the Ai'riri, two belonging to the Atẽpá, and finally by the two Tírowa who were about to receive the name. The last dancer was the boy who was to receive the name Tebe.

When each of these had performed the identical dance, this phase of the ceremonies was considered closed. Symbolic of its closure was the fact that cross pieces were immediately tied between the finishing posts so that the aperture between them was barred.

Third Phase

First Day: Tebe

The final phase of this whole complex of ceremonies lasted five days. On the first day the men adjourned to their clearing to continue singing and dancing while putting the finishing touches to their masks. In the afternoon the Tebe ceremony began. The meat which the family of the prospective Tebe had received from the formal distribution at the end of the communal hunt had been carefully dried in the sun by the women of his household. It was now brought to the centre of the village and placed there for everyone to see. Then it was picked up and carried to the house of S'rizamdí, one of the two Ai'riri age-set men who were sponsoring the initiation ceremonies. He acted as distributor for it and gave it away to all those who crowded into the hut. Everybody came for a share, with the exception of the Atẽpá age-set, who remained working on their dance masks and the Tírowa who remained in the bachelors' hut.

That evening the prospective Tebe (Genealogy 3: 84) was brought into the centre of the village and decorated with the utmost care by S'rizamdí. Stripes of latex were applied to his stomach, onto which tufts of cotton down were stuck. He was painted all over and then dressed in a *wamñõrõ* mask, so that his face and arms protruded through the opening at the front. Cotton bands were tied around his head and feathers were stuck into this head-dress to form an upright comb at the back of his head. Finally he was given a long pliant cane to hold like a wand in his right hand.

S'rizamdí, who did the decorating, was also painted scarlet all over. Similarly the makers of the regalia, men of the Tebe's lineage, appeared in full ceremonial paint to await the arrival and dressing of the Tebe himself. When he was dressed, Sië'mõwë, who normally carried the grass cape in the initiates' processions, appeared in full ceremonial paint with his hair tied up in a sheath into which was inserted the usual scarlet macaw's feather.

Sië'mõwë[1] sat down before the finishing posts of the initiation races. An outsize grass cape was put over his shoulders, such that three people had to help him up when he wished to stand. Tebe then tapped the cape with his wand and whistled in the ceremonial fashion. Sië'mõwë was helped up by members of the Tírowa, and he then set out in a ceremonial circuit of the village, starting at the bachelors' hut and finishing at the chief's hut. In front of him walked the body of the Tírowa. He was followed by the two Tírowa who were to receive the name of Páhiri'wa, bearing the scarlet poles with the double-barrelled flutes attached to them, which are the emblems of the age-set undergoing initiation. Behind them came Tebe and behind him came the Atẽpá age-set in full paint.

This procession stopped before every other house in the village, where the cape-bearer sat down and Tebe repeated the ceremony of tapping the cape and whistling. When they had completed the circuit of the village they started back again in the opposite direction. Meanwhile Tebe's kin wailed noisily. After the procession had traversed the village arc a few times, the members of the Atẽpá took it in turns to tap the cape instead of Tebe. At the end of that circuit the Atẽpá then left because

[1] Who was an affine of the prospective Tebe.

they had to go and sleep in the bush to guard the *wamñõrõ* masks. The others continued to go in procession throughout the night. During the early hours of the morning some of them went to snatch a little sleep in the bachelors' hut. The cape-bearer too was tired by the strenuous task of carrying the heavy cape and went to his hut to get some sleep. By about 3 a.m. there were only three people still processing: Tebe, one of the Páhiri'wa, and the leader of the Tírowa age-set, who was by this time carrying one of the lighter grass capes for the tapping before each hut. Before dawn the rest of the initiates re-assembled and the cape-bearer returned with the heavy ceremonial cape, so that at sunrise the ceremony was still being performed in the proper way. Soon after sunrise the officiants were dismissed by the mature men.

Second Day: Páhiri'wa

The following day was devoted to the Páhiri'wa. The men went into the bush as usual and soon all of them had their dance-masks ready and fully painted. Meanwhile the women of the Ai'riri age-set painted themselves in the way that men normally do for ceremonies (scarlet on the belly and on the back) and went off to a spot some distance from the men, where they sang the song which the Ai'riri had sung every day of the second phase of the initiation. The men could hear them from their retreat in the bush and the sound caused them great amusement.

In the *marã* where the men were assembled each one took his dance mask, left the clearing, ran back and circled about Páhiri'wa, and then danced and sang as on the previous days. This was done with the utmost solemnity, unlike the usual atmosphere of Shavante 'formal' occasions, which tend to be both noisy and chaotic.

The men now gathered at the edge of the clearing and the Páhiri'wa danced. The senior man who still bore the name Páhiri'wa in the village was a member of the Tẹrã age-set. He therefore danced alone. He was followed by the single surviving Páhiri'wa of the Ai'riri. Two Páhiri'wa of the Atẽpá then danced, and finally the two recently appointed Páhiri'wa of th Tírowa, the only members of the initiates' age-set who wer present.

Both dancers and spectators wore white bark-cloth wristle

and anklets during the dancing. The dancers put on deer's hoof rattles around the right leg. They squatted down with set expressions, faced left, and stamped the right foot three times. Then they faced right and stamped the same foot three times. They then shook the right leg to make the rattle sound, and finally danced all round the clearing in a most athletic fashion, lifting the right knee as high as possible and bringing it down again with as much force as possible. The new Páhiri'wa did not wear ordinary deer's hoof rattles for their dance. Instead they were provided with leg ornaments consisting of cotton bands from which hung small chains of *scleria* beads, ending in deer's hooves with small parrots' feathers inserted in them.

At midday two processions emerged from the huts of the recently appointed Páhiri'wa. Each was led by the young Páhiri'wa himself, carrying the scarlet lance and the double-barrelled flute of the initiates. The loads of meat which these two households had been apportioned for this occasion were carried out and laid in the centre of the village, together with flat maize cakes some three feet square, baked by the kins-women of the Páhiri'wa. An excited crowd gathered around this display of food, but nobody partook of it. Instead it was taken in charge by the two senior Páhiri'wa, one belonging to the Tẹrã age-set and the other (who was sponsoring the initiation ceremonies) to the Ai'riri. The meat and the maize cakes were carried to their respective houses and left there.

The lances, with the flutes dangling from them, were planted on one side of the central space in the village, which had been freshly cleared. A clean sleeping-mat was placed in front of them.

The two junior Páhiri'wa knelt down in front of the lances and were elaborately decorated by the older incumbents of the name, while a large crowd containing all the influential men in the village watched and gave advice. The boys were painted and then given their bark-cloth anklets and wristlets, their ceremonial leg rattles, and finally head-dresses consisting of cotton bands around the head with long holders inserted in them containing macaw's feathers.

As soon as the youngest had been decorated, the senior Páhiri'wa danced in the same way as they had done during the morning. The dancing took place before the new incumbents, who remained kneeling throughout the performance. The first pair of dancers were the two Páhiri'wa from the Tẹrã and Ai'riri respectively. They were followed by the two from the Atẽpá. Finally the two Tírowa rose from their mat and performed the dance.

All the initiated men now adjourned to the clearing in the bush where the dance-masks were hanging. At a given signal they raced into the village, where they rushed round anti-clockwise as before, with the Ai'riri Páhiri'wa at the centre of the circle. They then formed a tight circle around him and danced, singing their song, but this time so low that it was almost inaudible to the spectators. This lasted only for a few seconds, after which they sprinted away to their houses, where they put their *wamñõrõ* masks indoors.

These masks were painted in three different styles corresponding to the three clans. Masks with vertical red stripes (*ĩ-wáwi*) were those of the Tpereya'óno. Those with horizontal red stripes (*ĩ-sihẹdẹ*) belonged to the Topdató, and those without stripes but with a long scarlet fringe at the bottom (*ĩ-sar'bepré*) to the Ẹ wawẽ.

That evening the Ai'riri danced for the last time. They performed their round dance as usual just before dusk and then they retired to their huts to paint themselves for a marathon bout of dancing which was to last all night. They re-assembled just after midnight accompanied by the women members of the age-set. All of them were painted in a black criss-cross design which gave them a skeletal appearance, and the eerie effect was increased by the fact that their faces were also painted in the same way or with one half red and one half black. Some of them had one eye picked out in the opposite colour (red or black) to that used on the rest of the face. All the men wore their cere-monial *sõ'rebzu* necklets, and carried some sort of instrument with them with which to make a noise, such as a rattle slung over the shoulders or even a cow-bell. The women were painted in the same way as the men but they did not wear the *sõ'rebzu* necklets. Instead some of them wore capibara incisors hung around their necks.

They danced, with pauses for rest, right through the latter part of the night until dawn was approaching. Most of the villagers came out to watch at one time or other so that the dancers were ringed with watch fires. Their voices got hoarser and hoarser. Even though they did not all sing all the time to accompany their dance, there was not one among them who could manage more than a croak by the time the morning star appeared. By then the chief and most of the older men had settled down by their fire near the dancers and were urging them to greater efforts. The dancers meanwhile kept an eager eye on the position of the morning star, and in the intervals between dancing and singing they kept up each others' spirits with assurances that dawn was not far away.

As soon as the sun had cleared the horizon they went into a particularly long spell of dancing, singing the complete song over and over again without any pauses in between. Then, at a given signal, the dance broke up, and the dancers, accompanied by as many of the older men as had manufactured *wamñõrõ* masks for the initiation ceremonies, all raced as hard as they could to their houses in order to seize the dance-masks and bring them into the centre of the village. The women also ran to get them and it was a point of honour with the men that they should outdistance the girls and prevent them from 'stealing' the masks from them. The moment the dance broke up, the girls and boys of the Tírowa age-set burst out of their houses wearing the *wamñõrõ* masks and ran towards the centre of the village. They were intercepted by the Ai'riri, who stripped them of their regalia and took the masks to the middle themselves.[1]

The masks were then collected in the mature men's circle, where the chief received them all and distributed them to the women who had taken part in the dancing.

Third day: Tçibị

The third day of the ceremonies now began. The Atẽpá appeared, their bodies smeared black with charcoal, wearing

[1] A mask had also been made for me, since I had been incorporated into the Ai'riri age-set. As I did not understand what was to happen when the dance broke up, I ran to my own hut in order to get a camera to photograph the next stage of the ceremony. This caused terrific excitement among the onlookers. One of the older men ran after me and directed me to go and fetch my mask. He sprinted by my side all the way to the house where it was lodged. As we ran up, however, one of the girls came out of the hut wearing it and raced towards the centre of the village. I had to run after her and take the mask from her in order to present it myself in the men's circle.

clean cords at their necks and waists, and with bark-cloth
anklets and wristlets. They carried bows and sheaves of arrows
in their hands. Some of them stood behind the finishing-posts
facing towards the centre of the village, while others took up a
position in line at right angles to them. The Tírowa now
emerged from the bachelors' hut, painted scarlet, and also in
their best cord ornaments. The female members of the Tírowa
age-set were also painted red all over and they too assembled
together with the boys—the first time they had ever taken any
part in age-set activities during the time I had been with the
Shavante. All the Tírowa formed a long line beside those Atẽpá
who stood behind the finishing-posts, and thus at right angles
to the majority of the latter age-set. The Atẽpá then sang the
song which the men had hitherto only sung while dancing with
the *wamñõrõ* dance masks. The Tírowa stood with folded hands
and bent heads, flexing their knees to keep in time with the
song. When the Atẽpá had finished singing they led the way
in single file to the hut of the chief's eldest son, and there the
performance was repeated. They sang to the Tírowa at the
four 'corners' of the village. They then led them back to the
centre of the village and sang a sixth and final time to them. In
the meantime the proceedings had been watched by the mature
men gathered around their fire in the centre.

As soon as the singing was over the Tírowa boys disappeared
into the bachelors' hut and the girls scattered to their respective
households. The Atẽpá went to sit at their meeting place to
gossip and watch what happened next, and the conduct of the
ceremonies devolved once again on the Ai'riri.

First, however, Suwapté, the chief's son-in-law (a member of
the Tẹrã age-set) went over to the bachelors' hut. He led the
Tírowa in the singing of a song and then took them to the chief's
hut on the other side of the village. There they sang the song
again, at the same time performing a dance consisting of stamping the feet apart and then scuffing them together. They sang
right round the village until they reached the bachelors' hut
again. One of the Ai'riri now went over and rehearsed a song
in the bachelors' hut and the same process was repeated.
Through the day this singing was kept up. At the end of each
round of the village the Tírowa would snatch something to eat
in the bachelors' hut or go out into the bush to relieve them-

selves before the next song leader joined them. There was never more than a few moments' interval between the circuits. After the song in the bachelors' hut itself the Tírowa would file solemnly over to the chief's hut and wait there while the Ai'riri man who was leading them strolled over at his leisure. As they sang round the village the Tírowa paraded from hut to hut with the utmost solemnity, looking neither right nor left. The Ai'riri (or group of Ai'riri) always brought up the rear of the procession and was much more nonchalant about the proceedings.

They kept up the singing until evening, when the mature men were gathering in their council. The Tírowa then retired to the bachelors' hut and stayed there. Sometime after sunset they were led out again to sing round the village. When they were half way round, all the men from both the mature men's and the young men's councils crept over to the bachelors' hut. They went crouching, as if they were stalking game, squatting down at intervals, speaking in whispers and giving evidence of great excitement. They squatted in a half circle facing the bachelors' hut and awaited the arrival of the Tírowa. As soon as the boys got there the two elders who normally direct ceremonial stepped forward. They were Apęwẽ, the chief and senior man of the Tpereya'óno, and Prapá, the senior man of the Ę wawẽ. They marshalled the initiates in a straight line before the bachelors' hut and made them squat down. Prapá went down the line and placed a bast circlet on the head of each boy. All the men then whistled in the ceremonial way, while the initiates remained squatting silently. It was explained to me that the whistling indicated 'tęibị', 'it is finished'. Prapá then removed the circlets and the men dispersed. The Tírowa remained in the bachelors' hut, tired out after their strenuous day of singing and dancing.

Fourth day: Ceremonial Run

At dawn on the fourth day the Tírowa emerged from the bachelors' hut and ran once round the village giving loud whoops. They were led by the two Páhiri'wa, who had the double-barrelled flutes bound round their necks. As they ran they kept their hands folded together and their arms straight, in the way that the Shavante do when they are running ceremonially. When they had made one circuit of the village and

arrived back at the bachelors' hut they came in solemn procession to the men's council, where all the mature men were
gathered around their fire.

The flutes were taken from them and handed over to the
chief, who then led them a little way apart from the others.
Under a barrage of advice from the onlookers he distributed a
long straw to each of the initiates. Under his direction they
held the straws in both hands and sighted along them as men
do when making arrows. They then gave a series of rapid spits
by oscillating their tongues between their lips. The chief took
back the straws, and this closed the initiation.

The bachelors' hut was immediately dismantled and all the
women of the village helped themselves to its thatch, for repairs
to weak spots in their own huts. The Tírowa, now fully initiated
young men, were given a brand from the mature men's fire so
that they might 'kindle their own fire' in their own meeting
place.

All the men now spent the morning preparing for the ceremonial run to be held on behalf of the Tírowa. The Atĕpá went
off to a spot quite far from the village to decorate themselves.
The Ai'riri (accompanied by their female members) went to
the clearing where the *wamñõrõ* masks had previously been
prepared and began to paint themselves in the same criss-
cross style they had used for their all-night dance. The Tírowa
assembled at a third clearing in the bush, where they were
assisted by the older men to get ready.

The elders held a council meeting where the Tírowa were
preparing themselves. Speeches were made about the forthcoming run and there was much comment about the arrangements. Meanwhile the Tírowa had their hair cut short to neck
length and the crowns of their heads freshly tonsured and painted
red. They were then painted red on the belly and on the back
and they put on fresh sets of cords. The chief personally super-
vised their preparations and when they were ready he prepared
a bitter infusion of tree-bark, of which they were obliged to
drink a little and with which he then washed each one of them
from head to toe.

A number of younger boys, those of the yet unofficial
Nodzę'ú age-set, and some who were even too small to belong
to that, also came to the clearing where the Tírowa were being

prepared. They were encouraged by their parents (more often by their maternal uncles) to dress up and take an unofficial part in the proceedings. They were painted in exactly the same way as the Tírowa and were similarly washed by the chief, but they did not wear the same design on their legs. They painted their legs in a herringbone style which had only aesthetic significance instead of with the two or three white stripes on a black ground, indicating an initiated man (or at least an initiate) who belongs to one of the ceremonial moieties. The mature men manufactured two miniature double-barrelled flutes for them to use during the run.

When the preparations were complete the Tírowa and Nodzę'ú walked in procession through the village, playing the flutes and whooping. After passing through the village they continued on towards the spot some miles away, where the run was to begin.

A little while later the Ai'riri (men and women) also processed through the village, but their manner of progression was different. They made as much noise as possible. Each of them had some sort of instrument (flutes, rattles, even mouthorgans) to make a noise with. They also carried branches of palm-fronds, as Shavante hunters sometimes do when stalking game in the open. As they came slowly forward they crouched down at intervals, sometimes 'freezing' behind their branches, exactly as if they were stalking. They followed the Tírowa to the starting point, where the Atẽpá were waiting, painted scarlet all over and wearing bright head-dresses of macaw's feathers. The Ai'riri women, however, left the file and hid at intervals alongside the path. The other women of the village stationed themselves along the path with gourds full of water with which to refresh the runners, for it was the middle of the day and the sun beat down fiercely on the participants. Many of the old men likewise waited by the trail for the runners to return.

In 1958 I probably missed an important part of the ceremonies, which took place without my knowledge at the starting point of the run. I observed it however in 1962 at Simões Lópes. On that occasion the young men's age-grade, decorated in their most impressive finery, constructed leafy shelters in which to 'conceal' themselves near the start of the course. When the procession of runners arrived the newly initiated boys and the smaller boys formed up in a line at the start. After them came the mature men's age-set which was sponsoring the proceedings, crouching and stalking just as they had done at São Domingos. When they passed the first place where the young men were concealed, the latter broke cover. In fact there was only one young man in the shelter, painted black all over. The rest were women of the same age-set, painted scarlet. The group followed its black leader in a circle, running in the ceremonial fashion with arms outstretched. The women then dashed off along the race course, while the leader sat down and wept. As the mature men reached the second place of concealment, the second group broke cover. They were all men of the young men's age-grade similarly led by a figure in black. After they had circled around they formed in line to do a stamping dance. While the dance was in progress the mature men gave a signal to the initiates, who dashed off down the course. The young men continued dancing until the initiates had a good start and then ran after them. Their black leader was left weeping at the starting point.

The age-sets then ran back to the village. First the Nodzę'ú came by in single file. As they passed, the watchers whooped and cheered encouragement and some of them ran a little way with them. The two elders, Apęwě and Prapá, ran quite a long way before stopping to await the 'real' runners. The Tírowa, Atẽpá, and Ai'riri age-sets all ran together. Each Tírowa ran on his own, accompanied by a knot of Ai'riri and Atẽpá who were 'running him in'. The Tírowa ran normally and silently, while the accompanying Atẽpá loped along in the ceremonial way, holding their arms straight, not flexing the elbows, and crouching lower over their stride than they normally would. Meanwhile the Ai'riri were not, for the most part, on the trail at all, but bounded along beside it making as much noise as they possibly could.

The watchers joined the procession and ran some way with it as its groups went past. The women ran along beside them, offering drinks to the runners or pouring water over their necks. The Ai'riri women, however, accompanied the procession as far as they could, screaming encouragement as noisily as the male members of their age-set.

When the runners arrived back at the village the Tírowa ran

straight through and out the other side to their clearing in the bush. The young men (Atẽpá) went to their meeting place in the village and the mature men went to theirs. The Tírowa then returned in procession and presented themselves to the mature men, who relieved them of all the ornaments they were wearing. They were then given permission to establish their own council within the village. They cleared a site for their meeting place so that it lay to the north of that occupied by the mature men, while that of the Atẽpá lay to the south. Over this site they erected a shelter. They were supposed to sleep together in this shelter until such time as the Nodzę'ú were formally inducted into the new bachelors' hut and the Atẽpá correspondingly received into the mature men.

In the early evening the Tírowa were all present in their shelter. The Ai'riri gathered at its entrance, while the rest of the mature men assembled at their fire. At the same time the Atẽpá went singing round the village as if to make a parade of their ceremonial energy. While the Atẽpá were engaged in this way the marriage ceremony already described in Chapter III took place for the newly initiated age-set.

Fifth day: The New Age-Set

At dawn on the fifth and final day of these ceremonies the mature men were gathered as usual round their fire in the centre of the village. The senior of the two Páhiri'wa in the Tírowa age-set stepped out of the shelter where they were all sleeping and took up a ceremonial stance. He was in full paint. His back hair was caught up and tied in a tail and both this and his fringe were powdered with *wede-dzu*. He carried a reddened *um'ra* club. While he waited, the girls of the Tírowa age-set came over and gathered by the Tírowa shelter (on the left, from the point of view of the mature men). Meanwhile the girls and boys of the Nodzę'ú assembled on the opposite side of the village (on the right, from the point of view of the mature men).

When the Nodzę'ú were all assembled, Páhiri'wa lay down his club, walked across, led out one of the boys, and brought him over to stand right in front of the mature men but with his back to them. He then returned to his position, took up his club and waited a moment. After the pause he laid down the club again, walked over and led out one of the girls to stand beside the boy. This procedure was repeated until all the Nodzę'ú were ranged in a line with their backs to the mature men and facing towards the opening of the village. Páhiri'wa then walked over to his parents' hut (the chief's hut), where his kinswomen wailed over him.

The Tírowa now came forward and took up a position such that they were in line behind the Nodzę'ú (also with their backs to the mature men). Most of them had combs and scissors. They set about dressing the hair of the Nodzę'ú, combing it and spitting on it and smoothing it out. The boys dressed the boys' hair and the girls that of the girls. After the dressing they cut tiny clippings from the hair of all the Nodzę'ú and each individual was given the clippings from his own hair to hold in his hand.

Suwapté, the chief's son-in-law, now came and collected all the clippings in a gourd bowl. He then stood before the children, so that facing him he had a line of Nodzę'ú, with a line of Tírowa behind them and the mature men of the community gathered behind the Tírowa. He engaged in a dialectic with the mature men which went something like this:

'Is this hair good?'
'No, it's horrible, throw it away . . . etc.'
'Who does it belong to?'
(A number of ribald answers.)
'Is this then the Nodzę'ú?'
'Yes, it is the Nodzę'ú.'
'Is the Nodzę'ú good?'
'Yes' (although the tenor of this reply was almost drowned by the barrage of ribaldry provoked by the question).

The Nodzę'ú were now formally in existence as an age-set. The villagers drifted away to their huts, except for the Ai'riri and the Tírowa, who went singing round the village together, and Suwapté, who sat waiting in the middle of the village with his bowl of hair clippings. The Nodzę'ú came back in ones and twos to pay him with feathers for his services.

During the day the Nodzę'ú, assisted and directed by Apęwę, who, it will be remembered, is also a member of that age-set, started on the construction of a new bachelors' hut on the side of the village opposite to that where the previous one had been.

Finally, that evening, just before the hour of the men's council meeting, the Ai'riri came to the centre of the village and waited.

PLATE VII

a. Boys in the bachelors' hut while out on trek

b. The newly initiated young men clip the hair of those entering the bachelors' hut

Four Tírowa emerged from their shelter, wearing bast head circlets and reddened neck cords with neck feathers. They walked slowly over, bearing their *um'ra* clubs, and sat down in the middle of the place used for the men's council. At once four Ai'riri came up behind them and took off their head circlets and neck cords. Each Ai'riri then put these on himself and withdrew. The Tírowa at once got up and returned to their shelter, and their places were taken by four more Tírowa, who were similarly served by four Ai'riri. When all the Tírowa had been relieved of their regalia by the Ai'riri, both age-sets started out together on a singing tour of the village. They sang first in front of the chief's eldest son's hut and continued in an anti-clockwise direction. Simultaneously the Atĕpá, who had been waiting in their meeting place, started singing round the village clockwise from the chiefs' hut. The two groups crossed (by design) exactly in the middle of the village arc.

When the singing was over the Ai'riri escorted the Tírowa back to their shelter. Various Ai'riri then harangued the Tírowa, telling them that they must be active and sing and dance much. The Nodzę'ú meanwhile gathered to sleep for the first time under the beginnings of the bachelors' hut they were building, although they had not been formally inducted as *hę'wa* and were still without penis sheaths. They, in their turn, were harangued by some of the older men. The initiation of the Tírowa was closed.

I shall discuss the structural implications of these ceremonies at the end of this chapter. Their symbolism is analysed in Chapter VII.

3. YOUNG MEN

After the completion of the initiation ceremonies and the joint marriage of their age-set, the boys who have passed through the bachelors' hut together become *ritai'wa* (young men).

Immediately they make *uibro* (war clubs) for themselves, if their kinsmen have not already manufactured these for them. The *uibro* is a light club of hard wood, knobbly at one end and pointed at the other. The point is hardened in the fire and a speckled design is burned into the finished weapon. It is the symbol of belonging to the warrior age-grade. A young man carries one on every occasion when he wishes to impress, and invariably when he goes out to sit in the meeting place of his age-set in the evening.

The right to sit in council in the centre of the village is the most cherished privilege of the initiated men. Those who have recently been initiated gather in their *warã* (meeting place) whenever there is an opportunity to do so, but especially at dawn and just before dusk. Normally there are two such council sites: one for the *predu* (mature men) and one for the *ritai'wa* (young men). There may temporarily be three during the period immediately following the completion of an initiation. At that time the initiates graduate to the status of young men; but the age-set already in the young men's age-grade is not promoted to the status of mature men until a new age-set has been installed in the bachelors' hut. There may be up to six months' interval between the end of the initiation ceremonies and the formal induction of the new *hę'wa* into the bachelors' hut. During this time there is no age-set officially in seclusion and there are correspondingly two age-sets in the young men's age-grade.

These age-sets however differ sharply in status. In a sense they are both marginal to their age-grade. The senior one is already thought of as in the process of passing into the mature men's ranks, while the junior one, although ceremonially admitted to young men's status, is not fully established in this position until its successors have occupied the bachelors' hut. Consequently such age-sets sit apart in separate councils, one on either side of the mature men's meeting place.

Members of the young men's age-grade (if they happen to be in the village) spend much of the day preparing themselves for their evening council. They oil their bodies and faces with a mixture of saliva and *babassú* or coconut juice. They trim their fringes, keep their eyebrows and eyelashes plucked and anoint and smarm their hair.[1] They put on fresh paint and frequently make themselves fresh cords to be worn at the neck, wrists, and ankles. When they have completed their toilet they can hardly wait for the sun to be low enough for them to go out to their meeting.

At last one of their leaders judges that the sun has sunk sufficiently far. He takes up his club and crouches for some time at the entrance to his hut looking out to see what is going on.[2] Finally he walks with great solemnity, his head bent and his club balanced in his right hand, over to the young men's meeting place. On arrival he plants his club erect in the ground and sits down in front of it. He then calls for the other members of the age-set to join him and they come over with equal solemnity. Their discussion is characterized by that elaborate protocol and absence of wider significance which is reminiscent of university debating societies. The mature men's council is by contrast more informal.

Frequently the *ritai'wa* will gather during the night as well. One of their number goes over to their meeting place and lights a fire if the night is cold enough to warrant it. He then gives the high pitched rallying call characteristic of the age-grade. Usually a number of his age-set fellows respond[3] and come out to join him. If there are a sufficient number of them and if they feel sufficiently energetic they then sing around the houses. Otherwise they just sit and talk.

There is no doubt that young Shavante much enjoy these nocturnal meetings and ceremonial activities, although they

[1] One of the most popular gifts that outsiders can offer to Shavante men is perfume, with which they anoint themselves and particularly their hair.

[2] Shavante always crouch in a doorway and look out before emerging from a hut. It is a precaution which they automatically observe against being taken by surprise. Nowadays it also serves the purpose of enabling them to see when the coast is comparatively clear, so that they can go from one hut to another with acquisitions obtained through barter without arousing too much interest among the other members of the community.

[3] It does happen that two age-sets are in the young men's age-grade and therefore using the same rallying call. In this case the listeners are obliged to identify the caller and thus work out whether the call is intended for them or not.

may occasionally find them rather a burden. Through their age-set they participate during this period in a social life of greater intensity than they have previously known or will subsequently experience. They are always together with the other members of their age-set. They sit talking with them at all hours of the day and night. They co-operate with them in their various tasks both in and out of the village. Most important of all, they parade together with them in the ceremonial singing and dancing which takes up so much of the young men's time.

These activities are in fact ceremonial displays. The young men are careful of their appearance at all times but they take particular care to look their best before they go out to sing and dance by day. They are proud to be thus engaged, for they know that they are being watched and admired. Furthermore they take a pride in the fact of singing and dancing by night for they know that the villagers will then speak well of them and comment on how virile and tireless they are that they can sing and dance when the rest of the community wants to do nothing but go to sleep.

The newly initiated Tírowa age-set was particularly enthusiastic in this respect. They sang round the village every single night after their initiation, and often two or three times in the same night, so that their last bout of singing seemed hardly to have finished before their leaders could be heard in their meeting place calling for the dawn council.

The young men may also on occasion be sluggish. When I was out on trek with one of the São Domingos bands, the Atẽpá age-set used to sing nearly every night. On the other hand, when I left that band and joined another one I discovered that the Atẽpá there were not doing anything at all. They never sang or danced. They did not even bother to meet in their own council. The few of them that did come to the centre of the encampment in the evenings were permitted, on sufferance, to sit and listen-in at the edge of the mature men's council. I asked the Atẽpá why they were so inactive and they complained that there were too few of them. But when I checked this, I discovered that there were almost as many in the band as there were with the first group I had accompanied, where the Atẽpá had been leading a busy ceremonial life. The sarcastic verdict of the mature men—that the Atẽpá were too sleepy—seemed

PLATE VIII

The young men dancing round the village

nearer the truth. In fact the leading spirits of the age-set were with the first band, its less active members with the second. When the two bands joined up again later, all the Atẽpá immediately resumed their corporate activities, and that very evening they assembled in full in a separate *warã*, distinct from the meeting place of the mature men.

It is frequently at this stage of his life that a young man satisfies any desire he may have to travel. He has no obligations which bind him to his own community and he is not usually sufficient embroiled in the factional disputes of the mature men to make other Shavante communities dangerous places for him. He can and does visit them, knowing that he will be received and made to feel at home by the members of the young men's age-grade wherever he goes.

The young men thus occupy an enviable position in Shavante society. They have no authority, but correspondingly little responsibility. They are fed and looked after by their kinswomen and need do in return only what they care to. They are sometimes directed to go out hunting by the mature men's council, but they consider this excellent sport, and anyway may disregard the injunction if they feel like it. When the community is out on trek they go ahead to select the next camping site. On the day when the group moves to it, they get up before dawn, take their bows and arrows and lead the way. All the packing-up is done by the women, assisted to some extent by the married men.[1] When the group reaches the new site it finds the young men already sitting self-importantly in their meeting place, usually under a shady tree. They remain there while the new camp is pitched and only when their respective families have constructed and moved into their shelters do they stroll over and make themselves at home in the space kept for them.

They are also regarded as the warriors of the community. They do not have to prove themselves by special deeds of valour so that they are shamed and inconvenienced by periods of comparative peace. They enjoy the prestige of being warriors, and therefore the potential fighting men of the community,

---

[1] The members of the young men's age-grade are, of course, also married. They have not, however, for the most part taken up residence with their wives and begun to lead the lives of married men.

simply by being in the young men's age-grade, and need never actually do battle to establish their reputations in the eyes of their fellow Shavante.

Since they are usually the most numerous age-set in any community and are considered the most bellicose, Shavante leaders also take care to ensure that the young men, or as many of them as possible, are their supporters.

All this is very flattering and it is therefore hardly surprising that the members of this age-grade are exceedingly vain. They are supposed, both collectively and individually, to embody a number of virtues which the Shavante particularly admire. They are supposed to be warlike and handsome. They are supposed to be fleet and good performers in ceremonial runs and log-races. They are expected to be energetic hunters, though in this they may without shame be surpassed by their elders, since the Shavante recognize that hunting requires experience as well as physical prowess. The whole community takes a pride in them when they dance and sing, especially if they do it during the night, for this means that they are alert and wakeful (*warĩ-ti*), and this is the Shavante ideal of manhood. On the other hand, the epithet *abtẹ-di* (sleepy, sluggish) is regarded by them as particularly opprobrious if it should be applied to them in earnest.

4. MATURE MEN

Shavante males are divided between the uninitiated and the initiated. The transition from the former status to the latter takes place when an age-set is promoted to the young men's age-grade. On the other hand, they are also divided into subordinate and executive (or potentially executive). The transition from the first category to the second takes place when an age-set is admitted to the status of mature men.

The second transition is less dramatic than the first, for it does not entail a radical change in the personal status of the age-set members. As mature men they must be married, but then they have already been married as young men. As mature men they are expected to live with their wives, but they may have started to do so already as young men.

Nevertheless, the social consequences of this second graduation are more far-reaching than those of the first. Before an age-set is promoted to the mature men's age-grade its members have no say in the life of the community. But as soon as it is promoted its members take part in the discussions in the village forum on an equal footing (at least in theory) with their seniors.

Anybody may speak in the council. In fact most people are speaking for most of the time, so that the proceedings sound to outsiders like an undifferentiated babble. All those who are *predu* (mature men), and who feel like it, may attend the meetings. They come bearing a deerskin, or perhaps a mat of some sort, on which to sit, and range themselves in a big circle in the centre of the village. They do not sit in any special order, but the members of the active age-sets tend to sit together. In São Domingos in 1958, for instance, the Ai'riri and the Tẹrã usually occupied segments of the circle while the others were mixed up indiscriminately.

The council meets almost every evening. The mature men enjoy their meetings as much as the young men do. The very fact of meeting emphasizes their seniority. Women and junior men are not supposed to approach the mature men's council nor to hear its debates. In fact women never do, and the junior age-sets would not dream of approaching either, unless they were specifically instructed to do so, for if they did they would invite a rebuke which would publicly shame them. Children, on the other hand, since they are both disobedient and certain of being treated with comparative indulgence, often hang around the mature men's circle. They are often told brusquely to go away and to respect the *warã*, but they rarely take any notice. If they are mainly girls they may even be chased away, though this does not often happen. Boys are occasionally tolerated and elder Shavante sometimes take a favourite son (but rarely a favourite daughter) into the council with them, where he is allowed to fall asleep in his father's lap.

The mature men enjoy these meetings for their own sake. It is in their councils that news is made public and gossip exchanged. Everything that happens in the community and in other communities is discussed there. Decisions affecting the whole community are taken and disputes are thrashed out. Therefore, wherever they are or whatever they may be doing, Shavante rarely forgo their evening meeting. Sometimes, if there is something important to be discussed, they may assemble for a council at dawn as well. More usually the dawn council is an informal gathering around a fire in the centre of the village. These are especially well attended during the dry season, when the nights get progressively colder. By July and August the piercing cold wakes most Shavante a couple of hours before dawn, and then the mature men, rather than crouch over the fires in their huts together with the women and children, generally make a roaring blaze in the middle of the village and sit talking round it until sunrise.

Very occasionally there is no meeting in the evening. This is usually due to bad weather but it can also be due to inertia or lack of numbers. I was once at São Domingos when the majority of the men were away. The chief, having some important news to discuss, went to the centre but nobody joined him there. He gave the rallying call and was subsequently joined only by myself and one other Shavante. We talked for a while, after which the chief loudly harangued the villagers and upbraided them for their idleness. This provoked spirited replies from various huts to the effect that people were busy and had no intention of coming to a meeting which was bound to be poorly attended. Apçwẽ was therefore obliged to return to his hut and wait for another opportunity to address the council.

Whenever the chief is present it is he who opens the discussion by rising in his place and making a formal speech. When speak-

PLATE IX

The mature men's council at dawn in São Domingos

ing in this fashion Shavante break up their discourse into short
phrases. Each phrase is then delivered as a rush of unaccented
words, with the accent falling on the final syllable of the phrase,
irrespective of whether it would have been accented in ordinary
speech. It is then repeated. From time to time the flow of
duplicated phrases is interrupted by a grunt and a longer pause
indicating a change of topic. His listeners meanwhile lounge
where they are and interpolate their comments, which are often
minor speeches in themselves, at the same time as he has the
floor. These interpolations are phrased as they would be in
every-day speech. The chief announces any news that may not
generally be known, comments on items of public interest, and
brings up issues which he thinks ought to be discussed. Sometimes, but not always, a senior man from one of the other clans
gets to his feet and 'replies'. The two speakers then face each
other, speaking simultaneously, and take up each other's points
antiphonically, while their audience keeps up a barrage of
comment. In São Domingos, when the *warã* was well attended,
it was nearly always Prapá, the 'father' of the Ẽ wawẽ clan,
who replied to Apẽwẽ in this fashion.

When the chief has finished speaking others may take the
floor. In certain circumstances men are bound to address the
council. A new arrival in the community, for example, must
stand opposite the chief and be his 'replier'. The chief makes a
formal speech, asking him his business and commenting on his
news as it is given. The other man may also deliver his message
in the formal style, but as often as not, if he is very junior or
perhaps not even a member of the mature men's age-grade at
all, he will say what he has to say in ordinary conversational
style.

Similarly, a messenger or returning traveller is bound to
report to the men's council at the first opportunity. Whenever I
joined one of the bands that were out on trek my guide would
be summoned to report on all the circumstances of our journey.
He would do so in minute detail, often repeating verbatim our
conversations of some days past and describing at length what
we had seen and what I had failed to observe. Such councils
were invariably uproarious occasions, as everybody was con-
vulsed with laughter at the most recent evidences of my
ignorance and naïvety.

In theory any mature man may rise to his feet and address his fellows once the chief has finished speaking. But in practice it is only men with a certain amount of assurance or prestige who normally do so, apart from those who are obliged to, in situations like those outlined above. When they take the floor they are invariably 'opposed' by a complementary speaker from another clan. It is only a chief who has the privilege of addressing the assembly on his own.

In São Domingos it was generally men from the five senior age-sets who addressed the assembly. The four most senior age-sets contained a total of seven men, all of whom would address the council on occasion, and five of whom did so regularly. The members of the fifth most senior age-set (Tçrã) tended to get up and speak less frequently, with the exception of Waarodí, the chief's eldest son, and his rival Suwapté, the chief's son-in-law. These two spoke regularly and invariably took the floor at some stage of every important debate. On the other hand, it was most unusual to see a member of the Ai'riri, the most junior age-set in the mature men's age-grade, get up and take the floor. Those who occasionally did so were Páhiri'wa and Sibupá, sons of the chief and, after Apçwẽ and Waarodí, the most influential men in the dominant faction.

A good speaker acquires prestige among the Shavante, but it is commonly only the men who already enjoy a certain esteem who will get up and speak. How then does a man become a well-known orator? If he is *ĩdzú*, an influential member of the dominant faction, already used to taking a lead in community matters such as ceremonial, hunting parties, distributions, and so on, then he may have sufficient assurance to begin his career as an orator in the men's council while his age-set is still the most junior among the mature men. This was the case with Páhiri'wa and with Sibupá. The majority of men do not make many formal speeches in council until after their age-set has sponsored an initiation ceremony and another age-set, junior to their own, has been admitted to the mature men's age-grade. It is at about this stage that they begin to feel their seniority and speech-making provides them with an opportunity to demonstrate it. A man who is not a member of the dominant faction, yet wishes to establish a position for himself in the community, must, about this time, give proof of his rhetorical powers. Later, when his age-set becomes even more senior, he will have had over ten years' experience of the men's council and will be on the way to becoming one of the elders of the community. Sheer seniority should then give him the necessary assurance to address the council, and it is in fact considered rather strange if he does not do so. An unwillingness to make formal speeches is for a man of this seniority tantamount to a withdrawal from the political life of the community. As Shavante grow older and less active they are more and more bound up in this life, and most of their energy and initiative is expended in intrigues for the acquisition of prestige and power or simply in intrigues for their own sake. A man who opts out of this competition and does not make his voice heard in council is in a sense emasculating himself.

There is thus a distinct correlation between the ebbing of the corporate social activities of an age-set and the emergence of its members as important individuals. When a new age-set graduates to the mature men's age-grade it retains its corporate identity and continues to act as a group both ceremonially and otherwise. Its members sit together in the council and rarely take it upon themselves to get up and speak, thereby singling themselves out from their fellows. This solidarity is maintained throughout the period when the age-set is the most junior in the mature men's age-grade. The group activities of the age-set as a separate entity (and not as representatives of the mature men) are especially marked at the time of the initiation following their entry into the senior age-grade. As we have seen, it is they who sponsor the initiation and they are required as a group to perform many of the ceremonies connected with it.

Once the initiation is completed, however, and a junior age-set has been admitted to the mature men, the sponsoring age-set is no longer required to perform any corporate ceremonial functions. It may, on occasion, act together as the Tẹrã did when they ran as a separate age-set in the running phase of the initiation ceremonies. In general, however, its members now tend to go their own way and the age-set is submerged in the age-grade of mature men. It is no longer held together by ceremonial obligations and the economic functions of the age-sets are in any case minimal. Men do not go hunting or collecting together with members of their age-set because they need to or because they thereby get a better bag. They do so because they enjoy the companionship of their age-mates. By the time an age-set has graduated to the second junior position in the mature men's age-grade its members are beginning to be less interested in hunting and running, in singing and dancing and in cutting a fine figure generally. They are, by contrast, more interested in the realities of prestige and power. If they wish to make a display, it is an oratorical display in the men's council. They are increasingly thinking in terms of supporters and opponents, i.e. in terms of lineages and lineage groups, rather than in terms of their age-set and its enjoyable but purposeless camaraderie.

Membership of an age-set is therefore of supreme importance to a man from the time when, as a child, he longs for his group of playmates to be officially recognized as an age-set to the time when, as a mature man, he and his age-mates sponsor the initiation of their alternate junior age-set. During this time he acts and enjoys acting as a member of a group. When his age-set no longer has any corporate ceremonial functions to fulfil he not only consorts less with the other members of it, except in the undifferentiated circle of the men's council, but it is as if he begins to act more as an individual and less as a member of this particular group. From this time on he is feeling his way towards personal eminence. Owing to the fissive tendencies in Shavante society analysed in Chapter V, he is able to do this only with the support of his lineage and of any other men who are prepared to throw in their lot with his lineage. Accordingly, older Shavante emerge as important figures in their own lineages and factions rather than as leaders of their age-sets.

5. THE POSITION OF WOMEN

A Shavante woman also belongs to an age-set. At the time when small boys are first inducted into the bachelors' hut and thereby incorporated into an age-set, the small girls who are of about the same age are also said to belong to the same age-set. Thus the respective ages and seniority of women as well as of men may be given by simply naming their age-set.

But age-set membership is not the same thing for a woman as it is for a man. Girls do not pass through the bachelors' hut and they do not share, except at one stage, in the initiation ceremonies. They are therefore excluded from the central features of the age-set system. They cannot be initiated, as the men are, because women are barred from attending the esoteric *wai'a* ceremonies to which initiation gives access. Nor can it mean the same thing to them as it does to their male coevals that their age-set is promoted to the *predu* age-grade, since women are also debarred from participation in the council which decides the affairs of the community.

We have seen that the female members of certain age-sets do in fact join the males for certain ceremonies. The women of the Ai'riri danced together with the men in order to sponsor the initiation of the Tírowa and they took a prominent part in the final stages of the initiation ceremonies. Similarly, the girls of the Tírowa age-set paraded in full paint together with the boys on the morning when the Tírowa were formally initiated. In the same way, both male and female Tírowa were called upon to cut the hair of the Nõdzę'ú, and both male and female Nõdzę'ú presented themselves for this rite on the occasion when the Nõdzę'ú were granted formal recognition as an age-set.

Apart from these occasions, however, women never accompany the male members of their own age-sets. Nor do they consort with their female age-mates when they go out collecting or swimming, the two important communal female activities. Instead they invariably go about their business together with the women of their own household, or at the most with those of their neighbouring households.

For a woman, therefore, membership of an age-set is comparatively meaningless. Yet if women are to be classified by reference to the age-sets (and the age-set system is an important classificatory device among the Shavante) then they must be ceremonially reminded at intervals of their age-set affiliation. Accordingly women join the men whenever a particular age-set participates in a rite which alters its social status.

Girls do not take part in the rites of induction into the bachelors' hut, since seclusion, initiation, and participation in the *wai'a* are all male activities by definition; but they accompany the prospective bachelors to the hair-cutting ceremony and thereby establish their membership of the same social stratum. They do not accompany the bachelors when they pass through their initiation ceremonies, but they parade with them on the day they are formally promoted to young men's status, and assist them on the day when they cut the hair of the age-set about to enter the bachelors' hut. The male members of their age-set are now in the young men's age-grade. They remain there until a subsequent age-set is initiated. When this takes place the young men *and the women of their age-grade* take part in the ceremonial run on behalf of the new initiates. Later on, the junior age-set in the mature men's age-grade sponsors the initiation of the age-set in the bachelors' hut. This sponsorship involves dancing for the initiates, accompanied by the female members of the age-set, and running the initiates in, accompanied by the female members of the age-set. Women thus put in a ceremonial appearance at all transitional rites for age-sets, even though they may not be fully involved in their central activities.

Meanwhile the stages of a woman's life are referred to in terms which roughly correspond to men's age-grades (Table 9). A girl baby is called *baono* and this term may be applied to any small female child, just as *watębremĩ* refers not only to a male baby but also to any little boy who has not yet entered the bachelors' hut.

adzęrudu refers to a sub-category of *baono*, i.e. to girls who are still 'children' but no longer babies. There are no explicit criteria for the application of the term. A little girl running about may be addressed or referred to either as *baono* or *adzęrudu* (more commonly used in the diminutive *dzęrtu-ri*). Similarly there is a word *ai'repudu* which denotes a corresponding sub-category of small boys, but it is used much less frequently.

Boys who are in the bachelors' hut are referred to as *wapté*. Girls of the same age-set are known as *soimbá*. Young men in the age-set which has most recently been initiated are *ritai'wa*. The women of their age-set are known as *adabá*. Finally mature men are known as *predu*. Mature women are generally referred to as *pi'õ*, which is the generic term for 'woman' but in a restricted sense means 'mature woman'.

At one level of contrast *pi'õ* thus means 'female' as opposed to 'male' (*aibi̧*). At another it means 'mature female' as opposed to immature female' (*adabá* etc.) Similarly *predu* only refers to a mature male as contrasted with an immature one. In a different context a woman who is *pi'õ* may be referred to as *predu* (mature) where a discrimination is being made between mature people (irrespective of sex) on the one hand and immature people (irrespective of sex) on the other.

But the sequence of women's age-grades is complicated by certain additional factors. A girl who is *adz̧erudu* may be addressed as *soimbá* if it becomes known that her husband has brought meat to her house which he himself has hunted.

Similarly, promotion from *soimbá* to *adabá* does not simply take place when coeval boys graduate from bachelors to young men. It should technically be brought about in a separate ceremony. In fact most Shavante communities I visited did not perform the ceremony frequently enough, so that girls were often referred to as *adabá* because their age-set was of the appropriate seniority rather than because they had been ceremonially introduced to the latter status.

I have never seen this ceremony performed, and the accounts I have of it are conflicting. They concur only in specifying that in the course of the ceremony names are conferred on the *soimbá* by the men. This is done by the representatives of the age-sets (I could not determine which) who hold the office of *aiuté'mañãrĩ'wa* or 'baby makers'.[1] The prerogative of officiating as 'baby makers' is held by one lineage at a time and this lineage is often referred to collectively as *aiuté'mañãrĩ'wa*.

According to one account of the ceremony the age-sets involved were the one in the young men's age-grade and the one most junior in the mature men's age-grade. They hunted for five days while the girls to be named remained in seclusion in their homes. On their return they performed a ceremony

---

[1] From *aiuté* = babe in arms + *mañãr* = make + *'wa* = personal suffix referring to the stem.

during which a tapir was buried and the girls were named. The *aiuté'mañãrĩ'wa* then danced with the girls in the centre of the village. At some stage in the dance the girls broke away and dashed to their huts pursued by the men. The girls ran inside but the men stopped short at the entrance and pounded on the thatch.

In another version the girls were named in what was virtually a preliminary to the jaguar ceremony (see Appendix 3). The jaguar ceremony is an elaborate deception which the *aiuté'-mañãrĩ'wa* carry out on the boys in the bachelors' hut. They are assisted in the deception by all men senior to the bachelors and the first phase of the ceremony involves the naming of the girls in the bachelors' age-set.

At the close of this ceremony the girls are considered as having graduated to the status of *adabá* and are now held to be physiologically mature. Some men even go as far as to say that women do not menstruate until they are *adabá*. What they really mean is that menstruation (i.e. physiological maturity) is not socially recognized until they are of this age-grade. In fact, as they well know, women invariably have sexual intercourse and even bear children before they are *adabá*, and virtually all of them will have had their first menses before becoming members of this age-grade. This is explicitly recognized by the fact that there is a term (*araté*) for a woman who has born a child. A girl who bears her first child while she is still *soimbá* will thenceforward be referred to as *araté* until she graduates to full maturity as *pi'õ*. Thus the social ratification of female maturity invariably postdates the biological fact, which possibly accounts for the individual onset of menstruation not being marked by any particular ritual.

It is not clear, however, what the wider implications of this *rite de passage* are. Shavante girls are, as we have seen, married when they are children. They are obliged to have sexual relations with their husbands before they are physiologically mature. By the time they reach the age-grade of *adabá*, then, they are married and they are no longer virgins. On the other hand, graduation to the *adabá* age-grade does not imply a mental maturity, a sort of graduation from girlhood to womanhood. The *pi'õ* are the only women who are mature in this sense, and they are described by the Shavante as *predu* (mature), the term which is also applied to the mature men. The *adabá* are not yet *predu* in this sense. In what way, then, are they associated with the *pi'õ* in opposition to all those girls who have not yet undergone the *rite de passage*, as the young men are associated with the mature men in opposition to all those boys who have not yet been initiated?

The only answer seems to be that they are named. The characteristic of the *soimbá* and those junior to them is, in the words of the Shavante, that 'they have no name yet'. Shavante consider them in some way unfinished as personalities. But to say that the bestowal of a name on a girl is a public demonstration that she is now a fully-developed person merely poses our problem in other terms. In what way is she more developed as a member of the *adabá* than as a *soimbá*? She seems to have no social or sexual prerogatives that she did not enjoy previously, and she is not even regarded as being fully 'grown-up', without specific concomitant obligations, for that comes later when she graduates to the *predu*.

The explanation seems to be that the girls' *rite de passage* is arbitrarily assigned to the transition from *soimbá* to *adabá* in order to coincide approximately with the boys' transition to manhood. This is consistent with the whole nature of the age-set system, which is founded on the boys' seclusion and initiation, and which is nevertheless consciously used by the Shavante as a model of their total society. If Shavante society is stratified in age-sets, then the women too must belong to one or other of these strata and their *rites de passage* must coincide with the passage from one stratum to another. If the boys in the bachelors' hut are regarded as being, in a sense, unformed by virtue of being uninitiated, then the girls of their age-set are also regarded as immature by association. But the immaturity of the girls has none of the sexual implications that it has for the boys. It is simply a structural requirement of the system, and is symbolized by the fact that they have no names.

As far as women are concerned, then, the age-set system is solely a classificatory device. Its importance does not lie in the fact that it assigns them to corporate groups, for their membership in their age-sets is largely passive, but rather that it assigns them to arbitrary social categories which are independent of their bio-social status.

6. PROPERTIES OF THE SYSTEM

Shavante boys (and by extension Shavante girls) become members of a named age-set at the moment when they are inducted into the bachelors' hut. Five years later their age-set will be promoted to the young men's age-grade. Five years later they will pass to the age-grade of mature men. Their age-set will remain in that age-grade thereafter, but every five years one more age-set will join the mature men and the most senior age-set will revert to the beginning of the cycle and be reincarnated in the boys who are entering the bachelors' hut. Since there are eight age-sets in all, it takes any one of them forty years to pass through all the positions of the cycle and revert to its starting point in the bachelors' hut. Shavante men do not live long, for reasons which will be discussed in the next chapter, so it is only an exceptionally old Shavante who will see the same age-set pass through the bachelors' hut twice in his lifetime or who sees his own age-set complete the full cycle.

In 1958 there was no man in São Domingos who had seen his age-set reincarnated. While I was there the Tírowa were initiated and the Nõdzę'u entered the bachelors' hut. Apęwẽ, the chief and oldest man in the village, was Nõdzę'u. In 1962 I found in São Marcos one old man still surviving from the Abari'u, which was the age-set in the young men's grade, and one from the Nõdzę'u, the age-set in the bachelors' hut.

Shavante are fully conscious of the cyclical nature of the age-set system and will, if pressed, explain that time passes in a series of such cycles, expressing its passage by a series of circles drawn on the ground. The cycles themselves are divided into periods corresponding to the passage of age-sets through the bachelors' hut.

Each of these periods, they say, is of five years' duration, and they count up to five and tick the years off on their fingers to drive the point home.[1] Within these periods they divide the years (*wahú*) into two halves: the rains (*tã*) and the dry seasons (*wahú*). These in their turn are subdivided into a number (up

---

[1] As far as I was able to check it, this five-year interval is in fact maintained. I know that among the São Domingos Shavante the initiation of the Atẽpá took place in 1953, five years previously to that of the Tírowa observed by me in 1958, because it was partially observed by the first outside visitors to their village. When I returned in 1962 they said they were planning to initiate the Nõdzę'u 'next year'.

to five) of moons (aamõ), and the period of a moon can be sub-divided into its phases, 'rising' (watobro), waxing (ĭdzáru), wan-ing (ĭdzáru õ), and 'setting' (dzebre). For lesser intervals they reckon in nights or 'sleeps' (abtẹ), which they count off on their fingers and toes.

In this way they have a rough and ready method of time-reckoning which can, albeit very clumsily, be used to specify time intervals of up to forty years. But in fact it is virtually never used. Shavante are content to look forward to the next rains or back to the last drought, but not beyond. Their plans are usually short-term. They make assignations by indicating a certain number of moons and the phase of the moon in which they wish to meet. They calculate their journeys and give details of their movements in so many 'sleeps'. I have found these calculations to be wildly inaccurate, but this circumstance does not worry them. They are not interested in accurate time-reckoning and their statements about time are not intended to be taken literally.

What does interest the Shavante is seniority, in other words relative rather than absolute time-spans, and these they are able to express in terms of their age-set system. A woman, speaking of her children, will specify their age-sets so that her interlocutor can place them socially. It is a curious fact that, in spite of the absence of tribal ceremonial or even of consultations on an inter-community level, age-sets throughout Shavante-land seem to be at approximately the same stage of the age-set cycle at any given moment. The news of the initiation cere-monies is brought from group to group, so that, although each community holds its own initiation, it is able to hold it within a short time of the ceremonies elsewhere. When I left the Shavante in 1958, for instance, the Tírowa age-set was reported to be still in the bachelors' hut at Marãwasede, where the initiation ceremonies were just beginning. At São Domingos the Tírowa had been initiated three months previously. At Santa Terezinha they had been initiated the previous year. The seniority of each age-set is thus roughly the same throughout Shavante-land.

This holds true even though the relative order of the age-sets differs among the Western and Eastern Shavante. For example a S'daro man from the Eastern Shavante will find when he goes to the Western Shavante that his coevals are also S'daro, but an Anõrowa from the east will find that his age-mates in the west are Ai'riri (see Table 7). Nevertheless, I have seen Eastern Shavante move into Western Shavante villages and be told that Ai'riri there were the 'same' as the Anõrowa in the villages they had left. So they were, in terms of seniority in the age-set cycle. Thus the Nõdzę'u were bachelors throughout Shavante-land in 1962. The 'young men' in the east were Tírowa, the 'young men' in the west were Abari'u. It was therefore structurally correct to say that the Eastern Tírowa were the same as the Western Abari'u.

Given that this age-set cycle is a constant for all Shavante, it would be possible for them to date past events or at least narrow down the time of their occurrence to a five-year span by using the age-set system as a mnemonic device. But they do not do this. Anything which took place before the particular cycle which a man knows during his lifetime is referred to as having happened duré-hę (long ago). More recent events are sometimes placed in the context of the age-set system and said to have taken place when such-and-such an age-set was in the bachelors' hut. Yet much more often these events too are relegated simply to duré-hę (distant past), duré-iri (not so distant past), or nimõtsi (recent past).

This lack of historical interest is at least partly explicable on structural grounds. With the possible exception of the age-sets themselves, the Shavante have no relatively stable corporate groups whose history might be remembered. The age-sets do not have their own histories, nor are they associated with particular characteristics. Patrilineages are, but they grow, split up, and disappear according to the political alignments of each community. Communities themselves are highly unstable. Whatever the reason for it, this shallow view of their own society is characteristic of the Shavante and must be clearly understood by anyone who wishes to grasp the articulation and functioning of their institutions.

Shavante do see the age-set system quite explicitly as a model of a certain kind. Let us first consider some of its functions before discussing its more general properties.

It is important to note that, although the system requires that every five years a fresh group of boys be brought in and all the junior age-sets promoted, there is nothing automatic about the process. All *rites de passage* on occasions when age-sets progress from one social status to another symbolically emphasize that the junior age-sets derive their corporate existence from the senior ones and graduate socially only by permission of the mature men. The mature men engage in a ceremonial debate as to whether a group of boys and girls shall be allowed to form a new age-set. It is the mature men who authorize the group of initiates to enter the bachelors' hut and thus to 'enter' the age-set system. Moreover, until the mature men have performed the induction ceremony the 'new' age-set is not even regarded as being officially in the bachelors' hut, although they may already have built it and be living in it. During the initiation ceremonies it is the mature men who symbolically sanction every progression of the initiates. They carry the *wamñõrõ* masks for them throughout the ceremonies. They are in attendance while their representatives place bast circlets on the heads of the initiates, which are subsequently taken back again after the whistling consecration. They are in attendance when the chief gives straws to the initiates in the final ceremony, and these straws are subsequently taken back again. They decorate the initiates for the race that is held in connexion with the ceremonies, and after the race they relieve them again of all their ornaments. It is repeatedly made explicit that the status of a junior age-set is granted to it by the mature men.

In a sense, then, the passage of an age-set through the age-grades is a linear progression. It represents a series of approximations to maturity. The reason for an age-set's being constituted in the first place is in order that its members may be prepared for initiation. After initiation it passes through the grade of what we may call 'warriorhood', but the young men in this grade, though they are much admired, are still subordinate and regarded socially as immature. Even when their age-set has graduated to the mature men's age-grade the members of it do not, as we have seen, enjoy the same status as their seniors. Full maturity is only attained when men have graduated to the seniority of elders within the community, i.e. when their age-set is one of the four senior ones. This is accompanied by a corresponding diminution in the corporate activities of their age-set. Such men have, so to speak, 'arrived', and they are no longer referred to by their age-set names but invariably as *predu*. In one respect, then, it could be said that the age-sets function in order to regulate the graduations between boyhood and elderhood. Once elderhood has been attained they become socially unimportant.

There is accordingly a certain amount of hostility between the *predu* (here meaning all the mature men) and the immature age-sets. The latter feel themselves to be underprivileged and frequently complain that the mature men take unfair advantage of their juniority. This attitude is especially marked among the *ritai'wa*. The boys preparing for initiation have such a subordinate status that they are usually prepared to accept the pretensions of their seniors, though they do grumble occasionally that the *predu* 'take everything' and 'give them nothing'. This refers particularly to distributions, either of food or of manufactured goods. The latter are invariably held in the mature men's council, and children come swarming to be on hand and receive the odds and ends that are left over. If the goods are not particularly abundant, then the mature men do not apportion any share at all to either the young men or the boys. At other times they send over small shares for the junior age-sets. The latter are prevented by their pride from competing with the children at the edge of the mature men's council. Instead they sit sullenly apart and complain to each other about the iniquities of their elders.

The *ritai'wa* feel particularly strongly about their position. Their members used to speak scornfully to me about what the mature men had decided, although they always conformed with these decisions if they were of the least importance. They frequently complained to me about how predatory the *predu* were. It was they who took everything that was going, I used to be told. Once when I was on trek with a group of Shavante, the members of the young men's age-grade came to me to complain that the manioc flour I had brought with me was being shared out only among the mature men. On the other hand, they claimed that most of my food was provided by members of their age-set. Both of these contentions were, as far as I could see, untrue, but they were indicative of the relations between the age-grades. Finally, and this is for them the hardest to bear, the young men feel sexually underprivileged. I have already described how their reaction to this state of affairs varies with their mood. At times they make a virtue of necessity and brag that they are so tough that they do not need women. At others they complain bitterly about the immaturity of their wives and about the rapaciousness of the mature men who have 'lots of women'. But Shavante young men do not enjoy the overwhelming prestige that is sometimes accorded to warriors in other societies[1] and, since they only have to wait five years in the young men's age-grade before they are promoted to the mature men, they are usually content to wait more or less patiently for their own turn to come.

The relations between age-sets are set out in Table 10. The members of an age-set refer to all age-sets much senior to them as *wahi'rada*. They refer to the alternate age-set immediately senior to them as *wanimñõhú*. The age-set immediately senior to them is *ĩhí'wa*. Their own age-set is *ĩ-útsu*. The age-set immediately junior to them is *siñõrã*. The alternate age-set immediately junior to them is *wanimñõhú*, and subsequent junior age-sets are *ropsõ'wa*. It will be seen that there are three types of relationship implicit in this scheme. There is the relation *wahi'rada: ropsõ'wa*, which is between distant age-sets separated by at least two intervening ones. There is the relation *wanim-ñõhú: wanim-ñõhú* which is between alternate age-sets, and there is the relation *ĩhí'wa: siñõrã*, which is between proximate age-sets. The two latter are the most important. Between alternate age-sets there is institutionalized co-operation and between proximates institutionalized competition.

We have noted how the Ai'riri in particular sponsored the initiation of the Tírowa at São Domingos in 1958. Equally significant was the antithesis between the ceremonial behaviour of the Ai'riri on the one hand and of the Atẽpá on the other. The Ai'riri ran as a group at the beginning of the proceedings on the first day of the initiation runs. Afterwards they withdrew in favour of the Tírowa. The Atẽpá, on the other hand, were conspicuously absent during the inaugural part of the ceremony. Later they would sometimes appear in full regalia on a day when only the Tírowa were required to run, and stage rival runs. They did their best to look better and to run better than their juniors. Similarly, during the final days of the initiation

---

[1] e.g. among the Nilo-Hamitic tribes of East Africa, see Bernardi, 1952: 327.

ceremonies it was the Ai'riri who took care of the Tírowa and led them through the ceremonial. The Atẽpá joined the Tírowa only on the occasion of the Tebe ceremony, when the grass cape was paraded round and round the village. Here the element of competition was again apparent. While the Atẽpá processed together with the Tírowa they took the conduct of the ceremony out of their hands. It was the prerogative of a Tírowa who had just received the name Tebe to strike the cape ceremonially with his wand. The Atẽpá, however, took it in turns to do this for him after the first round, and the Tírowa were not left in charge of the proceedings until the Atẽpá had retired for the night. During the race held just after the initiation, knots of Ai'riri ran behind each Tírowa encouraging him with noise. The Atẽpá, on the other hand, took care to wear their finest regalia, including hair sheaths with long head-dresses of macaw's feathers. They ran ceremonially and in dead silence, making a striking contrast to the Tírowa, who trotted along as best they could in the company of their noisy sponsors. On the final day of the ceremonies the Ai'riri took the Tírowa singing round the village, while the Atẽpá sang round the village in the opposite direction.

Only once was there some ambiguity concerning the role of the Atẽpá *vis-à-vis* the Tírowa. On the third day of the initiation ceremonies the Tírowa (both boys and girls) were sung round the village by the Atẽpá. This is paralleled, however, by the role of the Tírowa towards the Nõdze'ú at the time when the latter received formal recognition as an age-set. Then it was the Tírowa who officiated for the Nõdze'ú at the hair-clipping ceremony. I would suggest that the hair-clipping was an act of ceremonial aggression, and that the Atẽpá singing at the Tírowa was likewise a symbolic confrontation of opposites—the Tírowa, painted red, starting their life as young men, opposed by the Atẽpá, painted black, who were finishing it. This symbolism is more fully discussed in Chapter VII, where I argue that 'singing at' must be distinguished from 'singing for', and develop the thesis that human hair is symbolic of aggressive action in Shavante ritual.

The relation of opposition between proximate age-sets could be seen as a function of the necessity to distinguish between them socially and ceremonially. It has been argued for some time that the simplest way to distinguish between categories is to oppose them. It is not therefore surprising that in an age-set system, where the structural position of each age-set is defined by contrast with that of its preceding and succeeding age-sets, the ceremonial relations between proximate age-sets should express this antithesis.

Yet the antithesis between the proximate and the alternate relation among age-sets is part of a wider dichotomy that pervades the entire age-set system. The Shavante, in common with all other Gê tribes, hold log-races in connexion with important ceremonies. The principle of these 'races' is that two lengths of palm trunk are cut at some distance away from the village and then carried back by two teams of racers. One man runs as fast and as far as he can with the heavy log on his shoulder, and when he gets tired he rolls it onto the shoulder of a fresh team-mate. The details of the ritual, for these races are ceremonies rather than purely athletic contests, need not concern us yet. It is the composition of the teams which is interesting. The members of half the age-sets run with one team while those belonging to the other half run with the other. Alternate age-sets are team-mates and proximate age-sets are invariably on opposite sides.[1]

Conceptually, then, the eight age-sets of the system are always divided into two sporting moieties. Once this distinction between a set of odd age-sets and a set of even ones (however the sequence is numbered) has been ethnographically established we are in a better position to consider the curious discrepancy between the age-set names of the Western Shavante and the age-set names of the Eastern Shavante. The two sequences can be set out thus:

Western Shavante		Eastern Shavante	
Moiety A	*Moiety B*	*Moiety A*	*Moiety B*
Anõrowa		Abari'u	
	S'daro		S'daro
Ai'riri		Anõrowa	
	Tẽrã		Tẽrã
Tírowa		Ai'riri	
	Atẽpá		Atẽpá
Abari'u		Tírowa	
	Nõdzẹ'u		Nõdzẹ'u

[1] I only saw two log-races at São Domingos and in those the racers were

It is at once clear that Moiety B is identical in both cases. Moreover, the sequence of Moiety A is also the same for the Western as for the Eastern Shavante. It is simply the intercalation of A and B that is different: as if these were two identical pairs of cog-wheels and one pair had slipped a single notch ahead of the other.

We shall later consider how this particular antithesis fits in with a pattern of antitheses that goes to make up the fabric of Shavante life. For the moment it need only be stressed that a certain type of antithesis is operative in the age-set system. Throughout the initiation ceremonies, which are the major institutional focus of the system, it was always this dichotomy between Moiety A and Moiety B, expressed particularly in the relation between sponsoring age-set + initiates on the one hand and intervening age-set on the other, which was expressed in the rites. It is further expressed in the fact that when the Tírowa 'kindled their own fire' in the centre of the village after initiation they did not do this at the spot where the Atẽpá, at that time still in the young men's age-grade, held their council. Instead they did so on the far side of the mature men's council and away from the Atẽpá. I was informed that the newly initiated age-set always did this, so that the position of the young men's council relative to the mature men's meeting place alternates with each successive initiation. Similarly the bachelor's hut is sited at one extremity of the village arc. When its occupants are initiated the hut is destroyed and a new one built at the opposite extremity of the semi-circle.

The final ritual which the sponsoring age-set performs for the initiates also expresses an antithetical principle, but this time it is a different dichotomy. I describe this ceremony as I witnessed it at São Domingos in 1958. At midday two members of the Ai'riri age-set came out in full paint and stationed themselves one on each side of the mature men's meeting place. One of them was from the Uhẽ lineage and he took up a ceremonial stance on the south-east side of the meeting space, facing north-westward; in other words, on the side opposite to the village

---

not divided strictly according to this rule. However, the Shavante at São Domingos and elsewhere are quite explicit that this is the rule according to which teams should be opposed. When I saw a log-race at Simões Lópes, the correct age-sets were assigned to each team.

segment on which his lineage was located, and facing towards it. Behind him stood Suwapté, the chief's son-in-law (belonging to the same lineage but to the Tẹrã age-set), to act as his second. The man who took up a ceremonial stance on the north-west side, facing south-eastwards, was a member of the Wamãrĩ lineage whose household was located in the south-eastern half of the village arc. He was seconded by Waarodí, the chief's son, who belonged to the same lineage, was a member of the Tẹrã age-set, and whose house was similarly in the opposite half of the village arc. These protagonists had their hair caught up ceremonially at the back, and those of the Wamãrĩ lineage had theirs liberally powdered with the magical *Wede-dzú* dust, in the manner that these lineage members affect on important occasions.

The Tírowa now emerged from their homes, either singly or in pairs, depending on how many there were in a particular house. They were painted red all over and wore head-dresses of tall macaw's feathers in special holders inserted in the customary balsa-wood plug tied into their back hair. Each of them carried a red *um'ra* club. Each one walked to the middle of the meeting space and sat down on his club. If the Tírowa was a member of the Tpereya'óno clan, then as soon as he was seated the Ai'riri who belonged to the Uhẹ lineage (Ẹ wawẽ clan) ran out in the ceremonial fashion, described a half-circle, and ended up behind the seated boy. He took off the head-dress that the Tírowa was wearing and ran back to his place. If the Tírowa was a member of the Ẹ wawẽ clan, then he was similarly served by the Ai'riri who was of the Wamãrĩ lineage (Tpereya'-óno clan). Only one of the Tírowa belonged to the Topdató clan, but since his father was adopted into the Tpereya'óno he had his head-dress removed by the Ai'riri from the Ẹ wawẽ clan.

When all the Tírowa had had their head-dresses removed they took their clubs and went to sit in their own assembly space. The seconds on each side then bound together the head-dresses which their principals had collected and which they had been given to hold. Each principal was now handed a single bundle consisting of all the head-dresses worn by the young men they had stripped. At a given signal the two men ran towards each other swishing the bundles of feathers from side to side, crossed over in the middle of the meeting space, and continued running to opposite sides of the village, where they disappeared into their own houses. They then sat down in their huts while their kinswomen wailed over them.

The significance of the weeping was to demonstrate that the Ai'riri had now performed their last rite on behalf of the Tírowa. The feathers which their representatives had collected were later shared out among the other members of the age-set in payment of their ceremonial services. The kinswomen of the principals wept over them because they had participated in a *rite de passage* for the whole Ai'riri age-set, which was now no longer the active junior age-set of the mature men's age-grade. It had completed the sponsoring of the Tírowa, and its place would be taken by the Atẽpá as soon as the latter were admitted to the mature men's age-grade. This ceremonial admission took place soon after my departure.

Note that in this ceremony, which marked the end of the Ai'riri sponsorship of the Tírowa, the opposition between clans was ritually re-introduced. Hitherto the Ai'riri had always acted as a corporate group which cut across distinctions of clan and lineage. They could do this because the age-sets are social strata in which all members of the community (and, conceptually at least, all members of Shavante society) are united at different levels in a series of graded solidary groups. But when an age-set reaches a certain stage in the cycle its members act less and less as members of the corporate group to which they belong through initiation, and more and more as representatives of a faction whose interests they seek to further. This is not a contingent tendency among certain groups of Shavante at certain times, but is clearly recognized as being a feature of their social system. Hence each age-set closes its active ceremonial life with a rite which divides it along clan lines.

The more sophisticated Shavante are quite aware of these two differing models of their own society. 'Age-sets are good' they say. Age-mates are referred to as '*zawi-di*' (friends), as opposed to members of other clans who are characteristically '*siti'rŭ'ti*' (angry, hostile). For the Shavante the age-sets represent an ideal of harmony whereas the clans represent the actuality of discord. If the social fission of the lineages triumphs in the end over the social fusion of the age-sets, then this is because the ideal cannot be realized.

V

THE POLITICAL SYSTEM

1. CLANS AND LINEAGES

SHAVANTE say there have always been three clans. Although I was given differing versions of how these clans came into being the stories all agreed on certain points. The founders of the clans came out of the ground in the very beginning when there was nothing (*ro b'badi* = everything empty). There were three of them and they founded respectively the Tpereya'óno the Ę Wawẽ and the Topdató. The three clans painted themselves differently and agreed to take each other's children in marriage for ever.

The Western Shavante versions of the story specify that this compact was between the Tpereya'óno on the one hand and the Ę Wawẽ + Topdató on the other. Both Western and Eastern Shavante insisted, however, that the Ę Wawẽ and the Topdató were distinct and always had been. One elderly Tpereya'óno man from São Marcos expressed the relationship of these clans to me this way:[1]

'I am Tpereya'óno and there is my affine. (He points at Sibupá [Genealogy 2:154] sitting opposite and also taking part in the discussion.)

Topdató are also affines. Our ancestors created the Topdató in order to mix up the Shavante, although we are all one. It was not a separate creation. We are all Shavante. At the very beginning kinsmen were grouped together. The Topdató were asked and they went with the Ę Wawẽ.

At the *oi'o* (ceremony) they were told not to be afraid. Shavante have always been divided—since the beginning.' (I interpolated: 'But are not the Topdató then Ę Wawẽ?')

'*No* (speaker's emphasis). Sibupá (speaker points again) is Ę Wawẽ. He is not Topdató. The Topdató are with the Ę Wawẽ.

---

[1] This is a verbatim transcript from my tape of our discussion. The informant is Meireles. (Genealogy 2:16) I have standardized the names of the clans, and use one form of each consistently throughout this book, to avoid confusion.

Our ancestors separated the Shavante in this way. The Topdató had their special face marks.

Then the Shavante separated into different villages.'

All my informants stressed the peculiar paint style of the Topdató by indicating with gestures how they made circles on their cheeks. In fact the name Topdató probably derives from this style, since it is a combination of *to* = demonstrative particle + *da-to* = eye, circle.[1] Ẹ Wawẽ comes from *ẹ* = water, river + *wawẽ* = old (but which may also be used as an augmentative). I am unable to explain the etymology of Tpereya'óno.

It is primarily by their paint that the clans are distinguished. The men of each clan are supposed to use the following designs on ceremonial occasions:

CLAN	DESIGN	POSITION
Tpereya'óno	♀♀♀	on the temples
Ẹ Wawẽ	⊓⊓	on the temples
Topdató	○	on the cheeks

Similarly we have seen that the *wamñõrõ* masks used during the initiation ceremonies were decorated in three distinctive styles, one for each clan. In actual fact men rarely use these clan insignia, even when they are taking part in ceremonies, and there is some confusion as to who would use which style for his dance mask. I shall argue that this is not evidence of a 'breakdown of the system' but, on the contrary, that the system itself requires such flexibility.

A clan is called *ĩ-snã'rda*, from *ĩ* = possessive prefix + *nã'rda* = root, stem.[2] Fellow clansmen are therefore people who stem from a common origin. But this fact is not expressed in speaking of them. They could be referred to as *ĩ-snã'rda-tdeʼwa*, which is a perfectly acceptable form in Shavante, and would indeed denote a class of people who had the common property of being

[1] This is clearly a cognate of the Sherente word *šiptato*, which is the name of one of their moieties. This moiety, like the Shavante Topdató, used a pattern of circles as its distinctive paint style.

[2] An alternative form is *wa-nnã'rda*, from *wa* = I (first person singular). The relationship term *ĩ-'rda* also derives from this notion, and refers to any person in the second ascending generation and upwards, or, loosely, an ancestor.

members of the speaker's *ĩ-snã'rda*. Instead, they are called *waniwihã*, which may be roughly translated as 'people of my side' or 'my kind of people'.[1] Similarly the generic term for everybody who is not of the speaker's clan is *wasi're'wa*, which can be approximately rendered as 'people separated from me' or 'others'.[2]

This we/they dichotomy is a crucial and pervasive distinction in Shavante thought and Shavante life. It is analogous to the distinction which Dumont has described among certain peoples of South India and which he has called a division between 'kin' and 'affine' (1953: 4; 1957a: 26–27). I prefer not to use the glosses 'kin' and 'affine' myself, since they are already infused with notions of consanguinity and affinity. Dumont pointed out that he was using these words in a special sense to refer not to genealogical relationships or relationships by marriage, but to the two sides in those systems of relationship terminology where any speaker classified all relatives into two antithetical categories. He would refer to one of these categories as 'terminological kin' and to the other as 'terminological affines'. But this did not prevent his analysis from being mis-understood, for example, by Radcliffe-Brown (1953), and I suspect that however much a writer tries to sterilize such notions as 'kin' and 'affine' of their conventional meanings the attempt can never be wholly successful. I shall therefore try to avoid these terms, even though they are in certain cases adequate transla-tions of *waniwihã* and *wasi're'wa*. Indeed, the fact that they are adequate translations in certain cases is all the more reason for avoiding them as glosses. Partial translations tend to become accepted as the primary meanings of words and this is perhaps the greatest single source of confusion in the whole of anthropol-ogy.

For the moment it is enough to say that Shavante regard fellow clansmen as somehow 'my people', as opposed to non-clansmen, who are 'others'. In the course of this chapter I hope to show just what this means and also how people come to be classified in either of these two major categories.

The most important sense in which fellow clansmen are 'my

---

[1] From *wa* = I + *niwi* which is a directional particle.
[2] From *wa* = I + *si're* = separate, divide (see 'Divorce') + *'wa* = suffix designating a person having the properties of the stem.

people' is that a person looks to them for support in matters which are potentially factional. Conversely, he anticipates hostility and opposition from people who are not of his clan. Non-clansmen are a class of people. They never act as a corporate group, even among the Western Shavante, where the moiety system would offer an institutional means of their doing so. Similarly, fellow-clansmen are a class of potential allies. They do not always act together and may, on occasion, even oppose each other. Yet according to Shavante ideology this should not happen. Shavante speak as if clansmen are always reliable friends (*zawi-di*), and when I asked in the course of my research what would happen if a man killed a fellow clansman I was assured that this could not and did not happen.

In 1958 I therefore assumed that those instances in my notes which referred to intra-clan fighting were based on misunderstandings. When I returned in 1962, I discovered that this was not so. I also discovered that the manner in which Shavante acted on their beliefs about the relationship between clans was both different from, and more complex than, the way in which I had supposed they did.

It would perhaps be more accurate to say that Shavante consider people of their own faction to be fellow-clansmen rather than to assume that they consider fellow-clansmen to be members of their own faction. In São Marcos in 1964 I observed the assimilation of a group of immigrants from Ẽ Tõ. It soon became clear that the majority of the inhabitants of São Marcos did not know the clan affiliation of many of the newcomers. They could guess at it but, as they expressed it, they 'did not know whose people they were'; or, alternatively, they 'had not seen them paint'. They could presumably have found out simply by asking. Since Shavante who arrive in a strange village are obliged to report at the first opportunity to the men's council, where they are 'questioned' by the chief on all their news, there is an excellent opportunity for a newcomer's personal status to be established.

But this is not done because clanship by itself is meaningless. It becomes significant only in context, and that context is supplied by the factional structure of the community, which is built out of, but does not necessarily correspond with, clan alignments. It is therefore less important for people to know whether a newcomer belongs to a certain clan than it is for them to know which lineage he is associated with. When he paints himself in the style of a given lineage, this is thus a public demonstration of a factional affiliation.

These distinctions are brought out in the collective words Shavante use (see Table 11). Any fellow clansman is potentially *waniwihã*, as opposed to *wasi're'wa*. But, unless he as an individual or as a member of a given lineage can be considered a member of the speaker's faction, he will not be classed as *wasiwadi*, and it is only *wasiwadi* who are normally addressed by relationship terms appropriate to 'my people'. At the next level of contrast *wasiwadi* (people of the speaker's faction) may be addressed by such relationship terms, or referred to collectively as *wasiwadi* in order to distinguish them from people closely associated with the speaker's own lineage. The latter (*wasisẽnẽwẽ*) are invariably addressed by the appropriate relationship terms, but can be distinguished from a yet more restricted class of people to whom a person feels he can actually trace genealogical relationships. These are referred to as *ĩ-hitebre*, if they are men, or *ĩ-hidiba* if they are women.

It is the lineage which is expected to act as a corporate group. A member of it cannot dissociate himself from the others on an important issue and still remain part of it. In these circumstances he must found a separate lineage or get himself adopted into another one. Sometimes a lineage becomes so small that it disintegrates and its surviving members are all incorporated into other lineages. But the expectation that members of a lineage will not actively oppose each other is much stronger than in the case of the clan.

Thus the lineages are the corporate groups on which the political system is based. It is true that Shavante, speaking loosely, sometimes refer to other communities collectively as being of such-and-such a clan; but, in doing so, they refer to the fact that the dominant faction in that community is of the clan mentioned. A faction consists of a lineage and its supporters, who may be other lineages of the same clan, other individuals, or even lineages of another clan. The dominant faction is of course the chief's faction and it may be referred to in conversation by the name of the chief's lineage. On the other hand, there may be no faction which is clearly dominant in a given community at a given time, in which case the major factions are likely to have their own 'chiefs'.

Lineages are invariably referred to by a soubriquet plus the suffixes -*tde'wa* or -'*wa*, which indicate collections of people described by the preceding name. The names in themselves have no latent significance nor are they ordered in any specific fashion. They appear to be no more than convenient appellations that refer to some characteristic of the lineage. As a result there may be more than one conventional way of referring to a certain lineage in a given community. At the same time, there is nothing to prevent different lineages from different communities being referred to locally by the same name. For example, a lineage of the Tpereya'óno clan in São Marcos (1962) was referred to as Páhiri'wa-tde'wa because its members were entitled to receive the name and office of Páhiri'wa. An unrelated lineage in Simões Lópes had the same name for the same reason. Yet the chief's lineage in São Domingos, which had abrogated to itself the privilege of receiving the name Páhiri'wa, was never referred to collectively by it.

In Table 12 I have set out the names and clan affiliations of the lineages in São Domingos (1958) and São Marcos (1962). It will be seen that lineage names are not limited to certain clans. The Tebe were Tpereya'óno in São Domingos and Ę Wawẽ in São Marcos. The appellation Wamãrĩdzu was applied to two lineages from different clans in São Marcos. I pressed for an elucidation of this apparent contradiction and was told that the Wamãrĩdzu people 'had been mixed (between the clans)' in this village.

Lineage names are thus contextual. Prapá, the senior man of the Dzutsi lineage (São Domingos, 1958), told me that his people had been Wamãrĩ 'a long time ago' and that they were not any longer. Meanwhile an elderly man who fled to São Domingos from Marãwasede was immediately accepted in the former village by the powerful Wamãrĩ lineage. Yet he assured me that there were no Wamãrĩ people in Marãwasede. He had become a Wamãrĩ in his new community.

The arbitrary and unsystematic manner in which these lineage names are applied may perhaps confuse the reader, but it may be some small consolation to him to learn that it also confuses the Shavante. A Shavante who arrives in a strange village must learn how its various groups are related factionally before he can act appropriately in the community. He may not even understand the discussions he hears in his own language, since they depend so much on contextual knowledge which he does not possess.[1]

This in itself is not particularly extraordinary. It must be well nigh universal for people to feel strange in unfamiliar communities. In our own society we are accustomed to the sensation of going to a place whose inhabitants share our nationality and our language and yet failing to understand the allusions in their speech or the matters they discuss. I stress this point in connexion with the Shavante, however, because it is often assumed that this does not happen in societies of such small size. It might be thought that the clan and lineage system of the Shavante could serve to define a person's status in any community with sufficient precision to make the assimilation of a newcomer almost automatic. Perhaps it could, but this is not the case. Nor does the relationship system have this effect, as we shall see later. These various systems act as sets of social co-ordinates that merely provide a matrix for actual situations. The context determines not only what a Shavante does, which could hardly be otherwise, but what he is.

In the next section I shall therefore examine in detail the factional structure of the village I knew best, São Domingos, to show how this system works. Meanwhile the names of the lineages and information as to where and how they occur are set out for convenience in Appendix 1.

---

[1] I found that Shavante could not understand my recordings of discussions made in other communities unless I gave them a great deal of background information. Shavante grammar, which leaves a great deal 'understood' and unspecified, also necessitates considerable contextual knowledge on the part of the listener.

2. SÃO DOMINGOS FACTIONS (See Table 13)

In 1958 there were between 200 and 220 people in this group and their base village comprised 17–18 huts.[1] There were 60–65 men, 75–80 women, and 70–75 children.[2] Fig. 4 shows a plan of the village. It will be seen that the huts were arranged in a semi-circle that opened towards the south-west, but there was no particular significance in this. Shavante invariably build their villages with the opening towards the source of water, in this case a small creek that flowed into the Rio das Mortes.

There are other regularities in the disposition of Shavante villages. The order of households around the village arc is strictly maintained, so that a given household group always has the same neighbours whichever way the village faces. Even if the semi-circle is turned 'inside out' this order remains constant. The bachelors' hut is invariably located some little way away from the others at one extremity of the crescent. The two end households of the village proper are referred to as *aamrã*, and they should be occupied by men of some prestige. They are normally the repositories of pieces of regalia used in the *wai'a* ceremony. Clans and lineages are not assigned determined positions along the semi-circle. Being patrilineal and uxorilocal they are necessarily distributed according to the households into which their male members have married. Thus the morphology of the village does not reflect the divisions of Shavante society in the explicit way to which students of Central Brazilian sociology have become accustomed.[3]

There is, however, a tendency for lineages to be localized in segments of the village semi-circle. This is not a rule, and it is not made explicit in any statement or idea about which part of the village should be the province of which clan or lineage. Yet men do not marry at random throughout the community. On the contrary, the male members of patrilineages tend to live in neighbouring households. They achieve this by consciously marrying women of a single lineage, preferably by a group of brothers marrying a group of sisters.

[1] One hut, located on Fig. 4 between houses F and G, was dismantled during my stay. Its inhabitants moved to Capitariquara.

[2] There was fluctuation in the population during my time in the field but the total never exceeded 220 or fell below 200.

[3] e.g. among the Bororo (Albisetti 1953), the Eastern Timbira (Nimuendajú, 1946: 79), and the Sherente (Nimuendajú, 1942: 17).

Consider the data presented in Appendix 4, which shows the composition of all households in São Domingos in 1958:

Household A. Wamãrĩ (TP)[1]

Apęwẽ (7) was chief of the village and most of the occupants were his sons.

Household B. Wamãrĩ (TP)

This household was established next to Apęwẽ's by Rĩtimõwẽ (110) the widow of Apęwẽ's brother. Some villagers claimed that Apęwẽ had 'married' her, as was his privilege. Her son (61) lived in household A and finally married a girl of that household (152). Such a marriage within the household could be arranged for him because of his close relationship to the chief.

Household C. Wamãrĩ (TP)

This household was occupied by two of Apęwẽ's wives who were no longer cohabiting with him (107 and 108). The men who married into A (141), B (144), and C (143, 145, 146) were all members of the Uhę lineage (EW).

Household D. Wamãrĩ (TP)

This household must originally have been of the clan of Apęwẽ's sister's husband (11). Now that he was dead and Apęwẽ's sister (10) aged, the senior member of it was 163, a Topdató clansman. But 163 had 'gone over' to the Tpereya'óno and been assimilated into the Wamãrĩ. Later, when even assimilated Topdató were purged, he fled and is now at Areões.

Household E. Wamãrĩ (TP)

The senior man of this household was originally 95, a member of the Dzutsi lineage (EW). 95 was killed when Apęwẽ purged the Dzutsi. The only adult male resident of the house was Apęwẽ's son (42).

Household F. Dzutsi (EW)

Prapá (91), the senior man of this household, is the leader of the Dzutsi and brother of 95, who used to live next door.

Household G. Wamãrĩ (TP)

Occupied by 57, the chief's brother's son, and his wives and children.

[1] I use the following abbreviations: TP = Tpereya'óno, EW = Ę Wawẽ and TD = Topdató.

Household I. Tebe (TP)

Occupied by 80, the sole adult member of the lineage, his wives and children, and son-in-law (114), a Dzutsi man.

Household J. Wamãrĩ (TP)

This household should have been Aiuté'mañãrĩ (TD), since that was the lineage of its senior man (162); but he had 'gone over' to the dominant Wamãrĩ.

Household K. Wamãrĩ (TP) / Wahi (TD)

In 1958 this house was evenly balanced between the hitherto dominant Wamãrĩ and the in-marrying Wahi. This was made possible by the fact that one of the Wamãrĩ men (47) had brought his wives to live virilocally with him, and the other (50) had not yet moved into his affinal household. This was, however, the Wahi corner of the village. The senior man of that lineage lived in L and that house was their meeting place. Young Wahi men (179 and 180) had married into K and it was assumed that they would soon be the dominant members of the household. The Wahi were subsequently extirpated, however, and I found in 1962 that the household was still run by 149 and her son 47.

Household L. Wahi (TD)

The senior man in the household was head of the Wahi lineage.

Household M. Dzutsi (EW)

This household was occupied by two Wamãrĩ girls and their stepmother. The men who had married them were Dzutsi.

Household N. Dzutsi (EW)

It will be seen from Genealogy 3 that the men who married into this household (68, 69) are in fact Wamãrĩ. I was told in 1958 that they were Ẽ Wawẽ clansmen, and therefore listed them as Dzutsi. Subsequently I discovered the error. I also discovered the reason for it. The men of this household had gone over to the Dzutsi and were classified as such by the community.

Household O. Dzutsi (EW)

The senior man of this household was 122, a prominent Dzutsi who was nevertheless sympathetic to the Wamãrĩ.

Household P. Wamãrĩ (TP)

The women of this house were Dzutsi and one of their brothers was still living there. But the household was clearly

Wamãrĩ, since the in-married husbands were influential members of that lineage. One of them was Waarodí (43), the chief's eldest son, who occupies the *aamrã* (end household) in his capacity as the second most influential man of the dominant lineage.

The dominant faction had therefore established themselves in houses A–J and had also taken over the *aamrã* at the opposite end of the village (P). The outsiders were congregated in houses K–O. The inhabitants of the village recognized this, and would talk of 'going over to the Wamãrĩ' when they meant going to any of the houses on the arc between A and J. The gathering place of the Wamãrĩ was in the chief's hut (household A).

Embedded in this Wamãrĩ part of the village was the entire Uhẹ lineage, whose members had married into households A, B, and C. They would gather informally in C, where there were no Wamãrĩ men living.

The meeting place of the Wahi was at household L, in the Topdató part of the village.

I found it difficult to understand the role of the Dzutsi. They were numerically the strongest lineage after the Wamãrĩ and they seemed to be concentrated at the south-eastern end of the village in houses M, N, O, and part of P. Yet they rarely gathered in each other's houses or showed any of the corporate spirit that characterized the other lineages. I put it down at the time to the personality of Prapá, the senior man in the lineage, who was extremely quiet and retiring. It seemed that this quality of his had enabled him to live to what was by Shavante standards a ripe old age, while his coevals had run foul of Apẹwẽ and been exiled or killed.

I discovered later that this was only partly the explanation. The Dzutsi had borne the brunt of the purge when Apẹwẽ had had eight men killed for 'murdering' his brother by sorcery. Those of them who were still in São Domingos were therefore still treading warily. They had not made common cause against the Wamãrĩ with the newly arrived Uhẹ, who were mostly young and inexperienced men. Nor did they throw in their lot with the Wahi. Perhaps this saved them in the long run, for the Wahi were subsequently wiped out. When the opportunity came, however, Prapá quietly persuaded a sizeable group to leave São Domingos altogether and move to Ẹ Tõ.

The opportunity the Dzutsi had been waiting for came in 1960, when the village at Capitariquara broke up. There was an influx of Shavante to São Domingos, which had been helping Capitariquara with its war on two fronts against Santa Terezinha and Areões. Some of the newcomers were lineage-mates of Prapá. The Dzutsi faction was thus reinforced.

At the same time the Wamãrĩ were losing their hold over the community. Some Wamãrĩ had died in an epidemic of influenza. The faction held the Topdató responsible and killed a number of them, including two who had 'gone over' and considered themselves Wamãrĩ. I could never determine exactly how many Topdató were killed at this time, for the enemies of the Wamãrĩ were eager to attribute every death which had occurred since my previous visit to the ferocity of the dominant faction. The Wamãrĩ assured me, on the other hand, that no Topdató had been killed by them. They insisted that the Topdató had suffered even more severely in the epidemic than they themselves had. It seems certain, however, that some Topdató were in fact killed, though some may have died of influenza. In any case the community as a whole was depleted and the Wamãrĩ found themselves without allies. Even their fellow clansmen were prepared to desert them.

At this point Prapá led about a third of the village over to Ẹ Tõ. He persuaded his sisters in household C to accompany him and thereby divorce Apẽwẽ. They went, taking their daughters and their young Uhẹ husbands with them. He took his 'daughters' (brother's daughters) from household E and his daughters from household F, and their husbands followed them though they were Apẽwẽ's sons. He took his brother's son (114) and he in his turn brought his wives and his in-laws, in fact the whole Tebe lineage, from household I. Finally the dissident Wamãrĩ from N also joined him, as did their brother, S'rizamdí (65), from P.

The case of S'rizamdí offers a clear demonstration of the contingent nature of Shavante alignments. He was a Wamãrĩ of considerable influence. He and Waarodí, the chief's eldest son, were married to two sisters and they occupied the *aamrã* at one end of the village. Yet S'rizamdí and his wife went with Prapá to Ẹ Tõ while Waarodí and his wife stayed. The social status of the wives, as full sisters, was identical. S'rizamdí, on the

other hand, differed from Waarodí only in his degree of closeness to the centre of power in São Domingos. He was not a
direct descendant of Apęwẽ, only a member of the chief's
lineage.

It is in retrospect significant that S'rizamdí and his brothers
from household N trekked in a different direction from the others
in May 1958. The village split at that time into four groups. Two
of them went on trek in the Serra do Roncador and later joined
forces and travelled back to São Domingos together. One resi-
dual collection of people remained in the village, and one small
group accompanied S'rizamdí along the east bank of the Rio
das Mortes. At the time I could not discover any particular
significance in these choices because I thought that they would
be dictated by lineage membership, which I imagined was
strictly genealogical. As soon as one appreciates, however, that
factional considerations determine lineage membership and that
this is a continuous process, it becomes possible to understand
Shavante decisions and the language they use to indicate their
social groupings. S'rizamdí's group of Wamãrĩ were already
beginning to act independently of the main faction.

When Prapá's people seceded, then, they removed households C, E, F, I, and N from São Domingos, plus S'rizamdí and
family from P. Household H died out. Household L was killed
off save for one in-married Wamãrĩ, who was its sole representative when I returned to the village.

At the time of my second visit there were accordingly ten
houses left in São Domingos and the population of the village
had shrunk to 110. The Wamãrĩ were still firmly established
as the dominant lineage, for there were few to oppose them.
The only other lineages still represented in the community were
respectively the Uhę and the Dzutsi, both considerably depleted.
The men of these lineages who had remained rather than move
to Ę Tõ did so for one of two reasons. Either they could not
persuade their wives to leave their kin and move to Ę Tõ, and
had no wish to go without them, or they preferred to throw in
their lot with their affines rather than move with their kin. In
any case, São Domingos in 1962 was one of the most homo-
geneous Shavante villages I have stayed in, factionally speaking.
It was as if the 'outsiders' had seceded in a body to Ę Tõ.

The Shavante saw it that way too, and they could not really

make up their minds as to whether Ẽ Tõ was a separate community or merely an appendage of São Domingos. I spoke to Prapá's son-in-law (42), who had moved to Ẽ Tõ to be with his wives, and he insisted that the move was simply to be nearer good hunting lands and good forest for planting. According to him it was a mere matter of convenience and there was certainly no ill feeling between São Domingos and Ẽ Tõ. Rintimpse, another Wamãrĩ, who had left Marãwasede for São Domingos and then moved from São Domingos to Ẽ Tõ, also insisted that relations between the two latter communities could not have been better. When I met him again in 1964, after he had fled from Ẽ Tõ to São Marcos, he told a different story. Apẽwẽ, he said, had always hated the people who went to Ẽ Tõ, and threatened to kill them all. Using the idiom of the lineages to express the current factional position he added that Apẽwẽ and his people were not real Wamãrĩ at all. They had stolen the Wamãrĩ. The only real Wamãrĩ were S'rizamdí, Sirimiramĩ, and those others who had seceded to Ẽ Tõ.

In fact, some of the Ẽ Tõ people were killed under mysterious circumstances. The Tebe lineage was annihilated. Most of the community moved to São Marcos. This was probably the work of Apẽwẽ, since there is little doubt that he did not look favourably on the village which had been carved out of his fief. It was virtually expected of him that he should move against it. When I visited other communities in 1962 I was told that Apẽwẽ was killing the Ẽ Tõ Shavante. I had just come from São Domingos/Ẽ Tõ and I knew that this was not true, but it was useless for me to say so. Shavante in the other villages 'knew' it was true. It was a clear case of a self-fulfilling prophecy!

3. THE SETTLEMENT OF DISPUTES

It is easier to explain who fights whom among the Shavante than to give a clear idea of what they are fighting about. In this section, therefore, I discuss Shavante disputes to try and show what sorts of issues pit one faction against another. I deliberately treat this as part of the 'political system'. The intimate connexion between law and politics is a commonplace, but in most studies there are good grounds, either institutional or analytical, for treating them separately. Among the Shavante, on the other hand, all legal 'cases' are political issues in the sense that they can only be heard in the men's council, where their resolution depends largely on the relative strengths of the factions. A dispute which does not become a factional matter is not technically a dispute at all. It has a status similar to that of a disagreement which has not been taken to court.

Everything which takes place in the community is discussed sooner or later in the men's council, simply as an item of news. Once it has lost its news value it is allowed to drop. It is only if the protagonists wish to pursue the matter that it becomes a dispute, to which the community as a whole, represented by the council of mature men presided over by the chief or chiefs, gives its serious attention.

Matters between women can only be considered or resolved by this informal court if they are presented by the men. But men take care not to get involved in female squabbles, which they consider laughable and unworthy of serious attention. So, if two women become involved in a dispute which does not concern the men, there is no forum in which it can be discussed and no institutionalized procedure for its resolution. As a result women occasionally come to blows, a thing men never do.

Example 1[1]: *Quarrel between Rēwawē and Wautomõwawē.*

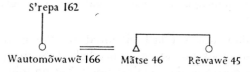

There had been a meat distribution in São Domingos after a steer had been slaughtered at the Indian Protection Service post.

---

[1] Serial numbers refer to Genealogy 3.

In the late afternoon all the households in the village were cooking their shares, in the largest pots they owned, over extra-large fires. It was the end of the dry season, when the hut thatch was brittle and moistureless and many of the houses were badly in need of repair. Suddenly S'repa's house caught fire. It flamed like a torch for no more than five or ten minutes before it was reduced to a smouldering heap. As the flames danced, excited Shavante made forays into the fierce heat, trying to salvage what they could before it was utterly consumed.

The bewildered inhabitants of the house were left sitting disconsolately among the few possessions that had somehow been saved. The women began to wail and the men tried to pass it off as best they could. Meanwhile Mãtse went next door to his sister Rêwawê and told her of all the foodstuffs, possessions, and ceremonial regalia he had lost. Rêwawê, unable to control herself, burst out of her hut and began to scream abuse at her brother's wife and mother-in-law for their carelessness around the cooking fires. The latter, who were already upset, replied in the same vein. Before long Rêwawê and Wautomõwawê were tussling on the ground. The men separated them, S'repa leading away his weeping daughter and Mãtse his still vituperative sister.

There was bad blood between these women for some time, yet the men never took up the issue. Mãtse had good grounds to feel annoyed. He had not only sustained considerable losses but he had also to help his father-in-law build a new house; yet, he did no more than grumble about the matter.

Example 2: Assault on an immigrant widow.

Some time before I arrived among the Shavante a woman who lived in São Domingos lost her husband. She had no married daughters to live with so she went to Santa Terezinha to live with her married son. In that community she had a liaison with one of the older men. His wives felt that he was neglecting them for her, so they sought out the widow and beat her up. The outraged widow moved to Capitariquara, swearing that she would get her kin to avenge her.

This affair was similarly ignored by the men. Even the woman's son took no action on her behalf. Such squabbles are enjoyed as gossip in the men's council, but no solution of them is either sought or expected. Into the same category came a fight which developed between a robust young woman and a spindly kleptomaniac whom the São Domingos Shavante tolerat because of his speech defect (probably due to a severe early attack of meningitis) and the feeling that he might have unusual powers.

Example 3[1]: Fight between Domitsiwa (123) and Pidzuiwẽ (66).

At a meat distribution in São Domingos Domitsiwa seized the entire head of a slaughtered steer and started to drag it away. A young girl, Pidzuiwẽ, also had hold of it and would not let go. Domitsiwa became infuriated and wrestled with her, pulling her hair in the manner characteristic of women's fighting. The men present roared with laughter, especially when they saw that the girl was by no means outmatched. Domitsiwa then broke away and seized a log to club her over the head, but she dodged and wrestled it from his grip. Only when he was frothing with rage and picked up an axe-head to throw at her did the spectators become alarmed and intervene. The Ai'riri Páhiri'wa, one of Apẽwẽ's sons and therefore an influential man in the village, stepped in and told him to stop. He was given the steer's head to calm him and allowed to depart.

This incident was the cause of much merriment in the men's council for days afterwards. The girl's kin saw no reason to make an issue out of it, however, and the matter was allowed to rest.

It is disputes between men which are really serious and in the settlement of which the chief must display his conciliatory talents. The commonest and easiest to resolve are cases of what may broadly speaking be called 'theft'.

The Shavante word *danipsaihuri*[2] refers to all classes of expropriation and covers 'taking', 'borrowing', and 'stealing'. It would be more accurate, then, to say that they think in terms of 'taking away' rather than of theft. They do not subscribe to the view that 'taking (something) away' without the consent of the owner is wrong in itself. Whether such an action provokes the owner to protest, or to do something to recover his property, depends on a number of contingent circumstances: what was taken, by whom, and for what purpose.

The commonest commodity which Shavante say has been 'taken' from them is food. Yet they would rarely wish to lodge a complaint in the men's council on this score. Fellow clansmen,

---

[1] Serial numbers refer to Genealogy 3.
[2] An alternative (third person) form is *sipsaihuri*.

fellow members of one's faction, kinsmen in other clans, all have some claim on one's food supply, so that if they 'take' food a Shavante will do no more than grumble about it, if that. If somebody who has no claims on one's food should 'take' some of it, this poses a problem. The plaintiff can make a complaint in the certainty that the issue will become a factional matter, or he can ignore it. He usually ignores it.

Similarly the 'taking' of artefacts which the Shavante make themselves is resented because of the inconvenience it may cause the owner. But these artefacts, being readily identifiable, cannot be expropriated in the full sense of the word unless the person who takes them leaves the village. Otherwise the owner can at any time inform himself of the whereabouts of whatever he has lost and demand it back from the taker. The taker invariably returns it rather than risk the censure of the community. He is, in any case, likely to be at least a lineage-mate of the man from whom he took the item in question, so that he is only exercising his right to borrow from a person who has an obligation to lend to him. Normally nobody would 'take' property belonging to someone in another faction unless that person was his sister's husband or, less commonly, his mother's brother. To do so in other circumstances would risk precipitating a factional conflict.

Danipsaihuri is thus regarded by the Shavante as irritating rather than illicit or morally wrong. It only becomes a serious matter when it is accompanied by some sort of 'intent to harm'. There is normally a presumption of such intent only when the taker is some person who has no claims at all on the owner, in other words, somebody in the category of *wasi're'wa*.

The introduction of manufactured goods has, however, introduced a new conception of property rights, and correspondingly a new category of *danipsaihuri*. If someone takes fish hooks or a knife from another, the owner cannot always identify his property again and cannot easily replace it. The taker can often make use of the item without this fact being reported back to the person from whom it was taken. Shavante therefore take care to guard this type of property as carefully as possible, and insist on exclusive rights in it. In 1958 the Downstream Shavante were still embarrassed by the possession of such valuables. They did not wish to carry them about on trek, and yet they did not dare to leave them behind in their huts for ear of having them stolen. They therefore took to leaving baskets, containing their manufactured possessions, in the care f the post or mission close to their base village. Even this measure was not always foolproof, for Indians were perpetually oming and going, and any Shavante could have free access to the room where these baskets were kept in order to get at his belongings. The missionaries or the Indian agent were not able to identify the property of individual Indians, and could not therefore ensure that a man took only what was his.

When a Shavante finds that somebody has 'taken' a knife or a pair of scissors from him, he will not just grumble, he will raise the matter in the men's council. Here it is discussed with a view to elucidating where and when he lost it and who could have taken it. Such discussions may drag on for weeks at a time:

Case 1: Theft of Suwapte's scissors.

Suwapte lost a pair of scissors while out on trek. He reported the matter in the men's council and it was discussed on a number of evenings. When the band with which he was travelling joined up with another band from São Domingos the case was reopened. The discussions were led by Suwapte, acting for himself, on the one hand, and a member of the Wamãrĩ on the other. The thief had not been identified and the scissors not returned when the two bands returned to São Domingos. On the first evening after their arrival the matter was reopened again, with Apęwẽ presiding. The culprit could not be identified, however, and Suwapte was finally persuaded to drop the case.

The chief usually leads such discussions and holds an informal court of inquiry to establish the identity of the thief. The skill with which Apęwẽ used his powers of oratory and moral persuasion to get a confession, or to get one of the thief's kin to inform on him, was apparent even to me, who could understand only half of what he said in his speeches. If the thief can be identified, the property is restored and the matter is considered closed.

A case of *danipsaihuri* that involves members of factions between which there is already bad blood can lead to serious consequences. The chief tries to 'talk out' the matter and restore harmony. If he is unsuccessful then the community as a whole takes measures primarily intended to restore peace rather than to restore property. So if the accused are stronger than the plaintiffs the easiest way to restore harmony is to side with the former. This may lead to the expulsion of the accusers, as in the following case:

Case 2: Theft of Wado's coconuts.

Wado accused Rupawĕ (of the Wamãrĩ) of stealing his coconuts. They quarrelled violently. The matter was discussed in the men's council, where the dominant faction supported Rupawĕ's protestations of innocence. Wado left the village.

The Shavante certainly value coconuts highly, both as food and because they use their milk as a cosmetic. Yet it would seem strange that Wado should challenge the dominant faction over the matter of a few coconuts. In fact he was already bitter against the Wamãrĩ, whom he accused of having killed his sister through sorcery. When I was investigating the incident, the Wamãrĩ admitted that Wado's sister had indeed been killed in this way and by them. It is against this background that the dispute over the coconuts has to be examined. Wado was a man with a grievance against the dominant faction, and the fact that he pressed an accusation of theft against one of its members would be taken as evidence of this grievance. The Wamãrĩ could therefore expect trouble from him. If he did not in some way obtain redress, which they were unwilling or unable to offer, he would be expected to try and get his revenge through sorcery. Under these circumstances the Wamãrĩ were probably making up their minds to get rid of him when he circumspectly forestalled them by leaving the community.

Shavante plaintiffs are not always as rash as Wado. They are often content to let their case drop if they sense that their own faction is not wholeheartedly with them. It is the chief's task to make sure that this is as easy as possible for them. He tries to persuade them to drop their case and not to harbour resentment against the accused, while at the same time trying to persuade the accused not to bear any grudge against the plaintiffs. It is in the best interests of the community that he should be successful in this endeavour. If the stronger party refuses to let bygones be bygones and moves for the expulsion of the weaker, then the community is numerically weakened. If on the other hand, the weaker are left harbouring a grudge then they will bring misfortune on the stronger through sorcery.

An accusation of sorcery is the most serious charge that one Shavante can bring against another, and is made extremely rarely in the men's council. Such matters may be discussed in private, but an accusation of this nature is a declaration of implacable hostility against the man concerned, and, if 'his people' side with him, against them too. The chief sees to it that, as far as possible, such cases are settled 'out of court', i.e., not brought up in the men's council.

Case 3: Waarodí[1] accuses Suwapte[2] of sorcery.

This case was never actually brought to the men's council. It was however, put about that Suwapte was a sorcerer and the matter was discussed in the Wamãrĩ lineage, where Waarodí was arguing that action should be taken. Apẽwẽ talked him out of bringing the matter up in council and eventually the charge was dropped.

The significance of this case is that Waarodí is Apẽwẽ's eldest son, and clearly his lieutenant. Suwapte is Apẽwẽ's son-in-law, a fiery orator and the leader of the Uhẽ lineage. The two men were at the time political rivals. I shall discuss their rivalry below. For the moment I wish to stress that most disputes among the Shavante are translated in the end into sorcery cases.

Even adultery only comes to the men's council when it has become a factional, and therefore probably a sorcery, matter:

Case 4: The chief who committed adultery.

Tomõtsu of the Topdató was in 1958 'chief' of Santa Terezinha. His authority was not firmly established, however. Both his wives died within a short time of each other. Their kin accused him of killing them through sorcery. They saw to it that he could not marry any other woman of their clan (TP). Tomõtsu seduced a Tpereya'óno woman, as a result of which there was nearly civil war in the community. The mission managed to prevent the fighting, but the 'outsiders' then left in a body for Capitariquara.

In this case the matter of Tomõtsu's adultery was not the major issue. The 'outsiders' felt that the chief was infringing their rights. They were powerful enough to challenge him but did not wish to do so in the mission, where he was supported

---

[1] Genealogy 3:43.   [2] Genealogy 3:141.

by the Fathers. Nor did they feel they could swallow the affront and carry on as if nothing had happened, since they felt that Tomõtsu had used sorcery against them in the past and would do so again in the future. They felt, therefore, that they must leave.

Similarly the only case of adultery which was decided while I was in São Domingos was really a trial for sorcery:

Case 5: The plaintiff executed.

S'rimri went about saying that Surupredu had seduced his wife. He thought that Surupredu had arranged for her to be selected as one of the women to be taken out for ceremonial sexual intercourse during the *wai'a*. Subsequently Surupredu fell ill and Mãtse developed a sore on his leg. The matter was discussed in council and this was taken as evidence that S'rimri was using sorcery against the Wamãrĩ. He was condemned to death and the execution was carried out by the Atĕpá age-set (the Young Men), who seized him when he was out hunting and killed him. Wamõrã, S'rimri's father's brother, who had spoken up for him in the council, fled to Capitariquara.

In this case S'rimri's kin (Topdató) did not stand by him. They were not only weak themselves, but S'rimri was a slow-witted man and his accusation a foolish one. If Surupredu had been having intercourse with his wife, then there was no need for him to arrange for her to be taken out in the *wai'a* ceremony. On the other hand, if he had merely had her during the ceremony, then there was nothing immoral in this and no stigma attached to either party. The story was implausible, and it may be that S'rimri's kin accepted the *prima facie* evidence of sorcery. It was therefore possible to get a conviction by the community instead of a split between factions.

More often than not, however, accusations of sorcery, and the attendant killings, have their own momentum. They are engendered by previous accusations and lead in turn to fresh grudges and further accusations:

Case 6: Execution of the killers of Juru.

Juru was the senior man of the Topdató clan and chief of the community which settled at Santa Terezinha. When he died his sons thought that members of the 'outsider' factions looked pleased, and had three of them killed.

Case 7: Tomõtsu executes his sister's husband.

Tomõtsu is the son of Juru at Santa Terezinha. When his brother died he accused his own sister's husband of sorcery, and had him executed.

Case 8[1]: Apẹwẽ executes those responsible for killing his brother.

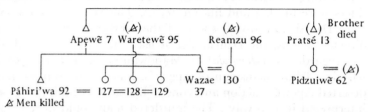

When Pratsé died, Apẹwẽ decided that his death had been brought about by sorcery. He therefore directed his supporters to kill those whom he considered responsible. Eight men were killed one night by the Wamãrĩ. Two of them were fathers of Apẹwẽ's sons' wives and a third was the daughter's husband of the dead brother himself. As a result a large number of men fled from São Domingos, some of them taking their wives with them.

This massacre horrified even the Shavante. I have heard it described in detail innumerable times and the accounts differ according to the point of view of the raconteur. Some say that the men were clubbed to death. Others insist that they were shot with .22 rifles, but this is usually a prelude to a sermon against the advisability of giving firearms to people such as Apẹwẽ and his supporters. Some make the occasion sound like a Shavante version of St. Bartholomew's night with shrieks and terror in the village, others convey the impression that the proscribed men were quietly dispatched and suggest that those who did not like it then left equally quietly the following day. Even the apologists admit, however, that it was an unusually serious killing and they do not deny that a certain Eniribowẽ (Genealogy 3:180) who was little more than a boy at the time was so disturbed by the event that he was found days later wandering through the forest in a state of shock.

All accounts agree on the basic facts of the matter, i.e. that Apẹwẽ felt his brother had been killed by sorcery and therefore took reprisals against the Ẹ Wawẽ in general and the Dzutsi

---

[1] Serial numbers refer to Genealogy 3.

lineage of that clan in particular. It is impossible to disentangle
the sorcery charge from its political implications. We cannot tell
whether Apęwẽ really believed that his brother had been
bewitched or whether he used his brother's death as a pretext
for moving against a strong 'outsider' faction which was
threatening his own. It is not even clear who the executed outsiders were in clan and lineage terms. The Shavante say they
were Dzutsi and always speak of the reprisal as having been
directed against the Dzutsi. Yet at least one of the men killed
was regarded as *ĩ-dúmrada*[1] by Manõwaupse (Genealogy 3:80)
who is a fellow clansman of Apęwẽ's. Since Manõwaupse has
deserted Apęwẽ's faction and gone to live at Ę Tõ, this could be
interpreted in two ways. The murdered man could have been
of the Ę Wawẽ clan and regarded as a sibling by Manõwaupse
because the latter had changed his faction, or he could be a
genuine sibling of Manõwaupse's who had also deserted his own
clan. The point is that his actual clanship cannot easily be
distinguished from his clanship by factional alignment. Thus
we cannot know whether all the men who were killed by Apęwẽ's
faction were actually related genealogically to the members of
the Dzutsi lineage. We can only be certain that the Shavante
saw them all as belonging to the Dzutsi faction.

It is also significant that Apęwẽ did not, as far as I have been
able to discover, bring his charge of sorcery against the Dzutsi in
the men's council. It is easy to see why. Whether or not he
believed that they were responsible for his brother's death, or
whether indeed the Dzutsi might privately have admitted this
responsibility, once the matter was raised in council it would
have led to a rift in the community. Apęwẽ could not hope to
obtain the conviction of a number of members of such a power
ful faction by the community as a whole. He therefore chose to
act in his capacity as a factional leader rather than as chief of the
community and eradicate his opponents.

A sorcery case is therefore a political matter. Indeed all
Shavante cases are essentially issues between groups rather than
disputes between individuals. A personal disagreement does no
become a dispute for adjudication in the men's council unless
and until it becomes a factional matter. Put another way, all
personal disputes which become cases in the men's counc:

---

[1] Some sort of sibling (See chapter VI).

become *ipso facto* factional issues. The factions act as legal 'persons'. There is no mechanism by which a member of a faction can bring a case against another member of it. Such disagreements have to be 'settled out of court', so to speak, usually in informal faction meetings. Should such a dispute become irresoluble, men may leave the faction thereby clearing the way for the matter to be brought in the men's council as an issue between factions.

The community as a whole can only take action against an individual if his faction disowns him. This is what happened to S'rimri (Case 5) and presumably also to the man who was executed in Case 7. In such cases it is again difficult to determine whether the faction did in fact disown the outlaw or whether it simply found itself powerless to do anything else but acquiesce in his punishment. Juru (Case 6) had the reputation of being a strong chief and it is therefore impossible to determine without a more intimate knowledge of the case whether his community outlawed and executed the men held responsible for bewitching him, or whether the killings were political murders through which his sons hoped to consolidate the position of their faction after the old man's death. Once a man is either disowned or abandoned by his faction, then he is virtually outlawed. Should there be a serious accusation made against him he can only flee to another community, for a decision to execute him inevitably follows.

4. THE POSITION OF THE CHIEF

Factionalism is a basic fact of Shavante life. It is part of the scheme of things, in terms of which people regulate their behaviour and order their conceptual categories. The factions are in perpetual competition for power and prestige and the ultimate prize of the chieftaincy.

It is hard to say what the powers of a chief are or even to determine who is a chief. Chiefs are not formally installed nor is there any procedure for electing them, appointing them or having them succeed to their office. They have no insignia and few prerogatives which mark them off from their fellows. They are in effect men who exercise leadership and thus lay claim to the status of chief. Not all leaders become chiefs, though, and it sometimes happens that a man will claim to be a chief and have his claim recognized only by part of the community. Where powerful factions are evenly balanced there may be more than one person to whom chieftaincy is ascribed.

Shavante find this quite natural since the chieftaincy is sanctioned by no more than a practical recognition of where power lies. Beyond this there is no independent legitimacy. Shavante recognize that influential men compete for the right to be known as chiefs, so that when one man tries to depose another who is generally considered a chief he does not act counter to their notions of correct behaviour. A chief is recognized as such so long as he is the head of a strong faction. If his faction should no longer be strong enough to maintain him in his position, then Shavante consider that he forfeits his right to the chieftaincy.

A chief is called *hę'a*. This is a referential title by which he is never addressed; nor is he often referred to by it. The term more commonly used in speaking of him and to him is *ĩ-mãmã* (a relationship term which includes such genealogical specifications as father and father's brother). In this context the term has both literal and figurative connotations. Literally he must stand in the relation of *ĩ-mãmã* to a strong lineage in order to aspire to and maintain his position. Figuratively the term expresses the Shavante idea that somehow the chief is *ĩ-mãmã* to the whole community. He looks after its interests, or as they put it 'looks well on it' (*ęmãdę'ę pse-di*).

He is the 'watcher' (*ęmãdę'ę'wa*) *par excellence*, and this quality of his is shared by his most influential aides. These are usually his sons and invariably members of his faction. They too are known as ǫmãdǫ'ǫ'wa, and the Shavante are aware that the word has a double meaning. They are the watchers in that they watch over the community, direct its activities, and exhort its members. They are also the watchers in the sense that they keep an eye on everything that takes place, and not only inform the chief about what happens in the community but effectively police it for him should the need arise.

Such influential members of the dominant faction are referred to as ĩdzu, the only honorific title, apart from hǫ'a, which the Shavante bestow. They are singled out for eminence while their age-set is still in the bachelors' hut. At this stage two of the boys are appointed by the chief to lead the age-set in all its activities. If the chief himself has sons of a suitable age, size, and character among the boys in the bachelors' hut, he will almost certainly nominate them. If not, he will select a pair of likely candidates from among the boys of his own faction. These boys, being immature, do not yet qualify for the status of ĩdzu, nor are they formally appointed to positions of leadership in their own age-set. They are simply called upon by their elders (and many of those who have dealings with the bachelors are themselves ĩdzu) to perform the leading roles whenever the activities of their age-set require it. During the years when the bachelors are secluded in the hǫ these boys are given every opportunity to exercise leadership and this usually comes naturally to them, since they have been brought up as chief's sons or at least as very close kinsmen of the chief. They learn to lead the expeditions which the boys themselves organize, principally hunting, fishing and gathering trips. They lead the file of initiates in the various ceremonies which are performed throughout their years in seclusion. It is they who bear the double-barrelled flutes and the lances, emblems of the hǫ'wa, in the culminating stages of initiation. They are expected to be the fleetest in the ceremonial races, and generally to set an example of physical prowess.

In São Domingos (1958) the leaders of the Tírowa age-set were both sons of Apǫwẽ. One of them, Baarodí, was the largest and most mature of the boys. The other, Bururewa, was certainly the quickest and most aggressive. Finally, the name ʔáhiri'wa was also bestowed on Bururewa, so that he took a prominent part in the terminal initiation ceremonies both in this capacity and as leader of the initiates.

The other boy in the Tírowa age-set to receive the name of Páhiri'wa was the son of Rupawẽ, who is the chief's brother's son. The members of the Atẽpá age-set who received this name at the previous initiation were also, respectively, the son of Apẹwẽ and the son of Rupawẽ. The one surviving Páhiri'wa in the Ai'riri age-set is also the chief's son. We have to go back to the Tẹrã age-set to find a Páhiri'wa who is not one of Apẹwẽ's sons. At that time, when the Tẹrã were being initiated, Apẹwẽ's age-set (Nõdzẹ'u) must have been in the same position in the cycle as that occupied now by the Anõrowa. In other words, Apẹwẽ had just graduated to 'elder' status and was beginning his bid for prestige. By the time of the next initiation he was able to procure the ceremonial preferment of one of his sons, and this pattern has been repeated at each subsequent initiation down to the present day.

The leaders of ceremonial in the 'active' age-sets were thus related to Apẹwẽ in the following manner:

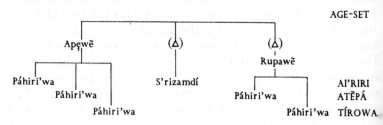

S'rizamdí was the only one who was not Páhiri'wa and who was neither a son of Apẹwẽ nor a son of Rupawẽ. He officiated during the initiation ceremonies in lieu of the second Páhiri'wa in the Ai'riri age-set, who is no longer at São Domingos. He earned this role by sheer force of personality. He regularly took the lead in age-set matters and spoke well in the men's council. At the same time he had a great gift for clowning, which made him as popular with his fellows as any Shavante is likely to be. It was therefore he who used to go each night to the bachelors' hut together with Páhiri'wa (Ai'riri) and blow the double barrelled flutes during the final stages of the initiation ceremonies. It was he who used to summon the Ai'riri to perform their dance in sponsorship of the Tírowa, and it was he who took the lead in the actual singing and dancing. In other words he performed all the general functions of a Páhiri'wa. He did not, however, perform any of the specific rites which only Páhiri'wa are entitled to.

Apęwẽ had thus abrogated to his lineage, and furthermore to two specific families within his lineage, the most important ceremonial office among the Shavante. This office is not, however, coincident with leadership of an age-set and the ascribed status of *ĩdzu*. Although all members of the dominant lineage are sometimes broadly referred to as *ĩdzu*, it is only certain of them who are *ĩdzu* in the technical sense and who will officiate at distributions and at important debates in the men's council. It is these latter who are indicated when the Shavante speak of the 'watchers'. Those of Apęwẽ's sons who are Páhiri'wa are also *ĩdzu* in this sense. The other Páhiri'wa are not.

At the same time there are certain important *ĩdzu* who are not Páhiri'wa. In the Tęrã age-set, Waarodí, the chief's eldest son, is one, and is the most important man in the community after Apęwẽ himself. In the Tírowa age-set there is Baarodí, who qualified for the status as soon as he completed his initiation.

From boyhood (*hę'wa*) the prospective *ĩdzu* are trained to lead their age-mates. Since they are at the same time the chief's closest kin, the chief is able to establish a pattern of authority for himself by seeing to it that his sons are the leaders at every level of the community. His own position is thus the sum total of his sons' statuses in their respective age-sets, and, through these age-sets, in the community at large. He is dependent on them for the maintenance of his prestige, and they derive their statuses in turn from his position as chief. In São Domingos we had a situation as appears on p. 194.

Apęwẽ is regarded among the Shavante as a particularly 'strong' chief. In other words he is at the head of a faction which is numerically strong, undivided, and which infiltrates his community at all levels. Yet his reputation for political murder leads one to suspect that this may not always have been the case. He certainly secured the chieftaincy by being the shrewdest leader of the most ruthless faction in competition for it. Both before and after he had established himself as chief of his group he was responsible for the killing or expulsion of those who stood in his way. He now seeks to ensure the continued dominance of his faction by using the age-set system to train his close kin as leaders in the community. This is the most he can do to guarantee that the succession continues in his patrilineage.

AGE-SET	ĨDZU	CEREMONIAL LEADERS	TOTALS OF MEN
NODZĘ'U ABARI'U S'DARO ANÕROWA	Apęwẽ's sons APĘWẼ	Apęwẽ's BS	7
TĘRÃ	Waarodí		7
AI'RIRI	Páhiri'wa Sibupá	S'rizamdí	16
ATẼPÁ	Páhiri'wa (Wazae)	Páhiri'wa	20
TÍROWA	Páhiri'wa Baarodí	Páhiri'wa	12

The method is, however, peculiarly effective, and it is one of the factors that make for stability in Shavante communities. It would require a man of unusual calibre or a combination of unusual circumstances to break the hold which Apęwẽ's faction has over the community at São Domingos. Apęwẽ is well aware of this, which is why he can afford to ignore the presumptive challenge of such a man as Suwapte. It is Waarodí, his potential successor, who is most concerned over Suwapte's pretensions, and is consequently the latter's bitter enemy.

In 1958 Apęwẽ's faction was in a stronger position than any other among the Downstream Shavante. By 1962 the secession to Ę Tõ had sapped the strength of his community, but there were no strong chiefs elsewhere to take advantage of its weakness. Marãwasede had been in the throes of its own power struggle since 1958 and was anyway fighting for its life against the Brazilians. Ęribiwẽ of Capitariquara had been a strong chief, but had lost his life by putting himself at the mercy of a hostile faction and his community had disintegrated. Tomõtsu had led his people out of Santa Terezinha and joined up with Ts'riñõ'a and his group. In 1962 they were at Areões, nervously waiting for Apęwẽ's attack.

The amalgamation of these factions in a single community

at Areões provides a good opportunity to see how Shavante themselves arrange a village from scratch. It will be remembered that Areões was abandoned in 1959 and its huts had lain empty for three years. When it was reoccupied, the Shavante moved back into the oblong houses which the American missionary had obliged their predecessors to build. They made no alterations beyond knocking loopholes in the walls, for they were preparing for an attack, and adobe huts are more traps than fortresses. Shavante houses are so loosely thatched that defenders can push great swatches of thatch to one side and fire through the apertures.

The missionary had also insisted that the huts at Areões should be built in two close, parallel lines (see Fig. 3). This had effectively distorted the traditional village pattern. In spite of all this, the mental picture of the traditional village remained with its new inhabitants. The man who showed me round referred to household A as the *aamrã* and pointed out that it was occupied by Tomõtsu, chief of the Topdató faction. Household M was also an *aamrã* and the home of Ts'riñõ'a, chief of the Tpereya'óno faction. My informant explained that the two *warã*, meeting places respectively of the Mature and Young Men should have been between the rows of houses, but that there was no room for them there. Similarly the bachelors' hut should have been at one extremity of the village, but that was where the administrative buildings of the Indian agency were located. Finally, the factions had occupied discrete arcs of the village 'crescent'. The powerful Topdató dominated one side of the arc, all houses from A to F. G to J were Ẹ Wawẽ houses and K to M belonged to the Tpereya'óno. Ts'riñõ'a was chief of these two clans, which combined loosely into a single faction. Areões was thus a paradigm of Shavante society, showing the three discrete clans and their arrangement in a dyadic system, complete with twin chiefs.

Among the Western Shavante the chieftaincy is rapidly losing its significance. Sõwa'õ was the chief at Simões Lópes, but he was replaced by his nephew Siriwaruwẽ, who was quicker to learn the ways of the white man. At the time of my visit the men's council rarely met and Siriwaruwẽ's role was more that of the steward of the Indian Protection Service post. Yet even at Simões Lópes Siriwaruwẽ's faction had consolidated itself in one segment of the village (houses A, B, C, and D) and occupied both the *aamrã*.

In São Marcos the process of dissolution of the chieftaincy was not quite so far advanced. There the chiefs were weakened for a different reason. There were too many of them. The comparative cessation of feuding as a result of involvement with the mission made it difficult for any chief to assert himself. The powerful A'e (TP) faction was led by Apęwẽ,[1] who bestirred himself from a most unchiefly indolence only to play football, which he did with passionate enthusiasm. Sibupá,[1] the chief of the Uhę (EW), was more like the old-style *hę'a*. Two influential newcomers, Sebastião of the Wamãrĩdzu (TP), and S'riwanoõwẽ of the Wamãrĩdzu (EW), were sometimes referred to as chiefs, since they had been redoubtable warriors in their time and still commanded their factions. There was even a fifth 'chief', a young man by the name of Piu, whose father had once been chief over the entire community. Piu was being groomed by the Fathers in the hope that he would one day be a link between the village and the mission.

The men's council still met irregularly in São Marcos and would occasionally even decide cases. It was indicative of Piu's status that he had little influence in that assembly and would not even be among the first to speak. Nevertheless, as the life of the village became increasingly integrated with the activities of the mission, the various 'chiefs' were coming to serve as orderlies, who received instructions and then arranged for them to be carried out by their people.

In São Domingos this representative function of the chief was minimal in 1958 and not substantially modified even in 1962 since the policy of the post was to interfere as little as possible with the Indians. On the other hand, a Shavante chief did not have to represent his community in its relations with other Shavante villages. There was no tribal council and no inter community consultation, so that chiefs would not normally meet each other. On the contrary they went out of their way to avoid each other. Alien communities could be dangerous places for them, as the story of Ęribiwẽ's murder proves.

A chief thus discharges the duties of his office solely within his own community where he is, by definition, the leader of

[1] Not to be confused with his namesake in São Domingos.

dominant faction. But his powers are surprisingly limited in view of the manner in which he attains and safeguards his position. In fact it is somewhat misleading to speak of the powers of the chieftaincy, even though I have for convenience described the office in terms of the Shavante recognition of where power lies. A chief, even a strong one like Apẽwẽ, cannot give orders in the sense that he may tell others what to do in the knowledge that they will be penalized for that specific infraction if they do not obey him. He has at his disposal only one ultimate sanction: the mobilization of his faction to coerce those who oppose him. Paradoxically, he cannot normally apply this sanction without the consent of virtually the whole community. If he did it would provoke a schism within his group and result in the expulsion or annihilation of his opponents, which would threaten the stability and numerical strength of his community. This in its turn would undermine the very basis of the dominance of his faction and consequently his own position as chief. Such measures can therefore be resorted to only in desperation or as a calculated gamble, aiming to establish the dominant faction at one blow in an impregnable position and hoping at the same time that the consequences will not break up the community itself. Apẽwẽ's purge of the Ẽ Wawẽ clan was a move of the latter type. The community survived it and his faction emerged stronger than ever. It is easy to appreciate the reasons which led him to take such a step, if we consider how much more dangerous a challenger a man like Suwapte would be today to the position of Apẽwẽ and his faction, had a large number of his clansmen not been eliminated from the community in one way or another.

When Shavante think of the powers of a chief, they think of the power of his faction; and their thinking about the relations between factions bears an intriguing resemblance to our own thinking about the relations between Great Powers. A dominant faction has at its disposal a 'massive deterrent', which is tantamount to making war on the rest of the community and can rarely be used. Much more important in every day situations, although overshadowed by the other in any general appreciation of a particular case, is the 'limited deterrent'. This is the ability of the dominant faction to use its prestige and its skilled speakers to have its enemies excommunicated should they for one moment forfeit the support of a sufficiently large group in the men's council.

The chief therefore influences public opinion far more than he issues orders. It is thus particularly important to distinguish between his power and his ability to influence others, which I call prestige. A man cannot aspire to the chieftaincy unless he has prestige and once he has achieved that status he can only function as a chief through the exercise of prestige. The reservoir of power which is his in his faction is the necessary condition of his becoming a chief but it is not a sufficient condition for him to be able to function effectively in the role. The strongest chiefs are not called upon to use their power just as the safest banks are not called upon to use their reserves.[1]

Prestige may be acquired in various ways. I have already shown how Apęwě selected his kinsmen for positions of leadership at an early age and in effect groomed them for prominence in the community. Men like Waarodí and Sibupá were *ĩ-dzu* because they were influential members of the dominant faction at São Domingos and as such they had prestige and could exercise its concomitant, influence. Yet there is nothing automatic in this process. If a strong chief patronised an *ĩ-dzu* who showed himself to be a poor athlete or, worse still, hesitant and a weak orator, the man's prestige would be negligible. The chief's patronage and the ascriptive title of *ĩ-dzu* represent a guarantee of prestige only if the client can display the necessary qualities.

These qualities are self-assertiveness, oratorical skill, athletic prowess and ceremonial expertise. The last named is the least important and in the unlikely event that it were developed by an individual who did not possess the others it would not gain him significant distinction. The other qualities usually go together too. A man is unlikely to be a good orator unless he is assertive and unlikely to be either unless he is (or has been) a good runner and hunter. A paragon of Shavante virtues would be a man who was fleet and a good hunter, who sang and danced well and who took the lead in communal activities by making impressive admonitory or hortatory speeches. But even a combination of all these qualities would not secure for him the title of *ĩ-dzu* if he did not belong to a chief's faction. He would

---

[1] I borrow this analogy from Parsons (1963).

certainly have prestige among his fellows but only the combination of prestige and political influence through a strong faction would earn him *ĩ-dzu* status. The most he could hope for would be to manoeuvre politically until his faction became strong enough for him to aspire to a chieftaincy or to the status of *ĩ-dzu* close to a chief.

Once a man has become chief (*hę'a*) he can make use not only of his prestige but of the coercive power of his faction. This may be very slight as at São Marcos where a number of factions are evenly balanced. Even when it is considerable, as at São Domingos, it cannot be used except as a last resort. In day to day matters then the chief must rely on his prestige to influence the community.

He does this primarily in the men's council where he is a principal speaker and which only a chief is privileged to address on his own. He brings up whichever matters he feels ought to be discussed and his views on them, phrased eloquently and forcibly, are those which the assembly hears first. They are not obliged to accept these views and they may and do argue with him and reject his suggestions.

Thus the men's council often overrules the chief on comparatively trivial matters. Over an important issue, however, he would be supported by the speakers of his faction and virtually certain to get his way in the end, unless the decision involved taking action against some segment of the community. Their representatives in the council would not, for obvious reasons, acquiesce in this, which would mean that the matter would have to be allowed to drop or the chief would have to resort to other means to gain his ends.

In practice, such an issue would not be raised at all in the men's council unless the chief were sure of getting sufficient support for his proposal that the community as a whole should act against the person or persons concerned. Otherwise the matter would be debated in the factional meetings in the chief's household.

But the majority of issues are not matters of life or death, such as murder or sorcery, the penalty for which is expulsion or execution. The chief spends most of his time making minor decisions on the basis of the discussions in council, and these the men of the community are only too happy to delegate to him.

He suggests when the group should move and where to. His suggestion is thoroughly discussed by the others and then he sums up the discussion and announces his decision. He makes ceremonial arrangements in the same way, first outlining how he feels about them, then listening to the comments of the others, and finally announcing what will be done. Nor is the listening to the general opinion a mere formality. Apęwẽ invariably modified his original suggestions if there seemed to be a majority in favour of the alteration. On other occasions, for example when he was directing ceremonial and there was no time for consultation with the mature men before he issued his instructions, he was sometimes shouted down if one of his 'orders' did not meet with the general approval.

One day, when the men were working on the preparation of their dance-masks for the initiation ceremonies, Apęwẽ announced that they should all return to the village and come back again in the evening. His remark was greeted by a shout of 'No, tomorrow!' and he hastily rephrased his instructions, saying 'We will all go back to the village now and return to the *marã* tomorrow'. On another occasion he directed two boys to join one of the files of initiates which was in procession round the village prior to one of the initiation runs. The boys set off accompanied by two others who were little more than toddlers and had been got up in their ceremonial paint for the occasion by their maternal uncles. Apęwẽ shouted after them 'No, no, only two!', whereupon there was a chorus of 'No! Go on! All four!' from the men sitting with the chief; and the children, after some hesitation, finally obeyed the crowd rather than Apęwẽ. Such instances could be endlessly multiplied.

In every-day affairs the chief is expected to suggest what should be done next. If the suggestion is acceptable, the men will pass it on to the rest of the village. If it is not, they will say so and the chief usually makes a fresh suggestion, incorporating the views which have been put forward. Even the final summing up, authorized by the men's council, is little more than a sanctioned suggestion. Men and women will comply with it if it suits them and ignore it if it does not.

Frequently, when the men got up from their evening council, dusted off their deerskins, and shouted their instructions about the morrow's activities for the whole village to hear, th

PLATE X

b. Apęwě at dawn holding court

a. Apęwě the Chief of São Domingos annointing boys before a ceremony

would provoke a bedlam of expostulation and dissent from the women. On one occasion they even postponed a ceremonial log-race they had intended to hold the following day because the women objected so violently.

Normally the chief, so far from acting simply as the leader of a dominant faction which can impose its wishes by force, functions as a focus for the entire community. He is its mouth-piece, and he tries, in his summings-up in the men's council, to put the general consensus of opinion rather than the views of any particular group. He is the representative of the community. Although he does not need to represent it before outsiders, he does so before its own members. To them he is the unique symbol of the integrity of the community over against other communities. It is for this reason that his most important ceremonial functions are those in which he acts as the embodi-ment of his community as opposed to its constituent factions.

He directs a communal hunt which is a community enter-prise. He directs the clearing, planting and harvesting for the same reason. All the elders advise him on the details of any ceremony he has to perform, even while he is actually perform-ing it. They tell him to do it this way, not that way, and order him hither and thither. He does as they say. Clearly, then, he does not officiate at these ceremonies because he is in a position of authority. Nor does he do so because he is better versed in the details of the ceremonial than any other person. In São Domin-gos, elders would sometimes demonstrate for Apẽwẽ what he had to do before he did it. Nevertheless it is the chief, sometimes assisted by another elder, who performs ceremonial acts such as the placing of head circlets on the initiates and taking them back again, because it is only he who can act on behalf of the com-munity as a whole. Where there is no single paramount chief, such ceremonial acts are performed by the senior chief of the village. He is the man who is tacitly accepted as being head of the strongest faction, even though that faction has not the power to establish itself in unchallenged dominance.

Nowhere is this characteristic of his office brought out more clearly than when he officiates at a ceremonial food distribution. Shavante usually take large kills to their own households, where first claim on the meat is the prerogative of the co-resident families. Hunks are meanwhile dispatched to relatives who are mother's brother or sister's child to both the killer and his wife and to the killer's parents' household. After these shares have been distributed, the killer has no further specific obligations towards his relatives. Nevertheless he may not decently refuse them if they ask for some of the meat, and they invariably come flocking, or at least send their children over, when they see a successful hunter returning. Shavante are therefore accustomed to making a lightning distribution of their spoils among the members of their household and their close kin, so that when others come to ask for some they can be told that it is all gone, or at the most given a nominal share. In addition to this they are passionately interested in meat and display a fervour in its acquisition which has to be seen to be believed. Thus any large-scale food distribution soon develops into a brawl, which may or may not be good-natured. Whenever the Indian Agent at São Domingos provided a steer for the whole community it was cut up by the older men. One haunch was given to the young men's age-grade, and then three or four of the elders would stand over the remaining portions, hacking off bits and distributing them as best they could, while the women and children scrambled all round them and even in between their legs.

The chief and the *ĩdzu* did not act as official distributors on such occasions because they were informal. Men who were *ĩdzu* often took a leading part in the killing and quartering of the animal, but they did so simply because they too wanted to be as near as possible to the source of supply, and their prestige enabled them to get closer than most. Once they were in the thick of things, however, they acted for themselves and for their closest kin. If such a man could get away with it, he would grab the whole liver and have his womenfolk scramble off with it. Another would try to get as much of the filet as possible, and so on until the animal was virtually torn apart. The chief's household thus invariably came off best; and, though care was taken that every household got some, and every child received at least a handful of meat or hide, the difference in the shares was such that some households would have meat sufficient for one or two days longer than others' portions would provide for.

Ceremonial distributions are quite different. The game is brought and placed at the feet of the chief, who stands leaning on a bow, as Shavante always do when they are at their most formal. When all the game is laid out the *ĩdzu* take up their stance in a half circle on either side of the chief. Each of them leans on a bow or club. The chief then directs the cutting up of the meat. This may be done by the *ĩdzu* themselves or by other men, but they do it according to the specifications of the chief, and with much less chatter than is usual on occasions of this kind. Finally, the game is divided into piles. This is also directed by the chief and is done as equitably as possible. It is important the piles should contain approximately equivalent amounts of meat, but no distinction is made between the various cuts. Neither the chief nor anybody else has the right to particular portions. When the division has been made, onlookers often suggest that such and such a pile is too small. The chief then holds a public consultation after the style of the discussions in the men's council, until it is decided if the pile really is too small for the number of people in the household for which it is destined and, if so, from which pile it should be augmented. He then directs one of his aides to transfer meat from one pile to another and this is done without any remonstration from those who stand to lose. Even his own pile is not inviolate and may be diminished in favour of another's. The representatives of the various households are then called forward and they bear away the spoils under his eye. I have never seen a ceremonial meat distribution presided over by more than a single chief, but Shavante told me that if a number of chiefs were present the procedure would remain the same. All chiefs would adopt the ceremonial stance flanked by their *ĩ-dzu*. The game would be placed in a pile between them and they would all direct its division as equitably as possible, taking into account the comments and protests of the spectators.

At a ceremonial distribution the chief therefore acts as the Shavante believe he should act—in the role of arbiter, with the impartiality which this implies. Such impartiality is, in Shavante eyes, the characteristic of a good chief. Although it is only formally required on specific ceremonial occasions, ideally a chief should practise it at all times. He is required, in his capacity as chief, to show tolerance and wisdom, to act as peacemaker and to drown discord in a flood of oratory. He should speak well, i.e., give good advice, which means advice to which people will listen. Otherwise the community runs the risk of being riven by factionalism. Shavante speak of such communities as those where men do not listen to the chief (ĩ-mãmã te-wapari õdi), and hold them in low esteem on account of their lawlessness.

A chief is therefore in a difficult position. The qualities ideally required of him and the behaviour expected of him while he is in office are diametrically opposed to those of which he had to make use when he aspired to the chieftaincy. Indeed, in a community where the dominant faction is not firmly established, they are opposed to the talents he must display in order to maintain himself in office at all. This accounts for the dual image of particular chiefs that we noted earlier. It also explains why chiefs tend to veer from one type of behaviour to its opposite. Sometimes they handle seemingly intractable situations with great patience and forensic skill. At others they deal summarily and ruthlessly with only incipient opposition.

5. INTER-COMMUNITY RELATIONS

The local factionalism of a Shavante community is inextricably linked with a broader system of alliances and enmities which pervades Shavante society. Shavante have kin in other communities and they know that they have potential kin (*waniwihã*) even in villages where they might not know a single person. This is an extremely important factor in their thinking. They feel that these other communities, however distant, are part of their social system. They not only speak the same language and share the same institutions, but they subscribe to the same set of ideas about the balance of power within the community and the possibility of secession from it. It is not even necessary to know where these other communities are. Many Shavante had only the haziest idea as to the numbers of their own people or the territory they occupied. They cross-questioned me about Shavante villages I might have visited far away, perhaps even in my own country, although they knew that that was across the water. They felt that what happened in other Shavante communities, however remote, potentially affected them, especially since they might wish to transfer to them at any time.

It did not greatly matter how much contact there was between the various villages, but it was very important to them that there might be coming and going between them. They regarded their villages as temporary aggregates which could at any time undergo changes in membership, perhaps even radical changes such as would alter the balance of power within them.

We have seen how the dominant faction in any community realizes that the minor lineages may and will secede if their rights are too grossly infringed. On the other hand, the dominant lineage must be perpetually on its guard to ensure that no minor lineage becomes strong enough, either of itself or at the head of a faction, to challenge the dominant group and wrest the chieftaincy from it. Correspondingly, every community automatically grants asylum to refugees or seceders from other groups.

This right of asylum is essential to the functioning of the political system. No matter how unwelcome individuals or groups may be to the dominant lineage, if they come seeking permission to take up residence in the community such permission is always granted. It is not granted because the Shavante feel that strangers have any morally or supernaturally sanctioned right to asylum, but as a matter of simple reciprocity. Refugees are granted asylum in order that those who grant it may also have the possibility of obtaining it in an emergency.

Such newcomers suffer no disabilities through being recent arrivals. They are accepted into the community on equal terms with the other members of their clan or faction. They may immediately side against the dominant group in the community which has adopted them. Equally they may be threatened with death, or flee to escape it, at the hands of the dominant group, only a comparatively short time after they have been accepted into the community. Shavante regard these vicissitudes as the normal hazards of life.

The position of alien lineages in each community is accordingly more important than it might have seemed from our analysis of intra-community relations above. The ambivalence of Shavante attitudes to outsiders was constantly brought home to me in São Domingos. Relations between this community and its neighbours, Marãwasede to the north and Santa Terezinha to the south, were bad. Consequently, whenever newcomers were seen arriving from either direction there was always much excitement, and the young men would invariably suggest that they should go out and kill the visitors. Equally invariably the newcomers were formally received and, if they had come to stay, were permitted to settle in São Domingos.

The reception given to one particular refugee from Marãwasede is typical of such arrivals.

In mid July 1958 I happened to be at the Indian Post on the banks of the Rio das Mortes when a Shavante man appeared on the far side and called across. I took him to be a man from our own village. I could not recognize him at that distance nor, as we shouted to each other, could I recognize his voice. He was obviously surprised to be answered in *a'wẽ* by a white man, but was too flustered at the time to ask questions. Instead he shouted urgently that we were to bring a canoe to fetch him quickly. When Shavante halloo to each other in this way their voices run up the scale to a high falsetto which carries far; they also mark the end of each phrase by dropping the voice on the final syllable to a normal, or sometimes unnaturally deep, note.

This man's voice cracked on the high notes and he could not manage the stops at all. I realized that he was both out of breath and frightened.

I persuaded the only Shavante who was at the Post with me to paddle the canoe across and meet the newcomer. After what seemed an interminable wait, for the single paddler made poor headway across the strong current, the canoe reached the other bank, and the boatman discovered that the new arrival was a member of his own lineage and a classificatory brother. He therefore invited him into the canoe and wept over him. The lamentations lasted for some minutes before the canoe was brought back to the near side again.

By this time other Shavante men had hastened up from the village. The newcomer was taken in charge by members of his own lineage, which happened to be the locally dominant Wamãrĩ, and the men walked in silence and in single file back to the village and over to the hut of the chief's eldest son, since the chief himself was away.

The visitor lay down on a sleeping mat and his lineage brothers and sisters sat on either side of him and wailed for about ten minutes until the tears dripped onto their chests and the mucus hung in strings from their nostrils.[1] When the weeping was over the wailers cleaned their faces with blades of grass and the men lay down beside their visitor. For some time nobody spoke. Finally Waarodí, the chief's eldest son, began speaking in a scarcely audible voice, using the formal manner. Not until Waarodí had finished addressing the visitor, asking him his reasons for coming and inviting him to tell all his news, did the latter begin to tell his story, also in the same formal style.

He explained that the people of Marãwasede were incensed with him; that he had run away in order to avoid being killed; that they had pursued him for more than a day along the trails; that they had fired arrows at him as he ran (he was nicked on

[1] This ceremonial weeping, or *Tränengruss*, as the German ethnographers called it, is very common not only in South America but also in other parts of the world (see, e.g. Friederici, 1906; Lehmann-Nitsche, 1936). Among the Shavante it is a *rite de passage*. In the case of a returning traveller it is a rite by which he is deprived of his status as a stranger and acquires a position as a member of the group. See Chapter VII for a discussion of this rite.

the shoulder and in the leg); and that he had finally out-distanced his pursuers and come to São Domingos without once sleeping by the way, and eating only what he could gather as he fled.

My knowledge of Shavante and the relations between São Domingos and Marãwasede[1] was not sufficient to enable me to follow the details of his speech, especially when it was delivered in this style. In any case the reasons he gave for his flight, which were heatedly discussed the same night when he had to report to the men's council, were only the efficient cause of his parti-cular desertion. During the discussion in council it was re-peatedly emphasized that the Shavante of Marãwasede were wicked and that they were killing many people (i.e., kinsmen of those present), so that, whatever the particular reasons for the expulsion of individuals from that community may have been, the general cause of the desertions of these men from Marã-wasede was that they were being squeezed out as a faction.

Páhiri'wa, the new arrival, told the men's council that all Apçwẽ's brothers were being killed in Marãwasede. It seems that the death of the chief of Marãwasede, a certain S'rizamdí, was the occasion of a struggle for power between lineages related to the Wamãrĩ, on the one hand, and the dominant lineage, who were probably Topdató clansmen, on the other. As a result a number of people had been killed and others had fled to São Domingos. Suwaiwe's father had been held respon-sible for the death of the chief because he was thought to have an interest in it, and was killed. Suwaiwe and his younger brother Buruwẽ therefore fled to São Domingos. Rintimpse was forced to flee as a result of the same disputes, followed by Probuwairõ and Wahipo. Páhiri'wa was thus the most recent arrival of a series.

These individual defections, as the result of a particular factional dispute, differ from the secession of a minor lineage or a section of it, such as had taken place previously when Suwapte and the other members of the Uhç left Marãwasede and came to São Domingos. As far as I could gather they were

---

[1] Shavante speakers and Shavante speech in general leaves a great deal understood. Verbs frequently occur without subjects; sometimes they are used in the active without objects because the listeners are able to follow from the context. Clearly this puts the anthropologist, whose contextual knowledge is always imperfect, at a serious disadvantage.

not chased out, but simply chose to transfer to another community, where Suwapte married the chief's widowed daughter. The other men were given much younger wives.

The recent history of the Downstream Shavante groups[1] shows even more clearly how fluctuations in community membership occur. Some of these details were given in Chapter I, but we are now in a better position to understand their significance.

About the time when Ẽribiwẽ's people made friendly contact with the Brazilians they were joined by Sebastião and his faction, who had come from the Upstream Region. Sebastião had had to leave in a hurry, for he had killed the chief of his village. The chief was the brother of Apẽwẽ, now chief of São Marcos, and father of Piu. He was also a fellow clansman of Sebastião, though of a different lineage. Sebastião's people accompanied Ẽribiwẽ to Capitariquara and remained there until Ẽribiwẽ was killed and the post itself destroyed.

The killing of Ẽribiwẽ, which touched off a series of battles among the Downstream Shavante, came as the result of a journey which this flamboyant chief made to Xavantina, together with an employee of the Indian Protection Service. It is important to know the unusual circumstances of the trip in order to understand what prompted Ẽribiwẽ, one of the shrewdest of the Shavante chiefs, to act as injudiciously as he did.

He apparently forced his company on the man from the Indian Protection Service in the hope that he could persuade him to buy him some 'balas' (literally 'bullets'), i.e., ammunition for his .22 rifle. This is extremely expensive in Central Brazil and beyond the means of most backwoodsmen. It was therefore especially prized as a gift by those Shavante who owned guns. Finally the Brazilian, wearying of Ẽribiwẽ's importunity, wilfully misunderstood him and promised him the 'balas', a word which also means 'sweets'. When Ẽribiwẽ was given a bag of sweets instead of the ammunition he was expecting, he flew into a rage and determined to get his own back not only on the man who had tricked him but on the Indian Service in general, which could no longer provide his people with the things they wanted.

In this frame of mind he made the otherwise inexplicable

[1] See Table 14.

decision to visit Areões and invite its inhabitants to join forces
with his own people in an attack on the Indian Protection
Service post at Capitariquara. Now the Areões Shavante had
previously seceded from his own village and presumably were
not allies of his. In any case, it was most unusual for a chief to
visit another community with the intention of haranguing it in
council.

His initiative was not well received by the chief of Areões,
who sensed a threat to his own authority. The discussion was
therefore going against Ẽribiwẽ when a number of recent
refugees from Capitariquara got up to say that he was responsible for the death of many of their kinsmen, that he was an evil
and scheming man, and that, so far from trusting to his leadership, they should kill him at once. These speakers won their
motion, and Ẽribiwẽ was killed.

Now the Areões Shavante realized there would be trouble
from Capitariquara. Some of them therefore set off to inform
their kinsmen in that community about the killing. The messen-
gers went to Capitariquara, ostensibly on a friendly visit, and
warned their kin to flee as inconspicuously as possible. They
did; but the dominant faction got wind of what had happened,
set out in pursuit, caught them up on the trail, and killed some
of the fugitives.

Now it was the turn of Areões to be incensed. Some days
later they sent a war party against Capitariquara, attacked the
village, and killed three people. A few months later Capitariquara attacked Areões.

As a result of these skirmishes the mission at Areões was
obliged to close down and the villagers eventually moved to
Santa Terezinha. Since the Santa Terezinha people were on bad
terms with Capitariquara they were natural allies. Together
they attacked Capitariquara once again, and precipitated the
dissolution of that community.

From Capitariquara Sebastião's faction moved to São
Domingos. The São Domingos Shavante feared the Santa Terezinha people as sorcerers, and had almost attacked them in
1957. Now in 1960 they joined forces with Sebastião and
planned in earnest to attack Santa Terezinha.

The attackers painted themselves for war and attacked at
dawn. They converged on the mission and the village from

three sides, and approached so silently that even the dogs did not bark. They took Santa Terezinha completely by surprise. One defender was killed at the moment of the attack when he came out to see what was happening. The rest dived into their huts or plunged into the river which was barring their egress on the fourth side. The attackers now controlled the village. Some of them lined the river bank and fired at those in the water, while others made preparations for flushing their enemies out of their huts.

Through the early morning there was parleying and desultory firing of arrows. The attackers' kin in Santa Terezinha acted as intermediaries between the contending parties and tried to make peace between them. Finally the missionaries covered the retreat of the Santa Terezinha chief and his faction into the mission buildings. They then offered presents to the attackers and managed to persuade them to return home.

But this was not the end of the story. Sebastião soon fell out with Apęwẽ in São Domingos and therefore took his faction off on trek to the south-west. There his men were surprised one day by their enemies from Santa Terezinha. They were apparently dividing their game, a task which generally engrosses Shavante to the exclusion of all else, and eight of them were killed before they could extricate themselves. The remainder fled to Xavantina. The whole Downstream Region was now dangerous for Sebastião's faction. Furthermore, they were cornered in Xavantina when the news reached them that the Santa Terezinha/Areões group was moving westward towards them. Sebastião therefore sent emissaries to São Marcos to ask if he could take refuge there, in the community whose chief he had murdered nearly a decade previously. It is indicative of how crucial the right of sanctuary is among the Shavante that this request was granted. Sebastião was, however, taking no chances. He took his people to São Marcos, but, in spite of the missionaries' guarantees that nobody would harm him, he was being exceedingly cautious in his dealings with Apęwẽ's faction.

There is thus an intimate connexion between inter-lineage or factional relations and inter-community relations. Shavante tend to identify communities with their dominant factions, but this is merely a manner of speaking. More commonly the relations between communities are not so clearly defined. It may happen that at a certain time a whole community comes to identify itself with its dominant lineage as against another community, but it is more usual for the relation between communities to be complicated by inter-lineage hostilities. For instance the dominant lineage in São Domingos (Wamãrĩ) regarded the dominant lineage in Capitariquara (Hu) as wicked and dangerous. Yet there is no doubt that Capitariquara was the place of refuge which most 'outsiders' (particularly Ę Wawẽ) from São Domingos chose when things went wrong for them. Again it was a group from Capitariquara that came and allied itself with São Domingos against Santa Terezinha, but not the same group as had previously been chased out of São Domingos when Apęwẽ purged the Dzutsi lineage.

When trouble was brewing between Areões and Capitariquara, the dominant faction at Areões tried to extricate its kin from what was to be an enemy village. Open warfare between the two communities really started only after the resident minor lineages had been to some extent purged. Once this war had started it could not easily be stopped. The Shavante have no customary manner of bringing such hostilities to an end. It is usually the minority groups in each community that take the lead in calming the bellicosity of the majority, so that peaceful relations may be re-established with their neighbours. Once this possibility has been removed, then there is likely to be perpetual warfare between villages until such time as internal frictions result once again in secessions and a re-ordering of the village compositions. So the war between Areões and Capitariquara (and their respective allies at one time or another) has continued for about five years. Yet the hostilities between São Domingos and Santa Terezinha were short-lived because each community contained sympathizers with the 'enemy', who did what they could to bring the fighting to a halt.

The presence of these refugees and stranger lineages in each community thus has a double aspect. They threaten the position of the dominant faction, and they may create bad blood between their community of adoption and their community of origin by speaking out against the village that has ejected them. Alternatively, they may have ties with factions in other communities which lead them to use their influence to prevent open warfare. The Shavante political system depends, therefore, on a delicate balance of power and of interests. An able man may be capable of upsetting this balance to his own advantage and of maintaining the *status quo* once he has done so. It is this desire to obtain followers and prestige, and at the same time to avoid being manoeuvred into a minority position, where even the ablest man is vulnerable to his enemies, that makes Shavante such gifted and constant intriguers. Shavante factionalism can thus be seen as a competition for leadership, with the position of *hę'a* as the prize. It is a competition in which all adult men are involved whether they like it or not, although some choose to play the game in earnest, while others allow themselves to be used by the players; and the stakes are very high indeed.

VI

THE RELATIONSHIP SYSTEM

1. TERMINOLOGY

THE Shavante could be said to have a Dakota-type relationship terminology,[1] in that it classes siblings and parallel cousins together and places all cross-cousins in a single category. I do not find such a label particularly useful, however. It is all very well to classify terminologies according to cousin terms if one wants to know something about cousin terms, but one should not make the mistake of assuming that such a classification will tell us much about terminologies. It has sometimes been thought that cousin terms are a crucial area of relationship terminologies and that other areas will vary concomitantly with them. But the assumption has remained undemonstrated, and I would certainly challenge it.

In any case I would argue that a useful typology of relationship terminologies would have to be based on the characteristics of terminologies as systems, not on one particular and supposedly diagnostic feature of them. Such a typology would be difficult to construct, for, in spite of all the talk about the advances made in the field of 'kinship', there are relatively few systematic studies of terminologies in the anthropological literature. All too often it is not clear from an ethnographic report what the principles of the relationship terminology are.

Perhaps the convention which has done most to obfuscate the understanding of relationship systems is that they should be set out as a list of native terms, each one matched to a number of genealogical specifications. It is a curious fact that anthropologists, who as a class make valiant, if spasmodic, attempts to understand the conceptual categories of the peoples they study, still cling to genealogies like a talisman. It was understandable that Rivers should have worked from genealogies in the Torres Straits. His training was in psychology and he had to invent his

[1] See Murdock, 1949: 125, 236.

field methods as he went along. But his papers on the 'genealogical method' (1900, 1910, 1912), which was little more than a
data-collecting rule of thumb, are to this day handed to
prospective anthropologists by their seniors to show them how to
set about the study of 'kinship'. So in study after study we are
told that some term (x) 'means', let us say, F, FB, FFBS,
FFFBSS.[1] If the ethnographer's information is full enough and
he gives us enough genealogical examples for the other terms,
we may then deduce that the term (x) refers to any male in Ego's
patriclan in the first ascending generation. But this information
should have been provided by the ethnographer in the first
place. An adequate description of a relationship terminology is
one which explains the rules according to which the categories
are ordered. The rule may be that each and every genealogical
specification on an Ego-centred kinship chart is in a separate
category; but even in this limiting (and to my knowledge non-
existent) case it is the *rule* which must be made clear, not the
fact that each term can be translated by a genealogical position,
which is simply a consequence of the rule. Concentration on the
rules (or principles) governing a terminology and less emphasis
on typical examples, which is what genealogical listings usually
are, would certainly improve the general standard of field
reports. It would render unnecessary the elaborate efforts which
'kinship' experts have to make to analyse other people's data
on relationship terminology, and might lead to the foundation
of a properly rigorous comparative study in this branch of
anthropology.

I shall therefore begin my analysis of Shavante terminology
by trying to set out the rules governing the distinctions between
their categories. These rules are fairly simple and they are
consonant with the social distinctions which I have discussed
in previous chapters. The fundamental discriminations in
Shavante relationship terminology are those which I have set
out in Table 15. In order to demonstrate them I have used a
binary matrix. This follows from the radical distinction which
Shavante make between *waniwihã* and *wasi're'wa*, a distinction
which is expressed in their relationship categories. The

---

[1] I use the convention whereby genealogical positions are rendered by
the first letter of each of their components, with the exception of Z = sister
to distinguish it from S = son. C = child (not cousin, which is a category).

Shavante therefore have a terminology which could be classed as a 'two-section system'.

The discussion of societies with what has been known variously as *dual organization, tweedelingen, Zweiklassensystem,* etc., has a long history. It was, I believe, Needham who introduced the term *two-section system*[1] to refer specifically to a system of relationship terminology organized in a binary matrix. The term does not refer, as previous concepts did, to the total social organization of a given people, but only to the structure of the relationship system. This point was brought out clearly by Dumont in his studies of South India (1953, 1957a, and 1957b) when he showed that what he called the Dravidian kinship terminology was a two-section system which could be used as a matrix for varying institutional arrangements.

The Shavante system bears a strong resemblance to Dumont's Dravidian systems, but there are also some notable differences, particularly in the 'affinal' section. In Table 15 I have included certain relationship terms in the matrix and listed others underneath. The terms in the matrix are only those which are in some way defined by it. For example, any female who is *waniwihã* to Ego and in the first ascending generation can be addressed as *ĩ-tebe*. The terms which I have listed below the matrix are those which denote sub-categories or single genealogical positions. I have throughout listed terms of address as used by a male Ego.[2] Their connotations are as follows:

1   *ĩ-rdá:* Any person who is in Ego's grandparents' generation or over.

2   *ĩ-nihúdu:* Any person in the second descending generation or below.

Waniwihã

3   *ĩ-tebe:* Any female in the first ascending generation who i. *waniwihã* to Ego.

4   *ĩ-mãmã:* Any male in the first ascending generation who i. *waniwihã* to Ego.

---

[1] See Needham, 1958: 210, 1960a: 23.

[2] There are very slight differences in the terminology used by a female speaker and the principles which govern it are virtually identical with those of the male terminology. I therefore give the female terms in Appendix rather than discuss them repetitiously in the text.

5 *ĩ-dúmrada:* Any person older than Ego who is in the same generation and *waniwihã* to Ego.

6 *ĩ-nõ:* Any person younger than Ego who is in the same generation and *waniwihã* to Ego.

7 *ĩ-'ra:* Any person in the first descending generation who is *waniwihã* to Ego.

8 *aibĩ:* Any male in the first descending generation who is *waniwihã* to Ego, with the exception of Ego's son.

9 *otí:* Any female in the first descending generation who is *waniwihã* to Ego, with the exception of Ego's daughter.

10 *ĩ-namté:* MZH.

11 *ĩ-pnẽ:* Any male who is a member of a lineage related to Ego's.

12 *pi'õĩtí:* Any female who is a member of a lineage related to Ego's.

Wasi're'wa

13 *wasiní:* Any person who is *wasi're'wa* to Ego.

14 *simẽnẽ:* Any person who is *wasi're'wa* to Ego.

15 *'rebzu:* Any person who is *wasi're'wa* to Ego.

16 *ĩ-nã:* Any female in the first ascending generation who is in Ego's mother's lineage.

17 *ĩ-datiẽ:* M.

18 *'rebzu'wa:* Any male in the first ascending generation who is in Ego's mother's lineage. Also MBW.

19 *ĩ-mãwapté:* MB.

20 *ĩ-'ra'wapté:* ZC when it is small.

21 *asimhí:* Any woman who has married a man in Ego's lineage, unless she is *ĩ-nã* to Ego.

22 *ĩ-za'mũ:* Any man who has married a woman of Ego's lineage.

23 *ĩ-mrõ:* wife.

24 *ĩ-mãpari'wa:* wife's parent.

25 *saihí:* WZ.

26 *ĩ-ãri:* WB.

The application of these terms serves as an excellent guide to those discriminations which Shavante find crucial when classifying members of their own society. In theory any Shavante could address every other Shavante by a relationship term. He only needs to know whether his interlocutor is *waniwihã* or *wasi're'wa*, and he can immediately place him in some sort of category. Note that there are more categorical distinctions on the *waniwihã* side, where a man will presumably have a clearer idea of people's relative ages and generational status, than in the *wasi're'wa*, where a term such as *wasiní* or *simẽnẽ* serves for all purposes. But we have already seen that it is not as easy as might be supposed for somebody to know whether others are *waniwihã* or *wasi're'wa*. If the speaker has always lived in the same community he will simply have grown up with this distinction and will know automatically how other people stand. If he moves to a strange community, then he must learn how to classify its inhabitants. His own clan affiliation and lineage membership will guide him in this, but they will not automatically determine it. It is the factional alignments that will, and I shall describe below how he learns to fit himself into them. For the moment it should be noted that, whereas every Shavante may theoretically address every other Shavante by a relationship term, he does not normally need to do so. The average person has everyday dealings with only a part of the village. It therefore causes no great difficulty for a new arrival if he does not know the proper terms for certain people, because they will in any case be the people he least needs to know them for.

In theory he could and should address anybody in his own clan by *waniwihã* terms. In fact he will do so only if they belong to factionally related lineages. So when I asked Apẽwẽ, one of the São Marcos chiefs, how he addressed Sebastião (who had killed Apẽwẽ's FB) he replied '*wasiní*'. Then I pointed out that Sebastião belonged to the same clan as he did and asked how, therefore, he could be *wasiní*. At that Apẽwẽ corrected himself and told me that Sebastião was really *wasi-wadí*, in this case the most distant 'own side' term he could find.[1] He emphatically denied, however, that Sebastião was his *ĩ-nõ*.

Similarly the members of the Topdató who were said to have 'gone over' to the Tpereya'óno (Wamãrĩ lineage) in São Domingos were addressed by members of that lineage as if they had been their own clansmen. Had these men been fully assimilated into the Tpereya'óno I think they would have brought up their children as Tpereya'óno, and in the next

[1] See table 11.

generation these children would have contracted marriages exactly as if they had been true Tpereya'óno.

But the process of separation between lineages of the same clan to the point where they intermarry, or assimilation of an alien lineage to the point where it is considered really part of the clan, takes some time. I suspect that, for a lineage to change clan in the full sense, its members must either emigrate to a new village or more than one generation must elapse. In the meantime a lineage may be regarded as having 'gone over' to another clan and the appropriate kinship terms used towards its members, yet it is still not quite on a par with its adoptive fellow clansmen. When the São Domingos Shavante trekked towards Cocalinho in 1960–1 they were hit by an epidemic of Asiatic 'flu. Since it attacked the dominant faction particularly, sorcery was at once suspected and the Wamãrĩ came to the conclusion that it was the Topdató who were responsible. Apẽwẽ therefore directed that certain of them be killed, including two Topdató who had 'gone over' to the Wamãrĩ and were theoretically their 'brothers'.

There are thus important discriminations made within the broad categories we have been discussing. Let us take the category ĩ-dúmrada as paradigmatic of Ego's 'own people' side of the terminology.[1] People who are members of Ego's lineage (ĩ-hitebre or ĩ-hidibá) will certainly be addressed or referred to as ĩ-dúmrada. They may if required be distinguished by the qualifier ubtábidi, which has the force of strengthening the term to something like 'very much ĩ-dúmrada'. Similarly wasisẽnẽwẽ are also ĩ-dúmrada since they are 'close kin', i.e. they belong to lineages closely related to Ego's. People in lineages which are not so closely tied factionally to Ego's are known as wasiwadí. They may be addressed as ĩ-dúmrada but are normally referred to as ĩ-pnẽ (male) or pi'õĩtí (female). Finally people who are only technically waniwihá by being in the speaker's clan, yet do not qualify as wasiwadí because they are not in his faction, will not be called ĩ-dúmrada at all. Shavante thus distinguish between lineage members, close factional relatives, distant factional relatives and potential factional relatives.

The position of the Topdató who had 'gone over' to Apẽwẽ's

---

[1] An identical analysis showing cross-cutting discriminations could be made for other waniwihá terms.

lineage in São Domingos was that of people who had been accepted as peripheral *ĩ-pñẽ*. They were addressed by the relationship terms which included them as 'Our People' by the dominant faction, but they were still only marginally so. Their situation was similar to that of a related lineage which might have been drifting apart, factionally speaking, from its fellows till it was on the border line of clanship.

On the 'Other' side, words like *wasini*, *simẽñẽ*, and *'rebzú* designate anybody who is *wasi're'wa*, but with certain exceptions. It would not, for instance, be correct for Ego to address his mother as *wasini*. She and the women of her lineage in her generation are *ĩ-nã*, although she may be singled out when addressed directly by using the term *ĩ-datiẽ*. Similarly the men of her lineage in her generation are all *'rebzu'wa*, although her actual brothers may be singled out as *ĩ-mãwapté*. They address their ZC reciprocally as *ĩ-ra-wapté*.

In Ego's and the first descending generation there are other exclusions from the general *wasini* category. Women who have married men of Ego's lineage are *asimhí*. Men who have married women of Ego's lineage are *ĩ-za'mũ*. But there is a modification of this rule. We have already seen that men who marry into a household are in an inferior status relative to the lineage which is 'owner' of the house at that time. Ego's FZH therefore married into a household where he was an outsider compared with Ego's F and FF. But all this probably happened about the time that Ego was born and in a household which is not Ego's. It was specifically in that context that the asymmetric relationships FF:FZH and F:FZH were established. The context of the relationship Ego:FZH is not the same, and Ego will therefore not normally address the senior man by the mildly derogatory term *ĩ-za'mũ*. Instead, he addresses him as *simẽñẽ*, as he would also anybody else who is of the 'Other' side.

Finally certain relatives are distinguished because of the specific ties which bind them to Ego as a result of his marriage. They are Ego's wife, his wife's parents, his wife's sister, his wife's brother.

There is a hierarchy of principles governing the application of these terms. In the first place there is a distinction made between *waniwihã* and *wasi're'wa*. But this is not the referent for those terms, such as *asimhí* and *ĩ-za'mũ* which do not connot people who have married Ego's *waniwihã*, but people who have married into Ego's lineage. Finally, the relationships which are distinguished from the general *wasiní* category as a result of Ego's marriage are determined by the composition of a man's wife's household.

A girl refers to a broad range of people as *ĩ-dúmrada*,[1] yet her husband will not address all of these as *ĩ-ãri*. Only her actual brothers, i.e. those who still treat her household as their own, will be so called. In fact the relationship between *ĩ-za'mũ* and *ĩ-ãri* is perhaps the axis of the household, and it can be shown that it is a domestic, and not specifically a genealogical, tie by the situation diagrammed in Fig. 7. This shows what happens when two men marry two girls of differing parentage but resident in the same house. Ego addresses his wife as *ĩ-mrõ*, his WB as *ĩ-ãri*, and his WF as *ĩ-mãpari'wa*. Since the other man who married a girl of this household must be at least a lineage mate of Ego's, he refers to him as (let us say) *ĩ-nõ*. But he does not call that man's wife *asimhí* (woman who has married into my lineage) but *saihí* (WZ), since in this case the household referent takes precedence over the lineage. Furthermore, he will address the brother of his *saihí* as *ĩ-ãri* and her father as *ĩ-mãpari'wa*. It is thus quite clear that the relationships

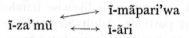

$$\text{ĩ-za'mũ} \begin{array}{c} \longrightarrow \\[-4pt] \longleftarrow\!\longrightarrow \end{array} \begin{array}{c} \text{ĩ-mãpari'wa} \\[2pt] \text{ĩ-ãri} \end{array}$$

are defined by the structure of the affinal household. Similarly *saihí* refers to any woman whom Ego's wife treats as *ĩ-dúmrada / ĩ-nõ* and who belongs to her household.

---

[1] See Appendix 2.

2. ROLES

There are considerable variations within these categories in terms of expected behaviour. For example, the categories *ĩ-'rdá* and its reciprocal *ĩ-nihúdu* are so broadly inclusive that they imply little more than the considerable seniority of one of the speakers. The only relatives who are expected to play a role entailed by this category are Ego's MF, MM, FF and FM; and of these it is the maternal grandparents who do so, much more often than the paternal ones. Given that the Shavante expectation of life is short, grandchildren usually lose their grandparents before they are very old, if they know them at all. A small child has quite a lot to do with his mother's parents who are in the same household as he is, and much less with his father's. In either case the relationship is thought of as one of affectionate indulgence on the part of the grandparent and privileged familiarity on the part of the grandchild.

I had plenty of opportunity to watch Apẽwẽ with his grandchildren in São Domingos, and noticed that his daughter's children regularly accompanied him about the place. When Apẽwẽ came over to sleep in our house he would often bring them with him to spend the night with us. Other older men sometimes took a co-resident grandson (DC) with them to the men's council. A senior man is likewise handed his food first and gets the best portions. Adult Shavante never finish any food that is given to them but always leave some and hand it on to a nearby kinsman. If a man has daughter's children with him, they always cluster round when he is eating and receive his left-overs. Son's children are similarly treated if they are present, but frequently they are not.

In the same way, the various categories on the *waniwihã* side are so broad that each one contains its own hierarchy of roles and concomitant expectations, following the lines of the distinctions we have already discussed with respect to *ĩ-dúmrada*. There are thus far-out *ĩ-mãmã* in related lineages whose position vis-à-vis Ego is little more than that of a senior man who is potentially an ally. Then there are the *ĩ-mãmã* of Ego's lineage of whom he sees a great deal. He should treat them with respect, consult them on important matters, and pay attention to their advice. They in turn should assist him wherever possible. One of these *ĩ-mãmã* is Ego's actual father, and it is with him that

Ego's ties are closest. He can be distinguished terminologically from other *ĩ-mãmã* by calling the others '*ĩ-mãmã amõ*' (*amõ* = other), but this latter phrase is not a relationship term in any useful sense. It is an explanatory locution corresponding to an English phrase such as 'mother's brother', which distinguishes a certain position within the category 'uncle'.

Whereas the discriminations on the *waniwihã* side are made by means of ever narrowing circles of 'closeness', on the *wasi're'wa* side the tendency is to pick out people or classes of people who have contracted specific affinal relationships with Ego or his lineage and distinguish them terminologically from the general run of 'Others'. People so distinguished fall, as we noted, into three classes: senior members of Ego's mother's lineage, people who have married into Ego's lineage, and members of Ego's wife's household.

Females who marry into Ego's lineage are an unimportant class. A man does not usually meet his *asimhi*, who live in a different household and towards whom he has no specific obligations that I could discover. Significantly, when a man marries into the same household as his brother, he does not call that brother's wife *asimhi*, but *saihi*. *Asimhi* therefore refers to someone married into the lineage but not co-resident with Ego.

Co-residence also influences the application of the term *ĩ-za'mũ*, which is characteristically used only for ZH and DH. *ZH is too senior and belongs to a different household. It could be argued that, in fact as opposed to theory, the household is the real determinant of both these categories; *asimhi* by exclusion, and *ĩ-za'mũ* by inclusion.

I have already discussed the critical significance of the *ĩ-za'mũ* (DH): *ĩ-mãpari'wa* (WF) and the *ĩ-za'mũ* (ZH): *ĩ-ãri* (WB) relationships. In Shavante thought they are the axis of the household. They therefore find it inconceivable that a man should be WB and ZH simultaneously to another man. Such a confusion of statuses would muddle up a relationship which is of great institutional significance, and would render social intercourse between the persons concerned almost impossible. A marriage is accordingly never arranged between a man and a girl if his uterine sister is already married to her uterine brother. Shavante refer to such marriages as 'bad marriages' (*was'té-di*).

When pressed to explain why they are 'bad' they say that they confuse things (*tsiwamnãr*) and we have already seen that this notion of confusion is the essence of their idea of incest.[1]

For the same reason men do not normally marry close classificatory 'sisters' of their sisters' husbands. Although such marriages do occur, they are infrequent because Shavante try to avoid them. I recorded the following instances in São Domingos (see Genealogy 3):

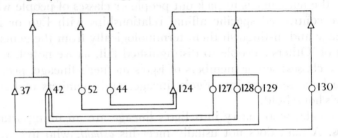

The explanation of this case is that the marriages 37 = 130 and 42 = 127, 128, 129 preceded the marriage 124 = 44, 52. Tsiriane (124) was a new arrival in São Domingos and he had not kept up his ties with his classificatory sisters 127, 128, 129, and 130. Tpereneõ (44) was widowed. Tsiriane therefore married her and treats 37 and 42 as WB. In other words, his relationship to his classificatory sisters is ignored. When Tpereneõ's younger sister (52) came of age, Tsiriane married her too.

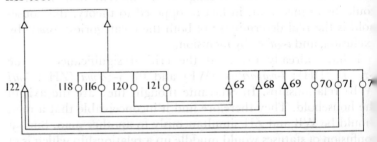

[1] Cf. Dumont on South Indian marriage (particularly among the Kallar) 'Everywhere there is a prohibition against marrying close parallel relative and a preference for cross-cousin marriage qualified by a dislike for th double cross-cousin variety. It is not that examples of such marriages are no occasionally found in genealogies, but there are rare and condemned every where in the same terms: *kuṇḍamuṇḍa cambandam*, 'ball'ball marriage meaning a 'muddled, tangled or confusing marriage'. (1957a: 13.)

The marriages of Ruzapré (122) and S'rizamdí (65) are the closest approach to sister exchange which I found in São Domingos. Originally S'rizamdí's brothers (68 and 69) were married to two sisters other than the ones shown in the diagram, so it was only the marriages 122 = 70, 71, 72 and 65 = 120, 121 which brought about undesirable confusion of statuses. It was resolved by Ruzapré's treating S'rizamdí as his WB without making the relationship reciprocal. This was because Ruzapré was married to S'rizamdí's uterine sisters and therefore into his household, whereas the latter was only married to Ruzapré's classificatory sisters. Subsequently the wives of 68 and 69, two Topdató girls, either died or were killed. They therefore took the opportunity to marry 116 and 118, young girls only recently matured, and the entire group (65 = 120, 121; 68 = 116 and 69 = 118) moved to Ę Tõ.

I noted two instances of similar exchanges in São Marcos (Genealogy 2). A man (154) married two classificatory sisters (27 and 26). At the same time their classificatory brothers married his sisters (29 = 153 and 20 = 152).

Again, a man (178) married a woman (46) and, at the same time, her classificatory brothers married his classificatory sisters (47 = 177 and 48 = 176).

I am not sure how these conflicts were resolved, since I was only in São Marcos for short periods of highly concentrated field-work and I did not discover these exchanges till after I had left. In the first case I would assume that since 152, 153, and 154 are uterine siblings and 29 and 20 the men marrying into the household, then 154 is the WB of 29 and 20. The second case is ambiguous, since neither side consists of a set of uterine siblings. Nevertheless, it is likely that the ambiguity would have been resolved by the means observed in the other cases, that is by ignoring the relationship on one side, and proceeding as if there had only been one set of marriages, establishing an asymmetrical relationship rather than some sort of exchange.

It can be said, then, that Shavante prohibit the exchange of uterine sisters in marriage and discourage the direct exchange of women between lineages because they hold the statuses of WB and ZH to be mutually exclusive. No person can occupy them both simultaneously *vis-à-vis* another, and they are terminologically distinguished. In the rare cases where a marriage that might entail confusion of these roles does take place, its terminological consequences are arbitrarily restricted and the ensuing affinal relationship defined by the exclusive application of one set of terms in preference to another.

Consequently no man can be both MB and FZH to another. These genealogical specifications fall into different categories. By corollary, MBW is also in a different category from FZ. The term for MBW is *'rebzu'wa* and is, in a technical sense, an extension. Shavante explained to me that the MBW was so called because *'rebzu'wa* was the name for the MB.

A MB has watched his sister's children grow up while he lived in her house and they are usually bound to him by close ties of affection.[1] He has probably dandled them as babies and played with them as young children. He is expected to decorate them with *urucú* as soon as they are able to run around, and he often pushes them forward to take their faltering part in ceremonies which they are properly speaking too young to attend, but at which their presence is tolerated. He gives his ZS his first neck-cord as a baby and should continue to make them for him throughout his life. These cords are known as *sõ'rebzu* and are a perpetual reminder to the wearer and the world of the bond between him and his MB, irrespective of whether the MB actually made them or not.[2] Later the MB bestows a name on his ZS at a ceremony which formally establishes their claims on one another. He is customarily referred to as a 'friend' (*zawi-di*) by his ZC. He is privileged to join in the weeping salutation with which a returning Shavante is greeted after any absence, and he will weep of his own accord if his ZC goes away for any length of time. He is given the choicest

[1] As mentioned in Chapter III.

[2] Should a man appear without his cord the circumstance attracts comment which is frequently derogatory to his maternal uncles. Suwapte set himself up as my *dañõ'rebzu'wa*, and saw to it that I was always wearing at least one of these cords. They are worn tightly about the throat. Once the knots have been tied, the ends are cut off so that it is impossible to unbind them. They can only be removed by being cut off. I found them extremely uncomfortable, especially after bathing (when they contracted). On two occasions I cut them off and went about without them. Suwapte was horrified and tied new ones on me the moment he saw I had removed them. Whenever I met Shavante from other communities and they saw me wearing the neck-cords they asked immediately 'Who is your *sõ'rebzu'wá*?'

tit-bits by his ZC whenever food is distributed and is expected
to return the compliment if his ZC comes to his house.

A person's MB, especially a man's MB, is thus seen by the
Shavante as an indulgent and protective figure; but they do not
consider him as in any way a 'male mother' (Radcliffe-Brown,
1952a). The only relative who is, perhaps, cast in that role is the
MZH. He is addressed by the term *ĩ-nãmté*, which is a contraction of *ĩ-nã* + *wapté* and could be translated as 'a sort of *ĩ-nã*'.
Yet even in this case a translation of 'male mother' would not
be wholly appropriate, since we have seen that the category
ĩ-nã is not identical with the specification 'mother'. In fact the
MZH is a 'sort of *ĩ-nã*' in a very special sense which has nothing
whatever to do with 'mother' in the sense in which Radcliffe-
Brown used the term.

The men who marry into a Shavante household in a given
generation are ideally full brothers, usually at least fellow
members of a single lineage and at the very least *waniwihã* to
each other. It is clear, then, that MZH must in some sense be a
'brother' of Ego's father. Ego therefore has two alternative
means of identifying him, as *ĩ-mãmã* (patrilaterally) or as
ĩ-nãmté (matrilaterally). I noticed that given individuals invariably used the term *ĩ-mãmã* for MZH if he was at the same
time their father's uterine brother. This might be called the
over-riding frame of reference. If MZH was, however, a more
distant 'brother' of Ego's father, then he might be addressed as
-nãmté, a category which stressed that Ego interacted with him
in the context of the household rather than in the context of the
lineage. In the household he was certainly *waniwihã*, but nevertheless associated with the mother's people. This would seem to
imply a serious contradiction, since the mother's people must
be *wasi're'wa*. Actually their status is ambiguous.

This is clearly brought out by the alternate term which is
used only to designate the uterine brothers of Ego's mother.
They are referred to as *ĩ-mãwapté*, a contraction of *ĩ-mãmã-
wapté*, 'a sort of *ĩ-mãmã*'. Like *ĩ-mãmã* they are entitled to
respect, and like them too they reciprocate with affection. The
MB may be more affectionate towards his ZC than some of the
latter's distant *ĩ-mãmã*, but there is little to choose between a
close *ĩ-mãmã* and an *ĩ-mãwapté*. There is therefore no contrast
between 'father' (typifying patrilateral kin) and 'mother's

brother' (typifying matrilateral kin), even though Shavante ideology is staunchly patrilineal. This is even more remarkable in view of the fact that there is a marked antithesis between WB and ZH. Clearly this 'affinal contrast' does not persist from one generation to another, for the opposition between ZH and WB is, from the point of view of the next generation, an opposition between F and MB.

There is thus no 'inherited tie of affinity' that defines the relationship of Ego to the members of his natal and affinal households. On the contrary, it is as if the members of a person's natal household were exempt from the unpleasant connotations of affinity, such as opposition, hostility, and malevolence. They are the only *wasi're'wa* whom he can treat as if they were *waniwihã*, and who will so treat him in return. Hence the ambiguity of a relationship such as *ĩ-nã*, which Shavante will classify, if asked, as *waniwihã* although it must logically be otherwise. Hence, too, the special position of *ĩ-mãwapté* (MB).

Since sister exchange is prohibited a man's MBD will not be his FZD. Both of these genealogical specifications fall into the category of *simẽnẽ/'rebzú*, which is the category from which a Shavante takes his wife. Yet the actual MBD is rarely, if ever, married. The reason for this should now be clear. The radical contrast in Shavante thought is between *ĩ-mamã* on the one hand, and *ĩ-mãpari'wa* on the other. The MB is assimilated to the first category and could not therefore be *ĩ-mãpari'wa* as well. A man will not therefore marry his MBD.

The case of the FZD is less clear. Such marriages are also rare. My genealogical information on the Shavante is incomplete, largely because the Shavante had such difficulty in thinking in genealogical terms for my benefit. Nevertheless, I recorded no instances of marriage with the actual FZD. This may be sheer coincidence. Shavante certainly do not forbid such a marriage, but I incline to think that they prefer to avoid a situation where Ego would become *ĩ-za'mũ* (DH) to someone (FZH) who could be his *ĩ-za'mũ*. Admittedly a man does not call his FZH *ĩ-za'mũ*, but this appears to be a courtesy out of deference to his seniority. The contradiction implied between the inferior status of FZH in Ego's F's household and Ego's then assuming a similar status *vis-à-vis* the FZH might be enough to discourage this type of marriage. The argument is not wholly satisfactory, but is the best interpretation I can give for the facts.

My genealogies do show marriages with close relatives, but they are never the genealogical cross-cousin or sister's child. A classificatory MBD (e.g. MFBSD) or FZD (e.g. FFBDD) or ZD (e.g. FBDD) is often married, but in such cases the previous relationship is superseded by the affinal one.

Finally, the position of the ZC further underlines the contextual nature of these categorizations. When he is very small he is addressed as *ĩ-ra-wapté*, the reciprocal of *ĩ-mãwapté*, which is explicitly 'a sort of *ĩ-ra*', and thus definitely somebody who is 'my people' to the speaker. This is consistent with the role of the MB and his status as an honorary *waniwihã*. But as the child grows older he or she will cease to be addressed by this term and will be called *'rebzú* or *simẽnẽ*. This change in nomenclature corresponds to the changes brought about in the MB:ZC relationship by the fact that the MB becomes progressively more involved with his affinal household and correspondingly has less to do with the children of his sister's house, and by the fact that the ZS 'grows away' from the MB as he becomes more involved with his own faction. A MB is always a friend, but for a man at least this friendship comes to mean less and less as he grows up. So a MB may intercede for his ZS if there is a factional dispute brewing, but once the matter has come to the men's council I have never heard a maternal uncle speak for his sister's son against the members of his own faction.

3. USE OF THE TERMS

Shavante in a strange community must acquire these points of reference—household, lineage, faction—before they can even begin to apply the relationship terminology. This is easily done if they have siblings in the village or people who are closely enough related to acknowledge them as lineage-mates. In that case they move in with their brothers or sisters and live with them until they have decided on their plans. A person who is not accepted by anyone in the village as a sibling has to look elsewhere for his household affiliation. He may be accepted as a MB or a ZC in a given household. Failing that he may be accepted as a sibling in a household that simply wishes to incorporate him into its faction.

The combinations of all these possibilities are perhaps best illustrated by a specific case. Rintimpse (Genealogy 2: 76) fled from Marãwasede to São Domingos early in 1958. He had no close kin in São Domingos but Apẹwẽ took him into his own house as an addition to the Wamãrĩ, presumably because he was an unattached Tpereya'óno clansman. In 1958 then Apẹwẽ addressed him as *ĩ-nõ* and he lived in the chief's house.

When I returned in 1962, Rintimpse had gone to Ẹ Tõ and married a girl in the household of S'riwanoõwẽ. The latter was the chief of the Wamãrĩdzu (EW) faction, which left Capitari-quara and joined up with Prapá's people to found the community at Ẹ Tõ. Rintimpse was still considered a Wamãrĩ in Ẹ Tõ, but when he came visiting in São Domingos I noticed that his relations with Apẹwẽ were cooler than they had been. Apewẽ had taken to calling him *ĩ-pnẹ̃*, although Rintimpse still addressed the chief as *ĩ-dúmrada*.

In 1964 I discovered Rintimpse in São Marcos, where he had recently arrived with a group of refugees from Ẹ Tõ. This group had been led into the Upstream Region by S'riwanoõwẽ himself and Rintimpse was still living in the latter's household. I had long conversations with Rintimpse in which he told me the news from Downstream, but when I tried to sound him out on matters in São Marcos he was at a loss. I therefore talked to the São Marcos people, trying to find out how they classified the newcomers.

Aniseto (Genealogy 2: 145) was one of my best informants. He belonged to the Uhẹ lineage of the Ẹ Wawẽ clan. He assured me that his people did not consider S'riwanoõwẽ's people proper *ĩ-dúmrada*, even though they were fellow clansmen. He addressed them as *ĩ-pnẽ* until he knew where they stood. As for Rintimpse, he was lumped together with S'riwanoõwẽ's people, even though he was married to one of their women. The Tpereya'óno lineages in the village all used 'Other' terms to refer to the newcomers, including, as far as I was able to discover, Rintimpse.

Rintimpse was thus in a situation where he was classed factionally with the very people who, in terms of marriage and household, were his affines. The situation of the Topdató who 'went over' to the Wamãrĩ in São Domingos was similar, but they had gone over of their own accord and used the appropriate terms to refer to their adoptive lineage. Rintimpse, on the other hand, still treated his affines as *wasi're'wa*, while not thereby being accepted as *waniwihã* by other members of the village.

Such a situation cannot last very long. I was only able to observe it because my visit to São Marcos, by a fortunate accident, came a couple of weeks after the arrival of the newcomers. Rintimpse would very soon have to gain admittance to one of the São Marcos factions or throw in his lot with his affines.

4. NAMES

I deal here with personal names as part of a general discussion of Shavante systems of classification and identification.

A Shavante boy is not named at birth. During his early childhood he will be referred to by kinship terms in his own household and as *bẹdi* by outsiders. He receives his first name when he is about five or six years old at a ceremony performed by his mother's brother. I have never seen the ceremony performed and believe that it is falling into disuse. My summary description of it is therefore based on accounts given to me by informants.

The boy's mother's brother's wife bakes a maize pie which is handed over to his father. The father then distributes it in his own natal household (i.e. in the boy's father's sister's household). The boy's hair is then bound up at the back and he sits down before his mother's brother, who dresses him in a *sõ'rebzu* necklet and bestows a name on him.

Note that the protagonists in the ceremony are F and MB, in other words ZH and WB, the crucial relationship in Shavante society. It establishes formally that the MB, who has now moved out of his ZS's household, has rights *in personam* over the boy. The outward sign of their relationship is the *sõ'rebzu* cords which a child wears from birth. When a child is given his *sõ'rebzu* necklet in the course of his ceremony it puts the MB:ZS relation on a formal footing. At the same time this assertion of the rights of the MB over the ZS is a limitation of the rights over him exercised by his father and his patrilineal kin. The ceremonial presentation of a maize pie by the MB's household to the FZ's household therefore has a twofold aspect. It indemnifies the boy's patrilineage for a restriction of their rights over him and it ceremonially emphasizes the common interest of both households in him. Shavante are explicitly conscious of this link that binds a man to his brother-in-law. When I visited their huts and talked to them they would, if their brothers-in-law happened to be playing with their children, point out the fact to me by saying 'That's his mother's brother'.

On the other hand, the bestowal of a name on a female child is not a ceremony involving the representatives of two kin groups, but is performed by the community as a whole through the agency of the age-sets. A girl's maternal uncle may play a part in the organization of the ceremony and the preparation of his ZD for it, but the ceremony itself does not establish his rights over her as opposed to those of her patrilineage. This is because women play no part in Shavante politics. They serve merely as perpetuators of groups which are at one and the same time factions and kin groups. Yet these are seen by the Shavante primarily as groups of males, so that inter-group tensions leave the women largely uninvolved. It is not, therefore, so important for a girl to have a formal relationship with one of her *wasi're'wa*, nor for the rights exercised over her by differing groups to be explicitly recognized in this fashion. She receives her name from the community as a whole, without reference to its factional divisions.

I received conflicting statements as to whether a boy's MB passed on his own name to his ZS or whether he merely bestowed a name. I suspect that originally a boy was expected to succeed to his maternal uncle's name. This is no longer so. Nowadays it does not seem to matter which name a boy receives. Adult Shavante rarely bother even to learn the names of the village boys, since all of them take fresh names on entering the bachelors' hut.

At initiation boys take what will be their third name, and they are supposed to assume a fourth when they graduate to the status of Mature Men. These names are not bestowed in sets so that a boy who receives one will necessarily receive certain others. Each name is supposed to cancel out previous ones. I was sometimes told, when I addressed a Shavante by what I thought was his name, 'That name is finished. My new name is . . .', yet I noticed that the villagers were as likely to refer to the man concerned by the old name as the new. In fact they were sometimes intensely interested when I told them of somebody else's 'new name', and told me that they had not previously been aware of it.

Theoretically, a man should assume a minimum of four names: in fact, most Shavante have not passed through so many by the time they reach maturity. Still, the process does not necessarily stop then. A man may assume further names if he so wishes. Apęwẽ in São Domingos took the name Rondón when he heard that General Rondón, the benefactor of the Indians, was dead.[1] His people still referred to him as Apęwẽ,

[1] The chief of a Sherente village similarly named his son Rondón in 1955 to honour the old man, who was at that time still alive.

but the old man would answer to Rondón without a flicker. Meanwhile the São Marcos Shavante worked themselves up into a fury of indignation when I spoke of Apẽwẽ (the chief of São Domingos). His name was not really Apẽwe, they insisted. He had stolen that name. His real name was Sipasé.[2] Suwapte similarly insisted that his name was really Nãtoptí. Suwapté was finished. Yet if I referred to him as Nãtoptí I was met with incomprehension.

The situation with women's names was even more complicated, in spite of the fact that a woman normally receives only one name. This name is bestowed much later than in the case of a boy. Women can grow up, by Shavante standards, without receiving a name, especially nowadays when name-givings are not frequently held.[3] Furthermore, I am certain that some Shavante women literally did not know what their own names were. One of my hardest tasks when trying to compile genealogical information was to identify the individuals on my charts. They were extremely shy about giving their names, and the normal answer to a direct request for such information from either man or woman was 'I have no name'. Yet I would sometimes sit and talk to the members of a family for a long time and slowly obtain the names of most of them, with the exception of one or two women who still maintained, in spite of their husbands' exasperated admonitions not to be silly, that they had no name.

Clearly women's names are not in everyday use. Nor do they appear to be designed for it. They are generally longer than men's names and many of them are polysyllabic tongue-twisters, which had to be repeated to me over and over again before I could even take them down.[4]

It would appear then that Shavante names are only partially, if at all, intended to identify particular individuals. Nor do they furnish an independent classificatory scheme. Among the Sherente each clan has its own set of names and naming is used as a means of establishing or changing clan affiliation. Among the Eastern Timbira the names a man receives determine his membership in various groups (Nimuendajú 1946: 77, 84, 95).

[2] This was in fact his previous name.
[3] I do not know if they were held any more frequently in previous times.
[4] e.g. Tsiñõtsémrõtõ, Rẽtsiwatsihú, Wautomõdañitsu'õ, etc.

The only Shavante names which have analogous functions are
Tebe and Páhiri'wa, whose incumbents belong to a society of
namesakes with the duty and privilege of performing certain
ceremonies.

There is a third possibility, which is that Shavante names are
linked to statuses and that the bestowal of them brings about
succession to the statuses they entail. This function is similar to,
but not identical with a system of names as a classificatory
device.[1] I could find no evidence to support this possibility.
Even if boys at one time regularly received their first name
from their maternal uncle, there is no way in which they
could be said to succeed to the status of the latter. On the
contrary, the importance of the link between MB and ZS
derives from the fact that a boy succeeds to the status of his
father which is the antithesis of MB.

The function of Shavante names is thus obscure. For men the
change of name seems to be more important than the name
itself. Similarly for women it is the naming rather than the
name which is remembered. There are indications in some of the
conversations I recorded that naming women may have been a
way of marking a special occasion. For instance, when the
Wamãrĩdzu peacemakers had re-established harmony after a
quarrel they were supposed to bestow names on a pair of women.
It is true that named women are as a class distinct from un-
named ones in that they are considered to be mature. Possession of a name is accordingly symbolic of maturity in much the
same way as wearing one's hair up instead of down may be in
other societies. Yet a name would seem to be a curious badge of
maturity since it lacks the elementary characteristic of insignia,
i.e. being obviously perceptible. Besides the 'maturity' of a
named woman among the Shavante is purely conventional.
Yet this is the only function of women's names that I have been
able to discover.

Men's names, or rather the changes in them, also reflect
their social status. Since it is important for the Shavante to
know whether a man is in the bachelors' hut, or Young Men's
age-grade, or whether he has graduated to the Mature Men,
these distinctions are made clear in a variety of ways apart

[1] Roger Keesing has developed this argument for the Eastern Timbira on
the basis of Nimuendajú's data. His paper is to be published shortly.

from the change of name. Yet it is consistant with the Shavante idea that a name is associated with a certain social status that when they change status they also change their name. Thus a man will often take a new name when he becomes chief.[1]

I am unable to explain why Shavante mark changes of status in this fashion. Indeed their use of name-changes as status markers raises the problem of whether their personal names should technically be called 'names' at all. Personal names must surely serve to identify persons. But the Shavante data is here ambiguous. Shavante names could be used in this way. In fact they are not. The problem is, are they intended to be so used? To this I can provide no answer.

[1] I suspect that this is when Apęwẽ (São Domingos) took that name.

5. PROPERTIES OF THE SYSTEM

Shavante are able to manage without making much use of personal names because they generally refer to people in terms of the system of categories I have been discussing. This system is ordered by a hierarchy of principles. The dominant one is the distinction between *waniwihã* and *wasi're'wa*. Discriminations are then made on the *waniwihã* side in terms of factional closeness, Ego's patrilineage being the minimal group which is so distinguished. Discriminations on the *wasi're'wa* side depend largely on the structure of Ego's natal household and of his affinal household.

Relationship categories are consequently not determined by the operation of a single principle at all levels of the terminology. Furthermore, there is no single set of behavioural expectations for most of the categories. It is obvious that every relative in a certain category will not act according to the conventional expectation of how such a relative should act; but it needs to be stressed that Shavante do not necessarily expect the same behaviour from all the members of each category. No Shavante would be so silly as to think that a distant *ĩ-dúmrada* should behave towards him in the same way as his own brother does.

Their relationship categories are classificatory devices, but the relationship terminology does not, as I have shown, make as many discriminations as the Shavante themselves wish to. These are effected by the use of modifiers, by manipulation of terms and by selectivity in their application.

Nevertheless, the overriding principle of the relationship terminology is the antithesis between *waniwihã* and *wasi're'wa*. This is the basic distinction which all other distinctions serve merely to modify. In this sense the Shavante have a two-section system.

It has sometimes been thought that because two-section systems established a radical distinction between one 'side' and the other, it would be inconsistent with their structure for discriminations to be made *within* the 'sides'. Thus Lévi-Strauss argued that a distinction between ZH and WB[1] among the

---

[1] He used the data in Nimuendajú's book (1942) and referred specifically to the terms *aimãplí* and *ĩ-zakmũ*. Nimuendajú, however, lists these terms respectively as:

aimãplí = parent-in-law and *ĩ-zakmũ* = ZH (man speaking) FZH; DH 1942: 24–25). Lévi-Strauss apparently confused *aimãplí* with *aikã-rie* which is listed as WB; WBC.

Sherente was one of a number of reasons for supposing that '. . . neither the terminology nor the marriage regulations coincide with an exogamous dual organization' (1952: 304). In fact, both the Sherente and the Western Shavante have had exogamous moiety systems and nevertheless made this terminological distinction. There is no logical reason why they should not, and I think I have now given an adequate ethnographic demonstration of how such a system works.

Lévi-Strauss's error, to which most writers on the topic[1] have subscribed, stems from a failure to distinguish satisfactorily between terminology and institutional arrangements. If two-section systems are seen as the expression of exogamous moiety systems, and exogamous moiety systems are represented by a model of two patrilines exchanging women or two matrilines exchanging men, then it follows that WB = ZH. But it does not follow that there can be no further modification of the rule that the moieties exchange women. They may exchange women with certain exceptions and these exceptions can be categorically distinguished.

The lesson of the Shavante terminology is that no single rule is applied uniformly throughout it. Its application is always restricted, or there are exceptions to it. Thus a two-section system may seem to 'require' that MB = FZH and FZ = MBW, yet these are distinguished. In spite of that, there is no distinction between MBC and FZC. This appears contradictory, and not so long ago I would have pointed to it as a contradiction in my own material. In fact it is not so. It is merely that certain rules are applied in a certain way at each level of the terminology, and they give this result.

In other words, if we know that a relationship terminology is a two-section system, this tells us something important about its structure but does not enable us to predict its details. There is, for example, no necessary contradiction in a terminology which is at once a two-section system and makes distinctions of the type known in Omaha or Crow terminologies.[2]

It should not therefore be supposed that there is little use in distinguishing a class of 'two-section systems'. All two-section

---

[1] Including myself (see Maybury-Lewis, 1960b).

[2] See Maybury-Lewis, 1956: 222. I propose to develop this point in my forthcoming book on the Sherente.

systems express by definition a major binary opposition in the societies which possess them, and it may be a fruitful line of inquiry to discover what sort of oppositions are thus expressed and under what circumstances.

Among the Shavante this opposition is between *waniwihã* and *wasi're'wa*, the content of which cannot be simply stated. It is partly factional, partly a matter of moieties (among the Western Shavante), partly a distinction between kin and affine. Indeed there are further aspects of it which are yet to be discussed. But enough evidence has been presented by now to enable me to state that this antithesis is a type of code or formula which permeates Shavante society. An understanding of the Shavante depends largely on an understanding of this code.

VII

RITUAL

1. OI'O

SHAVANTE are unable or unwilling to explain their own ceremonies, which makes it correspondingly difficult to begin an analysis of them. They say simply that they are *wẽ da*, literally 'to make beautiful'. When they talk about them they discuss how the participants performed, whether, for example, the boys sang well or the men ran properly. They would ask me eagerly if I did not think their rituals were beautiful and press me to tell them which aspect I found most attractive. It was clear that they regarded them as a major form of aesthetic expression.[1]

Their ceremonial could be compared to classical ballet in Europe. The performers try to create a harmonious whole which is aesthetically pleasing to the spectators, by acting out a series of highly formalized patterns. I call these performances ceremonial because they possess a symbolic significance which transcends mere representation in context. A Shavante who performs the *da-prabú* dance snorts and stamps and acts the part of an angry man, yet I would say that in so doing he was performing a rite. The *da-prabú* is a traditional performance to which a conventional symbolic meaning is attached by other Shavante, but this meaning can be expressed as a symbolic statement of something in the social order which transcends the particular context of the dance.[2] In analysing Shavante ritual I shall therefore seek to understand the language of these symbolic statements.

I begin with the *oi'o* ceremony outlined in Chapter IV because it is a relatively simple one to understand. Its details were, briefly, as follows: the boys in the bachelors' hut pain

---

[1] The Shavante word for a ceremony is *dasĩpse*, from *da* = a prefix referring to the first person singular + *sĩ* = a reflexive particle + *pse* = good. A ceremony is therefore something which makes oneself good.

[2] In this I follow Leach who expressed the point very well in *Political Systems of Highland Burma* (1954: 10–14).

themselves red and are equipped with reddened *um'ra* clubs. They are then separated into two groups, one at each end of the village crescent. From there they are led into the middle of the village, formed in two lines, and instructed to duel with each other under the supervision of their elders.

For this ceremony, at least, the Shavante have a rationale. It is, they explain, to make the boys strong. They use the adjective *t'té* (-*di*), which has connotations of 'resistant' or 'tough' in the same way that a hardwood tree is tough, difficult to cut.

The boys, for their part, are painted scarlet with *urucú*, which is the normal ceremonial decoration for people in the bachelors' hut. Shavante consider that *urucú* and redness in general have beneficial, creative properties. We saw in Chapter III that a man will paint his ear-plugs with *urucú* and take care to wear them during intercourse if he wishes to procreate a child. At the same time they make an explicit connexion between *urucú* (*bę*) and the sun (*będę*). Things which are bright red in colour may be referred to indiscriminately as *pré* (red), *bę* (*urucú*), or *będę* (sun). Red is their favourite colour and is characterized as beautiful. Above all it makes a person strong. Shavante used to importune me especially for red clothes 'to make them strong' (in the same way as red paint presumably would). Thus sun, *urucú*, and redness are all part of a single conceptual complex which the Shavante associate with good, life-giving properties.

I thought for a time that their word for 'penis' was identical with their word for *urucú*, but on subsequent investigation I discovered that they were in fact homonyms. There is a slight difference in pronunciation between *bę* = *urucú* and *bį* = 'penis', which I had assumed to be non-significant, but which the Shavante assured me made them into different words. Nevertheless, they say that urucú 'makes children', so I feel justified in arguing that in Shavante thought

$$bę \ (urucú) \text{ makes children}$$
and $\qquad bĩ \text{ (penis) makes children}$
therefore $bę = bį$.

When the boys are painted red, then, this is symbolic of generative power. There are also indications that the class of *wapté* (boys in the bachelors' hut) are thought to possess special creative powers. The person who creates things in Shavante myths is often a *wapté*. I shall discuss this aspect in Section 3.

The boys carry *um'ra* clubs which are the badges of their status. There are three major types of club among the Shavante, each one associated with (but not necessarily used exclusively by) one of the age-grades. *Um'ra* are associated with boys in the bachelors' hut and are not in fact ever used by anybody else. They are small, from two to three feet long, light, polished smooth, and kept red with urucú.

The Young Men's age-grade characteristically use the *uibro*, which Shavante think of as an aggressive or war club. When they speak of refugees who have fled from the community they often say 'they were frightened of the *uibro*'. In one instance (the killing of S'rimri) people said that he had been 'killed with an *uibro*', although I know from eyewitness accounts that he was actually shot to death with arrows. The *uibro* symbolizes aggressive power, and references to it are not descriptive statements about the instrument used in particular situations, but *clichés* which the Shavante use to express the idea of force. The shape of the *uibro* is peculiar. It is made from a young tree so that part of the root can be left as a knob at one end of the club, rather like the knuckle on the end of a bone. The club is then hardened by being exposed to the heat of the fire, and the opposite end of it sharpened to a point. Shavante do not plane it and smooth it carefully but leave the surface of it knobbly and uneven, containing all the original knots in the wood. They then burn spots onto the outer surface. The resultant artefact is usually slightly curved, rather light, and looks exceedingly crude in its worksmanship.

In the days when Shavante were fighting the Brazilians they usually left numbers of *uibro* by the corpses of people they had killed. As a result these were the first Shavante artefacts to become known to the outside world. I examined a large number of them from the collection of the Museu Paulista in 1954 and was struck by their curious design. At that time these clubs were thought to demonstrate that the Shavante were exceedingly primitive, because they were assumed to be incapable of manufacturing more polished articles such as had been collected from neighbouring tribes. Since they were apparently war clubs which had been left at the scene of a skirmish I suggested[1] that

---

[1] In a paper ('Akwẽ-Shavante Clubs') read at the XXXI Congress of Americanists, São Paulo, 1954.

they were perhaps throwing clubs and hence lighter and more curved than the weapons of the other tribes of the region.

This suggestion was quite incorrect, but the facts which prompted it—the unusual features of the *uibro*—do call for a special explanation. Shavante can and do make beautifully polished clubs, decorated with the woven bastwork which is characteristic of the whole Central Brazilian region. These clubs, known as *brudu*, are generally pointed at one end (which is used as a digging stick) and broad at the other (which is used for striking). They are characteristic of the Mature Men's age-grade. The fact that they do double duty as weapon and digging stick is symbolic of the fact that Mature Men are, by definition, both fighters and providers in the household.

Young Men, on the other hand, have not moved into their affinal houses and are thought of as the independent warriors of the community. Their *uibro* are associated with this aggressive characteristic, and they are fashioned in a special way to give them a phallic character. The knobs at the root of the club represent human testicles and the club itself a human penis. Shavante do not explicitly say so, but they do say that the *tsi'uibro* emblem used in the *wai'a* ceremony is a phallic symbol. Since the prefix *tsi-* is associated with passage from one state to another, it is clear that the *uibro* and the *tsi-uibro* are in Shavante thought on some sort of phallic continuum.

I suggest that the *um'ra*, from which this discussion started, represent by contrast some sort of free-floating generative power without specific genital connotations. This would be appropriate for the boys in the bachelors' hut, who are regarded as sexually potent (they must wear the penis sheath) but not sexually active (they do not wear ear-plugs).

In the *oi'o* ceremony itself the boys act out the pattern of opposition which is the *leitmotiv* of Shavante society. They congregate first at opposite ends of the village, then they are ranged in two opposing teams. Shavante refer to these teams as *vaniwihã* and *wasi're'wa*. I thought at first that the categories referred to clansmen and non-clansmen, and therefore cross-questioned my Shavante informants about how such a dyadic ceremony could take place when there were three clans in the community. The answers I received were vague and confused, which is understandable, since the question started from a false premiss. In fact *waniwihã* and *wasi're'wa* in such contexts refer to the two broad factional classes which constitute any Shavante village—the insiders and the outsiders. This opposition is not only expressed ritually in the 'toughening up' ceremony of *oi'o*, but also in every single debate in the men's council, where a man from each category stands up and the two speakers oppose each other rhetorically.

It is interesting that the boys gather at each extremity of the village before the duelling starts. This might suggest that the two ends of the village were associated with the opposition between *waniwihã* and *wasi're'wa*. In fact, as we saw in Chapter V, Shavante feel that the ceremonial end houses in the village should both be occupied by chiefs. In a situation where the power of the factions is evenly balanced the village would actually have more than one chief, and there would thus be a chief from one faction at one end of the crescent and a chief from another at the other.[1] It would seem that ideally the Shavante think of their village as evenly divided between *waniwihã* and *wasi're'wa*, so that each extremity would be associated with one category; and it is this ideal balance which is expressed in the *oi'o* ritual. In reality most Shavante communities are dominated at a given moment by one of the factions, and this faction will, if it is strong enough, annex both ceremonial end houses.

[1] As there were at Areões when the new community was established in 1962 (see Fig. 3).

2. LOG RACES

Shavante, in common with all the other Gê tribes, hold log races in connexion with important ceremonies. They do not hold them as frequently as some Timbira peoples, with whom it is almost a daily affair. They do not even hold them as frequently as the modern Sherente, who have clung tenaciously to log-racing though they have discarded most of their aboriginal ceremonial. However, Shavante feel that a *wai'a* cannot be performed without a preliminary log race. A log race should also be held at some stage of the initiation ceremony.[1] It may be held in conjunction with other ceremonies too, but *wai'a* and initiation require a log race as part of their proper ritual.

The decision to hold a log race is announced in the men's council on the night before the proceedings.[2] On the day of the race the Young Men's age-grade go out into the savannah and cut lengths of *buriti*-palm trunk at some distance from the village. These are generally about three feet long. The cutters take care that the sections are of approximately equal length and thickness, but there is none of the elaborate testing of their respective weights which sometimes characterizes Sherente log races. If one log is noticeably heavier than the other, this does not bother the Shavante. The logs are neither painted nor decorated, but are left, one on each side of the trail and parallel with the path.

In the early afternoon all the men go out to the logs, though not all of them go right to the place where the logs are lying. Many of the older men take up positions by the side of the trail and wait for their log to reach them, so that they may not be obliged to run the full course. The members of the Young Men's age-grade always go right to the start as a point of honour.

At the starting point the racers divide up into two teams. These should theoretically unite alternate age-sets into a pair of age-moieties, but this may not actually be done. The race

[1] The log race for initiation at São Domingos (1958), described in Chapter IV, was held some time after the close of the initiation proper. Instead, it was run as a preliminary to the *wai'a*; but the *wai'a* was specifically 'for the initiates' and could therefore be seen as an epilogue to the initiation ceremonies.

[2] Though it may be altered. We saw in Chapter V how Apęwẽ announced the time of a log race one evening in São Domingos, but was shouted down by the people, mostly women, in the surrounding huts. He hastily changed his instructions.

then starts as three or four men heave each log onto the shoulder of the first man who must carry it. Both log bearers set off along the trail, bent over, half sprinting and half staggering as fast as they can go. Whenever the man carrying the log is seen to be tiring, another one offers to take over from him; sometimes other men offer themselves, regardless of whether the log bearer is tiring or not. The log is then rolled from one carrier's shoulder onto the other's without either of them stopping running, and the fresh man puts in a terrific spurt while he is still able to. Meanwhile his team-mates bound along by the side of the trail, threading their way through thickets of trees and leaping over stunted bushes. When the teams arrive in the village they deposit one log in the Mature Men's meeting place and the other in the Young Men's meeting place.

During the first race I saw at São Domingos there was a mishap. One of the change-overs was bungled and a log rolled off its receiver's shoulder, crashing to the ground and bruising the foot of another runner, who was too slow in leaping out of the way. It took a few moments for it to be hoisted onto the shoulder of a fresh runner, and the loss of time meant that this team was left irrevocably behind. They made frantic efforts to catch up and members of the leading team even dropped back and offered themselves as bearers of the second log, in order to try and lessen the distance between them, but it was no use. The leading log arrived some time ahead of the second one.

Immediately the Mature Men gathered in their meeting place and held a lively post-mortem. They accused one of their number of not having exerted himself sufficiently and of taking the log only once. There was an argument about the Tírowa age-set, which had just graduated to the status of Young Men. Some of their elders insisted that they had been helped too much, that they had not carried the log fast enough or far enough, and so on. But the most important recriminations concerned the dropped log, on the subject of which a heated argument developed. Finally it was decided that the log race had not been successfully performed and that another one should be held before the *wai'a* could be celebrated.

This underscores the fact that these log races are not, properly speaking, 'races' at all. It is immaterial for the Shavante which log wins, so they do not mind if one log is heavier than the other and there is no contradiction implied by members of one team helping the other. The whole performance is a rite. It should be carried out with the maximum of exertion and co-operation by all concerned, since this in itself is aesthetically pleasing (*wẽ-di*). Furthermore, Shavante men take a pride in running well and they use the same word (*t'tẽ'di*) to indicate this quality of tight, controlled speed as they do to indicate tightness or hardness in people and things. A log race serves as a demonstration of the male virtues Shavante most admire—hardness and fleetness.

At the same time, it is more than a mere demonstration of strength and speed. If it were no more, it would not matter whether one log fell behind or not. But the Shavante have a notion of 'the proper performance' of the rite which includes the idea that the logs should remain close to each other. Each team should exert itself but neither should outdistance the other. So we come back to the idea of equilibrium, to the cancelling out of opposites, which seems to be the basic pattern in so many Shavante institutions. But in this case the opposition is not between *waniwihã* and *wasi're'wa*, but between two age-moieties.

Shavante age-moities resemble Sherente sporting-moieties in that their sole function is to distinguish between the two teams which carry the racing logs. It cannot therefore be argued, as it could for the Timbira, that one of the functions of log racing is to identify specific corporate groups, for Shavante and Sherente racing groups exist only to race. I would suggest instead that these racing moieties exist for the sole purpose of ordering Shavante and Sherente men according to a principle which is distinct from the major cleavage in their society. Sherente society was divided into two exogamous moieties, and the fissive implications of this distinction were potentially as grave for them as the distinction between *waniwihã* and *wasi're'wa* is for Shavante. Sherente men were therefore redistributed on cere-monial occasions into sporting-moieties which cross-cut the exogamous moieties just as Shavante age-moieties transect the opposition between factions. It is quite natural that Shavante should use their age-set system as a vehicle for the promotion of social harmony in the way I here suggest, since, as we have already seen, they conceive of the system itself as harmonious and fusive, in opposition to the division between *waniwihã* and *wasi're'wa*, which is factitious and divisive.

3. INITIATION

Initiation is the occasion for the most elaborate cycle of ceremonies which the Shavante perform. It is second in importance
only to the esoteric *wai'a* and equally rich in symbolic significance. I have described these ceremonies in Chapter IV, so we
are now in a position to consider their symbolism.

They start with the piercing of the initiates' ears and the
insertion of miniature ear-plugs. The cylindrical plugs are said
to pierce the lobes of the initiate's ears just as his penis may now
pierce a woman in the act of intercourse. Ear-piercing is thus
the symbolic conferring of manhood. Boys are conventionally
thought to be sexually capable when they enter the bachelors'
hut, which is why they must wear a penis sheath. But it is not
till they wear their ear-plugs that they are men in the sense that
they are socially permitted to exercise their sexual potency.

Immediately their ears have been pierced the initiates enter
the stage of the immersion ceremonies. In order to understand
these rites we must first consider the mythical precedent for
them. There are a number of stories in my collection of Shavante
myths which refer to a boy who immerses himself in the water.
They can be reduced to four main variants which I shall set
out schematically.[1]

(1) Tpemrã struck the ground and water gushed out, covering the earth. This was the Ẽ Wawẽ.[2] His father asked him
where the Shavante were going to live now that he had made so
much water. Tpemrã, however, remained in the water. His
father and brothers tried to persuade him to come out and go
with them, but he would not. He remained in the water with
his wives and created many things. His *ĩ-amõ* came to visit him
and Tpemrã turned him into a frog.

(2) S'ribtuwẽ cut off a piece of his mother's vagina, stuffed it
with *babassú* nuts, and ate it. He persuaded all the other *wapte*
to do likewise. Then he refused to go on trek with his father and
his brothers. Instead he went to live in the water, where he
created many things. He created women and married them. He

---

[1] An analysis of the full texts is in preparation. Here I use only a précis
of each myth.

[2] Refers here to the major river in the speaker's habitat. Shavante
nowadays use the term solely as a name for the Rio das Mortes.

refused to come back when his brothers asked him to. When his *ĩ-amõ* came, he turned him into a frog.

(3) Prinẽ'a created many things. He went out to hunt jaguar but the jaguar wept and he did not kill it. Out on the savannah he was so parched with thirst that he lay down to rest. Water poured out of his nostrils and covered the earth. All his companions could then slake their thirst.

(4) Prinẽ'a was one of two *wapté* who created many things. The other was S'ribtuwẽ. After creating many things and hunting much game they flew away like birds into the sky.

The essential elements of (1) could be stated as follows:

Boy   creates water
       rejects his kin
       lives in water and creates things
       turns his affine into a frog.

Story (2) is structurally identical, save for the addition of the boy's action towards his mother. Thus

Boy   eats mother's vagina
       rejects his kin
       creates water and lives in it
       creates many things
       turns his affine into a frog.

Story (3) can be expressed as:

Boy   creates many things
       spares jaguar
       creates water.

Finally, story (4) concerns two boys, one with the name of the hero of (2) and one with the name of the hero of (3), and can be expressed:

Boys   create many things
       kill much game
       turn into birds.

Versions (2), (3), and (4) are stories told about a single pair of protagonists and version (1) is virtually identical with (2), so I feel justified in treating these myths as a single complex of related stories bearing on one theme. The theme is that of creativity and in each case it is somebody from the class of *wapté* (bachelors) who is the creator. Not only does he create, but in three of the four variants he creates water, dramatically and apart from all his other creations. In (1) and (2) he then lives in the water, where he grows beautiful and sleek and fat. His hair grows long (down to the middle of his back) and shiny, and when people come to visit him they admire him. That is why his affine comes to see him, in the hope that he too may be permitted to live in the water and grow beautiful in the same way; but he is tricked by the creator, who turns him into a frog while pretending all the while that he is making his hair grow long and beautiful. Clearly this myth is related to the immersion ritual just as it is related to the other myths in the complex.

An analysis of the elements of this complex, in so far as they bear on the initiation ceremonies could be undertaken as follows. *Wapté* are associated with creativity. There is some indication that incest is also associated with creativity, since, on the basis of the Freudian equation between eating and copulation,[1] the act of eating the mother's vagina could be interpreted as maternal incest. Now the *wapté*, however they may have come to be creators, create water. This is seen as a different element. In (1) the boy's father specifically asks what is to become of them all now that he has covered the earth with water. In (3), similarly, the water extends over the whole earth. The *wapté* then lives in the water, thus setting himself apart from other people. I would argue further that this going to the water in versions (1) and (2) is the equivalent of taking to the air in version (4). In each case the *wapté* is categorically distinguished from his fellows by leaving their element (land) altogether.

This physical separation from other men is reinforced by a social separation. In the first two versions much of the narrative is taken up with overtures from the boy's kin, all of which are rejected. He refuses to go with them and even more emphatically rejects his affine by turning him into a frog. Significantly the versions which do not mention the incident of the affine are similarly lacking in details of the pressure put on the *wapté* by his kin. He emerges then in the true classical sense of the hero as

---

[1] There is, of course, considerable evidence to support this equation and many languages use the vocabulary of eating as a circumlocution for copulation. Unfortunately I cannot document this specifically for the Shavante.

a 'man set apart,' who has moved into a separate physical element and rejected all aspects of the social world.

I would suggest, then, that the immersion ritual which starts the initiation cycle is intended to endow the initiates with the heroic qualities of their mythical prototype. As *wapté* they have certain potency ascribed to them, which is symbolized in the scarlet paint they wear on ceremonial occasions and the red *um'ra* clubs they carry. During their immersions they symbolically re-enact the separation of the creator *wapté* from his fellow men.

During the next stage of the ceremonies the initiates, and on occasion also their seniors, make public demonstrations of fleetness. When the phase is ceremonially opened, all the men who take part are painted red. When it is closed they are painted black. This is consistent with the opposition between these colours in Shavante thought, for red is associated with creation and therefore with beginning, while black is associated with destruction and therefore with ending. I shall have occasion to refer to this antithesis later.

Another dichotomy is expressed in the actual organization of the runs. It is the privilege of a single lineage to carry the *no'oni* cape at the head of the initiates' procession before each run. In theory, then, the names Páhiri'wa and Tebe should be conferred on members of a different faction, so that their incumbents are invariably *wasi're'wa* to the cape-bearers. This provision may be violated in practice, as indeed most provisions may, by a particularly strong faction which succeeds in abrogating to itself the ceremonial offices which should rightfully belong to the opposition. Even in São Domingos, however, the Tebe and the Páhiri'wa came from Apęwẽ's dominant Tpereya'óno faction and the ceremonial cape-bearers were drawn from the Dzutsi lineage of the opposite Ę Wawẽ clan.

The cape-bearers open the running phase of the initiation and start each individual run. It is the Tebe and the Páhiri'wa respectively who close it. In São Domingos it was the Páhiri'wa who danced before the finishing posts and then flung the cape down between them in a gesture which symbolized their closure. In Simões Lópes it was the Tebe who performed this rite. In any case the Tebe perform the ritual circuits of the village, during which they tap the cape borne by its ceremonial cape-bearer.

This brings the running phase of the initiation to an end, and the Páhiri'wa should dance in the village on the following day.

In this way the complementarity of *waniwihã* and *wasi're'wa* are ceremonially emphasized. Their joint participation is required ideally for the ceremonies to be properly performed. Most of the ritual, however, serves to underline the relationship between age-sets and age-grades and thereby to ignore the factional distinction.

So the age-set which is finishing as Young Men sings at the age-set which is being initiated. Appropriately enough they are painted black to symbolize the end of 'warriorhood' and the others are painted red to symbolize their entering into that status. Similarly, as we have seen, the sponsoring age-set always acts 'with' the initiates who are their alternate juniors, while the Young Men always act ceremonially 'against' them. In the final run which marks the entry of the initiates into manhood their sponsors run with them, literally accompanying each boy and whooping and exorting him. The Young Men, appearing in this capacity for the last time, are decorated in their best finery and run with a savage determination to outdo their successors in beauty and speed. Yet their representative, painted black, remains at the start of the race and weeps, thereby symbolically marking the transition of his age-set from one age-grade to the next.

I have not so far said much about the *wamñõrõ* dance-masks, except to point out that they are manufactured by the members of the sponsoring age-set, a process which is exceedingly laborious and long drawn-out, and are run into the village on the final day of the initiation. Yet the masks are vital to the ceremonies. The whole complex which I have here referred to as 'initiation' is spoken of by the Shavante as '*wamñõrõ da*' (to make masks). They are at once the prerogative of initiated men and the symbolic instruments of initiation. They could be said to be in some way symbolic of initiation itself.

Let us consider this equivalance. The masks themselves are said to be '*wapté ĩ-wa'ru da*' (to make the *wapté* mature). The maturity attained by initiates after these ceremonies entails marriage and the contraction of specific affinal relationships. This is admittedly only for males, but then I have already shown that although girls are formally 'initiated' with their male coevals, this is merely a classificatory convention. The real initiates—those whose status changes as a function of the ritual—are the boys.

The *wamñõrõ* masks are manufactured for the initiates by the mature men. Yet through the initiation ceremonies the mature men's age-grade is represented by its junior age-set. It is they who 'dance for' the initiates every night and morning; who dance throughout the final night on their behalf, and seize the masks from them at dawn; who sponsor them on every ceremonial occasion. Furthermore they appear at the climactic moments of the ceremonies in a special paint. Their bodies are decorated in a criss-cross pattern of stripes and their faces are black with perhaps an eye picked out in red, or black on one side and red on the other. The effect is intentionally weird and the Shavante say that it is 'to frighten' (*pahí-da*).

I could not get a clear statement from the Shavante as to their ideas about the provenance and function of the dance which the sponsoring age-set performs daily for the initiates. They told me, however, that it came from the spirits. Similarly the *wamñõrõ* masks were associated with a class of spirits which the Shavante called *wazepari'wa*. These spirits were supposed to be attracted to the place where the masks were hung out during the manufacturing process, so that the young men had to sleep out and guard the *wamñõrõ* to prevent their being stolen, or literally 'spirited away'.

I obtained nine dance-masks, three from each clan, by barter after the ceremonies in São Domingos in 1958. They were carefully bound around a pole for me by Apęwẽ himself, who took great care to see that they were not spoiled in the process. When the village went on trek I travelled to Santa Terezinha and was away for some time, leaving the masks in my house, which was 'closed' as were most of the other huts in the community. I got back to São Domingos a few days before the villagers returned from their trek and discovered that the masks had gone. I took the matter up with Waarodí, Apęwẽ's eldest son, who had not trekked with the others, and he told me simply that the *wazepari'wa* must have claimed them back. In actual fact Waarodí himself had sold them to a Brazilian who visited the Indian Protection Service post. When the others came back I brought up the question in the men's council. Waarodí explained that the *wazepari'wa* had taken the masks and his explanation was accepted as the most probable one. I am sure that this was not a matter of factional convenience either. Men who had no great liking for Waarodí agreed, when I spoke to them about it, that it was to be expected that the *wazepari'wa* would steal them.

I would suggest, then, that the initiation ceremony, its sponsoring dance and its masks, are all associated with the *wazepari'wa*, and that it is therefore to the *wazepari'wa* that we must look for an understanding of them. The *wazepari'wa* are supposed to inspire fear, so the sponsoring age-set adopts a terrifying paint. They are characteristically stealthy, so the sponsoring age-set moves, at the climax of the ritual, in the 'stalking' fashion I have described. Finally, I shall argue in the next chapter that the *wazepari'wa* are associated with affinity as opposed to kinship. It is thus consistent with this whole pattern of ideas that they should be associated with initiation and the contracting of affinal ties.

PLATE XI

Pi'u dancing at the young men at the climax of the wai'a

4. WAI'A

Initiation not only confers maturity on a man but it entitles him to participate in the most important ceremony of all, the *wai'a*. I know of at least three kinds of *wai'a*. There is one which is performed for the sick, one performed for the arrows, and one performed for the masks (*wamñõrõ da*). The first one seems to differ in important respects from the last two.[1] It is a public ritual where men *and women* sing by the patient's house all night and the senior celebrants suck out his malady. They dance for him too, but both the singing and the dancing differ from the songs and dances I have noted in connexion with the other *wai'a*.

The *wai'a* for the arrows is a shorter version of the *wai'a* for the masks, which includes a certain amount of ritual concerned with the initiates. The ceremony for the arrows can be held at any time but was usually performed when the Shavante were trekking in a region rich in arrow canes. A full *wai'a* for the masks, on the other hand, is invariably held in conjunction with initiation and involves a long period of preparation for the initiates before the ceremony proper.

It is strictly forbidden for women and children to see these latter *wai'a*. They may not approach the places in the forest where the men can be heard singing, and when it is time for the secret rites to be performed in the village they must remain inside their huts and not look out. But during the *wai'a* I observed that these prohibitions were more conceptual than absolute. One of the senior men went all round the houses of the village, adjusting the thatch over the window openings so that there could be no peeping. He seized any girls who were loitering outside their huts and thrust them indoors before securing the brushwood over the entrances. All the same, he did not hurry to complete his round before the rites had actually started, so that women and girls could and did peep. It seems that the prohibition was a symbolic assertion of the esoteric nature of the ceremony, rather than an attempt to prevent women from seeing what was going on. Similarly Shavante tell blood-curdling stories of what they would do to a woman who ventured into the jungle where the *wai'a* was being celebrated. They claim that she would be manhandled, raped, and disfigured. In fact,

---

[1] I have seen one full *wai'a* and part of another, but have never witnessed *wai'a* for the sick.

though women do indeed keep away from the ceremony, I believe that such treatment would only be meted out to a woman who deliberately set out to infringe the prerogatives of the initiates by spying on them. An accidental passer-by would in all probability merely be hustled away, even if she did happen to glimpse the forbidden rites. This would be consistent with the fact that men take more care to stress that the uninitiated are not supposed to watch than to ensure that they do not watch. At one stage of the ceremony the 'forbidden' emblems are actually flaunted in the faces of the women, so it is likely that women as a class know what they look like. At another stage some women are actually introduced into the proceedings and accompany the men, while the others remain battened in their huts.

The preliminary stage of a *wai'a* for the masks involves the preparation of the initiates. Each boy has already been assigned to one of the ceremonial moieties which function only during the *wai'a*. It is the elders who let it be known which moiety a boy belongs to, and they are guided solely by the need to maintain approximately equal numbers in them. The moieties are called Udéhẹri'wa (wood-cutters) and Umrẽ-tdé'wa (gourd people), and are distinguished by the number of stripes which their members paint on their legs. On all ceremonial occasions Shavante men (and uninitiated boys too) paint their legs black with charcoal on a latex base. The black area extends from just below the knee down to their white ankle cords. Members of the Udéhẹri'wa moiety make three longitudinal stripes on this black base by drawing three fingers carefully up from the ankle to the knee on each side of the leg immediately after the paint has been applied. The Umrẽ-tdé'wa make only two stripes in the same way.

The boys now embark on a fast under the supervision of the older men.[1] The Umrẽ-tdé'wa sit together on a row of mat and the Udéheri'wa sit together at a separate place. At one ceremony in São Marcos their relative positions were as illustrated on p. 257

The Umrẽ people carry dance rattles while the Udéhẹri people take with them their reddened *um'ra* clubs.[2] At interval

---

[1] I have never seen the preliminary fast before a *wai'a*.

[2] It is possible that the moiety names are derived from these artefacts, fc *umré* means a gourd and dance-rattles are made out of gourds, while th

throughout the day the Udéheri get up and form a line in front
of the Umrẽ. They then dance towards the others and back
again, cradling their clubs in their arms. When they stop
dancing they remain opposite the Umrẽ, who dance right round
the Udéhẹri, bending low and beating time with their rattles.

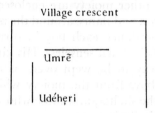

When the Umrẽ regain their position, both groups of boys return
to their mats and sit down. They remain out in the hot sun all
day, repeating this pattern at intervals. They are not allowed to
eat or drink at all during the daytime and they may not bathe
for the entire period of their fast.

Kinswomen of the boys try to make things easier for them
by dashing out to them with gourds of water whenever the men
are not around. But the men keep a look-out posted in a tree
for just this eventuality, and when he shouts they come running
from wherever they may be and dash the gourds to the ground.
It is only an agile sister and a quick mother who manage to get
a few drops of water donated before the ban is enforced.

The men meanwhile gather in their meeting place in the
jungle and sing, emerging at intervals to 'dance at' the boys.
This dance, which is characteristic of the *wai'a*, is known as
da-prabú (stamping on the feet). The dancer advances, stamping
right up to his subject and then engages in partial retreats and
lunges forward. His whole posture is aggressive. He adopts a
scowling expression and stamps furiously, raising his knee as
high as he can and pounding the earth just before the man he is
dancing at, often pounding the latter's instep as well. He snorts
and flails his arms, working his shoulders in a pantomime of
attack. The person who is danced at remains motionless in the
ceremonial stance, eyes downcast and body relaxed. He should
not move a muscle or flinch, even if the dancer tramples him.

---

other moiety name (wood-cutters) could refer to the clubs. I cannot support
this suggestion with any other evidence.

After some days of fasting the boys are weakened from exposure and coated with the dust which is kicked up during the dances. Then the men announce that the next stage of the proceedings will take place. Accordingly the boys from one moiety build a shelter in the village space and rather to one side. The boys from the other moiety are enclosed in it.[1] The men emerge from the forest and dance around the moiety that is 'out'. In the course of the dance each boy in turn rears up, whirls around, and then falls down senseless. His kin then revive him and he is taken away to be wept over, bathed and fed. The following day the boys from the moiety which has been thus danced over enter the shelter, and those who were in the shelter come out and are similarly treated.

The boys now sit on mats outside their huts. At nightfall they are led by their fathers into the forest, where they are told to investigate strange huddled shapes which turn out to be men hiding under leaves. These men hand them ceremonial arrows which they are told to carry back with them and place in forks by their mats. They then sleep beside the arrows to guard them. Next day they shuffle forward a few paces, dragging the arrows towards the centre of the village, and then shuffle back again. They keep up the process all day until they reach the men's meeting place at nightfall. There they lay their arrows down so that their points all touch in the centre of the circle.

After these preliminaries the boys and men paint and prepare themselves for the *wai'a* proper. This consists of two separate rituals, one involving the killing of Simihẹpãri and one involving the activities of the *pi'u* spirits. It is not clear whether both of these rituals should be performed in a properly constituted *wai'a* and whether they should be performed in any particular order. I have corroborated the details of each, however, and shall therefore describe them as I witnessed them in São Domingos in 1958.

Long before dawn the mature men were singing in their meeting place. At the end of each song they chanted in unison 'U, hẹ, hẹ, hẹ . . .' in a staccato, breathless fashion.[2] Two or

---

[1] During a particular *wai'a* in São Marcos the Umrẽ built the shelter and the Udéhẹri were the first to be enclosed in it.

[2] Sherente use a similar call ('hui, hui, hui') then they perform a ceremony to conjure up the spirits of the dead.

three of them went over to the shelter where the newly initiated Tírowa age-set were sleeping and stamped in among them, snorting ferociously. If any of the sleepers were slow to get up, they were seized and dragged out of the shelter and their sleeping mats hurled after them.

Just before dawn the men adjourned to the forest to sing. Four *dzę'wa* (rattle-bearers) sat in a tight circle in the middle of the clearing. Two of them were Umrẽ and two of them Udéhęri. They had *uibro* clubs such as are normally the badges of the Young Men's age-grade planted behind them. They led the singing, marking time with their rattles.

The same song was repeated over and over throughout the day, with short pauses. It differed from the songs Shavante usually sing in that it was rather more tuneful, and the middle passage of it was a diminuendo in which the singers dropped their voices from the customary bark to little more than a whisper.

The senior men of the village would sit close to the rattle-bearers and the more junior age-sets further away. The young men, who were also present in the clearing, placed their sleeping mats at the edge of it and kept a little apart from the mature men. Only the rattle-bearers remained there constantly. Others came and went as they felt inclined.

At mid afternoon four of the young men, two from each moiety, were selected by the rattle-bearers to carry the ceremonial emblems later in the ritual. The rattle-bearers then took their *uibro* clubs under their arms and led the celebrants in procession into the village. There they formed a half circle before the end house of the village.[1] The four leaders produced tiny whistles made out of lagenaria pods and blew a blast on them to open the proceedings. The men then sang the same song that they had been intoning all day and, with the exception of the rattle-bearers, danced. The dance consisted of clasping the hands over the abdomen and rhythmically bending and flexing the knees in a stylized representation of sexual intercourse.

The whistles were then blown again and many of the celebrants broke ranks and dashed to the huts at the end of the village, where they stamped and snorted and pounded on the

[1] Belonging to Waarodí.

thatch. This was brought to an end by another blast on the whistles and the men resumed their dancing.

At this point the four men selected from the two moieties ran ceremonially (i.e. with arms held straight) out of the village. When they returned some time later the two Umrẽ were carrying ceremonial arrows known as *ti-pe*, and the two Udéhẹri were carrying the phallic emblems known as *tsi-uibro*. They formed up in front of the dancers and joined in the dance, holding the objects in their right hands and waving them backwards and forwards with an undulating motion as they danced.

The dance was performed at the four 'corners' of the village[1] and then once again at the first point. Afterwards the men gathered in their respective meeting places, except for the two who were carrying the *tsi'uibro*. They rushed into the end house where the dancers had been singing and flaunted the *tsi'uibro* briefly before running out again. The women came to the door of the hut as they left, making motions with their fire-fans as if brushing something away. The runners dashed in and out of a number of houses in the village, from each of which the women emerged and vigorously repudiated them. Then they raced into the forest again in the direction from which they had brought the emblems.

Now the leaders of the *wai'a*, still carrying their war clubs, trotted off along the trail after the bearers of the *tsi'uibro*. They were followed by all the celebrants in single file. I was not permitted to accompany this part of the ceremony. According to my informants, however,[2] the celebrants made contact with Simihẹpãri, who is very fierce. They fought him and killed him.

---

[1] i.e. by the end house, at the point where the straight edge of the row of huts begins to curve, at the point where the curve begins to straighten out in the other arm, and at the other end house.

[2] The São Domingos Shavante were exceedingly reluctant to discuss this episode and so my information in 1958 was substantially incorrect. In 1962 I found certain Shavante groups who had so far lost interest in the *wai'a* as to be willing to discuss the impersonation of Simihẹpãri frankly. One Western Shavante group had even permitted the Salesians to make a film of the meeting with Simihẹpãri, which I saw in São Paulo. It corroborated my informants' stories: Shavante impersonate Simihẹpãri and paint themselves black with a lurid pattern of white stripes. They give the *ti-pe* and the *tsi'uibro* to the celebrants of the *wai'a*. Afterwards the celebrants return and there is a mock battle. Simihẹpãri growls and roars and rushes at his adversaries, who finally overcome him, beat him to the ground, and kill him.

Then they buried the *tsi'uibro* in simulated graves covered with brushwood and returned to the village.

They returned in solemn procession, the junior age-sets first and the senior behind, with the ceremonial leaders at the rear. The leaders sat down in the Mature Men's meeting place, the huts were opened, and they were brought cooked food from all the houses to pay them for their services.

That night the men's council did not discuss normal business. The elders sat in a closed circle and conversed in whispers. They did the same the following night, after a day of rest when the men had gone hunting and fishing to provide food for the ceremonial leaders. After a while they whistled in the ceremonial fashion and the Young Men then came over to the Mature Men's meeting place and joined the junior age-sets on the edge of the circle. The chief then delivered a short harangue and dismissed them. Shortly afterwards the junior age-sets also departed, leaving only the elders to discuss the details of the ceremony in private.

The following day the elders adjourned to the clearing in the forest, where they were brought venison and fish. The senior man of each ceremonial moiety ate some of the food and it was then given to the rattle-bearers, who divided it into two equal piles. They ate first and were followed by the other members of their moieties.

Throughout the day the rattle men led the singing again. Meanwhile a man painted black from head to foot lay well concealed in a thicket and sounded his horn. He represented the *pi'u* and the melancholy hooting of his instrument was supposed to strike terror into the uninitiated. The younger men worked on the preparation of the *ti-niptoro* arrows, which had long thin wooden points attached to their canes. Each one had two feathers affixed to the other end, but these were more decorative than functional, so that the artefact was not really 'feathered' like a true hunting arrow. Its shaft was decorated with snakeskin and clippings of human hair.

At mid afternoon, when the arrows had been completed, all the men assembled in the clearing. The members of the young men's age-grade, including recent initiates, then stood forward in threes and were danced at by their seniors. Afterwards each of them had a black stripe painted on his belly from the navel down to the pubes. When all the men were satisfactorily painted a small group went off to the village and I was obliged to accompany them, since I was not permitted to witness the next part of the proceedings.

The men took out one of the women who had been selected for this *wai'a* and escorted her into the forest. They then returned twice more for other women, so that eventually they had taken a woman from each clan. The three women were obliged to have sexual intercourse with the celebrants of the *wai'a*, on completion of which they were painted scarlet and given the same black leg paint as the men wore, down to moiety markings. They also wore white bark wristlets and anklets just as men do for the *wai'a*.

Once more the celebrants entered the village led by the rattle-men, carrying war clubs. This time they danced first in the centre of the village, and when the dance was finished broke up into two groups which rushed about for a moment and then gathered round one rattle-bearer each. These two groups[1] all did the stamping dance, without directing it at anybody in particular, until the leaders whistled for them to stop.

Then the celebrants, accompanied by the women they had co-opted, danced round the village as they had done on the first day, except that in this case the four young men in front danced with *ti-niptoro* arrows. The women were still not permitted to leave their huts when the dancing was finished. Instead, the newly initiated young men sang the *wai'a* song round the village throughout the night. All night too the *pi'u* kept up its mournful hooting.[2]

At daybreak all the men came out in the middle of the village again and waited, tense and expectant, until they heard a

[1] They were casual conglomerations, not divided by moieties.

[2] When the men adjourned to the men's council to discuss the day's ceremonies it was apparently decided that I should be accepted as a *wai'a* celebrant. I think the Shavante had felt embarrassed about my position during the ceremonies. On the one hand, I had been incorporated into the Ai'riri age-set and allowed to participate in the sponsorship of the Tírowa. On the other hand, I was clearly uninitiated, and Simihẹpãri would kill an uninitiated man. Nor could they be quite sure that I would not be shocked by the ritual rape. They therefore waited until these two episodes were over and then decided to make amends to me. One of the chief's sons danced at me, and was so carried away by his performance, which lasted longer than the others I had seen, that he finished by seizing my head in his hands and biting me on both cheeks until he drew blood. He and his father then

whistle outside the village. At once all the young men shouted
'*U, hę, hę, hę* . . .' and fanned out over the middle of the village.
Each whistle from the forest was answered in the same way,
amidst mounting excitement. At last the black figure of the *pi'u*
appeared at the edge of the village and fired one of the ceremonial *ti-niptoro* arrows into the air. The young men dashed for
it. The first to get a firm hold on it had the privilege of trotting
into the centre and presenting it to the elders. He then waited
there with downcast eyes while the *pi'u* rushed up and danced
at him. There was more than one *pi'u*, and also other men (not
pi'u), hidden among the trees firing arrows. So the *pi'u* were
dashing backwards and forwards dancing at the young men
as they received the stream of arrows.

When they had all been fired Prapá collected them into a
bundle and danced round the village showing them to alternate
houses, just as the *tsi'uibro* had been flaunted on the first day.
Then the *ti-pe*, the *ti-niptoro* and the whistles, all items that the
uninitiated should not see, were put carefully away. The huts
were unblocked and the *wai'a* was over.

I do not claim to be able to elucidate this complex ritual in its
entirety, nor could the Shavante provide me with an explanation
of it on which to base a subsequent analysis. I think, however,
that we have by now achieved a sufficient general understanding
of Shavante society to be able to embark on a contextual
analysis of the various elements of the *wai'a*, and that this in
turn will provide an explanation of its symbolism.

Consider first the ceremonial moieties. They are ritually
opposed to each other only at the time of the boys' fast. What is
it about that ceremony which requires a system of moieties, and
why will not the customary dichotomy between *waniwihã* and
wasi're'wa serve, as it does in the *oi'o*? The other context in which
the Umrĕ-tdé'wa and Udéhęri'wa have differential functions
is in the *wai'a* proper, when representatives of the former dance
with *ti-pe* arrows and representatives of the latter dance with the
tsi'uibro. Furthermore, these emblems are associated with the
figure of Simihępãri. The clue to this whole ritual complex lies
therefore in a structural definition of Simihępãri.

---

harangued me, telling me that I was now a *wai'a'wa*, that I could participate
in the rituals, and that I must keep them secret from women and other
uninitiated people.

In Shavante myth Simihẹpãri is referred to as a good hunter; he is so fleet that he brings back much game. He is also very fierce, so fierce that it requires a considerable amount of courage and aggressive spirit for Shavante to go out and face him in the *wai'a*. This comes out very clearly in the account of a *wai'a* ceremony which one of my informants gave me, and which I recorded at the time. I reproduce his version verbatim, to give an idea of how Shavante themselves conceive of the *wai'a*.

Wai'a

We went after Simihẹpãri. There he was growling and roaring. We chased him till we were tired. Many Shavante ran to get *ti* (arrows) and *tsi'uibro*. Then they painted and decorated themselves to be very fierce (*pahi da*). Simihẹpãri ran among them and they were frightened. They ran away. They ran to the village.

(Questioner asks: Did you run fast?)

Yes, we did.

(What were the names of the people with you?)

Butsi, Wa'airi, Babatí.

(Who else of ours (*waniwihã*)?)

Urasé.

(Prasé?)

No, Urasé. It is a different name. He was killed.

Then the *tsi'uibro* were brought into the village and were danced round fiercely (*was'tere-di*). The women were pushed into the huts. Then we sang.

(He sings.)

(Questioner: Which age-sets were making the *wai'a*?)

The old Tẹrã. Also the Tírowa and the Ai'riri.

(How about the S'daro?)

The S'daro were just children then.

(Did you often have a *wai'a* in those days?)

Often. Then everybody danced with the *tsi'uibro*. They are fierce and ready to fight. They will fight and then return home. They are fierce, just like wild pig. They are really fierce (*saihí-ti*). They go out after Simihẹpãri and catch him. They beat him to the ground. Simihẹpãri crawls about.

(Questioner: Did they have their heads whitened (i.e. with *wededzu*)?)

Who?

(The *wai'a'wa*?)

Yes, they had their heads whitened.

(Did you stay there too?)

Yes, I stayed there. I stayed there to seize Simihẹpãri and fight
with him.
(Noises to describe the slaying of Simihẹpãri.)
(Questioners: Where were the women?)
Which women?
(Were there no women there?)
(Embarrassed) Yes. There were women. (Laughs.) The padres
don't like that. The Shavante are still very fierce when they return
home and take the women. Now they have finished with Simihẹpãri.
OOOH OOOH   (Noise of *Pi'u*.)
Now the Shavante ran out again. They stopped. They had been
fasting. They had only eaten a teeny bit—just like children. They
were all very fierce. Then they seized him.
(Questioner: Whom?)
Urasé. They seized him and flung him in the water.
(Noises—Urasé being flung in the water.)
The *wai'a'wa* were still very fierce. Then they went into the jungle
and stayed there. I was there too, watching. The Nõdzẹ'u were very
fierce. They were all very tough (*sipt'té'wa*).

In this *wai'a* the celebrants go out to meet Simihẹpãri, who
is fierce and frightens them. They return to the village with the
ti-pe and *tsi-uibro*. In *wai'a* nowadays it is the men who represent
Simihẹpãri who actually hand these emblems to the celebrants.
In the story the celebrants then work themselves up to a pitch
of ferocity such that they can return and kill Simihẹpãri.
Ferocity is the keynote of the whole account. The narrator
mentions no less than nine times that the protagonists were
fierce or acting fiercely. They demonstrate their ferocity in
three ways, by killing Simihẹpãri, by raping the women, and
by killing one of their own number. The time of a *wai'a* was in
fact, and to a certain extent still is, a time when factional
disputes were likely to come to a head. When the men of the
village had worked themselves into such a state of excitement,
they were prone to settle old scores, so that a *wai'a* was frequently accompanied by a killing. This was not, however, part
of the ritual, whereas the killing of Simihẹpãri and the rape of
selected women was.

We have established that the *wai'a* is a ritual of ferocity. This
ferocity is communicated by Simihẹpãri to the celebrants and its
symbols are the *ti-pe* and the *tsi-uibro*. But we already know that
the Shavante think of the *tsi'uibro* as a phallic symbol. It can

therefore be taken to represent the sexual aspect of ferocity—broadly speaking, sexual power. By contrast the *ti-pe* represent the non-sexual aspect of ferocity, aggressive power. Since it is characteristic of sexual power that it be generative, it seems that the Shavante, in distinguishing between *ti-pe* and *tsi-uibro*, are distinguishing between generative and non-generative power or, as Freud would have put it, between sexuality and aggression.

The whole Simihẹpãri ritual is thus a communication of power to the *wai'a* celebrants. But Shavante distinguish two aspects of this power, the sexual or creative, which is symbolized by the *tsi-uibro*, and the aggressive or destructive, which is symbolized by the *ti-pe*. It is this complementarity which is the essence of the antithesis between the Umrẽ and Udéhẹri moieties. So not only do Udéhẹri men carry the phallic emblems in the *wai'a* but Udéhẹri boys dance during their fast with red *um'ra* clubs, the symbols of free-floating generative power. Not only do Umrẽ men dance with the arrows of aggression, but Umrẽ boys during the fast encircle their opponents and shake their dance rattles at them.

This interpretation does have the advantage of rendering the other major elements of the *wai'a* immediately intelligible. The ceremonial leaders carry *uibro* clubs throughout the proceedings, and we have seen that they are symbols of sexuality + aggression. When the celebrants enter the village they perform a sexual dance and then rush to pound on the thatch of the surrounding huts where the women are confined. Finally, the combination of sexuality and aggression could hardly be more aptly expressed than in a ceremonial rape.

The significance of the *pi'u* can be analysed along similar lines. Shavante say that they are black all over and that they make a buzzing noise. They come only when summoned by the singing of the *wai'a* celebrants. Shavante fear them because 'they fight a lot', yet a meeting with the *pi'u* 'makes a man strong'. The *wai'a*, then, is a rite in which the *pi'u* are conjured up, just as Simihẹpãri is also summoned. The Shavante both fear this contact, which is dangerous and perhaps terrifying, and welcome it because it confers strength. *Pi'u* communicate with Shavante in two ways, by firing *ti-niptoro* arrows at them and by dancing at them. I suggest that these rites are symbolic of the transfer of aggressive power from *pi'u* to *wai'a* celebrant.

Such an explanation of the relationship of the *pi'u* to the Shavante permits us to make an analysis of a separate set of rites, those concerned with hairdressing. It will be remembered that the *ti-niptoro* arrows, which symbolize whatever is communicated from *pi'u* to Shavante, are trimmed with snakeskin and human hair. Consider other hair rituals:

(1) The mature men cut the hair of the initiates just before they complete their initiation.

(2) The age-set which has completed its initiation clips the hair of the age-set which is about to enter the bachelors' hut.

(3) Mourners shave their heads completely.

(4) Men bind up their hair during ceremonial and warfare.

(5) Men powder their hair with magic substances during ceremonial and warfare.

It is not easy to interpret Shavante hair symbolism in terms of the common element in these situations. In my view this is because there is no single common element present. Leach has suggested (1958) that there is considerable ethnographic evidence to support the symbolic association of hair with libidinous energy, and indeed this equation is often made in psychological interpretations of symbolism. But Shavante hair symbolism does not appear to be sexual, or, at least, the connexion is not demonstrable. Mourners who shave their heads, for example, are not subject to sexual prohibitions. On the other hand, boys in the bachelors' hut, who must remain chaste, do not cut their hair short. Their hair is indeed cut by the Mature Men, but this is done at the moment of initiation, i.e. at the very moment when they are no longer under any social constraint to remain continent.

I would argue instead that much hair symbolism among the Shavante must be regarded as representing 'free power (aggression) as distinct from sexuality' (Leach, 1958: 160). This hypothesis accounts for the ritual in instances (1), (2), and (3) above, as well as for the human hair on the *ti-niptoro* arrows.

We have seen how the older men dance at the younger throughout the *wai'a*. I maintain that this is a demonstration of the power (aggressive) of the elders and a communication of it to their juniors, who cannot become full *wai'a* celebrants without this rite. By analogy, when the mature men clip the hair of the initiates previous to the ceremonial run that closes their initiation, this is explicable as an act of aggression—a symbolic exercise and communication of power.

Similarly, we have noted (Chapter IV) that there is a logical connexion between distinction and opposition. Furthermore, proximate age-sets are distinguished through opposition. So, when the initiated age-set clips the hair of those who are about to enter the bachelors' hut, this may be interpreted once again as a symbolic act of opposition (aggression).

Finally, the shaving of his head by a mourner is, according to this interpretation, an act of auto-aggression. It should be classed as a rite of self-mutilation without specifically libidinous connotations. Such rites are widely enough reported in the ethnographic literature, and are to be found in particular among the Apinayé (Nimuendajú, 1939: 151), close neighbours of the Shavante.

Note that, in the contexts we have been discussing, it is the cutting of the hair which is of symbolic importance, not the hair itself. Hair clippings in the *wai'a* thus represent hair-cutting and therefore aggression. The actual hair is not thought to have any special properties. Hair clippings are not used in sorcery, nor are they disposed of very carefully. Hence rituals which involve hair but not hair-cutting come into a different category. Nor are they very important.

Shavante do not use different styles of hair-dressing to indicate different social statuses, and we have seen that hair-dressing does not have specifically sexual connotations for them. They are therefore free to attach some other meaning to hair symbolism. When a man binds up his hair, this has no more significance than that he is 'ready for action'. It may have a practical advantage in that the hair does not get into his eyes during whatever activity he is preparing for, but the act of binding it back has a symbolic significance equivalent to 'rolling up one's sleeves' in our society, or, in the more poetic Biblical terms, 'girding up one's loins'. Similarly, it is the hair which is powdered with magical dust during ceremonies, and especially in warfare, because this is the easiest way of making a public demonstration that one is using it!

The *wai'a* is thus a ceremonial complex, during which

Shavante conjure up certain beings or spirits in order to acquire power from them. From Simihẹpãri they acquire generative power and destructive power; from the *pi'u* they acquire bellicosity. The combination of these powers is in Shavante thought the essence of manhood. That is why manhood presupposes and entails participation in the *wai'a*.

5. THE MEANING OF RITUAL

In this chapter I have tried to explain the meaning of Shavante rituals by contextual analysis of the symbolism employed. I wish now to consider two major implications of this approach. The first of these can best be demonstrated by means of an example.

The rite of ceremonial weeping among the Shavante is performed on the following occasions:

(1) On greeting a returning kinsman.

(2) While the Tebe procession goes round the village.

(3) After the Páhiri'wa had danced.

(4) At various stages of the initiation ceremonies.

(5) After the sponsoring age-set has performed the final rite for their *protégés*.

(6) After death.

Shavante explanations of the rite differ in each case. For (1) they say they weep because they have missed their returning kinsman. In cases (2), (3), and (4) they say they weep because they are happy that the Tebe/Páhiri'wa initiate has taken part in the appropriate ceremony. In the case of (5), however, they say they weep because they are sad that the sponsors have taken part in the appropriate ceremony. Finally, in the case of (6), they say that they weep because they are sad *and* because they miss their dead kinsman.

The emotional 'meaning' of the rite is different in various cases. It is even different for different people on the same occasion. We know that the Shavante make a sharp distinction between kin and affines. We know that they customarily feel solidarity with the former and hostility towards the latter. In view of this, it seems unlikely that a man's parents and his wife's brothers, both of whom weep over his corpse, are similarly disposed towards him when they bewail his death. An analysis of the rite in terms of the 'affective dispositions that regulate the conduct of persons to one another' (Radcliffe-Brown, 1948: 245, 239–46) is therefore hardly an analysis at all. It amounts to a statement that people are expected to behave towards each other in certain customarily defined ways, and that ceremonial weeping disposes them to do so by emphasizing the social relationship or the change in the social relationship between person and person. In other words we know that two people stand in a particular social relationship to one another. We know that they weep together. We therefore deduce that the weeping reinforces the relationship and establishes or revives the sentiments on which it depends.

But we have left the central problem unsolved. We still do not know how ritual weeping can be the expression of a tie of solidarity as well as a tie of hostility. We do not know how it may express relationships characterized by sadness and relationships characterized by happiness, how it can express nostalgia for what is irrevocably gone (the dead) and nostalgia for what has now returned (an absent kinsman). We do not know, in fact, the common denominator of the contexts in which Shavante weep.

Yet this common denominator is hardly recondite. To any anthropologist familiar with the work of Van Gennep it is at once obvious that ritual weeping in situations such as I have described is a *rite de passage*. Radcliffe-Brown perceived this, and it is implicit in his analysis of the rite among the Andaman Islanders quoted above. He did not, however, develop this line of argument, preferring to concentrate on the pseudo-psychological explanations which I have rejected.

Among the Shavante, those who weep make a public declaration of the changed or changing status of a close relative. The returning traveller passes from the status of a stranger to that of one of the group into which he is received (cf. van Gennep, 909: 51–53). A boy graduates to the status of Tebe or of 'áhiri'wa. At each stage of the initiation ceremonies the initiates leave behind one status and are ritually received into another. An age-set marks, by the performance of the last rites of sponsorship on behalf of the initiates, its own graduation from the ceremonially active groups. Death is yet another graduation.[1] Each of these graduations directly affects a small circle of the close relatives of the person concerned. It is they who 'announce' it by means of weeping. Their affective state has no direct bearing on the custom. It could be investigated, but only by an entirely different type of analysis made for different

[1] Cf. Hertz (1928a: 86): '. . . en d'autres termes, la mort, aux yeux des primitifs, est une initiation'.

purposes, that is by a psychological investigation that aimed to discover how Shavante feel about, and during, ritual weeping, rather than a sociological one that aims to explain what it is that is made public in the rite. Nor is it possible to explain by means of such a sociological analysis why the Shavante signal changes of social status by weeping, rather than by dancing or shouting or destroying their own possessions or any other public demonstration. The techniques of social anthropology cannot, as Leach has pointed out (1958: 160), establish the relationship between public and private symbols, between social states and psychological states. They can only seek to demonstrate the conventional, public meaning of symbols.

There is however a well-known ambiguity in this use of 'meaning'. Meaning for the society which performs the ritual or meaning for the analyst of it? It is unlikely that a Shavante either could or would analyse the symbolism of the *wai'a* in the way I have done. Does this indicate that the symbols do not mean what I say they do *to the Shavante*? If not, then in what sense can they be said to 'mean' what I say they mean, and to whom?

It has, I think, been sufficiently well established that people may be unaware of important facts about their own society. This does not mean that these facts cease to be true. When Hollingshead (1949) and Warner (1949) published their classic studies of American towns they set out to demonstrate that, in spite of the talk of a classless society, the communities they described were effectively stratified. Many of the inhabitants of those communities professed to be unaware of this stratification, but the sociologists argued that they nevertheless tended to behave as if they were aware of it.

I have deliberately chosen this simple—one might say simplistic—example to make my point. If people behave as if they are aware of the model, then their actual degree of awareness of it becomes of only secondary interest. It is these 'as if' models which Lévi-Strauss called 'unconscious models' (1953). People are unaware of the principles, or, at any rate, cannot make the principles explicit, but these principles nevertheless regulate their behaviour.

But this brings us to the most important problem of all. What evidence have we for assuming that the principles do in fact have the effects we claim for them? In my example of the class system in a theoretically egalitarian community the model derives support from data relating to educational possibilities, interaction frequencies, notions of prestige, and so on. It is much more difficult to demonstrate that Shavante hope to derive two types of power from the *wai'a*.

That is why I have, at the risk of boring the reader, included detailed descriptions of the ceremonies I discussed and, in so far as I was able to, of Shavante attitudes towards them. I have tried to treat each rite as a neutral symbol and to deduce its significance from the contexts in which it appears. My entire analysis of Shavante ritual therefore depends on my preceding analysis of Shavante ideas and actions, for it is on this preliminary elucidation that my understanding of the 'context' of the rite is based in each case.

My conclusions may be neo-Freudian, but this does not establish their validity. It only shows that two independent and mutually exclusive types of enquiry may produce the same kind of result.[1] Indeed I believe that my conclusions are valid just because they do not follow from premises about the universal meanings of certain classes of symbol, as psychoanalytic interpretations tend to, but because they are derived from premises which are strictly Shavante. Thus Róheim's interpretations of Australian ritual (1945) may be correct, but I would not agree that he succeeded in showing them to be so. They could only be demonstrated by some sort of Australian analysis analogous to the Shavante analysis I have presented.

I would take issue with some structural analyses on similar grounds. Lévi-Strauss' interpretations of Gê societies are cases in point.[2] They may be correct, but the evidence adduced to support them is sometimes inadequate. In my critique of them (1960) I stressed the importance of establishing the context, because in my view this is the best way we have of establishing the hypothesis. I hope that I have been sufficiently successful in doing this here to establish that the dialectical character of some of the ideas I describe comes from the Shavante and not from me.

[1] A similar confluence of a sociological analysis with a psychological argument is found in Leach (1958) where he takes up a theme treated by Berg (1951).

[2] See particularly 1952, 1955, 1956, 1965.

VIII

COSMOLOGY

1. SORCERY

IT is impossible to understand Shavante cosmology without first dealing with their views on death and the hereafter. Yet a discussion of death entails a discussion of sorcery. Much of the preceding analysis has been concerned with Shavante factionalism. We have seen how factions tend to counterbalance each other in Shavante communities and how the processes of law and the maintainance of order depend largely upon this balance. We have seen too how the relations between clans, and concomitantly those between 'Our People' and 'Others', are those of hostility, actual or potential. Such hostility may be expressed in sorcery (by the weaker against the stronger) or in accusations of sorcery, followed by killings or expulsions (by the stronger against the weaker).

Shavante do not invariably attribute sickness and death to evil agencies. They have some understanding of contagion and are aware, for example, that if they consort with a Brazilian who has a cough, then they too are liable to catch it from him. Should they catch his cough, they will not believe that he has bewitched them unless they have good reason to. The proviso—'unless they have good reason to'—is very important. A Shavante man believes that he always has good reason to suspect his affines of harbouring evil intentions towards him. When a man dies, then, Shavante seek to explain the circumstance by searching for its cause in the probable malevolence and sorcery of his factional opponents, particularly those to whom he was linked by specific affinal ties.

On the other hand, when a woman or child dies, Shavante do not normally look beyond the physiological reasons for death. They may do so on occasion, however. We saw in Chapter V how, when Tomõtsu's wives died in Santa Terezinha, this was interpreted by his affines as evidence of his trying to harm them through sorcery. This emphasizes my point. When Tomõtsu's wives died, people did not try to imagine who would wish to harm *them*, but rather which man could harm which other men *through* them.

Sorcery is thus a masculine activity and it is a function of the tensions between categories of males in Shavante society. A man's death is explained in terms of sorcery, unless he has been killed in an inter-factional dispute or executed. In such cases there would be no suspicion of sorcery, since the obvious suspects would belong to the group which had a hand in the killing. They would have no need to use sorcery against their enemy if they were going to club him to death anyway. Shavante would, on the contrary, consider this as proof that they were not using sorcery against their victim. This accounts for the fact that suspicions of sorcery are mainly harboured by the dominant faction against members of other factions. Members of the dominant faction in any community may, and do, employ sorcery against others in minor factions. But they do so only in comparatively trivial situations where they could not be sure of persuading their kin to take physical action against their enmies. A child's or a woman's death may be accepted as requiring no further explanation, or it may be considered as a by-product of the sorcery practised by men and aimed against other men.

Shavante also fear the canalized malevolence of neighbouring tribes. They are, for instance, afraid of their traditional enemies, the Karajá, who afflict them, so they believe, with sickness and death. Shavante scorn the fighting abilities of the Karajá and, until recently, considered all of them to be fair game. I suspect that many Shavante still do. They fear them because they despise them as weaklings. Shavante reason that the only way the weaker can retaliate against the stronger is by supernatural means. In their own society this is the only way that members of a weak faction can strike at the members of a strong one. It is consistent with this belief that they should feel themselves bewitched by the Karajá.

The belief is lent further support by the fact that, when the Shavante venture over towards the Araguaia river and into the neighbourhood of the Karajá, they usually contract some sort of infection. The Karajá themselves are more prone to infection than the Shavante, since they live in close contact with the Brazilians. A Shavante who visits them comes back, as often as not, with a cold. Sometimes he comes back with influenza and infects his fellow-tribesmen. When the Shavante of Santa Terezinha trekked towards Cocalinho in 1957 and met a camp of Karajá on the beaches opposite the settlement, they were infected with influenza, which they believed that the Karajá had inflicted on them.

The Karajá are thus credited with the possession of some diffuse and unspecified malign influence. Shavante call this *simię-di*, the same word which they apply to sorcery in their own society. Yet they deny that the Karajá know the uses of *suprá-was'té-di* (bad dust) or of *wede-dzu* powder, the commonest substances manipulated by Shavante sorcerers. The Karajá do not, according to them, 'do' anything to bring misfortune on others. They are bad and therefore they radiate malevolence. The Karajá are thus the closest approximations, in Shavante thinking, to what may be called 'witches' (cf. Evans-Pritchard, 1937: 387).

Shavante do not admit that there are people in their own society who have in themselves the power to harm others. They believe that Shavante are only able to inflict sickness and death on other Shavante by the exercise of certain rituals involving the manipulation of magical substances or implements. These substances are powders, which may be used both offensively and defensively. The possession of such a powder does not therefore brand a man as a sorcerer, except in the technical sense that he has the paraphernalia of sorcery at his disposal. He would not be considered as *simię*, unless it were thought that he was using these powders offensively. Indeed on certain occasions they are used quite openly. Men participating in ceremonies will often powder their hair with *wede-dzu*. Men going on a war-party do likewise, and men who are mobilizing to defend their community would be sure to do so, otherwise they would not be in a state of total preparedness.

It is the use of *wede-dzu* or of other forms of 'bad dust' in conjunction with specific rites which the Shavante consider as constituting sorcery (*simię-di*). They are understandably secretive about these rites. It was extremely difficult for me to obtain even a general description of them, and impossible to obtain a demonstration. Nor did I ever succeed in watching the preparation of *wede-dzu*, which is a type of sawdust extracted from particular woods. All male Shavante know how to make it and use it and they pass on the information from father to son. They insist, however, that no spells are employed either at the preparation or at the activation of it. It is operated by throwing it (or making as if to throw it) at the victim, while the sorcerer lurks in hiding. It may also be blown in the general direction of the person it is intended to injure. It seems that the blowing of a magical powder is merely a convenient method of propelling it in the right direction. The action of the breath is not essential to the performance of the rite, and the Shavante do not believe that the act of blowing is imbued with any particular power when performed in a ritual context.

Note.
physical
agency.

The propulsion of a magical powder in the direction of the ← victim is the most important technique of sorcery, but it is not the only one. A man also manipulates his ear-plugs with a view to afflicting his enemies. The ear-plugs used for this purpose are reddened with *urucú*. Clearly then this creative power can also be used for nefarious ends.

Surupredu, for instance, told me that Tsimõ was mean (*zoĩti-di*) to him. He therefore took out his ear-plugs and asked them to make a sting-ray wound the other man. It did so, and Surupredu felt satisfied. He could afford to tell me of this comparatively minor matter, since he belonged to the dominant faction and Tsimõ did not. I was also, to a certain extent, identified with the dominant faction and Surupredu used to address me as *ĩ-dúmrada* (elder sibling). He therefore considered it unlikely that I would repeat his words to Tsimõ. Even if I had, there was little the other could have done about it, save try and retaliate through sorcery himself. The risk of his doing this was anyway an ever-present factor in the social situation and would not have been appreciably heightened by hearing gossip from Surupredu.

Shavante claim likewise to be able to set alligators, *piranha* fish, snakes, and jaguars onto their enemies by addressing themselves to their reddened ear-plugs. I have even heard it claimed that this technique could make rain or drive away a storm. On the other hand, the users of 'bad dust' generally have a more noxious end in view. They hope to afflict an enemy with a long and painful malady, and generally also to bring about his death. Such an enemy is invariably *wasi're'wa*. It is therefore possible to interpret the prominent part played by a dead man's affines at his mortuary rites as a public assertion that they, who might otherwise be suspected of complicity in his killing, are innocent of intent to harm him (cf. Malinowski, 1929: 137).

2. DEATH

When an adult man dies, he is laid out in the hut of his wife's parents, and the event is made known by the wailing of his wife and of those of his male affines who are resident in his wife's household, or who still consider his wife's household to be their home. As soon as the fact of death is established, his parents, his uterine siblings, his children, his mother's brothers, and his sister's children (if they are adult) are obliged by custom to gather round the corpse and weep. A woman is, of course, laid out in her natal household, since she never resides anywhere else. She is usually bewailed by her parents, by her uterine siblings, her children, her mother's brothers, her sisters' children, and her husband.

A person who does not actually die in his own household is brought back and laid out there to be bewailed by his family, if this is at all practicable. Sometimes, if he has been killed in an inter-factional dispute and his close kinsmen have fled, or if he has been executed, he is buried outside the village without any wailing over his body. Nevertheless, those who stand in any of the relationships to him which have been mentioned above will bewail him in the customary fashion, either in the village to which they have fled or simply in their own huts, if they have not been obliged to seek refuge.

The wailing is a stylized weeping, identical with the rite of weeping when greeting a returning kinsman or when emphasizing the passage of kinsmen from one social status to another. It is, however, intensified on the occasion of death. It is louder and more violent and it lasts very much longer. On the two occasions when I heard mourners wailing in this fashion they kept it up for a full twenty-four hours without stopping. That is to say, individual mourners may have paused for a while, but there was never a moment of silence for a full day and a night after the death. At the end of this period the mourners were so hoarse that they could do little more than croak. Then there was a respite. In one case there was no more weeping for the few hours of darkness left. The mourners took up their wailing again at dawn and wept intermittently throughout the whole day. In the other, the family continued to weep, but with brief periods of silence, for another twelve hours after the original period of concentrated lamentation.

The wailing therefore lasts for about a day and a half after the moment of death. The fact of death is established by the cessation of breathing. Shavante then feel for the heart, and, if that has stopped too, they begin to wail. '*moto der*', they say, meaning 'gone dead'. The same phrase can also be applied to unconsciousness or an unusually deep sleep and Shavante believe that the soul leaves the body on such occasions. Once the heart has stopped, however, they know that the soul will not return and it is on this account that they start to weep. During the weeping the mourners crouch round the corpse and rarely stir away from it. The possessions of the deceased—his sleeping mat, weapons, and ceremonial ornaments, in the case of a man; her gourds, firefans, carrying-baskets, in the case of a woman—are torn apart or broken in pieces and put onto a big fire which is kindled in front of the hut.

Aboriginally, then, there can have been no question of inheritance. Nowadays, manufactured articles are not always destroyed at the death of their owner. The disposal of them is, however, not yet of any great importance. Shavante told me that a man's children and sisters' children would have first claim on his possessions after his death. His uterine siblings would also be entitled to a share. The introduction of comparatively imperishable and irreplaceable articles, which require to be handed on to the deceased's kin, is so recent that the Shavante I knew had not yet developed an institutionalized set of inheritance rules.

While the immediate family of the deceased is wailing and burning his possessions, anyone else who feels like it may also weep ceremonially. Apęwẽ, the chief of the São Domingos Shavante, wailed in his hut on the occasion of both the deaths which took place while I was present. In each case the dead child's father was a Topdató clansman, incorporated into the Tpereya'óno clan. One of those who died was Apęwẽ's sister's son's son. The genealogical relationship of the other one to him was much more remote and I was unable to trace it. It is fairly certain that Apęwẽ did not weep for them either in the capacity of a relative or as a fellow-clansman, but rather as chief of the community. He had likewise retired to his hut to weep on other ceremonial occasions, such as the processing of Tebe and the completion of various stages of the initiation.

Other Shavante not in the house of mourning also wept for a
little while on the occasion of the deaths I witnessed. But these
weepers who were not of the immediate family of the deceased
did not continue their wailing for very long. They had all fallen
silent after half an hour at the most. Since the deaths took place
at night I was not able to identify exactly who wept for the
children and who did not. In any case, outside the immediate
circle of mourners who keep up their lamentations for the full
period, the identity of other weepers is of little significance.

Those who take part in this ceremonial wailing may be
actuated by a genuine sadness, but this is not a necessary condition of their performing what is a customary rite. Long after the
death those among the bereaved who really feel a sense of loss
will wail whenever they come to think of the departed. This is a
spontaneous emotional release, although it is expressed through
the same type of wailing as is customary in ceremonial situations. Anything which reminds a Shavante of a lost relative may
provoke demonstrations of grief for years after his or her death.
One woman always wailed when she heard an aeroplane
because there had been one passing over when her husband
died. Another man went to fantastic lengths to obliterate all
traces of his deceased wife, for everything that reminded him of
her caused him acute sadness. He even set out along the trail of
the last trek on which she had accompanied him and destroyed
all the shelters she had built, so that he would not happen upon
them later and feel sad.

While the family of the dead man are bewailing him, his
corpse is prepared for burial. The children whose funerals I
attended were buried by their parents and their parents'
siblings. My informants told me, however, that a man is
normally prepared for burial and actually buried by his *ai'ãri*
(WB), or, in the absence of living brothers-in-law, by other
members of their lineage. A woman is similarly buried by her
husband's lineage.

The cemetery is usually close to the village. At São Domingos
it was among the trees and bushes near the edge of the cleared
village space and some twenty yards from the half-circle of huts.
The corpse is wrapped in a sleeping mat and placed in a perpen-
dicular grave in a semi-erect position. The freshly dug earth
is then piled on top of it and is covered with a mound of

brush-wood, both to mark the spot and to keep out carrion animals. When the burial party have completed their work, they return to the hut from which they bore the deceased and join the mourners who are still wailing there. At the funerals I observed, the corpse was buried within a few hours of death, without waiting even for daylight. Shavante do not, to my knowledge, practise secondary burial.

Some of the relatives of the deceased should now cut off all their hair. If it is a child who has died, in the sense of someone who is unmarried and resident in his or her natal household, then only its parents will be expected to shave their heads, though its mother's uterine brother may also do so. If the deceased was a married man then his wife and children will shave their heads, and possibly also the other affines who live in her house. His own parents are not expected to. On the other hand, if a married woman dies then her parents are expected to cut off their hair, as also is her husband and her children, but none of her husband's kin. It is thus within the household of the dead person that full mourning is observed.

Those relatives who bewail the deceased observe a two-day seclusion immediately after the death. During this time they sit wailing without eating or drinking or bathing. They leave the hut of mourning only to bury the body and when they are obliged to in order to relieve themselves. When the period of ceremonial weeping is over they take up their normal life again, and, so far as I was able to discover, are subject to no further restrictions.

Meanwhile, if the deceased should have been physically (as opposed to supernaturally) done to death by other Shavante, then the killer or killers are obliged to go into seclusion as well. A killer bleeds himself by making a series of lateral incisions across his chest and upper arms with the claw of an animal. These incisions must be deep enough to bleed profusely and they leave parallel scars across the chest when they have healed. The killer remains in his hut for a few days, neither eating nor drinking nor bathing. He does not speak to those about him. Socially he ceases to exist. I was unable to establish the exact length of his period of seclusion, but it does not last more than five days at the most. Nor was I able to obtain any information about his ritual re-instatement. Shavante said simply that after his seclusion he would go down to the river and bathe. He would then eat and drink and once more take part in the social life of the community.[1]

[1] Neighbouring Gê tribes also oblige a killer to go into seculusion (see Nimuendajú, 1939: 128; 1942: 78; 1946: 154 and Lowie 1946b: 498). Among the Sherente, a killer made incisions on his chest and stomach in the same way as is still done among the Shavante (Nimuendajú, 1942: 79).

3. COSMOLOGY

I cannot give a complete account of Shavante cosmological ideas. I doubt if any Shavante could. My knowledge of their language was never in any case such as would enable me to press my investigations of topics which the Shavante themselves found hard to express and unattractive to discuss. They gave an impression of having comparatively little speculative interest. Even in 1962, when I finally managed to persuade the old men to sit down and tell me stories, their tales were more often than not interminable onomatopoeic narratives of fights and hunting exploits. Only when they were pressed did they haltingly and with much reflection give me some details about the creation of the world; and unless I maintained a barrage of questions they would slip into one of the familiar myths about the origin of fire or the origin of maize that I had already heard innumerable times before.

I do not propose to undertake a full-scale analysis of Shavante myth at this point. Such an analysis is in preparation and will be published separately. I shall merely outline some Shavante cosmological notions which can be gleaned from my limited corpus of stories. They had, for example, no standard answer to the question 'Who made the world?' Nor was this simply a matter of the question's being meaningless to them. Different informants did indeed answer it, and they gave me differing accounts of the creation.

When Shavante speak of creation they make no distinction between creation out of nothing and creation in the sense of transformation. They use certain phrases to designate a creator, such as *romn'nãrdá'wa* or *roptó-n'nãrdá'wa* or *romn'nãrdá'mañãrĩ'wa*.[1] Such a creator may have participated in the creation of the world *ex nihilo*. Thus old Aihí're at São Marcos put it for me this way:[2]

Aïwamdzú was his name. He was the creator. Hireroi'wa too. Also our ancestor Aïwamdzú.
(Questioner: Where did they come from?)
They came from over there. (Gesture.) The world was empty

---

[1] Derived respectively from *ro* = everything + *n'nãrdá* = root or origin + *'wa* = personal suffix; *ro* + *podo* = create + *n'nãr'dá* + *'wa*; *ro* + *n'nã'rdá* + *mañãr* = make + *'wa*.

[2] I quote verbatim from the tape of his conversation with other Shavante.

then. He was creator too of the Sirentdé'wa. Our ancestor Aïwamdzú came out of the earth. The world was created because in the
beginning there was nothing. He was a Shavante.

(Questioner: How about the creation of women?)

They appeared. He had three wives and two children. He came
out of the earth. At that time the world was empty, empty. The
world was truly empty.

(Questioner: Where did he come out?)

Over there.

(Questioner: Where was that?)

Over by the Ẽ Wawẽ.

Then the east (lit. the beginning of the sky) was not created. At
the east there was spirit. From the east there was creation. The
woradzú pré were created. The whites and their towns were created.
The north and the south (lit. both sides) were created too.

Then he went on at once to tell the story of Tpemrã which I
listed as version (1) of the rationale for the immersion ceremonies. Tpemrã too was a creator—but he was a *wapté* who was
already living in a world peopled with kin and affines. If my
informant felt there was any distinction to be made between
these two types of creation, he gave no sign of it. Indeed, they
may be considered as on a par with each other. Aïwamdzú was a
creator but he did not actually create the world. He appeared
at a time when the world was empty and everything was being
created in it. Tpemrã appeared sometime later but was perhaps
equally a creator.

The problem of creation out of nothing, which exercises such
a perennial fascination in many religious and philosophical
schemes, does not seem to concern the Shavante. Their only
mention of it is in narratives such as Aihí're's above, where it is
stated that everything had a beginning and left at that. Most
Shavante creation stories are concerned with metamorphosis or
discovery.

So a young girl discovers maize, which is given to her by the
parakeets. A young boy discovers fire, which is given to him by
the jaguar. Both of these are origin myths in the sense that they
deal with the transformation of men from animal to human.
Before they possessed maize and fire the Shavante could eat
only rotten wood (like animals), which was soft enough to chew
and required no preparation. When they had acquired maize
they had proper food. When they had acquired fire they could

prepare it instead of eating it raw. The stories thus express the passage from a state of nature to a state of culture. The origins of nature itself are not something about which the Shavante find it useful to speculate.

They believe that this natural order of things was at some time created and peopled with Shavante who are of cthonian origin. As soon as they had emerged from the ground they divided into three clans, which have therefore been part and parcel of Shavante society since the beginning of time. Meanwhile, various mythical heroes are thought to have been creators in the sense of transforming the world, creating its fruits, and so on.

But these creation legends are 'just so' stories. Their protagonists are not invoked by the Shavante in any other context save that of the mythical rationalization. They are not held up for emulation nor turned to for assistance. There is not even general agreement on who the protagonists were. Aihí're mentioned Aĩwamdzú and Hireroi'wa as having been there at the very beginning. On another occasion he referred to Siridzí-ri as the creator because he had founded the Tpereya'óno clan. Similarly Rãrite and S'repá, the founders of the Ę̃ Wawẽ and Topdató, were mentioned as creators, all of them in addition to the hero-creators mentioned in Chapter VII. Meanwhile other Shavante suggested that S'rizamdí and S'ritomõzasé were also creative heroes.

In this plethora of heroic figures there is no single one I could discover about whom a series of legends was told. Nor, curiously enough, was there any cycle of legends concerning a pair of heroes who complement each other. This is remarkable in view of the importance of such cycles among the Timbira and the Sherente. The Sherente myths concerning Waptokwa, the sun in human form, and Wairíe, the anthropomorphic moon, are a central feature of their world view. Not only are these figures regarded as the founders and, in some sense, as the patrons of the exogamous moieties, but in story after story their characteristics are shown to be antithetical and complementary. Furthermore, Waptokwa was until recently worshipped as the supreme creator, who could intervene decisively in the affairs of the tribe.

The closest that the Shavante ever came to a narrative concerning a pair of heroes was in the story I listed as version (4) of the rationale for the immersion ceremonies. There S'ribtuwẽ and Prinẽ'a created many things before flying up into the sky. It is true that these figures are mentioned more than once as the protagonists of creation myths, but they do not normally appear as a pair. In any case Shavante do not think of these figures as exercising an influence over their day to day lives.

The entities which do exercise such an influence are the various classes of spirits. I know of at least four such classes: Simihẹpãri, the *pi'u*, *wazepari'wa*, and the spirits of the dead (*da hiebá*). I have already considered the relationship of the first two to the Shavante. They are strong and fierce, and they come when they are summoned by the singing of the *wai'a* celebrants, who then derive power from them.

Shavante also seek assistance from the spirits of the dead, particularly dead kin, who are regarded as especially benevolent. Once a soul has established itself in the community of the dead it can come and go with impunity. When it comes back to visit the living, Shavante are not afraid of it, since such souls are generally thought of as having the well-being of their kinsmen at heart. In cases of illness they can sometimes be relied on to 'look over' the patient and make him well again, and they are the source of other minor favours and benefits. But their powers are limited. In really vital issues, the Shavante intercede ceremonially with 'stronger' spirits. There is therefore no 'ancestor worship' or 'cult of the dead' among the Shavante. Their acts of worship, or rather of communication with the supernatural, are directed towards spirits of a different order.

Nevertheless, Shavante seek and welcome the advice and assistance of the souls of their dead kin. They invoke it, however, informally and only in situations with which their spirits are believed to be able to cope. We have seen how their help is sought in cases of sickness. If an important member of the community is very ill and the souls of his kinsmen seem powerless to help him, then a *wai'a* is held on his behalf. The *wai'a* is thus an appeal to a higher power, whereas men turn to the souls of their departed kin for assistance in the petty misfortunes and perplexities of everyday life. A man who is unlucky on the hunt is likely to ask the spirits of his kin to guide him to game. Another, who does not know whether to make a certain journey or whether to accompany one band on trek rather than another, will try to obtain their advice on the matter. I am not sure whether women too may communicate with the spirits of their kin. I have never heard of their doing so and I know of no woman who has had clairvoyant experiences; but there is no reason why they should not, since it is only participation in the ritual of the *wai'a* which is restricted to initiated men.

The dominant lineage in São Domingos, the Wamãrĩ, took their name from the cylinders of polished wood, somewhat resembling relay batons, by means of which they communicated with their dead kin. A cylinder could be hung either over the grave of a dead kinsman, usually of a father or father's uterine brother, or over the sleeping-mat of its owner. The owner then visited or received a visitation from his dead kinsman in the course of a dream. Such meetings were always happy occasions, though tinged with the sadness of nostalgia for the departed. A man felt strong after such an encounter and better able to face life.

Other lineages did not have any paraphernalia to assist them in meeting their departed kinsmen. These meetings did, however, take place, either by chance or because a man longed to see a particular spirit and concentrated so hard on him that he eventually appeared to him in a dream.

The spirits would sometimes give advice to their *protégés*. They might alternatively accompany them on their dream journeys, showing them what to do in particular situations or where to find specific things, such as game trails or fording places of difficult stretches of water. Other spirits taught their *protégés* songs, the singing of which would bring them good fortune. It is songs such as these that men teach to the boys in the bachelors' hut and which subsequently come to be 'sung round the village'. Finally, some men were taken by their guardian spirits along the trails which led towards the village of the dead. I never met anyone, however, who claimed to have been there and back. The distance, Shavante told me, is much too great. A man begins to feel frightened that he will never get home again, and always turns back long before he has reached 'the beginning of the sky'.

It is only the souls of the dead who ever complete this long journey. Shavante believe that the soul leaves a man's body at the moment of death and sets out for the village of the dead. This is not the only time it leaves his body. It may do so during sleep or unconsciousness or a trance. Its journeys are then correspondingly shorter and, of course, it always returns to its carnal envelope at the end of them. Dreams and hallucinations are therefore explained as experiences of the soul during its periodic wanderings outside the body. At death it leaves the body for the last time.

The journey to the home of the dead is a long and perilous one. The soul is guided on its way by the souls of kin who have preceded it. They try to guard it from the dangers that beset it, for if a person's soul were killed before it reached the community of the dead, then it would be obliterated for ever. It would be equally terrible for the soul to get lost before it had established itself among the dead, for then it might wander between the living and the dead, perpetually at the mercy of those dangers which threaten it in its marginal state.

Shavante believe that evil-doers and wicked people never reach the village of the dead. They are destroyed on the way, despite the efforts of their guides, or they are kidnapped by the *wazepari'wa*. There is some suggestion that the soul of an executed man is carried off by the *wazepari'wa* to become one of themselves and never reaches the village of the dead. For instance, chief Ẽribiwẽ, who was killed in Areões, was said by some to have gone to these spirits. But the two children who died while I was at São Domingos were said to have gone to join their kin in the village of the dead.

Once the soul has arrived in the village of the dead, its troubles are over. It is a huge village, situated at the 'root of the sky' and as far to the east as it is possible to travel. It is built on the same pattern as those of the living, but with more houses than have ever been seen in a single community before. It is a place of abundance, where life is easy and food plentiful and the souls of the dead spend their time there singing and dancing.

The *wazepari'wa*, on the other hand, are the antithesis of the spirits of the dead. They are malevolent, where the dead are benevolent. Their visits are feared, where those of the dead are welcomed. They are even located geographically at the opposite pole. The Eastern Shavante told me that they were to be found at the 'end of the sky', or as far west as it is possible to go.

They appear in various disguises, all of them terrifying. Sometimes they are like ordinary mortals, but their long matted hair hangs down to their waists and partly conceals their faces, which are indescribably sinister. At others they appear like ferocious warriors, their hair bound up at the back and their faces contorted. Sometimes they turn into animals. They are particularly fond of changing into *jaburu* birds, whose cry, sounding rather like 'pi-ã', the Shavante regarded as an especially evil omen, even a presage of impending death. Shavante do not regulate their behaviour according to such omens, however. They neither practise divination nor seek auguries concerning a future course of action.

wazepari'wa prefer to roam about at night, but they can also be met with by day. Lone hunters occasionally meet them and are invariably terrified. They either flee blindly from them or are transfixed with fright and unable to move. They are frightened because *wazepari'wa* have the reputation of carrying off mortals, both while they are still alive and while their souls are journeying to the village of the dead. Shavante tell each other stories like the one about the child who was spirited away by them, or about the man who pierced his foot and could not walk, so that his hunting companions left him in the shelter they had constructed. When they returned that night, they found that the *wazepari'wa* had spirited him away. Such stories enhance the reputation of these spirits, so that strange noises and inexplicable thefts are usually put down to their agency. Shavante often pestered me to give them torches, so that they could switch the beams on to prowling *wazepari'wa* on dark nights and shout at them to go away and leave the encampment in peace.

Despite the fear inspired by these spirits, Shavante believe that there are some men who regularly commune with them. Such men do so for the same reasons as others try to contact the spirits of the dead, for help and counsel and the power to foresee the future. The only man in São Domingos who was generally thought to be a communicant of the *wazepari'wa* was Domitsiwa, the man who was abnormal through meningitis. He certainly talked in his sleep and probably had fits of some sort. The Shavante believed that on these occasions he was entering into contact with the spirits, and it was his hut-mates who most

persistently begged me for torches. The ascription of this
relationship with the *wazepari'wa* to Domitsiwa inspired his
fellows with a certain respect for him. They tolerated him and
his abnormality, and even his kleptomania, for the *wazepari'wa*
are noted thieves, so that it was only natural that their *protégé*
should have the same propensity.

But the *wazepari'wa* are not merely dangerous spirits who are
invoked or avoided at the individual level. They play, as we
saw, an important part in the initiation ceremonies. The age-
set which sponsors an initiation impersonates the *wazepari'wa*.
They sing songs and perform dances which come from the
wazepari'wa. They brandish dance-masks which are closely
associated with the *wazepari'wa* and which have to be guarded,
so that the latter do not take them away. I have argued that
these masks are symbolic of initiation itself, and therefore of the
affinal ties which are contracted at initiation.

This association of *wazepari'wa* with affinity is confirmed by
the characteristics of the spirits themselves when seen, as contrasted with the characteristics of the souls of departed kinsmen.
The former are malevolent, the latter benevolent. The former
steal, the latter confer benefits. The former terrify, the latter
console. The *wazepari'wa* even live at the end of the sky, whereas
the souls of the dead live at its beginning, and we have seen
that end and beginning are ritually represented by the colours
black and red, which the Shavante in turn associate with bad
and good. This association of *wazepari'wa* with badness is
further demonstrated in the Shavante notion that evil-doers do
not reach the village of the dead, but go (or are taken) instead
to join the *wazepari'wa*. We know by now that to the Shavante
way of thinking the most likely people to fall into the category
of evil-doers are affines. Similarly, and by contrast, they think
of the village of the dead as essentially a place where a person
goes to join his kin.

I pointed out to my informants that if everybody's kin went
to the village of the dead, then logically everybody's affines
must be there too. They admitted the truth of this but replied
that in the village of the dead there was no sorcery and no
fighting. These are the characteristic modes of relationship
between a man and his affines, so in Shavante thought heaven
is a place where affinity has been exorcized.

This series of antitheses may be summarized as follows:

wazepari'wa	*da hiebá*
malevolence	benevolence
taking	giving
terrifying	consoling
ending	beginning
(death?)	(life?)
west	east
affinal place	kin place
affines	kin
wasi're'wa	*waniwihã*

The paradigm has to be slightly modified for the Western Shavante. They are organized in exogamous moieties. The members of each moiety claim that their dead go to the beginning of the sky and the dead of the opposite moiety go to the end of the sky. The *wazepari'wa* live away somewhere different —they did not know where. But the *wazepari'wa* are still in every other way antithetical to the *da hieba*. The Western Shavante have not only exorcized affinity in heaven, they have done so by ensuring that heaven is a place where there are no affines (cf. Lévi-Strauss, 1949: 616–17).

IX

AKWẼ-SHAVANTE SOCIETY[1]

1. SOCIAL STRUCTURE

W E are now in a position to consider the structure of Shavante society and to discuss some of its wider implications. I believe, and in this I follow Lévi-Strauss (1953: 525) and Leach (1954: 5), that the most useful conception of social structure is that it is a model or logical construct in the mind of the anthropologist. It would not make much sense, according to this usage, to say that an anthropologist in the field was 'studying social structure'. One could only say that he was collecting data on, for instance, social relationships or social institutions. When he ordered those data in the form of a model which purported to demonstrate certain crucial relationships in the society studied, the model could then be called the social structure of that society.

This, or a similar view of structure is the point of departure for structural anthropology, by which term I refer to the efforts of certain scholars, notably Lévi-Strauss, Leach, Dumont, and Needham, to develop methods of formal analysis that would enable social systems to be represented by highly abstract models. This approach differs radically from the Radcliffe-Brownian view of structure which dominated social anthropology at one period, but the nature of the difference needs to be clarified.

Radcliffe-Brown suggested that social structure should be viewed as a 'network(s) of relations connecting the inhabitants (of any convenient locality of suitable size) amongst themselves and with the people of other regions' (1952b: 193). Unlike culture, which he described as a 'vague abstraction' (1952b: 190), structure was a 'concrete reality' which could be directly apprehended by the observer and therefore described in a proper scientific spirit (1952b: 190, 192). He maintained that

[1] Parts of this chapter were incorporated in a paper read in Moscow 1964 (see Maybury-Lewis, in press).

it was important to distinguish structure from 'structural form' and that, while structure was the existing concrete reality which was directly observed, it was nevertheless structural form which a field-worker described (1952b: 192). By structural form he meant the general form of a relationship, as opposed to particular instances of it, or the general form of a pattern of relationships, as opposed to a specific concatenation of them.

These ideas, expressed in the illusively limpid style for which Radcliffe-Brown was well known, are somewhat imprecise. The word 'structure' might seem a poor choice for what turns out to be an aggregate of observed actions. Radcliffe-Brown reversed the conventional meanings of the words 'structure' and 'form', and used the first to connote the actual perceptible appearance of a thing and the second for the pattern which could be identified as the thing in the abstract. In his terminology 'structural form' is the abstraction which would most closely correspond to what I have termed 'structure'. Yet Radcliffe-Brown did not make much use of this concept in his work. He everywhere speaks of 'social structure' when discussing the societies which he proposed that anthropologists should devote themselves to classifying and comparing. As a result the sort of structural analysis which he and other like-minded anthropologists engaged in was not carried on at a very high level of abstraction. 'Social structure' was generally used as a blanket term to designate social institutions or social groups.

One other important characteristic of this approach was Radcliffe-Brown's conviction that every society had a structure which could be determined by inspection, much as the bone structure of a vertebrate may be described by examining its skeleton. This view, so far from contributing to a science of society as he had hoped it would, tended to freeze anthropological thinking and imprison it in its own classifications. When Radcliffe-Brown classified Australian societies (1931) for example, he did this in terms of such institutions as patrilineal or matrilineal descent, moiety systems, and marriage sections. Yet he clearly felt that in so doing he had once and for all demonstrated their 'structure'. From this it followed that attempts to look at these societies from another point of view could only be wrong and he resisted them vigorously (1951, 1953).

The merit of structural anthropology is that it offers a way out of this dilemma by positively inviting anthropologists to break away from their customary and often *a priori* views about the significance of social institutions, and to see whether, by thinking them out anew in formal terms, they can come to fresh conclusions. The social structure of a society is taken as an explanatory hypothesis about it, not a descriptive anatomy of it.

I would add that such a hypothesis is usually only one of a number of possible hypotheses. Some societies may, to all intents and purposes, be rendered intelligible by a single model. Even so, I feel it is important to bear in mind that this model is not the only explanation of the data; rather it is considered, at a certain time and for certain purposes, to be so far and away the best explanation that it can be treated as the only explanation of them. This may seem a tedious piece of hair-splitting, but we shall see its significance with regard to the Shavante in a moment. All too often the glittering certainties of today become outworn theories of tomorrow, and I feel it is incumbent on the scholar to bear this possibility constantly in mind.

One of the weaknesses of current structural anthropology is the tendency of its practitioners to insist on single model analyses of social systems. Lévi-Strauss has, for example, published stimulating interpretations of certain Central Brazilian societies (1952, 1955, 1956), but I cannot share his faith that the models he presents correspond to the 'real' structure of the societies he discusses. I tend to be something of an agnostic in these matters and would prefer to argue that they are provocative hypotheses and no more.

I offer my analysis of Shavante social structure in the same spirit. This book is little more than an argument that Shavante society can best be understood in terms of the dichotomy between *waniwihã* and *wasi're'wa*. I have tried to document this argument as fully as I can. In the next Section I consider how far such a model may be said to 'explain' Shavante society.

2. DUAL ORGANIZATION

The most immediately striking feature of Gê societies is their proliferation of moiety systems. Nevertheless, Lévi-Strauss pointed out in 1952 that perhaps this 'dual organization' had been over-emphasized. He followed up this suggestion in a later paper (1956), where he argued that the obvious complementarity of exogamous moiety systems was not necessarily the crucial factor in understanding societies of the class which had hitherto been known as 'dual organization'. He tried to show that in certain cases an asymmetric model could explain a wider range of social facts than the conventional symmetric one, and from this he argued that societies which had been thought of as symmetric should be treated for analytical purposes as limit cases of an asymmetric type of social organization, whose characteristics he briefly outlined.

Dual organization, according to this argument, is not a synonym for exogamous moieties. It is the name for a type of social organization which expresses a fundamental dyadic principle. This principle may be expressed in an exogamous moiety system, but, according to Lévi-Strauss, it can only be fully understood in terms of other principles operative in societies that not only lack exogamous moieties but possess asymmetric institutions, which had previously been held to distinguish them sharply from dual organizations.

I propose to reject the second part of the argument, on grounds which I have already made clear elsewhere (1960c). But I shall follow up two of Lévi-Strauss's points. In the first place, I agree with him that so-called 'dualistic societies' should not invariably be interpreted in terms of a single, symmetric model. I would not, however, replace one orthodoxy by another and insist that they be interpreted as limit cases of a triad.

Secondly, it seems to me that any analysis of moiety systems leads inescapably to Lévi-Strauss's conclusion that they do in fact express some sort of dualism which may be expressed by some other means in the very same society, or by other means in other societies. Consider the Gê data. If we stick to the concept of dual organization that equates it, as Rivers did (1914), with exogamous moieties, then we are obliged to conclude that the Sherente and the Western Shavante are examples of dual organization; that the Eastern Timbira peoples are doubtful;[1] and that the Apinayé, Kayapó, and Eastern Shavante are not.

This would not seem to be a particularly useful distinction. The Apinayé, for example, share a set of symbolic and spatial ideas associated with agamous moieties very similar to those possessed by the Eastern Timbira and the Sherente.[2] In all three societies moieties were localized on opposite sides of the village, associated with opposite points of the compass, with Sun and Moon respectively, and so on through a series of analogical antitheses. A more fruitful line of enquiry would be to treat them as variations of a single institutional complex. The case of the Eastern and Western Shavante is even more obvious. In sum, we have good reasons to believe that we are dealing with a set of closely related institutional patterns. Our problem is to try and explain the variations, and we are not helped in this by a formulation which distinguishes certain societies as being of a completely different type.

The implications of this conclusion are far-reaching. If dual organization is held to be synonymous with exogamous moieties, then one of the terms is superfluous, but at least we know where we are. If, however, dual organization is merely the socio-logical expression of a dyadic principle then what are the characteristic features of those societies pertaining to this class? One must entertain the proposition that this principle may be expressed otherwise than in moieties, whether agamous or exogamous. Lowie's remark, intended as a *reductio ad absurdum*, that if any opposition was a dual organization, then the distinction between Republicans and Democrats could be taken as an example of it, now has to be taken seriously. Why not? And why could this dyadic principle not be expressed in the ideas of a society without any corresponding oppositions between groups? Lévi-Strauss has, after all, argued that the symbolic opposition between the centre and the periphery in a Trobriand village, the two directions in which men and women can conceptually be said to circulate in Indonesian prescriptive

[1] Nimuendajú stated that they had exogamous moieties (1946: 75), but subsequent field-workers have cast doubts on whether the moieties were actually exogamous or not (personal communications from William Crocker and Jean Carter).

[2] See Nimuendajú, 1939, 1942, 1946.

marriage systems, and the exogamous moieties of the Bororo are comparable dualisms (1956).

In my view such an approach renders the discussion of dual organization vacuous. Such dyads are obviously all members of the class of dyads. But if it is held that they pertain to a distinct class of societies that we find it convenient to label as dual organization, then a demonstration of their common sociological properties must at some stage be offered. After all, it can be maintained that to distinguish by means of antithesis is one of the fundamental procedures of human thought. Aristotle certainly thought so,[1] and Heraclitus went even further. He believed that the oppositions inherent in the *logos* characterized not only human thought but the whole scheme of things.[2] In fact this notion of cosmic dualism permeates the whole of Western philosophy from Heraclitus to Hegel and Marx, and is hardly absent from Eastern philosophy either.[3] It was specifically taken up in the study of categories of thought by the French sociologists of the early twentieth century.[4] It follows from this that most human societies could be expected to give conceptual or institutional expression to some sort of dyadic principle. A conclusion that most human societies were therefore dual organizations would be, as philosophers say, only trivially true.

I think that a more useful concept of dual organization is that it is an ideal type corresponding to a theoretical society in which every aspect of the social life of its members is ordered according to a single antithetical formula. The discussion of whether or not a given society is a dual organization or whether dual organizations exist then becomes irrelevant. Instead, anthropologists might consider how far a particular dyadic model was explanatory of a given society; or, to put it another way, what range of rules, ideas, and actions was rendered intelligible by the model and, equally significantly, what range was not.

According to these criteria Shavante society would seem to

---

[1] The Categories (Chapters 10 and 11).
[2] See Kirk: Heraclitus, the Cosmic Fragments (1954).
[3] See Granet, 1950: 115–48.
[4] e.g. Durkheim and Mauss (1903), and especially Hertz (1928b). For further discussion of the point see Needham, 1960b: 104 and Maybury-Lewis, 1960a: 42.

approximate to the ideal type. It could be presented as a set of institutions modelled on a series of analogical antitheses:

HOUSEHOLD	Those married in	Dominant lineage
	Outsiders	Insiders
	Subordinate	Superordinate
COMMUNITY	They	We
	Opposite faction	My faction
RELATIONSHIP	They	We
TERMINOLOGY	Marriageable	Not marriageable
COSMOLOGY	Wazepari'wa	Spirits of the dead
	Affines	Kin
	WASI'RE'WA	WANIWIHÃ

This is the major dichotomy running through the Shavante scheme of things, but it is not the only one. I have argued that their central ceremony, the *wai'a*, can be interpreted as a ritual during which two types of power are communicated by supernatural beings to the celebrants. Its paradigm could therefore be set out as follows:

Sexual power	Aggressive power
tsi'uibro	ti-pe
Udehẹri moiety	Umrẽ moiety

Finally, even the age-sets which in Shavante thought counteract the split between *waniwihã* and *wasi're'wa* divide into age-moieties for log races. Admittedly most of Shavante ceremonial is conducted by the age-sets, but as soon as men become senior enough to take an active part in factional politics they cease to participate in age-set activities and take their obligations to their faction more seriously than their obligations to their age-mates. It could be argued, then, that the age-set system is, in a sense, a subordinate institution and that the best explanatory models for Shavante society are all dyadic ones.

These models are not explanatory in a predictive sense. An appreciation of the distinctions I have outlined would not enable an outsider to predict Shavante attitudes and behaviour very well. To do that he would require rather more complex models, such as the ones I discussed in my analysis of the political system and of the relationship system. But these models would be derivative, mere elaborations of the basic dichotomy. In short, the dyadic model may not tell us all we need to know about the Shavante, but, on the other hand, we cannot properly be said to 'know' anything about them except by reference to it.

3. COMPARATIVE

All the Gê tribes do not appear to have applied the dyadic principle in such a thoroughgoing fashion as the Shavante. A binary model still has some applicability among the Sherente. Unlike the Shavante, their whole scheme of antitheses was related to their exogamous moieties. Nowadays moiety exogamy is a thing of the past and young Sherente cannot even remember which moiety they are supposed to be in. Yet they continue to use a two-section relationship terminology, applying one set of terms to members of those clans who would in the old days have been in Ego's moiety and the other to members of the clans from the opposite moiety.[1]

The Sherente data appear to confirm my hypothesis concerning the relative importance of the age-set system and the factional system among the Shavante. Nimuendajú visited the Sherente in 1937 and was impressed by the wide range of activities controlled by the men's associations, which he correctly suggested had developed out of an age-set system (1942: 59, 64). By the time of my visit to the Sherente, in 1955, the associations were moribund; and in 1963, when I revisited them, they were a piece of quaint folklore in the memories of older men. Among the Sherente, then, the influence of the dyadic moiety system has outlasted that of the associational (age-set) system. Nowadays Sherente factions form in each community in a manner analogous to Shavante factions, so that the political system of the Sherente closely resembles that of the Eastern Shavante. This is not surprising, since the Sherente and the Shavante are so closely related.

Research among the Northern Gê has obliged us, however, to place these dyadic systems in a new perspective. Preliminary reports from the Kayapó, the Apinayé, and the Eastern Timbira appear to indicate that, while these binary oppositions are of some importance, they do not have the explanatory power that they possess for the Shavante. This is not the place to discuss the social structure of these other tribes. Separate studies of them are to appear shortly, and that will be the time to undertake a full-scale comparative analysis. But the fact that the Northern Gê may be less dualistic than the Shavante (and possibly the Sherente) has some implications for the present

[1] See Maybury-Lewis (1965: 222).

enquiry. After all, the Northern Gê (Kayapó, Apinayé, and Eastern Timbira) are closely related to the Central Gê (Shavante and Sherente). These peoples form part of a single cultural complex. If the Shavante, then, have developed one set of institutional possibilities to a greater extent than have their neighbours, it should follow that the other tribes have concomitantly developed certain features which are either absent or subordinate in Shavante society. An examination of the ways in which they differ from the Shavante could then be significant not only in a comparative sense, but also as an indication of the set of alternatives from which Shavante institutions have been derived.

The most obvious way in which the Northern Gê differ from the Central Gê is in the rule of descent. Nimuendajú stated unequivocally that the Apinayé and the Eastern Timbira were matrilineal. The Shavante and the Sherente are staunchly patrilineal. It is possible to pass this off by arguing that a rule of descent is quite arbitrary and, in a formal sense, a society may choose one as easily as another. Yet such an explanation is too facile. If these tribes all belong to a single complex, then these apparently antithetical descent systems should at the very least provide food for thought.

Closer examination shows that they may not, in fact, be so sharply distinguished as was at first supposed. For example, affiliation to most of the important groups in Eastern Timbira society was by name. A person received a set of names and they determined which groups he or she would belong to (Nimuendajú, 1946: 80–82). Affiliation to the Apinayé 'marriage classes'[1] was by a principle of parallel descent, such that a man succeeded his father and a woman succeeded her mother. There were no descent groups in either society. Matrilineality was confined to the moieties which were categories of people, and it has lately been questioned as to whether it was in fact the rule which constituted even these.[2] What is established is that among the Apinayé and Timbira peoples the nucleus of the household is a group of matrilineally related women. In fact matrilocality is

[1] I have argued elsewhere that these were not in fact marriage classes (Maybury-Lewis, 1960b).
[2] By members of the Harvard-Central Brazil Project, who are at present working on these tribes.

really a more meaningful concept for these societies than matrilineality. This interpretation is supported by evidence from the Kayapó, who practise matrilocal residence in the absence of unilineal descent groups.[1]

These reassessments of the Northern Gê material enable us to see the link between their institutions and those of the Central Gê. I commented earlier on the curious anomaly of uxorilocal residence among the Shavante, which caused each young husband to venture out into a household of hostile affines. It is now clear that this is all part of the Gê pattern. In every Gê tribe studied so far the household has contained an extended family whose nucleus was a matriline of women. This is true even for the Shavante and the Sherente, where the custom serves to fragment the important, named patrilineages.

Given this basic pattern, the major difference between the tribes are in the ways in which they regulate succession. Thus there was a tendency among the Eastern Timbira for a man to succeed to the status of the maternal uncle who named him, just as the woman succeeded the paternal aunt who named her. In other words men were likely to be recruited matrilineally and women patrilineally. Among the Apinayé there is evidence that some sort of recruitment was patrilineal for men and matrilineal for women. The Shavante and the Sherente, with their insistence on patrilineal descent groups, ensured that a son succeeded to the status of his father. Yet this patriliny was not so significant for women. Among the Shavante they were largely excluded from lineage affairs. They were not embroiled in factional disputes nor suspected or accused of sorcery. One might say that in Shavante society women were not wholly identified with their patrilineage. Since they lived matrilocally, there is therefore a sense in which they could be said to succeed to the status of their mothers, a situation which is not too far removed from that of the Apinayé

Thus we conclude that these societies are not so much representatives of distinct types of social organization as variations on a single sociological theme. One constant element in the pattern appears to be the matriline of females in the household groups, a conclusion which effectively disposes of arguments about the *a priori* inevitability of patrilocal residence

[1] Personal communication from Terence Turner.

among hunting and gathering peoples.[1] To use a Marxist terminology for a moment, this appears to be a basic element of the Gê substructure, just as an ideology of dual organization is, in some form or other, an important element of the superstructure.

These societies are also ranged on another continuum, which is not explained by any of the arguments I have so far advanced. We have seen that perhaps the most important sense in which 'My People' are distinguished from 'Others' in Shavante society is that the former are potentially members of My Faction whereas the latter are potentially Enemies. The formation of cliques, interest groups, factions, lobbies, and so on is an inevitable consequence of social life and just as universal as, say, that old anthropological favourite 'the prohibition of incest'. What is remarkable about Shavante factions is not their existence, but the extent to which they dominate the life of the tribe, and, given this domination, the fact that they are then structured in an analogue to a two-party system.

The dyadic model of Shavante society which I presented in the previous section does not in any useful sense 'explain' the factional system. On the contrary we saw in Chapter V and VI how the categories associated with this binary opposition were often adapted to pre-existing factional situations. Factionalism is thus a fundamental fact of Shavante life, on a par with, and independent of, any dualistic ideology. This limits the type of explanation one can give of it. I have, for example, demonstrated how dualism works among the Shavante. In the absence of historical data I can make no statements about the development of this pattern. An answer to the question 'Why do they have it at all?' can only be sought in extended comparative analysis, such as is being undertaken by the members of the Harvard-Central Brazil Project. Similarly I have been able to describe Shavante factionalism, but any explanation of why this type of institutionalized hostility should pertain among the Shavante must wait for a comparative study.

I can, however, venture a hypothesis. Nimuendajú mentioned that the Sherente were quarrelsome and intriguing, and contrasted them in this respect with the Eastern Timbira (1942: 15). My experience among the Sherente was the same. I noted the high incidence of factitious quarrels among them in 1955–6 and

[1] See for example Murdock, 1949: 213–14.

found that this was not the case among the Krahó (Eastern Timbira) among whom I spent a short period in 1956. The two peoples were well aware of this difference between them and expressed it in their stereotypes concerning each other. The matter began to interest me seriously when I had worked among the Shavante and recorded the data on which my analysis of Shavante factionalism is based. I remembered then that the Kayapó too had a ferocious reputation for internecine warfare, and this was subsequently confirmed by Terence Turner in the field.

We can, then, range the societies for which we have the best data as follows: severe factionalism, involving frequent violence, killings, and the break-up of communities occurs among the Shavante, Kayapó, and Sherente. Factionalism is by all accounts less severe, or absent altogether, among the Eastern Timbira peoples.[1]

It might be supposed that this can be explained by the fact that any man in Timbira society must belong to a number of differently constituted corporate groups (Nimuendajú, 1946: 77). If the members of these groups are assumed to have moral obligations towards each other, then it is correspondingly difficult for factions to form, since such obligations must in theory bind members of opposing factions. But such antidotes to factionalism exist both among the Shavante and the Sherente. The Shavante regard their age-set system as a counterweight to factionalism. They line up in age-moieties for log races and are redistributed in ceremonial moieties during the *wai'a*. The Sherente had strong allegiance to their 'men's associations' and belonged throughout their lives to one of the two sporting moieties for log racing (Nimuendajú, 1942: 59, 71). Yet these institutions do not prevent Shavante and Sherente men from seeking prestige through the factional system at the expense of the good-fellowship of their age-sets or associations or ceremonial moieties. The comparative harmony of Timbira society

[1] This assertion is based on the observations of Nimuendajú, which are supported by statements from Jean Carter for the Krĩkati and Julio Cesar Melatti for the Krahó. It seems to hold true also for the Apinayé, who could perhaps be bracketed with the Eastern Timbira in the following argument, but I prefer to concentrate on the Timbira, for which better data are currently available.

cannot therefore be explained simply in terms of corporate groups that transect any would-be factions.

Another plausible hypothesis could be that factionalism would be more severe where it was based on unilineal descent groups, which would give automatic continuity to the factions. This does not fit the data, however. It is true that the Timbira do not have clans or lineages which could compete with one another, but then neither do the Kayapó, where internecine warfare is almost an institution in itself.

Paradoxically, the one institution which is found in all three of the societies with severe factionalism, and yet is absent among the Timbira, is the men's house. I had assumed, because the Shavante and the Sherente said so and I had no reason to doubt their information, that this was an institution which counteracted disharmony. A reconsideration of it in the light of this suggestive correlation leads, however, to a diametrically opposed interpretation.

In the Central Gê men's houses boys were trained not only in ceremonial and the virtues of co-operation, but also in manliness. Among the Shavante this was expressed in wakefulness, which is why age-sets (especially the one in the men's house or bachelors' hut) sing round the village during the night; in fleetness, which is why the initiation ceremonies consisted to a large extent in a series of flat races; and in bellicosity. We have seen how this bellicosity is conventionally ascribed to the Young Men and how they carry the *uibro* club as symbolic of it. We have noted too that the Shavante have ceremonies of aggression in which initiated men ritually attack or dance at uninitiated boys. In the most important ceremony of all women are ritually raped by the men in a demonstration of the twin powers of sexuality and aggression.

Now ceremonial aggression against women is also common to the three societies with severe factionalism and absent among the Timbira. The Kayapó have a ceremonial rape similar to the Shavante rite and the Sherente men's societies would ritually threaten the women's society and mime the killing of a woman. The argument to this point can therefore be summed up as follows: in those Gê societies where a high value is placed on bellicosity as a form of manliness this is inculcated in the boys during their time in the men's house, and later given ritual expression in aggression against uninitiated outsiders, particularly women.

From this it may be argued that the expression of this bellicosity is unlikely to be confined to ritual situations. It is, in all three of the societies under discussion, the characteristic mode of relationship between men of a community and outsiders not of the same community. It seems also to be the characteristic mode of relationship between men of each faction within a community and those of other factions. I would suggest that this is because, in each of the three societies, there exists a strong consciousness of the antithesis between the terms of an opposition which consistently involves Ego and his own (We) against the rest (They). Among the Shavante we have a dichotomy between *Waniwihã* and *Wasi're'wa*, formally expressed in the two factions of each community. A similar dichotomy among the Sherente has given rise to an informal two-faction system in each village. Meanwhile the Kayapó, according to Turner, stress the opposition between the two men's houses which any properly constituted village should have and between which there is hostility, both conventionally and actually.

The Timbira, though they do not stress the virtue of bellicosity or have a men's house which teaches it or gives it ritual expression, do on the other hand have a strong sense of the opposition between antithetical social groups. This supports my contention that these binary oppositions do not explain Gê factionalism any more than they are explained by it. They are models of the same order of abstraction. An emphasis on bellicosity as a positive trait is an axiom of Shavante life. So is their ideology of dualism. The Timbira have much of the dualism without the bellicosity. The Shavante, however, stress aggression and it is therefore expressed in the hostility between We and They.

I seem by roundabout means to have come back to my original premiss that 'factionalism is a fundamental fact of Shavante life, on a par with and independent of any dualistic ideology'. But the digression was not wasted. In the first place, it has served to confirm the independence of factionalism and dualism and the fundamental nature of these principles in an analysis of the Gê. Secondly, it has enabled us to view the age-set system of the Shavante in a new light. While the Shavante think of it as a vehicle of harmony, it nevertheless appears to be the very institution that inculcates the values of aggression, which lead to disharmony in their society. I suggest that such a conclusion would not have been reached by an analysis of Shavante society taken in isolation. It is the comparative material which enables us to reach it.

In this connexion another concomitant variation in the Gê data is of considerable interest. I have claimed that the three societies with a high incidence of factionalism all value bellicosity and inculcate it in their men's houses. Now the institutional arrangements of all three of these tribes are such that a man finds himself forced into an anomalous position.

The Shavante and the Sherente emphasize their patrilineal descent groups, yet practise uxorilocal residence after marriage. I have shown the crucial importance of the household group for the Shavante and wish now to stress these findings. The Shavante household tends to stay together in spite of the cleavage within it. It is the unit of production and consumption. When the community splits up to go on trek a household always remains intact with one band. When there is a major schism in the community, whole households often emigrate to other villages. The relationship terminology, by means of which a Shavante categorizes his fellow men, takes especial account of those people who are co-resident with him. For a young Shavante the tensions of affinity are exorcized at least for those affines who live in the same house as he does. And yet they are only partly exorcized or, I should say, suppressed. When conflict erupts, it is the close affines in the household who are suspected and accused, even done to death. For Shavante and for Sherente there is thus strain and ambiguity in the male role consequent on a man's belonging to one group and living with another.

Turner reports an analogous situation for the Kayapó, where a man is expected to have some allegiance to his cognatic kin and yet is taken away at an early age to live in one of the men's houses. It can and does happen subsequently that he must, in a conflict situation, choose between his kinsmen and his 'groups' in the men's house.

The common element in all of these situations is the strain and ambiguity inherent in the male role. I would suggest that this role conflict is related to the valuing of bellicosity and the institutionalization of aggression, and that it is in this set of factors that an explanation of the high incidence of factionalism among the Shavante, Sherente, and Kayapó should be sought.

Among the Timbira, on the other hand, there are no calls on a man's allegiance which conflict with those ties that bind him to his matrilocal household group. This conclusion may be of wider comparative interest in view of the matrilineal tendencies of the Timbira. Some writers have argued that there are inherent strains in the male role in matrilineal societies because authority is in the hands of males while status is transmitted in the female line.[1] Yet among the Gê the Eastern Timbira are the most matrilineal people and their society appears to afford less strain in the male role than is the case among neighbouring tribes. Admittedly the demonstration is not conclusive, since we have already shown that the 'matriliny' of the Timbira is poorly established and not a very dominant principle in their social arrangements. Nevertheless, the Timbira case is suggestive. It indicates that it is not the rule or principle itself that may determine the stresses and strains of a social situation but the manner in which the rule is applied.

All this may seem rather obvious. If I restate it here it is because social anthropologists, in their proper concern with the rules of society, often neglect or ignore the manifold possibilities of their application. That is why I have set out the rules of Shavante society in some detail and then discussed the application of them in a number of crucial domains. In this final section I have indicated that there is more than one way of approaching the data I have presented. The type of analysis used must in the last instance depend on the type of question one wishes to answer.

But explanation is a matter of infinite regress. At this point further explanations of Shavante society must await further research on the Gê, for which I hope this book may serve as the point of departure.

[1] See for example Richards, 1950, Schneider and Gough, 1961.

APPENDIX 1.

LINEAGES

1. A'e. From *a'e* = scleria bead necklace. Worn characteristically, but not exclusively, by members of this lineage during ceremonial.

   SÃO MARCOS, 1962/64. Chief's lineage of the Tpereya'óno.

2. Amur. Derivation unknown.

   SANTA TEREZINHA, 1958. Reported as a lineage of the Topdató clan.

3. Aiuté'mañãrĩ. From *aiuté* = baby + *'mañãr* = makes. Members of this lineage name girls during the Jaguar ceremony.

   SÃO DOMINGOS, 1958. A small lineage of the Topdató, which later became extinct.

   SANTA TEREZINHA, 1958. Dominant (chief's) lineage of the Topdató.

   CAPITARIQUARA, 1958. Reported as present.

   SÃO MARCOS, 1962. Lineage of the Tpereya'óno, recently arrived from Downstream. Its leader was considered a chief.

4. 'Badzí. From *'badzí* = cotton; probably a reference to ceremonial regalia.

   MARÃWASEDE, 1958. Reported as present.

5. Dahçiwaro. Derivation unknown.

   SANTA TEREZINHA, 1958. Reported as present.

   CAPITARIQUARA, 1958. Reported as present.

6. Da'rã (also Wa'rã). Derivation unknown. Possibly from *da-'rã* = head, or from *asada* = mouth + *'rã* = black. The Asada'rã (cf. Sherente moiety Sdakrã) are noted for the beauty of their ceremonial paint. They make their faces scarlet with *urucú*, except for the mouth, which is painted black, as also are the belly and forearms. They are supposed

to dance during the Jaguar ceremony. I never met any lineage which was referred to by this name. However, the Da'rã are also supposed to officiate during the Jaguar ceremony.

SÃO DOMINGOS, 1958. A small lineage of the Tpereya'óno clan.

7. Dzutsi. From *dzu* = magic powder.
SÃO DOMINGOS, 1958/62. Lineage of the Ẹ Wawẽ clan.

8. Hu. From *hu* = jaguar. Hu people are said to be 'friends' of the jaguar species. They do not have special functions at the Jaguar ceremony, however.
SANTA TEREZINHA, 1958. Reported as present.
CAPITARIQUARA, 1958. Reported as the lineage of chief Ẹribiwẽ.
MERURE, ? . Reported (1962) as annihilated in this village because they were suspected of sorcery.

9. Ĩwede. From *wede* = wood.
MARÃWASEDE, 1958. Reported as present.

10. Páhiri'wa. Derivation unknown (from *pahí* = straw + *ri* = diminutive + *'wa* = suffix indicating a person ?). Members of this lineage are entitled to receive the name Páhiri'wa and to perform the ceremonial functions it entails.
SÃO MARCOS, 1962/64. Chief's lineage of the Tpereya'óno (see A'e).
SIMÕES LOPES, 1962. Lineage of the Tpereya'óno clan.

11. Tebe. From *tebe* = fish (?). This lineage has the prerogative of receiving the name 'Tebe'; its members so named have the right to exercise the ceremonial functions which go with the name.
SÃO DOMINGOS, 1958. A small lineage of the Tpereya'óno which was extinct by 1962.
SANTA TEREZINHA, 1958. Reported as present.
SÃO MARCOS, 1962/4. Chiefly lineage of the Ẹ Wawẽ clan.

12. Uhẹ (also 'badzí-pré). From *uhẹ* = pig. *'badzí* = cotton + *pré* = red. Refers to the ceremonial regalia especially associated with (but not exclusively worn by) members of

the lineage, consisting of head circlet and necklace of reddened cotton, the latter trimmed with peccary hair.

SÃO DOMINGOS, 1958/62. Lineage of the Ẹ Wawẽ clan.

SÃO MARCOS, 1962/64. Chiefly lineage of the Ẹ Wawẽ (see Tebe).

13. Uhẹdẹ. From *uhẹdẹ* = tapir.

MARÃWASEDE, 1958. Reported as present.

14. Wahí. From *wahí* = snake. Members of this lineage are said to have a special relationship with snakes such that snakes will not bite them. This is believed to have originated at a time when there was much sickness. Shavante went out to look for snakes. They found a rattlesnake which rested its head on the shoulder of each man in turn without biting him. They returned home and told what had happened, and from that time onward could cure the sick.

SÃO MARCOS, 1962/64. A small lineage of the Ẹ Wawẽ.

CAPITARIQUARA, 1958. Reported as present.

SÃO DOMINGOS, 1958. A small lineage of the Topdató which had been annihilated by 1962.

15. Wamãrĩ. From *wamãrĩ* = a polished, wooden cylinder. Members of this lineage are supposed to have clairvoyant experiences if they hang the *wamãrĩ* horizontally at the head of their sleeping mats. They can likewise communicate with dead kin by planting a war club by their grave with the *wamãrĩ* affixed to it crosswise.

SÃO DOMINGOS, 1958/62. Dominant (chief's) lineage of the Tpereya'óno.

SIMÕES LOPES, 1962. Lineage of the Ẹ Wawẽ.

16. Wamãrĩdzú. From *wamãrĩ* + *dzu* (see Dzutsi). Members of this lineage are supposed to act as peacemakers. When fighting threatens to erupt, two Wamãrĩdzú come out with their crowns painted red and their hair plastered with *ĩ-dzu*. Their bodies are painted black. They harangue the men in council until peace has been made.

SÃO MARCOS, 1962/64. Lineage of the Tpereya'óno recently arrived from Downstream. Its leader was considered a chief. Lineage of the Ẹ Wawẽ.

APPENDIX 2.

RELATIONSHIP TERMINOLOGY

Terms used by a female Speaker

1. *ĩ-rdá*: Any person who is in Ego's grandparents' generation or over.
2. *ĩ-nihúdu*: Any person in the second descending generation or below.

WANIWIHÃ

3. *ĩ-tebe*: Any female in the first ascending generation who is *waniwihã* to Ego.
4. *ĩ-mãmã*: Any male in the first ascending generation who is *waniwihã* to Ego.
5. *ĩ-dúmrada*: Any person older than Ego who is in the same generation and *waniwihã* to Ego.
6. *ĩ-nõ*: Any person younger than Ego who is in the same generation and *waniwihã* to Ego.
7. *ĩ-'ra*: S, D, ZS, ZD.
8. *aibį*: Any male in the first descending generation who is *waniwihã* to Ego.
9. *otí*: Any female in the first descending generation who is *waniwihã* to Ego.
10. *ĩ-namté*: MZH.
11. *ĩ-pnę*: Any male who is a member of a lineage related to Ego's.
12. *pi'õĩti*: Any female who is a member of a lineage related to Ego's.

WASI'RE'WA

13. *wasiní*: Any person who is *wasi're'wa* to Ego.
14. *simęnę̃*: Any person who is *wasi're'wa* to Ego.
15. *'rebzu*: Any person who is *wasi're'wa* to Ego.
16. *ĩ-nã*: Any female in the first ascending generation who is in Ego's mother's lineage.

17. *ĩ-datię*: M.

18. *'rebzu'wa*: Any male in the first ascending generation who is in Ego's mother's lineage. Also MBW.

19. *ĩ-mãwapté*: MB.

20. *ĩ-'ra-wapté*: HZC when it is small.

21. *asimhí*: Any woman who has married a man in Ego's lineage, unless she is *ĩ-nã* to Ego.

22. *ĩ-za'mũ*: Any man who has married a woman of Ego's lineage. Also DH, ZDH.

23. *ĩ-mrõ*: Husband.

24. *ĩ-mãpari'wa*: Husband's parent.

25. *saihí*: SW, ZSW.

26. *asaí*: HZ.

Terms used to refer to dead relatives (man or woman speaking)

1. *ĩ-'rdá* becomes *wahi'rdá*, a term which is also used to refer to ancestors in general.

2. *ĩ-nihúdu* becomes *ĩ-nihudú*.

3. *ĩ-tebe* becomes *wat'pé'wa*.

4. *ĩ-mãmã* becomes *wapto'wa*.

5. *ĩ-dúmrada* (male) becomes *dé'wa*.

6. *ĩ-dúmrada* (female) becomes *wañõhidiba*.

7. *ĩ-nõ* (male) becomes *ĩ-zemãrĩ'wa*.

8. *ĩ-nõ* (female) becomes *ĩ-piñã*.

9. *ĩ-'ra* becomes *siñõ'ra*.

10. *'rebzu* (*'rebzu'wa*) becomes *iñimñõ'rebzu*.

11. *i-mãwapté* becomes *iñímamatã*.

12. *asimhí* becomes *ĩ-amõ'wa*.

13. *ĩ-za'mu* becomes *sa'u'wa*.

14. *ĩ-mrõ* becomes *ĩ-amõ'wa*.

15. *ĩ-mãpari'wa* does not change.

16. *saihí* becomes *ĩ-sani'wa*.

17. *ĩ-ãri* becomes *ĩ-ãri'wa*.

APPENDIX 3

THE JAGUAR CEREMONY

I secured only one account of this ceremony, from Meireles at São Marcos in 1964. He described one in which he himself had taken part some years previously. A younger Shavante was present during the telling of it and he asked questions and occasionally explained aspects of the ceremony to me. My paraphrase of the recorded conversation follows. Remarks included in brackets are editorial comments made in the course of the narrative either by Meireles or by Fernando.

This ceremony was for the jaguar and to name the women. The Dzutsi'wa[1] led the singing. They started one morning and continued all through that day and the following night. Next day two Aiuté'mañãrĩ'wa[1] came out and sang. They hid some gourd flutes in a *buriti* palm. (Fernando: They were hidden there for the girls to fetch) Then the boys (*wapté*) came out of the bachelors' hut. They were told by the men (Fernando: by the Dzutsi'wa) to paint themselves red. When they were all painted they went out hunting tapir. Now the men in the forest blackened themselves, covering their hands and faces with charcoal and painting two white spots on their faces. They got together and practised their call "a,a,a," and "kai, kai, kai." Women too tried out the call but the men laughed at them because they did not get it right. Then the women painted themselves with stripes. One of the men made a speech saying that the boys ought to be summoned. The men sat there giving their call, singing and beating time with rattles of pig's teeth. The boys were very frightened. (Fernando: because the men were all painted black and were very fierce). (Meireles: All the men were there, from all the age-sets. It was beautiful. It was to name the women). The Dzutsi'wa sang again. Then the Aiuté'mañãrĩ'wa went out after the jaguar and called them 'Wi, wi.'[2] The jaguar were wearing necklets with macaw's

[1] See Appendix 1—Lineage Names.
[2] A way of saying "come here!"

tail feathers dangling from them and they were singing in the forest. Two Shavante were storks (Portuguese: Jaburu). They rushed towards the jaguar and fought. The feathers got broken. (Meireles, in answer to my question: The women's part of the ceremony is over now. They have names. Only the boys are still out there). That night the boys did not sleep and neither did the jaguar. The boys sang all night. Early in the morning the Aiuté'mañãrĩ'wa went and got them out. They gave their call. The Aiuté'mañãrĩ'wa led them out after the jaguar, now urging them on, now telling them to wait, now pretending to be frightened, building up the suspense. Then they climbed trees to survey the land while the boys waited below. The Aiuté'-mañãrĩ'wa spoke in squeaky voices, urging the boys to go carefully. (Meireles: It is all a trick that they play on the boys). The jaguar were roaring (realistically imitated) and the Aiuté'-mañãrĩ'wa wept. They knew that all the jaguar were up in the trees but still they urged the boys to wait. Then they hunted down the jaguar with clubs (*brudu*). It is a beautiful ceremony.

APPENDIX 4

COMPOSITION OF HOUSEHOLDS IN SÃO DOMINGOS AND Ẹ TÕ

(Adult members only)

The letter assigned to each household corresponds to its designation in figure 4 (São Domingos) or figure 5 (Ẹ Tõ). The numerals identifying individuals refer to Genealogy 3.

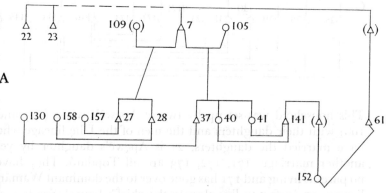

The nucleus of the household is the chief (7) and his sons and daughters. Note that he has three sons and one nephew living virilocally in his house instead of moving out to their wives' households. 22 and 23 were refugees from Marãwasede who lived here in 1958. In 1962 they were living at Ẹ Tõ (household X).

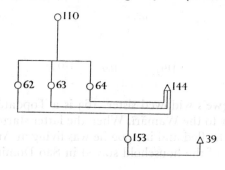

110 is the chief's brother's widow. In 1958 she had just established her household next door to Apęwẽ's and it was assumed
that he was intending to marry her. In 1962 some claimed that
she was in fact his wife, although Apęwẽ himself denied it. I
could not confirm this since she was away from the village at
the time of my visit. 39 is another of Apęwẽ's sons who is
technically living uxorilocally but spends most of his time in
household A.

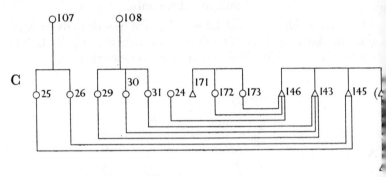

This household was set up by two of Apęwẽ's wives (107 and
108) with their daughters and the men of the Uhę lineage who
have married the daughters. 24 is Apęwẽ's daughter by yet
another marriage. 171, 172, 173 are all Topdató. They have
no parents living and 171 has gone over to the dominant Wamãrĩ
lineage, so prefers to live close to the chief's house. (See household R.)

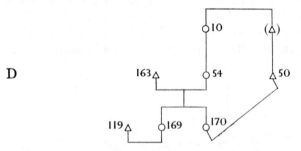

10 is Apęwẽ's widowed sister. 163 is a Topdató clansman who
went over to the Wamãrĩ. When the latter started killing off the
Topdató he fled and in 1962 he was living at Areões. The other
members of the household stayed in São Domingos. 50 treated

163 exclusively as WF, even though the latter was his classificatory ZH.

E
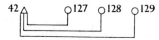

In 1958 this household was occupied solely by Apęwẽ's son (42) and his three wives. Their father (whose brother lived in F) was killed when the Wamãrĩ purged the Dzutsi. (See household S.)

F
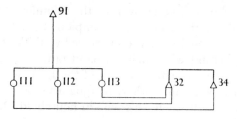

Occupied in 1958 by Prapá (91), his daughters and sons-in-law (sons of Apęwẽ). (See household T.)

G
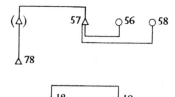

H

This household was set up in 1958 (at the end of my stay) by some refugees from Marãwasede. At one time there were four adult men living there but I could not obtain full data on their relationships with other people in São Domingos. They were accepted into the Wamãrĩ. The household had died out or moved away by the time I returned in 1962.

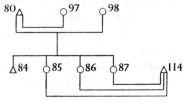

(See household U.)

J

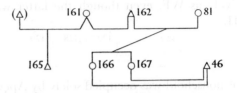

In 1958 this house was located next to I because 81 was the sister of 80, the senior man in I. Her husband (162) was a Topdató who had gone over to the Wamãrĩ. He was subsequently killed. She therefore accompanied her brother and the rest of his household when they moved to Ẹ Tõ. Her daughters remained behind with their husband (46). 165 was the son of 161 by her first husband, a man of the Ẹ Wawẽ clan. In 1958 he lived here with his mother. In 1962 his mother was dead and he had gone to live with his wife in household O.

K

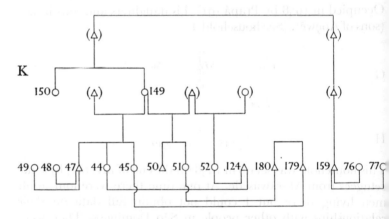

This household was established by the widow (149) and her children by two previous marriages. In 1958 her sister (150) was living with her husband in household H. She came to live in K after her husband's death. At that time the younger generation in the household consisted of two sons, 50 (unmarried) and 47 (married to two fatherless sisters); two daughters married to a pair of Topdató brothers; and a daughter and a step-daughter married to a man from the Ẹ Wawẽ clan. There was some suggestion that this man (124) had gone over to the Topdató but the Topdató sons-in-law were killed soon afterwards and he was not, so I presume that he managed to reverse this conversion in good time. In 1962 the household had been joined by 159 and his wives. He moved in with his 'FZ' since he had no closer relatives in the community. Meanwhile, 50 had married into household D.

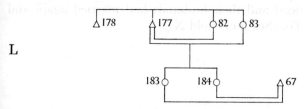

In 1958 this was the household of two Topdató brothers (177 and 178), one of whom was unmarried since he was rather simple though far from feeble-minded. When the brothers died or were killed the widows of 177 accompanied their brother (80) to Ẹ Tõ. In 1962 only 67 and his wives were occupying the house.

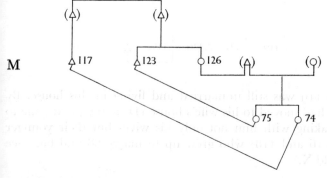

In this household 126 was sister to 123 and 117 and step-mother to their wives. This was an advantageous arrangement for the men, for they did not have to move in with their father-in-law but could in Shavante terms have the best of both worlds by staying with their sister and yet simultaneously being married without thereby acquiring any affines. 123 probably managed this because he suffered from a speech defect and other Shavante feared him on the grounds that he communicated with malevolent spirits. He was dead in 1962 and 117 had married his widow.

N

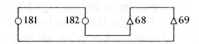

In 1958 this household was composed of two Topdató sisters married to a pair of dissident Wamãrĩ brothers. By 1962 the sisters were dead and their husbands had married again and moved to Ẹ̃ Tõ. (See household X.)

O

P

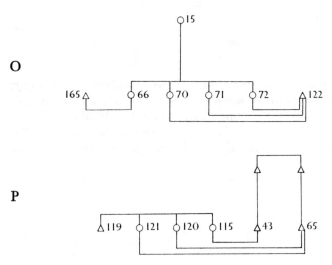

In 1958 119 was still unmarried and living in this house. By 1962 he had moved to his wife's house (D) and 65 had gone to Ẹ̃ Tõ, taking with him not only his wives but their younger sisters (116 and 118) who grew up to marry 68 and 69. (See household X.)

Ę TÕ

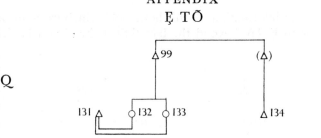

Q

I do not have complete information for this household which had not come to Ę Tõ from São Domingos. Some of its members subsequently went to São Marcos so that S'riwanoõwẽ (99) appears in Genealogy 2 as number 191. 131 was killed by the Wamãrĩ (?) from São Domingos some time after 1962.

R This house was originally household C in São Domingos. In 1962 I found that one of the older women (108) had died and the entire group of Topdató siblings had either died or been killed (171, 172, 173). One of the in-married Uhę men (146) was also dead. His brother (145) married the one surviving widow (24) so that at that time 145 and 143 had three wives each. Similarly 156 had matured sufficiently to marry two wives, about whom I could discover little.

S This house was originally household E in São Domingos and had an identical adult composition in 1962.

T This house was originally household F in São Domingos. Its composition in 1962 was the same except that a group of three sisters (33, 35 and 36) were additionally resident there. I did not meet them and could find out little about them save that their father, now dead, had been an Ę Wawẽ clansman. The two brothers who had married into this household (32 and 34) originally had two wives and one wife respectively. They married the newly arrived group of sisters and redressed this imbalance, ending up with three wives each.

U This house was originally household I in São Domingos and had retained the same composition at Ę Tõ, except that 84 was in the process of removing to his wife's house (W).

V   I have no information on this household which came from down river to Ẹ Tõ, beyond the fact that its head was Pediri (90).

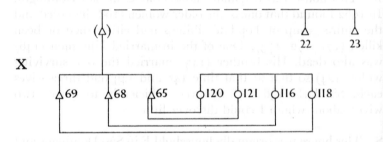

W

I have incomplete information on this household which also came to Ẹ Tõ from down river.

X

This household consisted of S'rizamdí (65) and his two wives who originally lived in São Domingos P; S'rizamdí's brothers from São Domingos N whose wives died (or were killed) and who married sisters of S'rizamdí's wives; and two refugees from Marãwasede who had been living in Apẹwẽ's house (A) before moving to Ẹ Tõ. The latter may have been married. I was unable to obtain this information. One of them, Rintimpse (22) later moved to São Marcos and appears as No 76 on Genealogy 2.

325

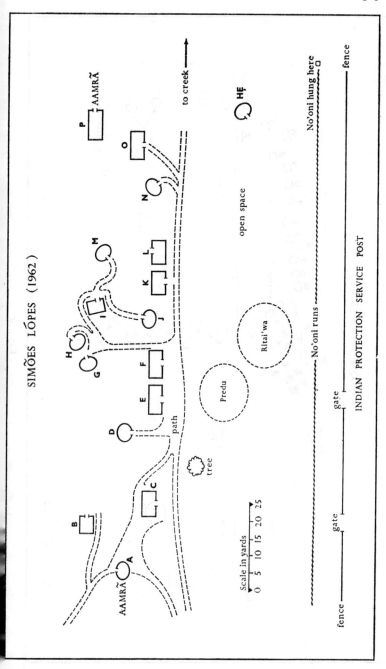

SIMÕES LÓPES (1962)

FIG. I

INDIAN PROTECTION SERVICE POST

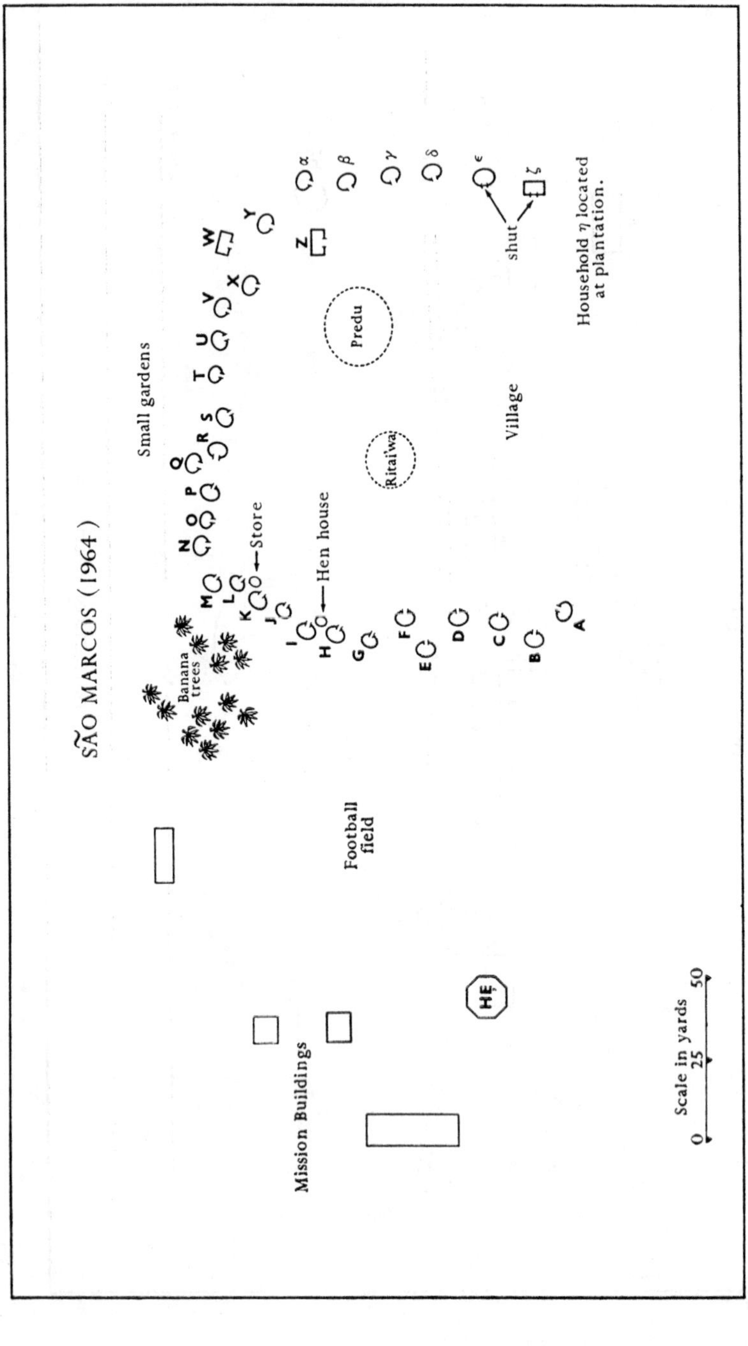

326

SÃO MARCOS (1964)

Small gardens

Banana trees

Store

Hen house

Football field

Mission Buildings

Predu

Ritai'wa

Village

Household η located at plantation.

shut

Scale in yards
0   25   50

Fig. 2

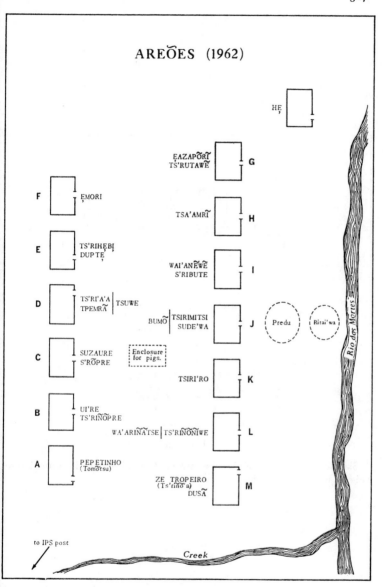

AREÕES (1962)

FIG. 3

Principal male members of each household are marked. Where names are separated by a vertical line, those to the left of it are the owners of the household and those to the right are in-married outsiders.

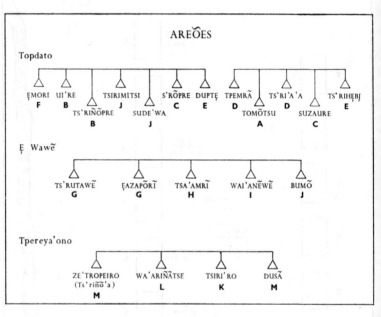

FIG. 3a

Skeleton genealogy of Areões (1962). Capital letters indicate houses (Fig. 3) where men reside.

329

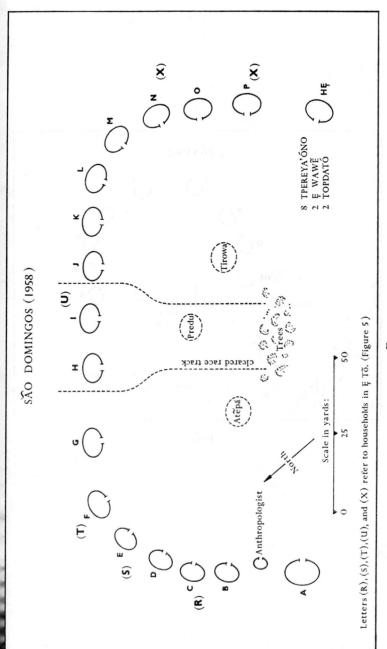

SÃO DOMINGOS (1958)

8 TPEREYA'ÓNO
2 Ę WAWĒ
2 TOPDATÓ

Letters (R), (S), (T), (U), and (X) refer to households in Ę TÕ. (Figure 5)

FIG. 4

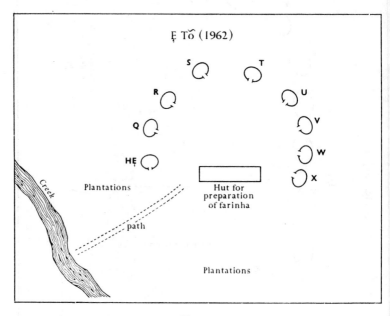

FIG. 5

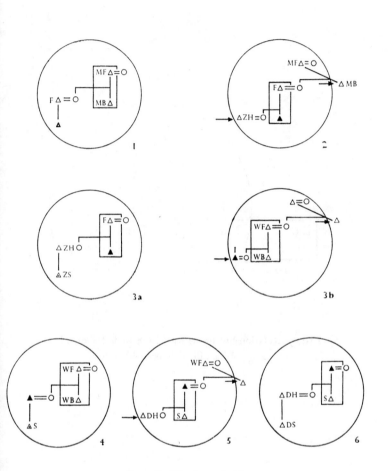

FIG. 6. The household

▲ Indicates Ego.
△ Indicates an immature boy.

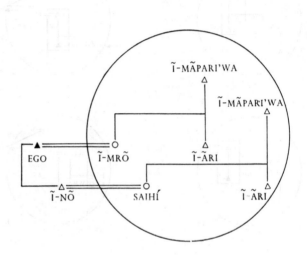

FIG. 7. Relationship terms used by a male for members
of his affinal household

TABLE 1

Shavante Communities

	1958	1962	1964
Western Shavante			
Xingu			
1. Batoví	No	300[1]	
2. Simões Lópes	information	175[4]	
Upstream			
3. Sangradouro	200[2]	175[2]	
4. Merure	200[2] São Marcos	300+[5]	350[5]
Eastern Shavante			
Downstream			
5. Areões	80[2]	175[4]	
6. Capitariquara	150[3]	—	
7. Santa Terezinha	100[3]	—	
8. São Domingos	220[5]	110[5]	
9. Ę Tõ	—	80[3]	
10. Marãwasede	?	150[3]	

[1] IPS estimate.
[2] Missionary estimate.
[3] My estimate.
[4] IPS count.
[5] My count.

Table 2

Some of the roots which form the basis of the Shavante diet

No. 1. Tomõtsú: usually of the size and consistency of a potato.

No. 2. Ponẽri: has a hard silvery skin, with eyes in it. Its consistency resembles that of an unusually starchy potato.

No. 3. Ude-du: long tuber with a rough, thick skin. Somewhat resembling sweet manioc (*Manihot aipi*).

No. 4. Wẹ: has a smooth, greyish skin. Its consistency when peeled is soft and starchy.

No. 5. Udzapodo: round, beet-like root. Its meat is crisp and it can grow to the size of a small pumpkin.

No. 6. Monihẹire-ri: a tiny root, collected in large quantities. When baked in the embers it has a taste and consistency similar to that of a roast chestnut.

No. 7. Tomõtsúihẹire-ri: a small bulb. It is now only eaten after being boiled for some time.

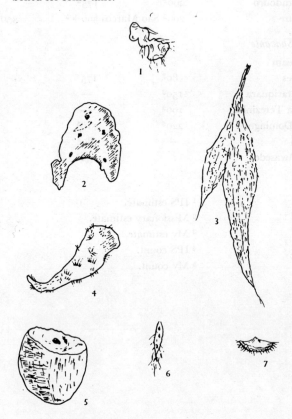

TABLE 5

SEASONAL ACTIVITIES SÃO DOMINGOS (1958)

	JAN.	FEB.	MARCH	APRIL	MAY	JUNE	JULY	AUGUST	SEPT.	OCT.	NOV.	DEC.
CLIMATE	HEAVY RAINS		LIGHT RAINS			DRY SEASON			LIGHT RAINS		HEAVY RAINS	
RESIDENCE	TREK	VILLAGE			May 1 TREK	June 24 VILLAGE	Communal Hunt 16/7 28/7 VILLAGE	Aug. 7 TREK		Oct. 20		TREK
AGRICULTURE		Harvesting Maize				Harvesting Beans Pumpkins Burning clearings					Clearing and Planting	
BASIC FOODS	CAROB / PIQUI		MAIZE		BABASSÚ		BEANS PUMPKINS	MANGOES	CAROB / BURITI	PIQUI		
						PALMITO ROOTS						
CEREMONIAL		Water Exercise / Ear Piercing INITIATION (1)			Wai'a (arrows)	Ceremonial Races June 24 INITIATION (2)	July 30 Finale	INITIATION (3)			Wai'a INITIATES	

TABLE 4

Polygynous marriages of prominent men

Community	Name	Number wives	Community average (Prominent)	Community average
Simões Lópos	*Siriwaruwẽ*	1	—	0.98
São Marcos	*Apẹwẽ*	2		
	Sibupá	2		
	Sebastião	1		
	Piu	1		
	S'riwanoõwẽ	3	1.8	1.25
São Domingos	*Apẹwẽ*	3		
	Prapá	1		
	Waarodí	1		
	Suwapté	2		
	S'rizamdí	2	1.8	1.65

This table shows the actual number of living wives married to various prominent Shavante at the time their communities were visited. Marital histories are not used because the data are incomplete. Men generally recognized as chiefs are in italic. Column three shows the average number of wives for marriageable men in the same community.

The recent arrival of S'riwanoõwẽ in São Marcos has disproportionately increased the average for prominent men in that community. In general it will be seen that men have more wives per capita in São Domingos and influential men also slightly more than influential men in other communities.

TABLE 5

Polygyny

Number of wives actually possessed by men at the time of this study

Number of wives	Simões Lópes (1962)	São Marcos (1964)	São Domingos (1962)
0	8	?	4
1	36	50	18
2	5	12[1]	14
3	1	2	10
Average number of wives per adult male	0.98	1.25	1.65

[1] Includes one man whose brother's widow lives in his household, although it could not be established that he had taken her as his wife.

The eight unmarried men in Simões Lópes were the marriageable members of the age-set which had just been initiated. They had not been married at the time of this study.

It was not possible to obtain complete data on the number and marital status of all the boys living in the school maintained by the mission in lieu of a bachelors' hut at São Marcos.

The four unmarried men at São Domingos were all refugees from Marãwasede.

TABLE 6

Sororal Polygyny

Community	Number polygynous marriages	Sororal	Partially sororal	Doubtful	Not sororal
Simões Lópes	6	6	0	0	0
São Marcos	14	10	0	1	3
São Domingos	24	17	2	3	2
Totals	44	33	2	4	5

TABLE 7

The Age-set System

Showing the relative positions of the Age-sets in 1962

Western Shavante			Eastern Shavante
São Marcos			São Domingos
(Abari'u)			
(Nõdzę'u)			(Nõdzę'u)
Anõrowa			Abari'u
S'daro	Mature		S'daro
Ai'riri	Men	Predu	Anõrowa
Tęrã			Tęrã
Tírowa			Ai'riri
Atẽpá			Atẽpá
Abari'u	Young Men	Ritai'wa	Tírowa
Nõdzę'u	Bachelors	Waptc	Nõdzę'u
(Anõrowa)	(Children)	(Watębremĩ)	(Abari'u)

TABLE 8

Initiation

São Domingos 1958

First Phase	February–March	Immersion exercises Ear-piercing
Second Phase	June 27–July 30	Daily running
Third Phase		
1	July 31	Tebe
2	August 1	Páhiri'wa
3	August 2	Tęibi
4	August 3	Ceremonial run Marriage of initiates
5	August 4	New age-set established

TABLE 9

Age-Grades

Male		Female		
Mature Men	Predu	Pi'õ		Mature women
Young Men	Ritai'wa	Adaba		Named women
			Arate	Women with children
Bachelors	Wapte	Soimba		Girls whose husbands brought meat
Children (Boys)	Watẹbremĩ	Baono		Children (Girls)
(Not babies)	(ai'repudu)	(adzẹrudu)		(Not babies)

TABLE 10

Relationships between Age-sets

Senior	Wahí'rada
Senior Alternate	Wanimñõhú
Senior Proximate	Ĩhí'wa
Ego's	Ĩ-útsu
Junior Proximate	Siñõrã
Junior Alternate	Wanimñõhú
Junior	Ropsõ'wa

TABLE 11. Shavante categorizations

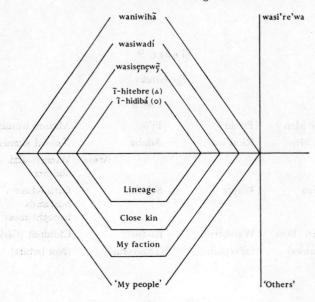

TABLE 12

Clans and Lineages

Village	Tpereya'óno	Ẽ Wawẽ	Topdató
São Domingos 1958	*Wamãrĩ* Tebe Da'rã	Uhẹ Dzutsi	Wahí Aiuté'mañãrĩ
São Marcos 1962	{ *A' é* { *Páhiri'wa* { *Aiuté'mañãrĩ* { *Wamãrĩdzú*	{ *Uhẹ* { *Tebe* Wamãrĩdzú Wahí	Hu

Lineages of chiefs are in italic

TABLE 13

São Domingos Factions 1958

Dominant Faction		Others	
Lineage	*Clan*	*Lineage*	*Clan*
Wamãrĩ	TP	Dzutsi	EW
Tebe	TP	Uhẹ	EW
Aiuté'mañãrĩ	TD	Wahí	TD

TABLE 14. Fluctuation in Shavante communities

Legend:

APẼWẼ, CHIEF

ẼRIBIWẼ CO-CHIEF?
CHIEF OF NEIGHBOURING GROUP?
LEADER OF DISSIDENT FRACTION?

—— TOP DATÓ FACTION SPLIT OFF

GROUP CAME WESTWARDS CIRCA 1930
FIGHTING NEAR MERURE 1936-1937
CLASHED WITH EASTERN SHAVANTE 1954

CONTACTED BRAZILIANS 1950? CLASHED WITH WESTERN SHAVANTE SPLIT UP
GROUP CAME EASTWARDS CIRCA 1950
JOINED FORCES

Year	Batoví	Simões Lópes	Sangradouro	Merure São Marcos	XAVANTINA	Areões	Capitariquara	S. Terezinha	São Domingos	Ẽ Tõ
1953									Founded 1953 Apẽwẽ, Chief	
1954								Founded 1954 Pepetinho, Chief		
1955	Founded 1955	Founded 1955								
1956			Founded 1956	Founded 1956		Founded 1956 Ze Tropeiro, Chief	Founded 1956 Ẽribiwẽ Chief Sebastião, Chief			
1957									Contemplated attack on Santa Terezinha 1957	
1958						Ẽribiwẽ killed '58 Attack Capitariquara	Areões Kinsmen flee, some killed 1958	Faction Secedes 1958		
1959					Sebastião's group to São Marcos	Mission closed, Shavante move to Sta. Terezinha '59	Drove out IPS post Community splits, Sebastião's group to São Domingos			
1960							Others to Ẽ Tõ 1960	Attack Capitariquara, 1960	Attack Santa Terezinha, 1960; Sebastião's group secedes, goes on trek 1960	Founded 1960
1961					Relocated in Areões 1961			Abandon Santa Terezinha, flee to Xavantina	Faction secedes to Ẽ Tõ 1961	
1962										
1963									Faction secedes to São Marcos	

TABLE 15. Relationship categories

2nd ascending	Ĩ-'RDA		

	WANIWIHÃ		WASI'RE'WA
	O Δ		

1st ascending	Ĩ-TEBE	Ĩ-MÃMÃ	
EGO'S	Ĩ-DÚMRADA Ĩ-NÕ		WASINÍ SIMĘNĘ̃ 'REBZU
1st descending	Ĩ-RA OTÍ | AIBĮ		
2nd descending	Ĩ-NIHÚDU		

1·ascending		Ĩ-NÃMTÉ	Ĩ-NÃ (Ĩ-DATIĘ)	'REBZU'WA (Ĩ-MÃWAPTÉ)	Ĩ-MÃPARIWA
EGO	PI'ÕITÍ	Ĩ-PNĘ̃	ASIMHÍ Ĩ-MRÕ, SAIHÍ	Ĩ-ZA'MŨ Ĩ-ÃRI	
1 descending			Ĩ-RA-WAPTÉ ASIMHÍ	Ĩ-ZA'MŨ	

REFERENCES

Albisetti, Césare, 1953. 'Il villaggio boróro', *Anthropos* 48: 625–30.

Almeida, S. R. F. de, 1869. 'Matto Grosso: Navegação do Rio Tapajoz para o Pará', *Revista do Instituto Historico e Geographico Brasileiro* 9.

Bachofen, J. J., 1861. *Das Mutterrecht*, Stuttgart.

Baldus, Herbert, 1948. 'Tribos da bacia do Araguaia e o Serviço de Proteção aos Indios', *Revista do Museu Paulista* (N.S.) 2: 137–68.

—1954. 'Os Oti', *Revista do Museu Paulista* (N.S.) 8: 79–92.

Berg, Charles, 1951. *The Unconscious Significance of Hair*, London.

Bernardi, B., 1952. 'The age-system of the Nilo-Hamitic peoples: a critical evaluation', *Africa* 22: 316–32.

Carlette, E., 1928. *Heróis Auténticos*, Petrópolis, Brazil.

Colbacchini, Antonio and Albisetti, Césare, 1942. *Os Boróros Orientais Orarimogodógue do Planalto Oriental de Mato Grosso*, São Paulo.

Dumont, Louis, 1953. 'The Dravidian kinship terminology as an expression of marriage', *Man* 54.

—1957a. *Hierarchy and Marriage Alliance in South Indian Kinship*, Occasional Papers of the Royal Anthropological Institute, No. 12.

—1957b. *Une Sous-caste de l'Inde du Sud: Organisation Sociale et Religion des Pramalai Kallar*, Paris.

Durkheim, Emile and Mauss, Marcel, 1903. 'De quelques formes primitives de classification: contribution à l'étude des representations collectives', *Année Sociologique* 6 (1901–2): 1–72.

Ehrenreich, Paul, 1891. 'Die Einteilung und Verbreitung der Völkerstämme Brasiliens nach dem gegenwärtigen Stande unserer Kenntnisse', *Dr. A. Petermanns Mitteilungen aus Justus Perthes' Geographischer Anstalt* 37: 81–89 and 114–24, Gotha.

—1895. 'Materialen zur Sprachenkunde Brasiliens: III Die Sprache der Akuä oder Chavantes und Cherentes (Goyaz)', *Zeitschrift für Ethnologie* 27: 149–62.

Evans-Pritchard, E. E., 1937. *Witchcraft, Oracles and Magic among the Azande*, Oxford.

—1962. 'Anthropology and History', in *Essays in Social Anthropology*, The Free Press, Glencoe, Illinois.

Frazer, Sir James G., 1910. *Totemism and Exogamy*, London.

Friederici, Georg, 1906. 'Der Tränengruss der Indianer', *Globus* 89: 30–34, Braunschweig.

Fock, Niels, 1960. 'South American birth customs in theory and practice', *Folk* 2: 51–69, Copenhagen.

—*Waiwai, Religion and Society of an Amazonian Tribe*, Nationalmuseets Skrifter, Etnografisk Raekke VIII, Copenhagen.

Fonseca, José Pinto de, 1867. 'Carta que escreveu . . . ao Exmo. General de Goyazes, dando-lhe conta do descobrimento de duas nações de índios (1775)', *Jornal do Instituto Historico e Geographico Brasileiro* 8: 376–90.

Fosbrooke, H. A., 1948. 'An administrative survey of the Masai social system', *Tanganyika Notes and Records* 26: 1–50.

Granet, Marcel, 1950. *La Pensée Chinoise*, Paris.

Greenberg, Joseph H., 1960. 'The general classification of Central and South American languages', in Wallace (Ed.): *Selected Papers of the Fifth International Congress of Anthropological and Ethnological Sciences*, 1956, University of Pennsylvania Press.

Gough, E. Kathleen, 1959. 'The Nayars and the definition of marriage', *Journal of the Royal Anthropological Institute* 89: 23–34.

Haeckel, Josef, 1939. 'Zweiklassensystem, Männerhaus und Totemismus in Südamerika', *Zeitschrift für Ethnologie* 70: 426–54.

—1952. 'Neue Beiträge zur Kulturschichtung Brasiliens', *Anthropos* 47: 963–91.

Henry, Jules, 1941a. *Kaingang*, U.S.A. (No place of publication.)

—1942b. Review of Nimuendajú: *The Apinayé*, in *American Anthropologist* 42: 337–8.

Hertz, Robert, 1928a. 'Contribution à une étude sur la représentation collective de la mort', in *Mélanges de Sociologie Religieuse et Folklore*, 1–98, Paris.

—1928b. 'Essai sur la prééminence de la main droite', in *Mélanges de Sociologie Religieuse et Folklore*, 99–129, Paris.

Hollingshead, A. de B., 1949. *Elmtown's Youth: the Impact of Social Class on Adolescents*, New York.

James, Preston, 1941. *Latin America*, U.S.A. (No place of publication.)

Kirk, G. S., 1954. *Heraclitus, The Cosmic Fragments*, New York.

Leach, E. R., 1954. *Political Systems of Highland Burma*, London.

—1955. 'Polyandry, inheritance and the definition of marriage: with particular reference to Sinhalese customary law', *Man* 199.

—1958. 'Magical hair', *Journal of the Royal Anthropological Institute* 88: 147–64.

Lehmann-Nitsche, Robert, 1936. 'Der Tränengruss im Alten Testament', *Baessler-Archiv* 19: 78–86. Berlin.

Lévi-Strauss, Claude, 1944. 'On dual organization in South America', *América Indígena* 4: 37–47.

—1948. 'La vie familiale et sociale des indiens Nambikuara', *Journal de la Société des Américanistes de Paris* 37: 1–131.

—1949. *Les Structures Elémentaires de la Parenté*, Paris.

—1952. 'Les structures sociales dans le Brésil central et oriental', in Tax (Ed.): *Indian Tribes of Aboriginal America. Selected papers of the XXIXth International Congress of Americanists*, 302–10, Chicago.

—1953. 'Social structure', in Kroeber (Ed.): *Anthropology Today*, Chicago.

—1955. *Tristes Tropiques*, Paris.

—1956. 'Les organisations dualistes existent-elles?' *Bijdragen tot de Taal-, Land- en Volkenkunde* 112: 99–128.

—1962. *Le Totémisme Aujourd'hui*, Paris.

—1965. *Le Cru et le Cuit*, Paris.

Lowie, Robert H., 1941. 'A note on the Northern Gê tribes of Brazil', *American Anthropologist* 43: 188–96.

—1946. 'The Northwestern and Central Gê', in *Handbook of South American Indians* I: 477–517, Washington.

Magalhães, Couto de, 1938. *Viagem ao Araguaya*, São Paulo (first published in Goyaz, 1863).

Malinowski, Bronislav, 1929. *The Sexual Life of the Savages*, London.

Martius, Carl Friedrich Phil. v., 1867. *Beiträge zur Ethnographie und Sprachenkunde Amerika's zumal Brasiliens*, Leipzig, 1867.

Mason, J. Alden, 1950. 'The languages of South American Indians', in *Handbook of South American Indians* 6: 157–318, Washington.

Maybury-Lewis, David, 1960a. 'The Social Organisation of a

346 REFERENCES

Central Brazilian Tribe: the Akwě-Shavante', Unpublished D.Phil. thesis, Bodleian Library, Oxford.

—1960b. 'Parallel descent and the Apinayé anomaly', *Southwestern Journal of Anthropolgy* 16: 191–216.

—1960c. 'The analysis of dual organizations: a methodological critique', *Bijdragen tot de Taal-, Land- en Volkenkunde* 116: 17–44.

—1965a. *The Savage and the Innocent*, London.

—1965b. 'Prescriptive marriage systems', *Southwestern Journal of Anthropology* 21: 207–30.

—1966a. 'Some crucial distinctions in Central Brazilian ethnology', *Anthropos* (in press)

—1966b. 'On Martius' distinction between Shavante and
—Sherente'. *Revista do Museu Paulista* (in press).

—in press 'Structural Anthropology and the Problem of Comparison', *Paper read at the VII International Congress of Anthropological and Ethnological Sciences*, Moscow 1964.

—with Neel, Salzano, Junqueira and Keiter, 1964. 'Studies on the Xavante Indians of the Brazilian Mato Grosso', *Human Genetics* 16: 52–140.

Métraux, Alfred, 1927. 'Les migrations historiques des Tupi-Guaraní', *Journal de la Société des Américanistes de Paris* 19: 1–45.

Murdock, George P., 1949. *Social Structure*, New York, 1949.

Needham, Rodney, 1958. 'The formal analysis of prescriptive patrilateral cross-cousin marriage', *Southwestern Journal of Anthropology* 14: 199–219.

—1960a. 'Lineal equations in a two-section system', *Journal of the Polynesian Society* 69: 23–30.

—1960b. 'A structural analysis of Aimol society', *Bijdragen tot de Taal-, Land- en Volkenkunde* 116: 81–108.

Nimuendajú, Curt, 1939. *The Apinayé*, Washington: Catholic University of America Press.

—1942. *The Šerente*, Los Angeles: Frederick Webb Hodge Anniversary Publication Fund.

—1944. 'Serente Tales', *The Journal of American Folk-Lore* LVII, No. 225, pp. 181–7.

—1946. *The Eastern Timbira*, Berkeley and Los Angeles: University of California Press.

Oliveira, R. Cardoso de, 1955. 'Relatório de uma investigação sôbre terras em Mato Grosso', in Simões (Ed.): *Relatório das Atividades do Serviço de Proteção aos Indios* 1954, Rio de Janeiro.

Parsons, Talcott, 1963. 'On the concept of influence'. *Public Opinion Quarterly*, XXVII: 37–62.

Peristiany, J. G., 1939. *The Social Institutions of the Kipsigis*, London.

Radcliffe-Brown, A. R., 1931. *The Social Organization of Australian Tribes*, Oceania Monographs No. 1, Melbourne.

—1948. *The Andaman Islanders*, Glencoe, Illinois: The Free Press.

—1951. 'Murngin social organisation', *American Anthropologist* 53: 37–55.

—1952a. 'The mother's brother in South Africa', in *Structure and Function in Primitive Society*: 15–31, London.

—1952b. 'On social structure', ibid., 188–204.

—1953. Letter: 'The Dravidian kinship terminology', *Man* 169.

Ribeiro, Darcy, 1951. 'Noticia dos Ofaié-Chavante', *Revista do Museu Paulista* (N.S.) 5: 105–32.

—1962. *A Política Indigenista Brasileira*, Rio de Janeiro.

Richards, A. I., 1950. 'Some types of family structure amongst the Central Bantu', in Radcliffe-Brown and Forde: *African Systems of Kinship and Marriage*, Oxford.

Rivers, W. H. R., 1900. 'A genealogical method of collecting social and vital statistics', *Journal of the Royal Anthropological Institute* 30: 74–82.

—1910. 'The genealogical method of anthropological enquiry', *Sociological Review* 3: 1–12.

—1912. 'The genealogical method', in Freire-Marreco and Myres (Eds.): *Notes and Queries on Anthropology*, 119–22, London.

—1914. *Kinship and Social Organisation*, London.

Róheim, Geza, 1945. *The Eternal Ones of the Dream: A Psycho-analytic Interpretation of Australian Myth and Ritual*, New York.

Sauer, Carl O., 1950. 'Geography of South America', *Handbook of South American Indians* 6: 319–344, Washington.

Schneider, David and Gough, E. Kathleen, 1961. *Matrilineal Kinship*. Berkeley and Los Angeles: University of California Press.

Simões, Mario F., 1955. 'Atividades do S.P.I.', in *Relatório das Atividades do Serviço de Proteção aos Indios* 1954, Rio de Janeiro.

Siqueira, J. da Costa, 1872. 'Compendio historico-chronologico das noticias de Cuyabá, repartição da Capitania de Mato-Grosso, desde o principio do anno de 1778 até o fim do anno de 1817', *Revista Trimensal de Historia e Geographia* 13: 5–124, Rio de Janeiro.

Szaffka, Tihamér, 1942. 'Sôbre construções navais duma tribu de índios desconhecidos do Rio das Mortes', *Revista do Arquivo Municipal* 87: 171–81, São Paulo.

Tylor, Sir Edward B., 1870. *The Early History of Mankind*, London.

Van Gennep, Arnold, 1909. *Les Rites de Passage*, Paris.

Warner, W. Lloyd, 1949. *Democracy in Jonesville: a Study in Quality and Inequality*, New York.

The following works, dealing either solely or in large measure with the Shavante, have been consulted. All three are superficial and full of misinformation:

Blomberg, R., 1960. *Chavante; an Expedition to the Tribes of the Mato Grosso*, London.

Fabré, D. G., 1963. *Beyond the River of the Dead*, London.

Miyazaki, Nobue, 1960. *Razoku Shabantesu* (The Naked Tribe: Shavantes), Tokyo.

INDEX

INDEX